RECOLLECTIONS OF
THIRTY-NINE YEARS IN THE ARMY

Recollections of Thirty-Nine Years in the Army

GWALIOR AND THE BATTLE OF MAHARAJPORE, 1843
THE GOLD COAST OF AFRICA, 1847-48
THE INDIAN MUTINY, 1857-58
THE EXPEDITION TO CHINA, 1860-61
THE SIEGE OF PARIS, 1870-71
ETC

BY

SIR CHARLES ALEXANDER GORDON, K.C.B.

GYAN

Published by

GYAN

Gyan Publishing House
5, Ansari Road
Daryaganj, New Delhi-110002
Phone: 011-47034999, 9811692060
E-mail: books@gyanbooks.com

Distribution Network
gyanbooks.com
India, USA, Canada, UK, Australia, France

ISBN: 978-81-212-7101-1 (PB)
First Published, 1898

2nd Impression 2024

Printed at: Gyan Press, Delhi.

RECOLLECTIONS OF THIRTY-NINE YEARS IN THE ARMY
Author: CHARLES ALEXANDER GORDON

RECOLLECTIONS OF

THIRTY-NINE YEARS IN THE ARMY

SIR CHARLES A. GORDON, K.C.B., SURGEON-GENERAL

(*From a Photograph by* MR. A. BASSANO, *Old Bond Street*)

Recollections of Thirty-nine Years in the Army

GWALIOR AND THE BATTLE OF MAHARAJPORE, 1843
THE GOLD COAST OF AFRICA, 1847–48
THE INDIAN MUTINY, 1857–58
THE EXPEDITION TO CHINA, 1860–61
THE SIEGE OF PARIS, 1870–71
ETC

BY

SIR CHARLES ALEXANDER GORDON, K.C.B.

"The story of my life,
From year to year, the battles, sieges, fortunes
That I have passed."
—*Othello*, Act 1, Sc. 3

London
SWAN SONNENSCHEIN & CO., LIMD
PATERNOSTER SQUARE
1898

THIS PERSONAL NARRATIVE

IS INSCRIBED TO

MY WIFE AND OUR CHILDREN

CONTENTS

THIRTY-NINE YEARS IN THE ARMY

CHAPTER I

1841-1842. *GAZETTED TO THE BUFFS. ARRIVE IN INDIA*

First Affghan War—Chatham—Fort Pitt—Supernumeraries—How appointed—Gazetted—Breaking in—Orders of readiness—Ship inspected—Embark—First days on board—Typical characters—Warmth—Our "tub"—Reduced allowances—Conditions on board—Amusements for men—For officers—"Speaking" ships—A dismasted vessel—First sense of responsibility—Indiscipline—Neptune—On board—Table Bay—Shore boats—Cape Town—Vicinity—Official duties—The ship *Lloyds*—An "old friend"—The 25th Regiment—The contractor—Botanic Garden—Eastward—Mutinous crew—Land ahoy—Terrible news—The Hooghly.

IN 1841 British and Indian troops occupied Cabul; but throughout Affghanistan the aspect of things political was alarming. In Scinde the Ameers were defiant and hostile. The Punjab in a state of disturbance and convulsion; law and order had ceased; isolated murders and massacres instigated by opposing claimants to the throne left vacant in 1839, and since that time occupied by a prince against whom the insurrectionary movement was now directed by chiefs, some of whom were inimical to British interests.

Military reinforcements on a large scale were dispatched from England. Great, accordingly, the activity at Chatham, then the only depot whence recruits and young officers were sent to regiments serving in India. The depot then at Warley was for soldiers of the Honourable Company's service.

Into the General Hospital at Fort Pitt were received military invalids from India as from all other foreign stations. There they were treated for their several ailments; thence discharged to join their respective depots, or from the service on such pensions as they were deemed entitled to by length of service and regimental character. Then the period of engagement was for life, otherwise twenty-one years in the infantry, twenty-four in the mounted branches.

B

There young medical men nominated for appointment to the army underwent a course of training, more or less long, according to individual circumstances, for the special duties before them; meanwhile they received no pay, wore no uniform; they dined at mess, paid mess subscriptions, and were subject to martial law.

Professional education included requirements for diplomas, and in addition, special subjects relating to military medicine, surgery, and management of troops. Nominations for appointments were given by old officers or other men whose social position was a guarantee in regard to character and fitness of their nominees for the position sought by them; certificates by professors and teachers under whom they studied were submitted to the responsible authority[1] at the War Office, with whom rested their selection. Thus in effect a combined system of patronage and competition was in force.

With anxious interest a small group of expectants awaited the arrival of the coach by which in those days afternoon letters and evening papers from the metropolis were conveyed. Eagerly was *The Gazette* scanned when, close upon the hour of midnight, the papers were delivered. Great was the pride and rejoicing with which some of our number read the announcement relating to them; great the disappointment of those who were not so included. The regiment to which I had the honour of being appointed was the 3rd, or "Buffs," the depot of which formed part of the Provisional Battalion then occupying Forton Barracks.[2]

The duties assigned to young medical officers were unimportant—initiatory rather than definite in kind. Careful watch and superintendence on the part of official seniors gave us an opportunity of learning various points relative to practice, as well as to routine and discipline, to be turned to account—or otherwise—in the career upon which we were entering. But the process of "breaking in" was not without its disagreeables. Courtesy towards young officers on the part of their seniors, military or medical, was a quality rare at Chatham, but where met with in isolated instances was the more appreciated, and remembered in subsequent years. The "system" of training in force tended rather to break than bend the sapling.

Thus did three months pass away. Then came an order of readiness to embark with the detachment of recruits next to sail. Although about to proceed with those pertaining to what was now "my own regiment," official regulations required that my appointment to

[1] Sir James McGrigor, Bart., Director-General.

[2] The date of appointment as Assistant Surgeon, June 8, 1841. My diplomas—L.R.C.S.E.; M.D. St. Andrews: both April, 1840.

charge of them should have the authority of "The Honourable Court of Directors," and that to obtain it, personal application must be made at their old historical house in Leadenhall Street—a formality which was gone through with ease and success. This is what the appointment in question implied:—Not only did I receive the free passage to which I was entitled, my daily rate of pay[1] running on the while, minus £5 deducted "for messing," but was privileged to occupy the second best cabin on board, and at the end of the voyage to receive in rupees a sum equivalent to fifteen shillings per head for officers and soldiers landed, and half a guinea for each woman and child. In those "golden days" the sterling value of the rupee was at par.

The ordeal of "inspection" was duly performed, the requirements on board declared "satisfactory," the formal report to that effect transmitted to the authorities. My personal knowledge of those requirements was absolutely *nil.* How much more definite that of other members of the Inspecting Committee, was soon to be judged of. For example: side or stern ports there were none, deck ventilators being considered sufficient. Food stores comprised casks of salted beef and pork; tins of soup and bouillé, potatoes and other vegetables, some dried, some tinned; pickles and lime juice, bread, otherwise hard biscuit, destined ere many weeks had elapsed to become mouldy and honeycombed by weevils. There were bags of flour, peas, and raisins; an ample supply of tobacco; also of rum and porter, to be issued to the troops as a daily ration. The water tanks and a series of casks on deck had been filled—so it was said—from the Thames below London Bridge, when the tide was at its lowest.

The day of departure arrived. The detachment of which I was an unit marched away from Chatham Barracks, through Rochester, Strood, and so by road to Gravesend. There it was conveyed on board the *Indian*; twenty-four hours allowed us to settle down on board; the ship then taken in tow by steamer; we are on our voyage.

A fortnight elapsed; we were no farther on our way than off the coast of Spain. The novelties of first experience afforded subject of observation and thought: those which most impressed us, the clear moonlight, the starry galaxy of the heavens, the Milky Way, the cloudless sky, the phosphorescence of the undulating sea through which our ship slowly glided; the masses of living things, chiefly medusæ, that floated fathoms deep in ocean. During daylight many land birds flew over us or rested on the rigging.

Small though our party was, it comprised its proportion of men

[1] *7s. 6d.*

typical in their several ways. The commander of the vessel, soured with life, disappointed in career, tired of sea life, but unable to quit his profession. One of the ship's officers, a young man of deeply religious convictions. An ancient subaltern, inured to the chagrin of having been several times purchased over by men of less service but more fortunate than himself in worldly means. The lady's man, pretentious and vapid, given to solos on a guitar; the instrument adorned with many coloured ribbons, to each of which he attached a legend; his cabin decorated with little bits of "work," cards, and trinkets, for as yet photographs had not been invented. The irascible person, ready to take offence at trifles, and in other ways uncertain.

A month on board; the Canary Islands faintly seen in the distance. Already heat and stuffiness 'tween decks so unpleasant that carpenters were set to work to cut out stern ports for ventilation. Our progress so slow that with all sails set a ship's boat was launched, in which some of our numbers amused themselves by rowing round the vessel.

Two months, and we still north of the Equator. Various reasons given for tedious progress, among others light airs, contrary winds, adverse currents. But none of these explained the fact of our being passed by vessels, some of which, on the horizon astern of us in the morning, were hull down on that ahead ere daylight vanished. That our ship was alluded to as "a worthless old tub" need now be no matter of surprise.

Not more than one-third of our distance to be run as yet got over; prospects as regarded the remainder by no means happy. The unwelcome announcement made that all hands, including crew and troops, must submit to reduced allowance of food and water. Of the latter, the full allowance per head per day for cooking and all other purposes was seven pints, now to be reduced to six. No wonder that the announcement was not received with tokens of approval.

Looking back to conditions as described in notes taken at the time, the contrast so presented between those which were then deemed sufficient for troops on board ship, and those which now exist may not be without some historical interest. Space 'tween decks so limited,[1] that with men's hammocks slung, those who on duty had to make their way along at night were forced to stoop almost to the attitude of the ordinary quadruped. The "sick bay" on the port side, close to the main hatch, directly exposed to rain from starboard; except a canvas screen, no separation between the quarters of unmarried and those of married; no separate accommodation for sick women or children; no prison set apart for the refractory. All over the ship myriads of cock-

[1] The hammock space per man was 9 feet × 1½.

roaches; these insects, especially lively at night, supplied to men and officers excitement and exercise, as, slipper in hand, they hunted them whenever the pale light given by the ship's lamps enabled them to do so. Cleanliness of decks and fittings was to some extent effected by means of dry scrubbing. The use of Burnett's Solution [1] substituted the odour of the compound so named for that of humanity. By means of iron fumigators in which was burning tar, the atmosphere of 'tween decks was purified, due precautions taken to minimise the risks of fire attending the process. Tubs and hose on deck supplied ample means for the morning "souse."

A carefully chosen library provided for the use of our men was placed on board by the Indian authorities; it was highly appreciated and generally made use of. Among the troops, games of all sorts were encouraged, their selection left to men's own choice. In working the ship ready hands were at all times available. Gymnastics and feats of strength were in high favour, and so, with the routine of guards, parades, inspections, and so forth, daytime was filled up. In the evenings, songs, recitations, theatrical performances, and instrumental music were indulged till the bugle sounded "lights out."

Officers had their ways of passing the time. They included games, gymnastics, bets, practical jokes (of all degrees of silliness), cock fighting, wild and dangerous adventures in the rigging, and on Saturday evenings, toasts, then usual on such occasions, enthusiastically "honoured." A weekly newspaper was set on foot; the works of Scott, Shakespeare, and Pope, among other authors, carefully studied, and discussions, more or less profitable, held on their contents.

Sighting, signalling, and hailing ships was a favourite amusement as opportunity occurred. By some of those homeward bound we dispatched letters, with passengers on board others we exchanged visits, strange as such ceremonies may seem to those now acquainted only with modern twenty-knot floating steam palaces. While paying such a visit to a ship five months out from China, we learned the "news" that Canton had been captured (on May 25–27, 1841) by the forces under command of Sir Hugh Gough.

In near proximity to the Equator we came upon a ship, the *Cambridge*, disabled, her topmasts carried away in a sudden squall two nights previous. The resolve to stand by and give assistance was quickly taken. Boats were lowered, parties of sailors and recruits, accompanied by some officers, were soon on board. Within a few hours defects were made good as far as that was practicable; meantime night had closed in, a somewhat fresh breeze sprung up, clouds obscured the sky, and

[1] Solution of chloride of zinc.

so the return to our ship was by no means accomplished without danger.

The distance to be got over was still great before the ship could reach Table Bay and renewed supplies obtained. The health of all on board had so far remained good, notwithstanding all the drawbacks experienced. The likelihood, however, that this happy state of things might suddenly come to an end became to me a source of what was the first sense of official anxiety with which I had been acquainted.

Excepting two somewhat elderly non-commissioned officers, specially put on board the better to ensure discipline among our recruits, all others were as yet but partly tutored in military duties and order. Unwilling obedience had from the first been shown by several of their number; then came irregularities, quarrels, and fights among themselves. Nor were the few married women on board ideal patterns of gentleness, either in speech or behaviour.

Among the crew were men whose antecedents, so far as they could be ascertained, were of the most questionable kind, and whose conduct on board had, from the first, been suspicious. Between them and kindred spirits among the recruits, it appeared that an understanding had been come to to have what they called "a disturbance" on board. Those intentions having come to the ears of the officers, with the further information that fully ninety men were implicated, preparations were made for emergencies: arm-racks fitted up in the saloon; fire-arms burnished; ammunition seen to; non-commissioned officers instructed as to their duties. But an occurrence which now happened distracted attention from the so-called plot, whether real or imaginary did not transpire.

Our entrance into tropical latitudes, some three weeks previous, had been duly announced by "Neptune," who, selecting the period of first night watch for the ceremony, welcomed us from amidst a flare of blue lights on the forecastle, on our coming to his dominions. Having done so, he returned to his element; his car a burning tar-barrel, which we continued to watch as it seemed to float astern, until all was darkness again. On board, "offerings" had to be made to the sea-god, half-sovereigns and bottles of rum, sent to the fo'c's'le, being those most appreciated.

While yet in the first degree of south latitude, the sea-god, accompanied by his court officials, announced their arrival on board, the whole personified by members of the ship's crew, appropriately attired in accordance with their respective official positions. The ceremony of "initiating" the "children" was quickly in progress, the chief ceremonies connected therewith including shaving, "bathing," besides some others by no means pleasant to their subjects. One of our young recruits strongly resisted the ordeal through which several of his comrades had passed. He succeeded in making his escape from his captors, and quickly mounting the ship's railing, thence plunged into the sea, to the consternation and horror of us all. The vessel was instantly "put about," a boat lowered, but search for him was in vain. The occurrence was, indeed, a melancholy outcome of what was intended to be a scene of amusement. But the spirits of young men were light, and ere many hours had elapsed, the song and dance were in progress, as if the event had not occurred. A Court of Inquiry followed in due time, and then the incident was forgotten.

We were now approaching Table Bay. Great was the interest and admiration with which we looked upon Table Mountain, as its grandeur became more and more distinctly revealed. Hardly less was our estimate of the Blue Berg range, by which the distant view was bounded. Soon we were among the shipping, and at anchor.

Our ship was soon surrounded by boats, that seemed to come in shoals from shore; some conveying fruit and curiosities for sale, others suspected of carrying commodities less innocuous in kind. But sentries, already placed at gangways and other points on deck, prevented traffic between our men and the small craft. The aspect of boats and their crews was alike new and strange to most of us: the former, striped with gaudy colours, red, black, and white; the latter, representing several nationalities, including English, Dutch, Malay, East Indian, and typical African, their several styles of costume no less various than themselves.

Some of our number, proceeding ashore, stood for the first time on foreign ground. Cape Town presented a series of wide, regularly arranged streets, intersecting each other, their sides sheltered by foliage trees. Flat-roofed houses, coated with white plaster, were nearly invariable in their uniformity. Great wagons, drawn by teams of oxen, from six to twelve in number—and even more—were being driven along by Malays, armed with whips of alarming proportions; though, fortunately for the beasts of burthen, they were little used. Crowds of pedestrians were on the thoroughfares, interspersed with guardians of the peace, the latter dressed after the manner of their kind in London. It was the month of December; but the temperature was that of summer; the heat oppressive, as we continued our excursion.

Part of that excursion was to Constantia. On the right, the great mountain, rising to a height of three thousand feet; the space between its base and the road along which we drove thickly covered by forest and undergrowth, the whole comprising oaks, silver and other pines, geraniums, pomegranates, and heaths, interspersed with herbaceous plants bearing gorgeously coloured flowers. At intervals there were richly cultivated fields and valleys; on or near them attractive-looking houses, many having attached to the latter no less handsome gardens. The road was thickly occupied by vehicles and pedestrians; among the whites, a considerable proportion of well-looking individuals of the fair sex. There was, in fact, a general aspect of activity and of prosperity.

The ordeal of "reporting ourselves" to the authorities was gone through: our reception by one, whose surname indicated Dutch origin, ungracious and supercilious; by the departmental chief so kindly, as by contrast to make an impression upon us, but partially inured to official ways as we then were. Meanwhile, the necessary steps were in progress for placing on board our ship the much-needed supplies of food materials and of water.

Among vessels that anchored in the bay during our detention, there was the ship *Lloyds*, having on board emigrants from England to New Zealand. When first they began their voyage, they numbered eighty women and 117 children; but so appalling had been the mortality among them that, of the children, fifty-seven had died. In all parts of the space occupied by passengers, sickness and distress in various shapes prevailed. Children, apparently near to death, lay in cots by the side of their prostrate mothers, whose feebleness rendered them unable to give the necessary aid to their infants. A state of indescribable filth existed everywhere; ventilation there was none in the proper sense. Women and children affected with measles in very severe form, that disease having been brought on board in the persons of some of those embarking; others suffered from low fever, and some from scurvy, which had recently appeared among them. The family of the medical man on board had suffered like the others, one of his children having died. On the deck of the ship lay two coffins, containing bodies of the dead, preparatory to being taken on shore for burial. The entire scene presented by the ship, the saddest with which, so far, I had become acquainted.

In Table Bay we again met the *Cambridge* already mentioned, that vessel arriving shortly after our own had anchored. In a sense we, the passengers of both, greeted each other as old friends; visits were interchanged, then leave was taken of each other with expressions of good wishes. By-and-by there came to anchor the ship *Nanking*, having on board recruits belonging to the service of the Honourable Company. Greetings and cheers were interchanged; for were we not all alike proceeding on a career, hopeful indeed, but as yet uncertain?

In the Castle, a short distance from Cape Town, the 25th Regiment, or Borderers, was stationed, and in accordance with the hospitable custom of the time, an invitation to dinner with the officers was received on board. The party on that festive occasion numbered seventy, the majority guests like ourselves, and now the circumstance is mentioned as showing the scale upon which such entertainments were given.

Invited to the house of an Afrikander Dutchman,[1] we found ourselves in large airy rooms, destitute of carpets, with polished floors; wall space reduced to a series of intervals between doors and windows; the arrangements new to us, but suited to climatic conditions of the place. Little attentions shown by, added to personal attractions of, lady members of the family naturally enough left their impression on young susceptibilities.

Very interesting also, though in a different way, was our visit to the house of Baron von Ludovigberg. Elegantly furnished, rooms so arranged as to be readily transformed into one large hall, everything in and around marking a life of ease and comfort. His garden, situated in Kolf Street, extensive, elegantly laid out, with large collection of plants indigenous and foreign; at intervals fountains and ornamental lakes. In the latter were thousands of gold fish, so tame as to approach and feed from the hand of an attendant; to the sound of a handbell rung by him they crowded, though on seeing us they kept at a distance. To the sound of the same bell when rung by us they would approach, but not come near the strangers.

Our voyage resumed, away eastward we sailed. Sixteen days without noteworthy incident; then sighted the island of Amsterdam, from which point, as the captain expressed it, he began to make his northing.

Another interval of monotonous sea life. At daybreak we found that in close proximity to us was a barque, the *Vanguard*, on board of which there was disturbance amounting to mutiny among the crew. The captain[2] signalled for assistance. A party of our young soldiers, under command of an officer, proceeded on board, removed the recalcitrant men to our ship, some of our sailors taking their place, and so both vessels continued their way to Calcutta.

Again was the unwelcome announcement made that short allowance of food and water was imminent, to be averted by progress of our vessel becoming more rapid than it had hitherto been. The

[1] Mr. Mechi.

[2] Captain Gurwood.

tedium of the voyage had told upon us; idleness had produced its usual effect. Chafing against authority and slow decay of active good fellowship became too apparent; all were tired of each other.

Another interval. From the mast-head comes the welcome sound, "Land on the starboard bow." Soon we come in view of low-lying shore, over which hangs a haze in which outlines of objects are indistinct. What is seen, however, indicates that our ship is out of reckoning; that, as for some time past suspected, something has gone wrong with the chronometers. Wisely, the captain determines to proceed no farther for the present, until able to determine our precise position. A day and night pass, then is descried a ship in the distance westward. We proceed in that direction, and ere many hours are over exchange signals with a pilot brig.

Twenty-four weeks had elapsed since the pilot left us in the Downs; now the corresponding functionary boards our ship off the Sandheads. We are eager for news. He has much to tell, but of a nature sad as unexpected. The envoy at Cabul, Sir William Macnaughten, murdered by the hand of Akbar Khan; the 44th Regiment annihilated, part of a force comprising 4,500 fighting men and 12,000 camp-followers who had started on their disastrous retreat from Cabul towards the Khyber Pass; one only survivor, Dr. Bryden, who carried tidings of the disaster to Jellalabad. Another item was that several officers, ladies, and children were in the hands of the Affghan chief.

Progress against the current of Hooghly River was slow, steam employed only while crossing the dreaded "James and Mary" shoal; for then tugs were scarce, their use expensive. Three days so passed; the first experience of tropical scenery pleasant to the eye, furnishing at the same time ample subject for remark and talk. On either side jungle, cultivated plots of ground, palms, bamboos, buffaloes and cattle of other kinds. In slimy ooze gigantic gavials; in the river dead bodies of animals and human beings, vultures and crows perched upon and tearing their decomposing flesh. Native boats come alongside; their swarthy, semi-naked crews scream and gesticulate wildly as they offer for sale fruit and other commodities. Our rigging is crowded with brahminee kites and other birds; gulls and terns swarm around. The prevailing damp heat is oppressive. Now the beautiful suburb of Garden Reach is on our right; on our left the Botanic Garden; the City of Palaces is ahead of us; we are at anchor off Princep's Ghat.

The "details," as in official language our troops collectively are called, were transferred to country boats o uncouth look, and so conveyed to Chinsurah, then a depot for newly arrived recruits. Our actual numbers so transferred equalled those originally embarked, two lives lost during our voyage being made up for by two births on board. Sanitation, in modern significance of the term, had as substitute the arrangements—or want of them—already mentioned; yet no special illness occurred; my first charge ended satisfactorily.

CHAPTER II

1842-1843. *IN PROGRESS TO JOIN*

Chinsurah—Cholera—Start—Omissions—Relics of mortality—Collision—Fire—Panic—Berhampore—The "garrison"—Crime and punishment—Civilities—Progress resumed—A hurricane—Cawnpore—Attached to 50th Regiment—The troops—Agra—Sind—Gwalior—39th Regiment.

FIRST impressions of this our first station in India, recorded at the time, were:—Houses of mud, roofs consisting of reeds, fronts open from end to end; members of families within squatting, infants sprawling, in a state of nudity, upon earthen floors made smooth and polished by means of cowdung applied in a liquid state; while to outside walls cakes of the same material are in process of drying, to be thereafter used as fuel by Hindoos. Gardens and cultivated fields abound; flowering trees and shrubs, cocoa palms, banana bushes, clumps of bamboo, rise above dense undergrowth of succulent plants. A heavy, oppressive atmosphere, pervaded by odours, sweet and otherwise, has a depressing effect, as if conditions were not altogether wholesome. European houses according to Holland model, terraces and gardens giving to them an attractive and elegant appearance, indicating the importance of the place while in the hands of the Dutch, prior to date[1] of the treaty in accordance with which it was by them exchanged for Java. An extensive range of spacious barracks and supplementary buildings added much to the beauty of the station.

Before many days were over several of our young lads had fallen victims to cholera. In this our first experience of that disease we had access to no one capable of giving aid and advice; we were left to individual judgment, and it altogether astray as to the appropriate method in our emergency. For a time, out of our small party death claimed several daily victims; young wives were thus left widows, young children orphans.

Glad to receive orders of readiness to resume progress by river to next stage of our journey. Then arrived two senior officers,—

[1] 1815.

one to take military command;[1] the other, departmental charge of our detachment. Country boats provided as before, others of better kind for officers. Our unwieldy fleet started at the appointed time;[2] the boats comprising it straggled irregularly across the river, and having gained the opposite bank, there made fast for the night.

Early next morning it was in movement. Mid-day heat became oppressive. One of the soldiers was prostrated by cholera, another by sun fever. Inquiry revealed the unpleasant fact that the "experienced" officer recently appointed for the purpose had made no arrangements whatever for sick. Those fallen ill were now sent in small boats back towards Chinsurah; and so we continued our river progress, steps being taken to have deficient requirements sent on without delay.

Next evening was far advanced ere they arrived. The numbers of our sick had increased, several deaths taken place, some with appalling rapidity in the absence of means of help. The great heat prevailing made early interment necessary. Graves had to be hastily made in groves of trees near the river bank; to them the dead were committed, our fleet continuing its progress, sailing or tracking[3] according to wind and current. After night had fallen, the blaze of funeral pyres on the river banks told their tale of pestilence.

For several days mortality was great in our small party, and among the native boatmen. As deaths occurred among the latter, the bodies were simply left on the bank to be devoured by jackals, dogs, and vultures, numbers of which were in wait for prey. Some of our boats sprung leaks, and so became useless; nor was it an easy matter to get them replaced. Men and stores had to be got out as best they could and disposed of among others—proceedings by no means easy under then present circumstances.

At last there came an interval in which the malign influence of our invisible enemy seemed as if withheld. While gliding upwards against the silent river current, suddenly from one of the men's boats there burst a mass of thick smoke, speedily followed by flame, and within the space of a few minutes nothing except the charred framework remained. How, or by what means, the occupants of the boat escaped did not transpire; that they did so was fortunate for themselves and satisfactory to all, though the accident, subsequently ascertained to have resulted from their own carelessness, destroyed their entire kits and other belongings.

[1] Captain Astier, 62nd Regiment.

[2] March 28, 1842.

[3] *i.e.*, drawn by means of ropes attached to their masts.

Short was our respite. Suddenly and fatally was our detachment again struck, several deaths by cholera occurring in quick succession. Our somewhat eventful "voyage" was near its end, when in mid-stream two of our boats came violently in collision with each other, considerable mutual damage being the result. An unfortunate panic occurred among the recruits on board, one of whom leapt overboard and so disappeared. Soon afterwards our journey was at an end, it having occupied eleven days; we arrived at Berhampore.

Near to the spacious range of barracks in which our young soldiers were accommodated were lines occupied by a native regiment,[1]—at that time reputed to be of distinguished loyalty to Jân Kompanee, with whose liberal dealings towards its own proper servants all were so well pleased. In others were invalids, soldiers' wives and children pertaining to regiments[2] employed in the war proceeding against China; many as yet unaware that they had been made widows and orphans by the climate of Chusan and coast generally.

Here the conduct of our lads—for they had scarcely become men—became so reckless that military discipline had to be rigidly enforced, while in many instances severe or fatal illness seemed to be the direct result of their own misconduct. As a ready, and as thought at the time effectual, means of coercion, corporal punishment was awarded by courts-martial. The ordeal of being present during its infliction was nauseating; but constituted as the detachment was, the punishment seemed to have been in all cases well deserved.

General Raper was the officer in political charge of the Nawab of Moorshedabad, then a boy of some ten years old. Several civilians high in rank, and a few non-official residents, for the most part connected with the manufacture of tussar[3] silk, resided at Berhampore. From several of them we young officers received much attention and kindness, not only in their own houses but on excursions organized by them for our special benefit. Prominent among those who thus befriended us, young "griffs" as we were, General Raper and Charles Du Pré Russell are remembered gratefully—even while these notes are penned, many years after the date and incidents referred to.

In due time the order arrived for us to resume our river journey, our destination Cawnpore; again country-made boats our means of transport. In the early days of August we started on what was to be in many respects a monotonous voyage, though not altogether without its excitement and stirring incidents. The general manner of our

[1] 21st.
[2] Namely, 26th, 49th, and 55th.
[3] *i.e.*, silk produced by the *Antherea paphia*, and allied species.

progress was that with which we were now acquainted. We were doomed, as before, to be at intervals stricken by cholera, which seemed to have its favourite lurking-places, generally at the foot of a somewhat precipitous alluvial bank. Night after night rest was disturbed or altogether banished by the sound of tom-toms, songs, barking of dogs, cries of jackals; sight and smell offended by funeral fires as they blazed in near proximity to us.

More than half our journey was got over without special mishap. Our boatmen observe that signs of coming storm appear in the sky; they prepare as best they can, but soon the hurricane is upon us. Boats are dashed against each other, and against the river bank; waves break over them, tearing away their flimsy gear, battering some to pieces, their inmates obliged to escape and save themselves as best they could. After a time there came a downpour of rain; then gradually the storm ceased, leaving several of our number boatless, and destitute of greater or smaller portions of our respective kits. Among others, I suffered considerably. A friend in need, more fortunate than myself, gave me hospitality on his boat until sometime thereafter, when, with others similarly situated, I chartered a budgerow. A few days after our mishap news reached us that a similar fleet to our own, with troops,[1] some thirty miles ahead of us, suffered very severely from the same hurricane that had struck us, a considerable number of the men in it having perished in the river.

Without further incident of importance we arrived at Cawnpore in the early days of November, our journey by river having occupied more than two months and a half, the date fourteen years before the terrible year 1857, when that station was to acquire the sad memory ever since associated with it. Anticipating the return to India of the force commanded by General Pollock from Jellalabad, the march to which place had restored British prestige from the temporary eclipse at Jugdulluck, Orders were issued to honour that army by an appropriate military display on the left bank of the Sutlej. Among the regiments assembled for that purpose, at Ferozepore, the then frontier station, were the Buffs. Orders had also directed that on completion of that duty they should march towards Allahabad and there occupy the fort, the detachment with which I was connected joining headquarters *en route*. For the time being we were attached to the 50th Regiment, and so continued during the remaining four months of the cold season.

Here took place the first initiation into their several duties connected

[1] Of the 50th and 62nd Regiments; more than 100 men were lost at Seckreegullee, that being the place where the typhoon occurred.

with regimental life of the young men belonging to our detachment, myself among them. Among the officers in the "Dirty Half-Hundred" who had served with it during the Peninsular War, when, on account of the continuous severe work performed by it, the corps obtained its honourable soubriquet, three[1] remained, looked up to with the respect due to, and then accorded to, distinguished veterans. Alternate with duties assigned to us, amusements filled up our time pleasantly. Gaiety was in full flow. Many were the joyous gatherings by which were filled the Assembly rooms—some years thereafter to be the scene of very terrible doings. Outdoor games and sports were the order of the day, the tract of jungle in Oude that stretched along the opposite river bank proving our most happy hunting ground. So it was that time passed pleasantly, if in an intellectual sense not very profitably. At the time alluded to traffic and communication with Oude was by means of a long bridge of boats, that bridge from their attack on which in subsequent days the Gwalior mutineers were to be driven by the forces under Sir Colin Campbell.[2]

A large force, comprising all arms, then occupied that important station. The impression made upon us, as for the first time we beheld the magnificent spectacle presented by general field-day parades and exercises, was never to be forgotten. The swarthy visages of the sepoys; their quaint uniforms attracted our notice. The solidarity of the 50th gave the impression of irresistible force. The rush of cavalry, as, like a whirlwind, they went at full charge, to a great extent concealed in a cloud of dust raised by their horses' hoofs; the magnificent and unsurpassed Bengal Horse Artillery, in performing the evolutions pertaining to them,—these incidents struck us with amazement and admiration. Little did we think that not many months thereafter we were to be even more struck with admiration at the brilliant performance of some of those very troops in actual fight.

A trip to Agra[3] introduced me to the experiences of *palkee dâk*. Travelling by night, the distance got over was about fifty miles; alongside trotted torch-carriers, the odours from those "pillars of flame" foul and offensive. During the day a halt was made at bungalows provided by Government for the use of travellers. Thus were four days occupied in making a journey of two hundred miles. In and near Agra various excursions were made and places of interest visited. In the fort had recently been deposited the gates of Somnath,[4]

[1] Colonel Wodehouse, Major Ryan, and Captain Tew.

[2] December 28 and 29, 1857.

[3] On the invitation of my friend, L. C. Stewart, 39th Regiment.

[4] Gates of Somnath—carried thence, A.D. 1024, by the conqueror, Mahmood of Guznee.

in connection with the removal of which from Ghuznee the bombastic proclamation by Lord Ellenborough was still subject of comment. The tomb of Akbar[1] and the exquisite Taj Mahal[2] were visited on several occasions. The scene presented by the latter, more especially as seen by moonlight, was extremely beautiful. The minarets and domes of the mausoleum, consisting of pure white marble; the long avenue of cypress trees by which it is approached; the fountains in full play; the ornamental flower pots,—made upon us an impression never afterwards to be forgotten.

With the regiments returned recently from Kandahar, aided by troops from Bombay and Bengal, Sir Charles Napier undertook an expedition against the disaffected Ameers of Scinde. In February, 1843, the battles of Meeanee and Hyderabad ended in defeat of their forces, Hyderabad occupied, the country being conquered during the succeeding month of March. Of that war it was said: "The Muhamadan rulers of Sind, known as the Ameers, whose chief fault was that they would not surrender their independence, were crushed."

In the neighbouring State of Gwalior events were in progress, the issue of which was destined to affect the 39th, the 50th, and the Buffs in a way not at the moment anticipated by either of those regiments. Early in February, the distant boom of heavy guns intimated to us at Agra that the Maharajah of Gwalior was dead, and had been succeeded on his throne by his adopted son[3] in the absence of a lineal heir. In such events there did not appear anything to interfere with the routine of pleasure in which so many young officers indulged; that routine went on uninterruptedly, for as yet with them the serious business of life was in the future.

Those were indeed the days of India's hospitality, alike in respect to individuals and regiments. For example: Three weeks had I been an honorary member of the "Dorsets'" mess, when the time of my departure arrived; yet to my request for my mess bill I received the reply, "There is none." Among the officers whose hospitality I had so long unconsciously enjoyed were two, father and son, both of whom I was shortly to meet under circumstances very different from those in which I had made their acquaintance.

[1] Akbar the Great, A.D. 1556–1605.

[2] Taj Mahal-Bibi ke Roza, or Crown Lady's tomb, erected over the remains of Mumtaz Mahal, the Pride of the Palace, wife of Shah Jehan. She died in childbed of her eighth child, A.D. 1629, at Berhampore in the Deccan, whence her body was carried and buried where the Taj now stands.

[3] The story of these events is concisely given in Sewell's *Analytical History of India*, page 244.

CHAPTER III

1843. *AT ALLAHABAD*

I join the Buffs—An execution parade—Remnants of 44th Regiment—Allahabad—Sickness—Papamow—Cobra bite—Accident — Natural history—Agriculture—Locusts—Hindoo girl's song—Society—Lord Sahibs—Their staffs—Rumours of war—Preparations—The start—Affairs in Gwalior—The Punjab.

EIGHTEEN months had elapsed since the day when we left Chatham to that on which we joined the distinguished regiment[1] of which I was a member, the manner of my reception kind and friendly. As the regiment passed through Cawnpore, a short halt was ordered to take place; the camp to be pitched on that part of the parade ground, afterwards to be occupied by the defences in connection with which the story of General Wheeler and his party has left so many sad associations. The object of that halt appeared in Division Orders—the carrying into execution of sentence of death passed by General Court-Martial on a soldier of the regiment convicted of murdering a comrade. This was to be the first regimental parade on which I was to appear. By sunrise the troops were in their places, so as to form three sides of a square, the fourth being partly occupied by the construction above which the fatal beam and its supports stood prominent. The procession of death began its march, the regimental band wailing forth the Dead March; then came the coffin, carried by low-caste natives; then the condemned man, ghastly pale, strongly guarded. Thus did they proceed until they arrived at the place of execution. The eyes of most of us were averted, and so we saw not the further details of the sad drama. Regiment after regiment marched past the structure, from which dangled the body of a man; thence to their respective barracks or tents, their bands playing "rollicking" tunes.

Pleasant as novel were the incidents of our march eastward along that most excellent highway, the Grand Trunk Road. The early rouse, "striking" tents, the "fall in," the start while as yet stars glistened in the sky and dawn had not appeared; then came the wild note of the coel[2] as herald of coming day; the gleam of blazing fire far ahead, indicating where the midway halt was to take place, and

[1] At the time commanded by Colonel Clunie.

[2] *Eudynemus Orientalis.*

morning coffee with biscuits was in readiness for all. Resuming the day's journey, we reached the appointed camp ground by 8 a.m. Tents were quickly pitched on lines previously drawn by the Quarter-master and his staff. Bath, a hearty breakfast, duty, shooting, and other excursions occupied the day, then early dinner, early to bed, and so ready to undergo similar routine on the morrow. In our progress we passed through Futtehpore, a place to be subsequently the scene of stubborn fight against mutineers in 1857.

Attached to the Buffs were the remnants of what had been the 44th Regiment, now consisting of a few men of whom the majority were mutilated or suffering from bodily illness; the party under command of Captain Souter, by whose gallant devotion to duty the regimental colour was saved two years previous when our force was annihilated near the Khyber by Affghans, directed by Akbar Khan.

Pârâg, as the locality of Allahabad was anciently called, is closely connected with Hindoo tradition, and still retains a sacred character. At the date referred to in the Ramayana it was a residence of a Rajah of "the powerful Kosalas," whose capital was Ajudyia, their country the modern Oude. Here it was that Rama and Seeta crossed the Ganges in their progress to the jungles of Dandaka, where shortly afterwards she was captured by Ravana and carried away by him to Lunka, otherwise Ceylon. Within the fort, now occupied by our regiment, is an underground temple dedicated to Siva, its position believed to indicate the point where the mythical Suruswatee joins the still sacred Ganges. On an enclosed piece of ground stands one of six pillars assigned to Asoka, B.C. 240, bearing an inscription of the period of Samudra Gupta, 2nd century A.D. That pillar, having fallen, was restored by Jehangir, A.D. 1605; the fort itself captured by the English from Shah Alum, A.D. 1765.

As the hot season advanced, severe and fatal disease prevailed alarmingly among our men, cholera and heat fever claiming victims after a few hours' illness. Treatment applied by the younger medical officers in accordance with theoretical school teaching was useless, nor was it till the regimental surgeon (Dr. Macqueen) directed us to more practical methods that anything approaching favourable results were attained. In these notes, however, the intention is to omit professional matters.

A full company of our men was sent to Papamow, situated on the right bank of the Ganges, six miles distant, the object being to afford additional space to those within the fort. Captain Airey, in command of the detachment, had been one of the hostages in Affghanistan to Akbar Khan, and utilised on that occasion his culinary talents by acting as cook to the party. For a time the men enjoyed, and benefited by their change to country quarters. Towards the end of the rainy season, however, malarial diseases attacked them to a degree larger in proportion than their comrades in the fort; consequently our detachment was ordered to rejoin Head-quarters.

A good deal of freedom was allowed to the soldiers when first sent to the country place above mentioned, one result being that crime was next to absent from among them. A favourite amusement was shooting in the adjoining woods and fields, and, unhappily for some of them, of bathing, notwithstanding strict orders to the contrary, in the Ganges, then in full flood. On one of those shooting excursions a soldier got bitten in the hand by a cobra, the reptile being immediately killed, and brought in with him. That the teeth penetrated was manifest by the wounds; yet, strange to say, no serious results followed—a circumstance accounted for only by supposing that the poison sacs must by some means have been emptied immediately previous. Of those who insisted on entering the river, some fell victims to their temerity.

The pursuit and study of subjects relative to natural history furnished those of us whose leanings were in those directions with continuous enjoyment and profitable occupation. Visits by friends and small attempts at hospitality came in as so many pleasant interludes. When neither of these was practicable, a good supply of books and papers gave us variety in the way of reading.

So time passed until the month of September, when the cultivated fields were covered by heavy crops special to this part of India. A sudden outburst of discordant noises induces us to quit our quarters in search of the wherefore. A dense cloud is seen in rapid advance from the south-east; myriads of locusts, for of those insects it is composed, alight upon and by their accumulated weight bear down the stems to which they cling. Next day a similar flight is upon us, devouring every green thing; eight days thereafter, a third, but it passed over the locality, obscuring the sky as it did so.

The regimental mess house occupied an elevated position adjoining and overlooking the Jumna, a short distance above the confluence of that river with the Ganges, a terrace pertaining to the building being a favourite resort whereon, in the cool of the evening, it was usual for the officers to enjoy the refreshing breeze, when there was any, and contemplate the unrippled surface of the deep stream as it glided past. On one such evening, while a number of us were so enjoying the scene, watching the lights of native boats secured for the night to either bank, and listening to that strange mixture of sounds to which natives give the name of music, a series of what appeared to be floating lamps emerged from where the boats lay thickest and glided along the stream. Here we witnessed the scene alluded to, and so graphically described by L.E.L.[1] in her version of "The Hindoo Girl's Song."[2] It was, in fact, the Dewalee Festival.[3]

Allahabad was the chief civil station in the provinces; the principal courts were situated there, the higher officials connected with criminal and with revenue administration having their residences scattered over what was an extensive and ornamental settlement. Some of their houses were noted for hospitality, and for more homely entertainments given for the special benefit of the younger officers. Of the latter, that of Mrs. Tayler[4] has left most pleasant recollections, the good influence exerted by that lady making its mark on some of us who might otherwise have had remembrances very different in kind. Among the most esteemed of the residents was Dr. Angus, "The Good Samaritan," as he was called. Hospitable to all; considerate to juniors; his good advice, and help in other ways, readily given to all who in difficulties applied to him.

Early in October, the Commander-in-Chief, Sir Hugh Gough, arrived *en route* north-westward. New colours were presented by His Excellency to a native regiment[5] of distinguished service in Affghanistan, the event celebrated by festive gatherings, in accordance with cus-

[1] Poor L.E.L.! Further memories of her will recur hereafter.

[2] The words are so beautiful and pathetic that I transcribe them.

> Float on, float on, my haunted bark,
> Above the midnight tide;
> Bear softly o'er the waters dark
> The hopes that with thee glide.
>
> Float on, float on, thy freight is flowers,
> And every flower reveals
> The dreaming of my lonely hours,
> The hope my spirit feels.
>
> Float on, float on, thy shining lamp,
> The light of love is there;
> If lost beneath the waters damp,
> That love must then despair.
>
> Float on, beneath the moonlight float,
> The sacred billows o'er;
> Ah! some kind spirit guards my boat,
> For it has gained the shore.

[3] *Dewalee*—Festival to Lakshmi, goddess of wealth and fortune.

[4] Mrs. Tayler, mother of Lady Hope Grant, then a young girl in England at school.

[5] 37th.

tomary usage. On the staff of His Excellency were two officers, both of whom subsequently attained high military distinction; the one Sir Harry Smith, the other Sir Patrick Grant.

Reports were "in the air" that a Camp of Exercise was about to assemble at Agra, as an experiment then tried in India for the first time. Bazaar report had it that the Buffs were about to be ordered on service, the scene and nature of which did not just then transpire. Meanwhile, responsible officers "saw to" the state of "brown Bess," with which weapon our men were then armed; to that of ammunition, and other necessary items of equipment. The arrival of part of the 29th Regiment, to take our place, next followed, and, simultaneously, came an order directing the Buffs to proceed to Kalpee, on the Jumna, thirteen days' march distant. A few days thereafter, published orders directed the organization of "the Army of Exercise" into divisions and brigades; still, there was no inkling of what was about to happen.

For some time previous evidences were manifest that all was not right in Gwalior; latterly report said that things in that State had settled down, terms having been come to between the young Maharajah and leaders of the disaffected. A few days thereafter, our preparations were renewed; our weakly men, together with soldiers' wives and children, arranged for to be left behind, and with a fighting strength of 739 powerful and seasoned soldiers, the regiment started fit and ready for whatever service might be required of it.

The actual state of affairs, above referred to, was briefly this:—The young Maharajah, known as "Ali Jah Jyajee Scindia," owed his selection to the widow of the deceased monarch of the same name, who died childless, she a girl aged thirteen, named Tara Bye. To the post of Regent, Mama Sahib, an uncle of the deceased monarch, was acknowledged by Lord Ellenborough through the Resident, against the wishes of the Maharanee; Dada Khasjee, steward of the Household, by the Maharanee. Thereupon, the Resident was ordered by His Excellency to quit Gwalior, and the Dada prepared his troops to oppose forces of the Company, if sent against him; hence the campaign now about to take place.

In the Punjab, conditions were at the same time most serious, giving rise to expectations of armed intervention there. For example:—On the 15th of September, 1843, was perpetrated the double murder of the Maharajah Shere Singh[1] and his son Pertab, at the northern gate of Lahore, the conspiracy which led up to that deed having been formed

[1] Shere Singh, an unacknowledged son of Runjeet, "the Lion of the Punjab."

by Dyhan Singh.[1] Next day Ajeet Singh, by whose hand the crime was committed, together with his followers, were attacked and put to death by Heera Singh, son of the deceased vizier, and his party. For a time a state of anarchy, with its attendant slaughter and rapine, prevailed within the capital. These having run their course, Dhuleep Singh, only surviving son of Runjeet, was placed upon the throne of his father, Heera Singh making himself vizier. Meanwhile, the Sikh or Khalasa army had become formidable under Lal Singh, a favourite of the Ranee;[2] as an outcome of a conspiracy among them, Heera was murdered, his place taken by Lal.[3] Nothing could then restrain their ardour but an expedition into British territory, for which it was well understood that preparations were in progress. The proceedings thus alluded to supplied ample subject for comment in the papers, and talk at social gatherings.

[1] Dyhan Singh, vizier of the above.

[2] The Ranee Jinda, mother of Dhuleep. She was now Regent.

[3] Subsequently Sikh commander at the battle of Ferozeshah, December 21, 1845.

CHAPTER IV

1843-1844. *CAMPAIGN IN GWALIOR. HURDWAR*

16th Lancers—Delhi—The city—Kutub—Feroze's Lath—Divers—Muttra—Affairs in Gwalior—Army of Exercise—Halt—City of Krishna—River Chumbul—Across—Sehoree—Before the battle—Battle of Maharajpore—The 16th—"The Brigadier"—Search for wounded—General Churchill—Lieutenant Cavanagh—The muster-roll—Next night—The killed and wounded—Resume the advance—News of Punniar—Queen Regent—Around our camp—Gwalior—The fort—Disarming the conquered—Breaking up—Repassing the field of battle—Meerut—The welcome—Writing to the papers—Native troops—Hurdwar—Religious festival—The Dhoon—Return—Batta—A native regiment disbanded—Unrest in Punjab—Rejoin the Buffs.

ON the day the Buffs began their march, I proceeded to join the 16th Lancers, to which distinguished regiment I had been, by General Orders, attached for duty. Ten nights were passed in travelling by palkee dâk. In early morning of the eleventh day the Kutub was seen in bold relief against the indistinct horizon, for the atmosphere was laden with dust. After a little time, the Jumna was crossed by a bridge of boats; then another interval, and I was hospitably received by Dr. Ross, to whom I had an introduction.

Various places of interest in the imperial city were visited in turn. The Jumna Musjid, or chief mosque, its domes and minarets imposing in their grandeur; the balcony in the Chandee Chouk, whereon, in 1739, Nadir Shah sat witnessing the massacre of the inhabitants; the palace of the once "Great Mogul"; the smaller building in its garden, within which had stood "the Peacock Throne"; the remnants of the crystal seat upon which, in ancient times, monarchs were crowned; those of numerous fountains; the Persian inscription, to the effect that "If there is an Elysium upon earth, it is this." But from the ruins around, frogs and lizards stared at us; the once gorgeous palaces, and all that pertained to them, were smeared over with filth.

At a distance of twelve miles from the city stands the Kutub, surrounded by numerous remains of buildings, the road through all that way being along a space covered by ruins of various kinds. The Cashmere gate of Delhi by which we emerged was then noted as the place where Mr. Fraser, Resident at the Court of the Emperor, was murdered, and where Shumshoodeen, the instigator of that crime, was executed; it was to become famous as the scene of severe but victorious struggle against the mutineers in 1857. About two miles onwards stood the ruins of an astronomical observatory, one of two of their kind in India, the other being at Benares. A little farther on was the tomb of Sufter Jung, minister to the princes of Delhi; then continuous ranges of ruins until we arrive at Feroze's Lath, a metal pillar, the history of which is somewhat obscure, but on which marks of shot indicate attempts by Nadir Shah to destroy it. Now we reach the Kutub, a pillar sixty-five yards in circumference at the base, the ascent within it comprising three hundred and twenty-nine steps, the exterior interrupted by four terraces. Legend relates that it is Hindoo in origin; history that its exterior ornamentation was seriously damaged by the Mahometan conquerors. Not far from it are the ruins of what would seem to have been a tower of still larger dimensions. In the vicinity of the latter a deep well, into which from a height of sixty feet natives dived, performing strange evolutions in mid-air as they did so.

From Delhi to Muttra the journey was made along by-paths across country. In camp near the latter-named city were the 16th, commanded by Colonel Cureton, and there I joined them. The fact had meantime been promulgated that the destination of "the Army of Exercise" was to be Gwalior. The force so named, 30,000 strong, was to be divided into two wings or corps, to enter that State simultaneously from two directions. That from the south and eastward comprised the Buffs, 50th Regiment, 9th Lancers, Artillery, Native Cavalry, and Native Infantry; that from the west, the 16th Lancers, 39th and 40th Regiments, a strong force of Artillery, 1st and 10th Regiments of Native Cavalry, 4th Irregulars, and several regiments of Native Infantry.

While arrangements for active movements were being matured, those of us on whom as yet cares of office had not descended, passed our time in visiting places of interest in and near the cities of Muttra and Bindrabund, both held sacred by Hindoos in relation to the life of Krishna. In the last-named city we were only permitted to approach the principal temple that stood close to its entrance gate, but from the distance we could see, stretching far away as it seemed to us, the vista of its interior, dimly lighted by hanging lamps; at its extreme end the emblem of the deity to whom it was dedicated, resplendent with gems and precious stones. Everywhere along the narrow streets and from the flat roofs of their houses armies of "sacred" baboons grinned and chattered at us. A picnic to some characteristically Indian gardens[1] adjoining the banks of the Jumna furnished us with another pleasant interlude.

[1] Belonging to Luckimchund, at one time a Government contractor.

The division of the force of which the 16th were part resumed its march; in three days arrived at its assigned position not far from Agra, and there encamped, pending the result of an ultimatum dispatched by the Governor-General to the disaffected Gwalior leaders. Meanwhile, arrivals of the high civil and military officials, additions to the force, salutes and festivities afforded all of us pleasant occupation and variety.

The answer of the chiefs arrives; its terms are defiant. War against the State immediately proclaimed[1] by Lord Ellenborough; portions of the force put in motion towards the river Chumbul, among them the 16th. The appointed rendezvous near Dholpore is speedily reached, and there we encamp.

A vakeel arrives in camp, bearer of a dispatch by which the leaders of Gwalior rebels submit proposals for peace, on their own terms. They are at once refused. By daybreak next morning the force is in motion. Three hours suffice for crossing the Chumbul, an operation effected without important incident; establishments follow without delay; camp is pitched on hostile territory. The aspect of our position and immediate vicinity presents uneven ground, intersected by deep ravines, destitute of roadways. Our halt is of short duration. Early next morning the force emerged on open country; in due time arrived in near proximity to the village of Sehoree, and there encamped.

Meanwhile, information was received that Gwalior forces were rapidly concentrating in our front. Officers on the staff of our Quartermaster-General reconnoitred the country to a radius of ten miles and more around our camp. Soon the "Chief"[2] issued orders that the march should be resumed next day, and the Mahrattas attacked if met with.

Conversation at mess turned upon the probable events so soon to transpire; extemporised plans by individual officers indicated the several views they entertained of what was to happen. The very young expressed hopes that the enemy would show good fight; some of their number speculated on the chances of promotion before them. Then broke in one of the seniors, who had gained experience of war in Affghanistan: "I have just been employed in making a few little arrangements in case of accidents." "Highly proper," remarked another, "for no one knows what to-morrow may bring forth."

At daylight on December 29 our force began its advance, its manner of distribution to make an attack simultaneously on front and flank of the position known to have been occupied by the Mahrattas

[1] December 20, 1843.
[2] Sir Hugh Gough.

the previous evening. But during the night they had taken up a new position, considerably in advance, and from it unexpectedly opened fire on our leading columns. The general force was at once directed upon the new position. Horse Artillery commanded by Captain Grant[1] at full gallop rode directly at the Gwalior battery; opened fire upon it with crushing effect, and within the space of a few minutes reduced it to silence. Having done so, away again at full gallop Captain Grant led his battery against one on the left of the former, that had meanwhile opened upon us, our infantry columns plodding their way, slowly but steadily, against its line of fire. Very soon that battery also was silenced. The infantry were at work with the bayonet with terrible effect upon the enemy, with very heavy loss to our own forces, in men, horses, and ammunition. A third battery began its deadly work upon other bodies of infantry, in motion onwards. Again Captain Grant led his troop against it with the same result; then arrived the infantry, including the 39th and 40th British regiments; then hand-to-hand conflict, and then—the positions were in the grasp of our forces.

While thus the conflict raged fiercely, the 16th, led by Colonel Rowland Smyth,[2] together with the two cavalry regiments[3] brigaded with them, were ordered to sweep round the rebel camp, cut off, destroy, or disperse those who, driven from their guns, might take to flight. The Lancers dashed onwards at the charge, the bright steel and showy pennants of their weapons seeming to skim the ground, while at intervals stray rebels fell lifeless. The Gwalior men, anticipating such a manœuvre, had taken precautions against its complete success; the position for heaviest guns selected by them had along its front a ravine of great breadth and depth. Upon its edge the cavalry suddenly came, nor is it clear by what means they escaped being precipitated into it. There was for a moment some confusion as the halt was sounded; eighteen guns directly in front, six others in flank sent their missiles through our ranks or high above them. To remain exposed to risks of more perfect practice would serve no good purpose; there was no alternative but to retire. The infantry were seen advancing; down one side of the ravine, lost to sight; up the further side, then onwards, into the batteries, and then—the fight was won.

When at first the 16th took the position assigned to them on the field, it may have been that my endeavours to discover what was subsequently called "the first line of assistance" were unsuccessful; it may have been

[1] Charley Grant Sahib, as he continued to be called many years afterwards when as a General Officer he commanded a Division.

[2] Colonel Cureton now acted as Brigadier in command of the cavalry.

[3] 10th Bengal and 4th Irregular Cavalry.

that they were not very keenly made, at any rate "the Brigadier"—for so was named the troop horse I rode—knew his right place in the ranks, and so enabled me to witness the events now described.

Returning to my proper duties, I joined the parties who traversed the field of battle in search of wounded. Great, alas! was the number who lay prostrate,—many dead, many more suffering from wounds. Among the latter was General Churchill, his injuries of a nature to make him aware that speedy death was inevitable. While being attended to with all possible care, he requested me to take charge of the valuable watch he wore, and after his demise to send it to his son-in-law, Captain Mitchell[1] of the 6th Foot, at that time serving in South Africa. During the night he died, and his request was carried out by me.

At a short distance lay, in the growing crop that covered the field of battle, Lieutenant Cavanagh of the 4th Irregulars, loudly calling to attract attention, supporting by his hands a limb from which dangled the foot and part of the leg, his other limb grazed by a round shot which inflicted both wounds, and passed through his horse, now lying dead beside him. He was taken to the hospital tents, where meanwhile wounded soldiers and officers in considerable numbers had accumulated. The surgeons' work begun, three[2] of us mutually assisted each other. The turn of Lieutenant Cavanagh to be attended to having come, he made a request that we should "just wait a bit while he wrote to his wife," for he had recently been married. This done, he submitted to amputation, and during that process uttered no cry or groan, though nothing in the shape of anæsthetic was given, nor had chloroform as such been discovered; then, during the interval purposely permitted to elapse between the operation and final dressing, he continued his letter to his young wife, these circumstances illustrating the courage and endurance so characteristic among men (and women) at the time referred to. His case was one of many men who had to be succoured that day.

Meanwhile the force was in process of encamping on the field so gallantly won; the 16th paraded for roll call, the band of the regiment playing "The Convent Bells," the notes of which long years thereafter recalled the day and occasion. Casualties[3] among the men were only

[1] Afterwards General Sir John Mitchell, G.C.B.

[2] Namely, Dr. Walker of the Body Guard, Currie of 16th Lancers, and myself.

[3] The strength of the opposing forces at the commencement of battle was: *British*, 14,000, with 40 guns; *Mahrattas*, 18,000, including 3,000 cavalry and 100 guns. The *losses* were: *British*, 106 killed, 648 wounded, 7 missing; total, 797. Seven officers were killed on the field or died of wounds. The *Mahrattas* sustained losses estimated at 3,000 to 4,000.

nine; but among the horses more numerous than they had been at Waterloo, where as Light Dragoons the 16th so highly distinguished themselves.[1]

The arduous and responsible work of the day over, those of us who could do so withdrew to our tents, our hearts full of gratitude to the Almighty for individual safety, there to obtain such measure of rest and quiet as under the circumstances was procurable; for all through the evening and early hours of night the bright glare from burning villages, the dense smoke from others, the dull heavy sound of exploding mines made the hours hideous. Such was the battle of "Maharajpore."

During the evening the mangled remains of what in the morning had been a band of brave men were committed to earth. With returning daylight the same sad task was continued, all possible honour being shown to the dead according to the rank they had held, from that of General Officer in the person of General Churchill, who had succumbed in the course of the night, to that of the private soldier. Meantime, in tents the work of attending to the wounded went steadily on. There, officers and men whom we personally knew, lay helpless; among them Major Bray, of the 39th, and his son in adjoining cots, the former terribly burnt by the explosion of a mine, the life-blood of the latter ebbing through a bullet-wound in his chest.[2] And there were many other very painful instances, to the aid of whom our best endeavours had to be directed.

It was for the time being impossible to carry on with the army, in its further advance, the large number of wounded with which it was now encumbered. A guard sufficiently strong to protect the extemporised field hospital having been detailed, the general force resumed its march, the intention being to press on as rapidly as possible to the capital. Along a tract of soft sandy country, oppressed by heat, exhausted by the fatigue of the previous day, the troops plodded their weary way, in their progress passing many relics of the recent fight, including shot, arms, shreds of clothing, dead bodies of animals and of men, etc.

At last the halt resounded from trumpet and bugle; for a time we rested as best we could, and then the tents having arrived we

[1] In repulsing a body of French Lancers in pursuit of a party of Scots Greys, for which, as marks of appreciation by the king, they were made Lancers and granted scarlet uniform.

[2] Many years thereafter I became acquainted with Colonel Bray, who obtained his commission "without purchase" in acknowledgment of services rendered by his father and brother.

encamped. Some further delay was rendered necessary by circumstances. During that and the succeeding day information was received in camp that while the battle was proceeding in the vicinity of Maharajpore, an engagement equally formidable took place between the Mahrattas and the force under General Grey at Punniar, on the eastern border of the Gwalior State; that in it the Buffs had sustained a loss in killed of one officer and thirteen men, in wounded of three officers and sixty men,—the casualties in the 50th being equally numerous.

The arrival in camp of the Queen Regent, together with her Sirdars, and the young Maharajah, the salute on the accession of whom some ten months previous has been already mentioned, caused no little excitement, and at the same time much speculation among us. Later on, however, the report spread that the result of their interview with the Governor-General was by both parties deemed satisfactory.

As some among us took rides in different directions around our camp, not an armed man was met with. In some of the villages visited individuals who had escaped the carnage of the previous day were found lying more or less completely stripped of clothing, and wounded, some of them dead. The villagers had fallen upon the fugitives, robbed them of all they possessed, then turned them adrift. They had failed, and they paid the penalty of failure.

The march resumed, the force in due time reached the immediate vicinity of Gwalior, and there encamped. The huge fortress seemed to tower above us, while the neighbouring hills looked as if from their summits a well-directed fire could have swept the country to a considerable distance around. Within a couple of days arrived the force under General Grey and the Seepree contingent under Brigadier Stubbs. Negotiations had so far advanced that the latter took possession of the fort, the camp of the former adding very considerably to the dimensions of the great canvas city already existing. Rapidly and completely did the routine of life to which for some time past we had been accustomed undergo a change: complimentary visits and entertainments, each regiment entertaining every one else and being in turn entertained by them. By the high officials durbars and receptions were held, to which ceremonials Representatives of Gwalior having given their presence, the fact that they did so indicated that the end of our expedition was approaching.

Connected with the strong fortress by which the city of Gwalior is dominated were many points of interest; among them the general aspect of decay as seen from without, the tortuous narrow lane that leads to it, the steep and difficult flight of stone steps by which the ascent must be made, and powerful gates that seemed to lead but to a mass of ruins. Within the defences we were face to face with remains of temples, pillars, and arches pertaining to edifices of the Jains;[1] there were remains of what had been reservoirs of large dimensions and beautiful workmanship, in some portions of which clear water glistened in the sunlight. Only one piece of ordnance was met with; it was an ancient gun, seventeen feet in length, and apparently capable of discharging a fifty-eight pound shot.

The process of disarming the Gwalior troops was next performed—somewhat slowly at first, and not without some risk of difficulty, but more rapidly as information circulated among them that they were to receive all arrears of pay due, and a certain number of them taken into the service of "the Company."[2] Then did they march to the places assigned to them in battalions, their bands playing what was intended to be "God Save the Queen"; finally laying down their arms and surrendering their colours, all of which, packed on elephants, were taken to the fort. The artillery and cavalry gave theirs up elsewhere.

The wounded from different regiments were collected in camp, those among them fit to undergo the journey towards Allahabad being dispatched thither by means of doolies and native carts (hackeries),—the orders of the Commander-in-Chief, as expressed by himself, being that their progress thither should be by "easy stages and intermediate halts." From Allahabad they were to be conveyed by means of native boats to Calcutta, and there embarked on board one or more of the most comfortably and well-equipped ships proceeding *viâ* the Cape to England. For those whose condition was more serious, accommodation was provided in camp, and in public buildings outside the city of Gwalior. Among those so left were three respected officers of the Buffs. Of these, Captain Chatterton and Dr. Macqueen shortly afterwards succumbed to the disease—induced by the trials of active service. The death of the third—namely, Captain Magrath—was attended by a little circumstance which showed that the spirit of romance persisted to the last in him. During the battle at Punniar, he, together with thirteen men of his company, were blown up by the explosion of a tumbril that they were in the act of capturing. Captain Magrath and twelve of the soldiers with him speedily succumbed, or were instantly killed. When his body was being prepared for burial, there,

[1] *Jains.* The origin of the sect of Buddhists so called dates from sixth or seventh century A.D., its decay in the twelfth or thirteenth.

[2] The "Gwalior Contingent" so established joined the mutineers in 1857, and took prominent part in the investment of Cawnpore.

over the region of the heart, was found a lady's glove; nor was it difficult, bearing in mind some of the most pleasant incidents at Allahabad already recorded, to indicate the hand to which the memento originally pertained.

A general parade of the combined forces now took place. On that occasion the young Maharajah accompanied the Governor-General, by whom, in the course of his address, sufficient was expressed to raise hopes that further service on the Punjab frontier was to be immediately undertaken. But this was not to be.

Disintegration of "the Army of Exercise" forthwith began, in obedience to orders issued. Starting on their return march, the 16th traversed the field on which, twenty-nine days previous, the battle already mentioned had taken place. At short distances over its extent lay bodies of men and horses far advanced in decomposition; fragments of natives and equipments everywhere. The village of Maharajpore reduced to charred ruins; in their midst numbers of dead bodies of those who had so manfully stood their ground and perished as they did so. In what had been a room or enclosure a confused heap of what had been men further testified to the obstinacy of the defence. In some places miserable-looking inhabitants were searching among the ruins for property and houses. Such was the wreck of battle.

Thence to Meerut the march of the Lancers was uneventful. Halts for a day were made respectively at Hattras and Alighur, associated as those places are with early campaigns of the century. At the latter fortress we visited the gate and approach thereto through which was made the historic charge by the 76th Regiment;[1] then the monument to officers and men who fell on that occasion, and at Laswaree soon thereafter. Twenty days *en route*; the 16th re-enter Meerut, whence they had started on service now happily performed. Very touching were meetings between wives and their husbands; though to younger and less thoughtful men the full significance of husband and father restored to those dependent on him had yet to be realized.

A series of entertainments, including regimental dinners and a station ball, welcomed the return to cantonments of the 16th and troop of Horse Artillery, now under Captain Alexander, that had so much distinguished itself at Maharajpore. Preparations rapidly pushed on for the annual race for "the Lancer Cup," and all seemed to settle down for the hot season of 1844, then fast approaching.

A young (Artillery) officer had the indiscretion to write to the papers a severe criticism—from his point of view—on the tactics to which, according to himself, was due the heavy cost in killed and wounded at

[1] Under Lord Lake, September 3, 1803.

which the recent victory had been gained. A second officer made open boast of the help he had given in preparing that letter, and both of them boasted pretentiously of what they had done. But soon the attention of the "authorities," including the venerable Commander-in-Chief, was drawn to the comments in question, with the result to the subalterns concerned that, as expressed at the time, they were "come down upon like a sledge-hammer." Popular verdict declared that the example set by them, if followed, would destroy all discipline.

The date on which, according to ancient custom, the great Hindoo religious festival of the year was to be held at Hurdwar was near at hand. As on similar occasions, arrangements were made to send to that place a small body of native troops, those detailed for the purpose being men of the 53rd N.I. and 10th Cavalry, I placed in departmental charge. Our march thither began in the middle of March. As we proceeded, we went along through a highly cultivated country, many of the fields covered with "golden grain," for it was the season of barley harvest. More and more distinct became the snowy peaks and precipices of the Himalayahs; denser and more dense the masses of pilgrims toiling their weary way to the sacred shrine, for the occasion was that of the greater fair known as Kumbh Mela, held every twelfth year.[1]

Situated directly on the right bank of the Ganges, where that river emerges from the Himalayahs, the surroundings of Hurdwar are extremely beautiful, comprising hill, valley, forest, and stream. At short intervals temples stand; ghats or steps that lead downward to the sacred stream are crowded with devotees. In the clear, rapid stream, men, women, children, and fish commingle—for, like the river, the fish are sacred. The hills immediately behind the town are of the Sewalik range. Along their face occur a series of what were roads, though now scarcely deserving the name; on either side of them are veritable rock dwellings, now occupied by Fakeers. To the geologist the same range has interest connected with the remains of extinct animals contained therein; among them, of Ganesa's elephant, that lived, died, and became imbedded in marshes subsequently to be upheaved and so form the range referred to.

On this occasion[2] an estimated number of two hundred thousand persons were assembled on and in the immediate neighbourhood of the

[1] The festival takes place on the first day of the (Hindoo) month Baishakh, that is, commencement of the Solar year (March–April) and anniversary of the day on which the river Ganges first appeared on earth. Every twelfth year the planet Jupiter being in Aquarius, a feast of peculiar sanctity occurs; the great bathing day, or Maha Mela, coinciding with the new moon.

[2] April 11.

ghats to take part in what was called "the great celebration." At a given signal by the Brahmin priests, the masses precipitated themselves into the river, there to perform their religious ceremonies. Of the number who did so, about fifteen thousand were women; but it was said that during some previous years female devotees had been fewer than heretofore. After nightfall the river was illuminated by floating lamps as already described in reference to the Jumna at Allahabad, the scene presented being, as on that occasion, very beautiful.

An excursion to a distance of twenty miles or so up the valley of the Dhoon, undertaken for the combined purposes of shooting small game and relaxation, introduced us to surroundings very beautiful in themselves, full also of living things, animal and vegetable, most interesting to lovers of Nature. From the point reached by us a striking view was obtained of the ranges on which stand respectively the sanatoria of Landour and Mussoorie, and in the further distance snow-covered peaks of the Himalayahs.

The *mela*, or festival, over, without mishap or outbreak of special sickness, our return march took place. The mid-day heat had become great; we were therefore glad to be again within comfortable houses at Meerut, provided with thermantadotes and tatties;[1] and so the temperature reduced from 105° F. in the open to 76° F. indoors.

Not long thereafter the greater number, if indeed not all of us, were gratified on reading, in Government Orders, the announcement that officers and men who had been present at the battles of Meeanee or Hyderabad, recently fought in Scinde, Punniar, or Maharajpore in Gwalior, were granted as a donation one years' batta, amounting in my instance, with relative rank of lieutenant, to Rs.700—a very welcome windfall.

Certain native regiments were at this time ordered to the first-named country. Rumour spread that peace having been established therein, the extra allowances granted to troops while war was in progress was to be discontinued. In the regiments alluded to insubordination immediately showed itself, in at least one of them to a degree bordering on mutiny. A general parade was ordered; the disaffected corps so placed as to be in face of artillery, on either side cavalry and infantry; thereupon the sepoys belonging to it laid down their arms, after which they were paid up to date and escorted out of the station. The officer commanding another corps took upon himself to get rid of the ringleaders without waiting for official authority for so doing. Thus was suppressed what for the moment threatened to

[1] Prepared from the roots of *Andropogon*.

become a somewhat difficult state of matters. This was in 1844. The terrible events of 1857 at the same station were in the future.

The state of unrest with reference to affairs in the Punjab continued to increase, the likelihood of war next cold season appearing the greater from the facts that military stores were ordered to be collected at Umballah and Ferozepore, means of transport arranged for, and troops of various arms warned to proceed towards the frontier. Meanwhile, Lord Ellenborough was recalled, and Lord Hardinge reigned as Governor-General in his stead.

At the end of April, in obedience to orders, I started away to rejoin the Buffs, who had returned to Allahabad. The first part of the journey thither was performed by horse transit, then recently introduced—the palanquin placed upon a four-wheeled truck or cart, drawn by a single horse at the rate of seven miles per hour; for as yet railways had not been introduced into India. The latter part of the journey was by ordinary "palkee dâk"; and so, in due course, I was again with the happy regiment to which properly I belonged.

CHAPTER V

1844–1845. *ALLAHABAD TO ENGLAND*

In charge—Routine—Orders for England—Volunteering—Getting ready—Departure—Chunar—Benares—Sarnath—Ramdeela—29th Regiment—Ghazepore—Buxar—Dinapore — Patna — Granary — 62nd Regiment — Cholera — Monghyr——Hospitality—Bhaugulpore—Rajmahal—A reckless soldier—Corporal punishment—Berhampore—A Gwalior hostage—Plassee—Transport—Party of 10th Regiment—"Rejected"—Chandernagore—Calcutta—Preparations—The bronze star—The "Monarch"—St. Helena—Garrison—Slave ships—Longwood—Napoleon's grave—Courage at sea—England.

ROUTINE of duty, and responsibilities connected with what was called "full charge" of the regiment, now devolved upon me. Much had to be learnt in respect to official matters relating to my new position, nor could it be so except from so-called "subordinates" attached in those days to hospitals pertaining to British troops; to them I had, therefore, to refer, and from them gain needed information.

The aspect of cantonments during the next few months much resembled that of the previous hot season: pleasure and gaiety at suitable times, but not to interfere with duty. Among the soldiers unhappily there occurred, as before, great sickness and mortality, the line of new-made graves in the cemetery filled the previous year, and then numbering sixty, being duplicated and exceeded by one on this occasion.

Late in September, orders of readiness to proceed to Calcutta, there to embark for England, were appreciated in different senses by the younger officers and by the older, the latter contrasting in their minds their relative rates of pay in India, where the rupee had its standard value, and at home. With few exceptions the juniors expressed themselves as delighted at the prospect.

Then came the customary order that, prior to its departure, men who so desired should be given the opportunity to *volunteer* from the regiment to certain specified corps whose period of service in India had yet some years to run. A special officer was appointed to superintend the proceeding. Applicants for the privilege were subjected to physical examination; their defaulter sheets and "small books" looked at, after which, if deemed eligible, and under forty years of age, they were accepted, and received a bounty equivalent in amount to £3 sterling. To those whose age exceeded that limit no bounty was officially given, but a corresponding sum was granted from regimental funds as they existed at the time. As an unfortunate part of the system the canteen was kept open throughout; there the bounty money was quickly spent, with the result that throughout the week devoted to "volunteering" scenes of irregularity became numerous; parades and discipline were in abeyance, drunkenness and riot took their places.

As the arrival of our regiment, and its return from active service, had been made the occasion for a round of entertainments, so was now its prospective departure; civil officials and officers of native regiments joined in turn to show attention to the Buffs, and thus testify good fellowship and friendly sentiments towards the corps. Then came the final official ordeal; namely, inspection by the venerable officer commanding the Division. General Watson, then said to be of the old school, had seen much war service; personally amiable, but so full of years that, on the occasion of the parade in question, he was unable to mount a horse, and so perforce witnessed the formality of the march past while he remained on foot.

Boats of the kinds already described now lay ready moored to the bank of the Jumna for our reception. The General gave as a last entertainment a sumptuous *dèjeûner*, to which were invited the principal officers, civil and military, of the station. Healths proposed and drunk to in champagne; good wishes expressed; leave-takings gone through; then all take their respective places; bands play "Auld lang syne," "The girls we left behind us," "Home, sweet home," etc.; we are speedily on board; the moorings untied; the "fleet" in movement with the placid stream; from the ramparts of the fort heavy guns fire a "Royal salute" in honour of our regiment. Thus begins the journey homewards.[1]

We are speedily at the fort of Chunar, built by the Mahomedan conquerors of India, from Hindoo temples destroyed for that purpose; captured by Major—afterwards Sir Hector Monro in 1764,[2] but still held semi-sacred by the descendants of those whose shrines were so desecrated. On an open tract of ground in its near vicinity, a series of barracks and small houses were occupied by pensioners of the East India Company.

Benares, viewed from the Ganges, is picturesque, and in some re-

[1] October 16, 1844.

[2] Or rather, fell into his hands as a result of his victory at Buxar.

spects beautiful. Houses of red sandstone, their fanciful windows, projecting balconies, and flat roofs, giving to them a character all their own. The city extends from the very edge of the river; its numerous temples and ghats—the latter crowded with devotees and others, wearing garments of many colours, giving the scene a picturesque aspect. Some of the temples and ghats present a dilapidated appearance; but others, especially that of Visheswar—dedicated to Siva—is resplendent with gold gilding. Another striking object is the Mosque of Arungzebe, erected in the reign of that monarch from Hindoo temples destroyed for that purpose. Near the golden temple, in the heart of the city, is the no less famous well, named after Manic Karnik, believed by votaries to be filled with "the sudor of Vishnu," and at its bottom to contain Truth. At a short distance is the Astronomical Observatory, erected by Jai Singh, A.D. 1693.

History records that this ancient city continued during many generations to be the metropolis of Aryan civilization in India. It was at Sarnath, a suburb of Kasi, as Benares was then called, that in the sixth century B.C. Gautama preached the doctrines of Karma[1] and Nirvana.[2] There Buddhism assumed its sway, which it retained till the fourth century A.D., when it gave way before a revival of Hindooism, in regard to which religion Benares has ever since been considered its most sacred city.

Here we first witnessed the celebration of the Ramdeela festival. It consists in a representation of the more important incidents connected with the abduction of Sita; the chase, the siege, and capture of Ravanu's stronghold; her rescue, the ordeal of fire, to test her purity, and reception by Rama. As noted at the time, the performances, interpreted by the light of legend, gave to them considerable interest.

Resuming our river journey, we met a fleet of boats similar to our own, having on board a party of the 29th Regiment, in progress towards the north-west. The effective portion of the regiment was marching to its destination from Ghazepore, at which place it had been stationed during the two years it had been in India. From a strength of close upon 1,200, it had been in that short time reduced, by fever and cholera, to little over 400 effectives. Alas! out of those remaining, great were to be the losses at Ferozeshah, and other frontier battles, then in the near future.

There was nothing in the aspect of Ghazepore, or the buildings connected with it, to account for the havoc in life and health sustained by the 29th Regiment. A large extent of grass-covered plain separates

[1] That each act in this life bears its fruit in the next.

[2] The attainment of a sinless state of existence.

the station proper from the river. On it stands a monument, erected in memory of Lord Cornwallis,[1] who died near this place, while in progress up the Ganges. That monument, surrounded by tamarisk bushes, above which its summit rises, bears upon it a memorial figure by Flaxman. The range of barracks and the church are the only other buildings that are immediately seen. A visit to the native town brought us to the ruins of what had been the palace of Mir Cossim Ali Khan, whose forces were defeated, and power destroyed, at Buxar, in 1764, by Major Munro. The graceful proportion of its pillars, arches, and general aspect struck us forcibly, though the building itself is in a state of decay, as are also the numerous smaller ranges by which, in former days, it was surrounded; nor is it more than eighty years since that decay began. Other points of interest connected with Ghazepore include the growth and manufacture of poppy and opium, roses and their otto. A breeding stud for cavalry and artillery horses is here maintained by Government.

Buxar, our next halting place, was one of three places at which breeding studs were maintained by "the Company," the other two being Ghazepore, already mentioned, and Haupur. It would appear, however, that all these are insufficient to meet the requirements of the army, and that consequently importation of horses from the Cape and Australia has had to be resorted to.

Dinapore, then occupied by European[2] artillery, one British and three native regiments of infantry, for the assigned purpose of guarding against possible incursion by the Nepaulese, whose relations towards the Government of India were somewhat strained. It was said that for a number of years the terms of the Treaty of 1816 between Sir David Ochterlony and the chief of the Ghoorkas were faithfully adhered to by the latter; but that in recent times signs of disaffection had begun to show themselves. As an outcome of the Treaty in question, some of the Nepaulese took military service under the Company, they being enrolled in what became known as Ghoorka regiments. For some reason, the nature of which did not transpire, several days elapsed before our journey was resumed.

Impressions of the place were not particularly favourable; that it has attractions of a kind, however, seems evident, as families and various retired officers were said to make it their residence. A few miles distant is the city of Patna—Pataliputra of the Hindoos, and Palibothra

[1] Died 1805.

[2] During the early wars by the East India Company the troops employed by it comprised men of various European nationalities, besides natives of the United Kingdom.

of the Greeks—famous in relation to British history as the scene of murder by Kossim Khan, in 1763, of 200 Englishmen, besides 2,000 sepoys; to become again noted in connection with events of 1857. On our way to and from that city we noticed by the roadside the now disused grain-store, erected in 1769–70, to receive grain against the great famine then prevailing in Behar, in respect to which it is related that "the tanks were dried up, the springs ceased to reach the surface, and within the first nine months of 1770 one-third of the population of Lower Bengal were carried off by want of food."

The 62nd, occupying barracks at Dinapore, entertained the officers of the Buffs on a scale of hospitality and in a manner to be compared only with regimental festivities pictured in the works of Charles Lever. "The Springers," as in those days they loved to be called, were under orders for Umballah, much delighted at prospects of service therein implied; for the state of affairs in the Punjab, already mentioned, had from day to day continued to increase in gravity. The feeling of gallant hilarity was expressed in a somewhat demonstrative manner in extemporary song by one of their officers in early morning hours, while mess had not yet broken up.[1] Of our festive hosts on that occasion scarcely one was alive fourteen months thereafter.

Resuming our journey, our fleet was moored about sunset under a somewhat high alluvial bank, such as in this part of the river course are of frequent occurrence. To several of our soldiers the result was fatal; during the night cholera attacked with violence, and claimed them as victims. As we continued on our way next day the malady seemed to be left behind us.

Monghyr, at which we speedily arrived, is interesting in several respects. To the cession of its rather imposing fort was immediately ascribed the massacre of our countrymen at Patna, as already mentioned. Near this place, in the year of that occurrence, 1763, a mutiny occurred, in which not only native but also European troops were concerned, nor was it until several of their number had been blown from guns by order of Major Munro, already mentioned, that the outbreak was suppressed.

At this place more hospitality was shown us. While yet at some distance from our halting ground, an invitation reached the regiment

[1] The officer alluded to, familiarly known as "Paddy" Graves, parodied a well-known soldiers' song of Peninsular days after this manner:—

"The Sixty-second Springers all—are
Going to march unto Umballah—r;
And the Buffs, that gallant band—are
Going to their native land—are.
Love, farewell."

from Mr. Hodson, then occupying the position of Joint Magistrate and Collector, that officers should dine with him; while to the soldiers, "refreshments" would be served on tables arranged for the purpose as near as possible to the boats. Thus did our host express the compliment he desired to show the regiment, and very highly were his successful endeavours appreciated.

Our next halting place was Bhaugulpore. There, in 1827, the Buffs were stationed, while as yet our frontier line was comparatively little advanced,—Bhurtpore only the previous year captured. In the range of hills that thence extend in a south-westerly direction are various wild Santhal tribes, very low in civilization, devil-worshippers by custom;[1] their weapons were chiefly bows and arrows; their own ethnic alliance believed to be Dravidian.

At the time referred to the number of steamers on the Ganges was small; the length of inland voyage from three to four weeks. Officers and others availing themselves of that mode of transit considered that they were travelling "by express." It was customary with some to spend the period of sick leave, extending in certain instances to six months, on board comfortably fitted up "budgerows" on the river; tradesmen also arranged the kind of boat so called as travelling shops, and these different classes of persons and craft gave certain variety to our river voyage. Arrived at Rajmahal, the former capital of Northern Bengal, but now a ruined mass out of which stood a few broken shafts of what had been pillars of black marble. The ruined palace dates back only to A.D. 1630. Sultan Shujah, by whom it was founded, elder brother of Arungzebe, was at the time Governor of Bengal. He was soon thereafter deposed by the latter-named monarch; fled to Arracan, and there perished miserably. When visited by Bishop Heber, the ruins of the palace were in comparatively good preservation; subsequently, however, their materials were utilised in the construction of the magnificent palace of Moorshedabad.

Two incidents now occurred, each characteristic in its way. A soldier having clandestinely obtained bazaar spirit, was thereby rendered drunk and desperate; boasting of his courageous deeds, he was challenged to "take a header" into the Ganges. He did so, and appeared no more. The other was the infliction of one hundred lashes on the back of a hardened old offender, simply as punishment, for none of those who knew the man expected that it would have any deterrent effect in the future.

Entering the Bhauguruttee branch of the Ganges, our fleet was soon

[1] In subsequent years large numbers of them were converted to Christianity; colonies established by them in Cachar and Assam.

at Berhampore,[1] whence I had started up the river little more than two years previous. Again, but now as one of a body of officers, I partook of hospitality shown to the whole regiment by General Raper. A breakfast given at the palace of the Nawab;[2] excursions by land and river, presentation to His Highness, permission to visit different parts of his palace, including jewel-room and its contents, were so many items connected with ovation given to us as representatives of a distinguished regiment. All this was wound up by dinner at the house of the General, followed by a "Reception," during which I had the pleasure of again meeting some "old" friends.

Among the guests at that Reception was "the Khasjeewalla of Gwalior," implicated, as we have seen, in the disturbances that led to the recent campaign in that State. For a time he was interned at Agra, but latterly had been "at large," under surveillance of our host; his demeanour towards those by whom the victory at Punniar was gained, by no means agreeable; but under the circumstances anything else could hardly have been looked for.

Resuming our journey, we soon arrived at and glided past the village of Plassee,[3] but the actual field so named had long since been swept away by the river by which we were being carried along. At Kulnah,[4] indications of flow and reflux of the tide were evident. There we met the fleet of boats, similar to our own, by which the 10th Regiment was being conveyed inland. Mutual salutations passed between us, but little at the time thought I of close association subsequently in store for me in relation to it. A short distance more, and we passed the village of Balaghurree, its inhabitants, those and their descendants, who, having been left by their relatives to die by the side of the river, were rescued through the good offices of missionaries.

We were nearing the end of this river journey. In quick succession

[1] In 1757 a stately range of two-storied barracks for "European" troops were erected at a cost of £302,278, the rupee then worth 2*s*. In 1834 they were abandoned on account of high rates of sickness and mortality among their occupants; average admission rate of 13 years per 1,000 strength, admissions 2,196, deaths 82. Of certain endemic diseases treated the rates of deaths to admissions were:—fever, 1 in 21; dysentery, 1 in 10; hepatitis, 1 in 9.

[2] Then sixteen years of age. His grandfather, Jaffer Ali, Wuzzeer of Suraj ood Dowlah, Nawab of Bengal, a member of the Imperial family of Delhi, whom Lord Clive defeated at Plassee in 1757. It is related that on that occasion Jaffer Ali bribed a number of Suraj ood Dowlah's troops; with them he deserted his chief and went over to the English side. Subsequently the Nawab was assassinated, and Jaffer Ali raised to a position he had no right to claim. Thenceforward the Nawab of Moorshedabad was an "ally" of the British Government.

[3] Plassee. From Palasa, "dâk tree," or *Butea frondosa*.

[4] Kulnah is 164 miles from the Sandheads.

our fleet glided past the important native towns of Bandel, noted on account of its Roman Catholic convent; Hooghly, for its college; and Chinsurah, already mentioned. Now we were off Chandernagore, on the battlements of which waved the tricolour. In 1757 that little settlement was captured from the French by Clive, aided by Admiral Watson, who, for the attack, brought thither his frigate carrying seventy-four guns—a feat not now possible because of the silting up of the river. The place was shortly afterwards restored to the French, to again fall to the British during the Revolutionary War, and finally to be ceded to them in accordance with the Peace Treaty of 1816.

We are well within the influence of the tide. As it recedes we are borne towards Calcutta. A forest of masts becomes more and more dense; tall chimneys on either bank tell of factories; the clang of hammers, of ship-building yards; the odour of tar, that we are nearing our port; and great is the surprise with which our north-country servants and followers look upon the unwonted sight. We pass the Armenian Ghat. It is an open space, on which various funeral pyres blaze and smoke; vultures and adjutant-birds are waiting for such human remains as may be left: the scene most unpleasant to look at. For many years past that which has just been alluded to has ceased to exist, a crematorium having taken its place. We arrive at Calcutta; the regiment lands, and marches into Fort William.

Preparations for departure proceeded rapidly, and with a will. Hospitality to the regiment and attentions in other ways were shown by some of the higher officials. At Government House some of us had an opportunity of being present at the dinners and balls, for which it was then, as since, well and favourably known; also at parties given by the Chief Justice Sir Lawrence Peel, in the spacious house occupied by him at Garden Reach.

The issue to men and officers of the Bronze Star respectively for Punniar and Maharajpore took place, but without pomp and circumstance such as most properly at the present time are observed on similar occasions. Being informed that the stars in question, composed of metal of Mahratta cannon that had wrought heavy injury to our regiments, were in readiness, in company with my friend Maude,[1] I drove to the Mint, and there, from two heaps on the floor, of those decorations, selected one each, leaving both for the purpose of our respective names being engraved on them. A few days thereafter we returned, and having received from an employé of that establishment

[1] Now, after an interval of fifty-two years, I still am proud to call him friend. Alas! since the above was written he has passed away.

the much-prized decorations, we placed them in our pockets, and drove back to Fort William.

Soon thereafter,[1] the Headquarter portion of the regiment was on board the *Monarch*, and away from India homeward bound. Our ship, one of a class by which troops were wont in favoured instances to be conveyed between England and her great Eastern dependency: graceful to look at, roomy, well fitted up, sumptuously provided—veritable floating palaces. The comfort of the soldier, his wife and children, secured to an extent that under subsequent regulations became impossible. With regard to officers, "stoppages" for messing was on the scale already mentioned. I became entitled to "head money," as on the outward voyage, notwithstanding that I was in the performance of my ordinary duties with my own regiment.

Nine weeks of uneventful life passed, and our ship was at St. Helena. Very shortly thereafter, parties of us, arranged for the purpose, landed at James's Town, the population of which seemed to consist almost entirely of mulattoes of low type, physically and intellectually; the balance were of pure negro type. We learned, moreover, that slave ships with their human cargo on board were from time to time brought to the island by British ships of war, very harrowing details being given of the sufferings of the unfortunate captives on board. At the time of our visit the garrison of the island comprised the St. Helena regiment and a battery of artillery.

An excursion to Longwood proved to be a somewhat arduous undertaking—carriages ricketty, horses like living skeletons, lame, and weak, the ascent steep, rugged. The six or seven miles to be traversed required several hours for completion of the task. At last we were at and within the barn-like, dilapidated building in which took place the closing life scenes of Napoleon; its surroundings a tangled mass of brambles and other shrubs. In the building itself his library room, then partly filled with hay; near it the stable, having stalls for six horses. In a pretty valley close by, under the shade of the then famous willow, was the open tomb whence the remains of the great Frenchman were removed in 1840 for transport to the banks of the Seine.

Continuing our voyage, an incident which happened during its further progress deserves record. While sailing under the influence of the trade winds, a sailor fell from aloft into the sea. Quickly were life-buoys slipped, the ship brought round, a boat lowered, while from top-gallant cross-trees an officer directed the crew

[1] January 19, 1845.

towards the man struggling in mid ocean. Soon, from the bows of the boat one of its crew dived, for the drowning man had already begun to sink; a brief interval, and both rescuer and rescued were hauled on board. With no loss of time the boat was alongside and on board ship, the man restored to animation and life by means used to that end. Many years thereafter, meeting Mr. Cloete, who performed the gallant act, we talked over the incident and its surrounding circumstances.

Another month at sea, and the *Monarch* swings at anchor off Gravesend; the Buffs, absent from England since 1821, disembark;[1] the ordeal of the Custom House gone through; the march on foot begun, for as yet a railway had not been opened. Evening was far advanced when the regiment arrived at Chatham, where it was to be temporarily quartered. In accordance with the routine of that day, nothing whatever had been prepared in barracks for our men, save that doors were open, displaying bare walls, bed cots devoid of mattress or bedding; while for the officers, not even quarters had been assigned; they were expected to look after themselves. Night had far advanced before duty rendered necessary by such a state of things was so far complete as to allow of our going in search of hotels in which to spend the few hours that remained till daylight. It was not till two o'clock in the morning that we had "dinner," in course of which various allusions were made to the "hospitality" accorded to us as a body on the occasion of our return, as contrasted with what we had experienced in India. Two days had to elapse before the regimental baggage arrived, though the distance over which it had to be conveyed was no more than ten miles; nor was it till then that straw for the men's cots was issued by the barrack stores, and they initiated into the art of stuffing their allotted quantities into their palliasses. This was the beginning of our Home Service.

[1] On April 29, 1845.

CHAPTER VI

1845-1846. *HOME SERVICE*

Leave Chatham—First railway experience—March continued—A comparison—Chichester—Soldiers' tea—Winchester—Forton and Haslar—Naval Hospital—Sikh invasion—Regiments to India—Experimental Squadron—Russians—Ibrahim Pasha—Regiments—Volunteer for West Coast of Africa—Leave the Buffs—Hounslow flogging case—Clarkson and slavery—Abolition.

TIME-EXPIRED and some other classes of men not conducive to regimental efficiency being discharged, soldiers and officers "set up" in respect to kits and equipments, the order to proceed to Chichester was received with acclamation, for in those days the reputation accorded to Chatham as a station was by no means flattering. At the end of May the Buffs marched merrily away; that is, marched on foot, for railway communication had not yet connected Chatham with the outside world. A few miles got over, and we were at Blue Bell Hill, the ascent of which revealed to us in great variety and luxuriance forest, flowers, and grass-covered patches; the summit reached, an extensive view of the lovely vale of Kent stretched away beneath us, and in our near vicinity the cromlech called "Kittscotty House"[1] attracted the notice of those among us who were of antiquarian tastes.

At Maidstone the regiment had its first experience of transit by rail The art of "training" and detraining troops had not yet been learnt; hence delay such as would now be culpable was unavoidable before soldiers and their baggage were in their places, and a start made. The line being open only to Redhill, all had there to alight, the short journey to Reigate being performed on foot. Arrived at that pretty town, we had our initiation into the system of billeting, the officers being "told off" to the principal hotel, the comforts of which made us speedily forget what-

[1] It is related that in A.D. 455 a battle took place near this spot between the Saxons under Hengist and Horsa, and the Britons under Vertimer, the latter being victorious; that among the killed were Horsa, the Saxon, and Catigern, the brother of Vertimer. One account relates that the cromlech alluded to is that of Catigern, Horsa having been killed at Horsted near Rochester.

ever disagreeables had attended the proceedings of the day. Continuing our journey, we arrived in succession at Petworth and Horsham, at each of which towns we similarly enjoyed our billets; thence to Chichester. The approach of a country gentleman to our Commanding Officer attracted our attention; the "halt" was sounded; the word passed on that, on hospitality intent, he had provided "refreshments" for all of us. His kind attention was highly appreciated, acknowledgments expressed, he himself invited to dinner with the officers at our new destination; then the march resumed, the Buffs marching into quarters at Chichester on the fourth day of their very pleasant journey.

Compared and contrasted with a march in India, that now over presented some striking points of difference, not the least of which were the absence of hackeries, bullocks, camels, elephants, and that heterogeneous collection of "followers" comprised under the name of "the bazaar." Instead of tents and camp fare we had comfortable if expensive entertainment at hotels, while our daily line of route lay through rich, varied, and beautiful English scenery. But some of our party looked back with fond remembrances to the freedom and feeling of exhilaration attending the early morning march in India, dusty roads and sundry other drawbacks notwithstanding.

The huts, literally "baraques," assigned to us were old, dating from the Peninsular War. From the restoration of peace they had been left unoccupied until quite recently, when they were utilised in the first instance for the temporary reception of men enlisted to form a new 44th Regiment, and subsequently by the 55th on its return from China. The officer[1] who held the position of Barrack-master boasted of a very honourable military "record," he having been, if not the very first, among the first to mount the breach at Badajos; yet, like many others of his day, he had been thrown on half-pay at the conclusion of the war, and so deprived of the chance of rising in the service. From the residents of the cathedral city and its neighbourhood our officers received much civility and hospitality. The cathedral, used as a stable in the days of Cromwell, but long since "restored," was often visited, the circumstance that it had been transported from Selsey to its present site adding to it many points of historical interest. But to some among us Chichester had the great disadvantage of not yet being in direct communication by railway with London, the journey to and from the metropolis having to be performed by coach. A Bill had then only recently been passed authorizing such a railway.

An event occurred while we occupied those huts which marked in its

[1] Lieutenant Graham.

way a stage in the advance of comfort and well-being of the soldier. Hitherto his "regulation" daily meals were only two; namely, breakfast at 8 a.m., dinner at 1 p.m.—an interval of nineteen hours being thus left during which he had to be without food, unless he happened to have spare money wherewith to supply himself at the regimental canteen or public-house in town. The obvious drawbacks of such a state of things had long been subject of representation, but hitherto unsuccessfully. Now, however, in 1845, authority was issued granting the issue to the men of a tea meal at 4 p.m. For a time the order was resented; that a soldier should condescend to *tea* was held to be against the natural order of things, and to mark effeminacy. Soon, however, the measure was appreciated by all, and drunkenness, at that time the bane of the soldier, underwent a remarkable decrease.

Winchester, to which we next proceeded, had "for ages" been looked upon as a favourite station by regiments. To some of us the many historical associations connected with that ancient city became so many sources of interest and objects of study. The commodious barracks, occupied by the Buffs and Scots Fusilier Guards stood upon the site of what had been a royal palace, and still earlier a castle. The city itself dates back to B.C. 800. The cathedral—to which our visits became very frequent—occupies a site whereon stood, during the years of Roman occupation, an altar to Apollo, and, in times still more ancient, one devoted to sun worship. Among other places of interest in and around the city were the buildings to which more particularly are referred the legendary stories of Saint Swithin of rainy fame; the ancient hospital of St. Cross, at which travellers might claim a dole of bread and beer; the world-famous school and college, both founded by William of Wykeham, A.D. 1324–1404. Among favourite walks was that to "the Labyrinth," on the summit of St. Catherine's Hill; several alongside the banks of the Itchin, sacred to the memory of Izaak Walton, and that to Twyford. In the churchyard of that place stood a remarkably fine specimen of a yew tree, such as, in times long gone by, were preserved in burial places, and so held in a manner sacred—for the purpose of supplying yeomen with long-bows, in the use of which weapon those of England so much excelled. The hill from which, in Cromwell's time, the city was bombarded was a favourite walk among us. So was the village of Horsely, some few miles distant; its church associated with the author of *The Christian Year*, the choir, consisting of various very ordinary musical instruments, including a violin and clarionet.

On a day late in January, 1846, the Buffs proceeded by rail to Portsmouth. Bitterly cold, wet and windy, was the weather; the streets of that great naval port in some places inundated by the tide, so that progress along them was by no means pleasant. By the floating steam bridge the harbour was crossed, our regiment divided so as to occupy barracks at Forton and Haslar respectively. With the companies proceeding to the latter place I was detailed for duty. The quarters consisted of huts, the one assigned to me so situated as to afford from its window a near view of Spithead, and of the magnificent and graceful sailing men-of-war vessels anchored there or manœuvring in the Solent.

An early opportunity was taken to visit the great Naval Hospital, near to which my temporary residence was situated; and although in these notes professional recollections are for the most part avoided, one of the results of that visit was sufficiently interesting to be made an exception to that rule. On a portion of the adjoining grounds, and set apart for the purpose, a considerable number of mentally afflicted patients, together with their attendants or keepers—their costumes in every respect similar to those worn by the patients—were engaged with apparent heartiness in what was a "rollicking" dance, to the notes of several violins, the performers on which were presumably patients and attendants. In the treatment of the patients all coercive measures were absent; free association among them was permitted from time to time, as we had seen; such of them as desired to work or labour were given every opportunity of doing so, and for the special benefit of those who desired to follow—in imagination—their seafaring life, a lake with its fleet of boats was provided. Such were some of the measures adopted in respect to this class of patients in 1846. The *Victory* and other "sights" connected with the great naval port were visited; but in respect to these it appears unnecessary to enter into details, except that all associations on board relating to England's naval hero were duly venerated.

Without previous warning news circulated that the Sikhs, in great force, had crossed the Sutlej, and thus invaded British territory. Then quickly followed intelligence that four severely contested battles against them had been fought, their forces defeated, Lahore occupied; Dhuleep Singh, a child, brought by his mother, the Maharanee, to the camp of Lord Hardinge, the Governor-General, by whom his "submission" was accepted. In those battles many officers fell, with whom, collectively or individually, we had but recently, as already mentioned, been most pleasantly associated, and whose fate we now mourned. As fuller details became known, it appeared that on December 12, 1845, the Sikh armies, under the command of Lal Singh, crossed the Sutlej, and by the 16th had strongly fortified a position taken up by them on the left bank of that river. On the 13th the forces under Sir Hugh Gough attacked and drove them from their position at Moodkee. Following them to Ferozeshuhur, at which place they had meanwhile entrenched themselves, he renewed his attack upon them on the 21st, the terrible battle which was to ensue continuing during that and two following days,—the issue, for some time uncertain, ultimately being in favour of our troops. There it was that the 62nd, with whom but lately we had been happy at Dinapore, having begun its advance against those entrenchments with 23 officers, lost 17 of that number—8 killed on the field and 9 wounded. But still another position, and it at Aliwal, was taken up by the retreating Sikhs, where, on January 28, 1846, they were attacked by the forces under Sir Harry Smith. There the 16th Lancers performed the gallant deed of charging through a ghola (or mass) of Sikhs, their substitute for a square; then repeated the charge, destroying the enemy thus rode down. In the performance of that heroic feat the regiment lost upwards of one hundred men killed and wounded—that is, nearly one-third of their effective strength. On February 10 the Sikhs were defeated, their forces destroyed up at Sobraon, though at very heavy cost in killed and wounded to the British. On that occasion the 50th lost in killed and wounded 12 officers, nearly all of whom were personal acquaintances, more or less intimate of my own, and in addition 227 men. The 10th Foot, with which I was destined to be subsequently associated, had in killed and wounded 3 officers, 3 non-commissioned officers, and 127 rank and file. Other regiments engaged suffered heavily, for the Sikhs contended for their nationality and class interests. The facts related give significance to the intentions of Lord Ellenborough expressed in Gwalior, to lead the troops thither direct upon the Punjab frontier. That plan was disallowed, and so two years were given to the Sikh leaders wherein to complete their arrangements for taking the offensive.

Orders from the Horse Guards directed that three infantry regiments —namely, the 8th, 24th, and 32nd—should proceed to India without delay. No less than six weeks elapsed, however, before they sailed, the circumstance itself illustrating the state of unreadiness for emergencies which then existed. The three regiments named were destined to take their parts in arduous service in India, the first at Mooltan, the second at Chilianwalla, the third at Lucknow.

The establishment of what was to be called our "Experimental Squadron" at this time was justly looked upon as an event of great importance. The fleet so designated consisted for the most part of sailing ships of war, but comprised also several steam vessels, propelled by paddles, the whole providing for spectators an unusual and magnificent sight as they lay anchored at Spithead.[1] Between the lines passed the Royal yacht, having on board Her Majesty the Queen. From the sides of each successive ship thundered salutes; from their decks rose strains of the National Anthem; from their yards, manned for the occasion, came hearty cheers of loyalty. A brief interval succeeded; then simultaneously, as if by combined movement, dropped the huge white sails; these gradually filled to the breeze; away glided the fleet, followed by hundreds of yachts, boats, and craft of all sorts. About this time also the then strange sight was for the first time witnessed of a war ship, the *Rattler*, sliding, as it were, out of Portsmouth Harbour, destitute of sail or paddle, the first of her kind propelled by the Archimedean screw.

The arrival at Spithead of the Russian war-ship *Prince of Warsaw*, having on board the Grand Duke Constantine, escorted by two other vessels, was to Portsmouth an event of interest and political importance. The officers of the Imperial frigate were entertained at dinner by those of the Buffs: an attention much appreciated by them. Next day a party of us were most civilly received on board their ship; in the course of that visit the circumstance made clear that our hosts were well acquainted with the English language, as also with insular manners and customs. But great was the contrast between conditions on board and those of the "Experimental Squadron." The Russian sailors untidy and slovenly in appearance, the terms of their service severe, inasmuch as after a period of twenty years in the Navy or Army the reward to which they had to look forward was—emancipation; for as yet they were serfs. According to their own accounts, the period of obligatory service by officers was twenty-one years. Leave of absence, if exceeding a total of one year during that period, had to be made up by them; and if on any occasion absent from their ships or regiments for more than four days, their pay for that time is withheld from them. We congratulated ourselves that our position was in those respects more fortunate than theirs.

About the same time Ibrahim Pasha came among us. The circumstance that the comfort or otherwise of travellers across the desert between Cairo and Suez depended much on measures directed by the Viceroy of Egypt, added to other considerations, no doubt moved Admiralty and Horse Guards to order that every attention should be shown to His Highness. Among other displays for his gratification

[1] July 15—under command of Sir Hyde Parker.

the troops in garrison were paraded on Southsea Common. As he rode along the line, the impression produced by his appearance and style was by no means favourable; about fifty years of age, bloated in aspect, cruel and relentless in expression, he looked in these respects a true descendant of his father, Mehemet Ali.

In quarters at Portsmouth were the 13th Light Infantry, then recently returned from India, their honours thick upon them, as "The Illustrious Garrison." The 74th, re-converted into Highlanders, paraded for the first time in their newly-acquired uniform. In those regiments and in the Buffs there was a large leaven of old soldiers who had not risen beyond the ranks; the majority of the non-commissioned officers were men whose locks were grey, some with sons serving as soldiers; recruits were relatively few in number; barrack-room courts-martial in full operation; crime, at least that *officially* brought forward, comparatively rare, though what in reality is quite another thing. That the regiments so constituted were capable of the most arduous service was proved by that of the Buffs in Gwalior, the 13th in Affghanistan.

The receipt from the War Office of a letter containing an offer of promotion conditional on proceeding to the West Coast of Africa, though a surprise, was not altogether an agreeable one, for hitherto the usual designation of that part of the world had been "The White Man's Grave." Official reports[1] regarding it referred to no later date than 1825; but this is the result of reference to them:—In February of that year a party of white soldiers, 105 strong, arrived at the Isles de Loss, near Sierra Leone; at the end of eighteen months 54 of their number were dead by fever, 8 by other diseases, 21 invalided back to England, 20 remained on those islands, scarcely any of them fit for duty. Then followed a table by which, at the Gambia, the annual mortality of white men was shown to have been at the rate of 1,500 per 1,000 average strength. On the other hand, the proffered promotion would advance me over one hundred and forty of my seniors; increased pay[2] would be an immediate advantage, and, in the event of survival, increased departmental position. The upshot of thought given to the subject was that, in the expression common to the time, I volunteered for the West Coast.

With regret and sorrow I ceased[3] to be a member of the distinguished old [4] regiment, with the traditions and history of which, like all its other members, I had become familiar. I had, moreover, formed

[1] Statistical Reports by Major Tulloch.

[2] Regimental pay, 7*s.* 6*d.* per day; mess and band subscriptions deducted from it.

[3] July 10, 1846, Staff-Surgeon, 2nd class.

[4] Dating back to A.D. 1572, when, under Elizabeth, the regiment was formed

friendships [1] such as subsequent experience taught me existed only between regimental officers during early life. The kindly expressions addressed to me by the Commanding Officer on the occasion of the farewell dinner, to which I was invited, impressed me in a manner not to be forgotten, and are here alluded to as indicating the relations then existing between medical and battalion officers.

No regular line of communication existed between England and the West Coast of Africa; consequently, when orders to embark were received, passage had to be negotiated for through the medium of a ship's broker, and so advantage taken of trading brigs or other small craft proceeding, at irregular times, on voyages thither, either from the Thames or Mersey. Several months elapsed before transport was obtained, and, meanwhile, time was spent in visiting places interesting in themselves or by reason of past associations.

At this time public attention became aroused to a state of ferment, ostensibly because of the death of a soldier of the 7th Hussars at Hounslow, after having been flogged to the extent of 150 lashes, in pursuance of a sentence to that effect by court-martial, for having violently and dangerously assaulted a non-commissioned officer of his regiment. Medical opinion differed *in toto* as to whether the death was, or was not, the effect of the corporal punishment. But the case was taken up and energetically debated, not only at public meetings convened for the purpose, but also in both Houses of Parliament. Whatever may have been its intrinsic merits, the case in question undoubtedly led to the introduction of a Bill, the outcome of which was that the maximum number of lashes to be inflicted was thenceforward reduced to fifty. Instead of "unlimited" service as heretofore, the period of a soldier's engagement was reduced to ten years; and so, it was hoped, encouragement held out for a better class of recruits to join the ranks; desertion would be diminished, and the general efficiency of the service increased.

In September, 1846, the death of Thomas Clarkson, at the age of eighty-six, recalled attention to the subjects of slavery and the slave trade, against both of which, for many years, his energies had been directed. It was in 1720 that English opinion was first drawn to the horrors incidental to that traffic. In 1787, by the efforts of Clarkson

out of the Trained Bands of London, its uniforms of Buff leather, whence its name, now a proud title.

[1] Now, alas! while these notes are being transcribed, only one remains; namely, General Sir Frederick Francis Maude, G.C.B. Only lately did my other great friend, Deputy Surgeon-General Bostock, C.B., Q.H.S., die. While the notes are under revision, Maude has passed away.

and Granville Sharp, a Society for total abolition of the system was formed. In the following year a Committee of the House of Commons was appointed to inquire into the entire system; but not for a considerable time could the objects of that Society be carried out, or members of influence be induced to take interest in the Anti-Slavery Association and its work. Suddenly, and as if through an accidental occurrence, public opinion was aroused; that accident, the seizure in the streets of London of an escaped slave, named Somerset—his late master, the captor. In 1792, Wilberforce carried a Bill for the gradual abolition of the slave trade. In 1805 the importation of slaves into British Colonies, recently taken from Holland, was prohibited; a Bill carried, by which such traffic after 1808 was declared illegal. In 1811 it was declared to be felony; in 1824 it was made piracy. In 1837, made punishable by transportation for life. In 1838, complete emancipation of slaves throughout all British possessions took place. We were soon to see the results of those measures in what had once been one of slavery's most active spheres.

CHAPTER VII

1847-1848. *COAST OF GUINEA. BARBADOS. ENGLAND*

Sail for Guinea—Arrive—Cape Coast Castle—Fantees—Some characteristics—Domestic "slaves"—Obsequies—First impressions—Tornado season—Sickness and mortality—Personal—Husband of L.E.L.—"Healthy" season—Amusements—Natural history pursuits—Snakes—King Aggary—Chiefs—Accra—Apollonia—Burying the peace-drum—Axim—River Encobra—The "royal" capital—Savage displays—Prisoners released—Scarcity of fresh water—The king surrendered—Brought in manacled—His atrocities—Retribution—Return march—Cape Coast—Fantee women—Force disbanded—"Reliefs"—Departure—Incident on board—Barbados—The island and its people—Compared with tropical India—Homeward bound—Arrive in England—Comments—Chartists—Leave of absence.

COLD, misty, and raw was the day in the first week of January, 1847, when, at Gravesend, a small party, of which I was one, embarked on the brig *Emily*, bound to Cape Coast Castle. Still more miserable the four following days and nights, during which the little vessel remained at anchor, a thick dark fog enveloping us; horns and gongs sounding at intervals, to avert a collision, if possible. At last the pall lifted, and we were on our way. My fellow-passengers, four in number, were three junior officers of the 1st West India Regiment, and the wife of one of them. The ship had a burthen of only 130 tons; no separate cabins, no accommodation suitable for officers, and none whatever for a lady. Around the cuddy, as the "saloon" was called, a series of bunks were arranged; one of these was told off to each of us, ingress being attained either feet or head foremost, according to individual fancy and agility. Every possible consideration was shown by all on board to the lady, whose sorry plight we all commiserated; hers was indeed a sad example of the discomforts to which a subaltern's wife was exposed. Our prospects so far were by no means happy, for the circumstance became increasingly plain that only "black sheep" were considered to be sent to "the Coast"; many years had to elapse before Africa was to spring into fashion.

Fifty-two days at sea—for steam communication with the West Coast was a thing of the future—and then the headland of Grand Drewin came in sight. That point sighted, our little ship glided along the coast, carried southward by the oceanic current at the rate of three knots an hour or thereabouts. Arrived in the roads of Elmina, at the time a Dutch settlement, we disembarked by means of small canoes, made by hollowing out a branch of the bombax or silk cotton tree, each canoe "manned" by three black boys, the eldest of whom did not apparently exceed twelve years of age. We made direct for the house of Mr. Bartels, not that we had an introduction to that well-known gentleman, but for the double reason that "everybody" did so, and that Elmina boasted neither of hotel nor other public place to which new arrivals could resort. The hospitable gentleman on whom we had thus thrown ourselves showed us every kindness. Next day means of conveyance to our destination were provided for us. Mine consisted of a long narrow basket, carried on the heads of two strong Africans, one at either end. In that way we travelled over some miles of roadless ground; in others along the sea beach left dry by the receded tide, and so arrived at Cape Coast Castle, the capital of our settlements on the Coast of Guinea.[1]

The fortress had in its day been used for many purposes, from the time when in 1610 it was erected by the Portuguese, and by them made use of as a slave hold, down to the present (1847). Captured by the Dutch from its original possessors in 1643, it was taken from the latter by Admiral Holmes in 1661; recaptured by the Dutch fleet under De Ruyter in 1665, but the same year ceded to England. In 1757 it was attacked unsuccessfully by the French, since which it has remained free from the din of war, although from time to time conflicts have occurred between the native tribes occupying the neighbouring districts. In 1672 the first African Company received a charter from Charles II. From that date till 1844 the fort continued in the possession of that Company and its successors; in the year named it came directly under the administration of the Colonial Office, as a dependency of Sierra Leone. At the time of our sojourn there, Cape Coast Castle was occupied by a portion of a West India regiment by officers belonging thereto, and to military departments; by the Governor, also by the "mixed court," by which law or justice, or both, were administered. A school for African children, the apartment being used for Divine service

[1] When the first Europeans trading between Benin and Palmas asked where the gold and produce offered them for sale came from, the natives answered, "From Jenné" (on the Niger, near Timbuctoo). Her name was thus given to the Gulf of Guinea, and, indirectly, to the English coin, the guinea. (*Timbuctoo the Mysterious*, by Felix Dubois, p. 172.)

on Sundays, was in close proximity to the billiard-room. An annexe ot the fort was utilised as a prison for the worst class of malefactors, and the native police in charge of them, the prisoners being engaged in chain gangs by day, working on roads and public works within the settlement. Since the days of slavery, what had been "barracoons" for captives have been transformed into water tanks for the supply abundantly provided by the rainy season.

The inhabitants of the territory around Cape Coast Castle and of the Gold Coast generally are in the mass known as Fantees. Originally dwellers in the regions beyond the river Prah, they were forced to cross it, and driven to the coast line by the people now called Ashantees, who took possession of and gave their name to the country so conquered. Although under protection of the British Government, the Fantee chiefs (in 1847) pay tribute to the Ashantee king, who still assumes suzerainty over them. That suzerainty, since 1826, has been maintained without right on their part, the Ashantees having in that year been defeated at Doodwa, near Accra, by a Fantee force, led by British officers. In the same year, however, though earlier in it, a small force,[1] under Sir Charles Macarthy, was disastrously beaten by the Ashantees. That officer, rather than fall alive into the hands of his enemies, is said to have shot himself; they to have devoured his heart, in the belief that by that act of cannibalism they might become endowed with the high attributes which they admired in him.

A noticeable characteristic of the people was the total absence among them of ceremony, rite, or other observance pertaining to religious worship. That certain phases of superstitious impressions existed among them was evident by their belief in "lucky" and "unlucky" days. Neither a fisherman nor bushman would proceed on their avocations on a Friday, as it was by them devoted to their "Fetish."[2] Although caste as understood in India is unknown among Fantees, the existence of septs or families approaches in some respects the social and religious divisions of the Hindoos. Each Fantee sept is distinguished by its special badge or armorial bearing, taken usually from some wild animal of the forest, as among Scottish Highlanders and other civilized nations, ancient and modern.

Ten years had nearly elapsed since slavery on the Gold Coast, as in all other British dominions, was abolished. In all but name conditions remained unchanged; former domestic slaves, now called servants, remained with their former owners, by whom they were housed, clothed,

[1] Mr. Barnes, with whom I was acquainted in 1847, had been with that force in 1826.

[2] From the Portuguese *Fetisso*, a spell, or charm.

and fed as heretofore. It was related that when, in 1838,[1] emancipation was proclaimed, the negroes here appealed against being "sent away," on the plea that they and their children had ever been cared for; that as freed men and women they were without country to return to, or means of earning their living, save with their old masters and mistresses. Their appeal was listened to, and now (1847), when asked jokingly, rather than in earnest, to whom do they belong, they answer proudly that they are "slave" of, say Mrs. Jackson, Mr. Barnes, Mr. Hutton, and so on, all highly respected residents of Cape Coast.

A "slave" girl of the class alluded to having died, ceremonies, elaborate in kind, took place over her body. Placed in a sitting posture, and so supported in a corner of a room, it was enveloped in a shroud of costly damask; the feet rested upon a cushion similarly covered; neck and arms decorated with heavy ornaments of solid gold; the body embellished by more or less artistic designs composed of gold dust applied to some adhesive material. In the mouth was a twig of shrub; on an adjoining table a goodly supply of rum and tobacco. On the floor of the room sat a crowd of female mourners, whose dirge was loud if not melodious. These ceremonies over, the dead, still covered with ornaments, was deposited in the grave prepared for it in the floor of the dwelling-house of the survivors; but, as stated to us, at the end of a year, the body would be "turned on its side to make it comfortable," and then the golden ornaments removed.

Two months had elapsed since our arrival, and impressions of the place were noted after this manner:—At the end of February, temperature in the shade between the moderate extremes of 84° F. and 86° F.; sky clear and cloudless, sea breeze recurring each morning, and continuing during the hours of daylight. Behind, and from close proximity to the town, the "bush" or dense forest begins; two inconsiderable hills, each surmounted by a "fort," dominate us. Some few roads or pathways extend in various directions inland and along the beach side to the Salt Pond, their borders lined with cacti and with flowering shrubs,[2] the occurrence of reptiles of various kinds, and creeping things innumerable, adding to our walks of interest and excitement in giving the former chase. Among the forest trees a species of bombax was a striking object, its branches so thickly covered with nests of the tailor-bird (*Ploceus*) that they touched each other, and looked not unlike a series of gigantic honeycombs. The absence of the bamboo was noted with surprise, considering the latitude of the locality. Nor was any

[1] From August 1, 1838, slaves became free.

[2] Thespesia, acacias, including the sensitive plant, abrus, convolvuli, palms, wild figs, tamarind, etc.

cultivated field to be seen, the explanation being that each year small patches of the bush are cut down, the ground cleared, crops sown or planted, and once gathered in the "field" is quickly restored to its original wild state till again required for agricultural purposes. Birds and butterflies, some of both highly coloured, dashed through or fluttered among the herbage, but no voice of song properly so called as yet came from the former.

With the advent of the tornado season, the face of nature underwent a sudden change. From the south-east came rapidly a mass of dense black cloud. As it seemed arrested overhead, it assumed the form of an arch; from its concavity forked lightning flashed, then heavy thunder rolled. The previous stillness gave place to a rush of wind at hurricane speed, followed by such a downfall of rain as we had never previously seen, even in India. A few repetitions of these, and the rainy season was upon us. Then suddenly cultivation was begun in places previously covered by bush; crops of Indian corn, yams (*Convolvulus Batatas*), ground-nuts (*Arachis hypogea*), and the castor-oil plant sprang up with a rapidity truly astonishing.

With the first regular downpour of rain came a serious change in health of our small party within the fort, also of the few settlers whose places of business were in the town immediately outside; and for a few succeeding months we were destined to realize the true significance of a sickly season on the Coast of Guinea. Fever in one or other of its local forms made its appearance, affecting the older residents in that of ague, while the newly arrived were attacked by the more violent form, called at the time their "seasoning," from which the chances of recovery were considerably less than those of death. Of the three officers and the wife of one who had been my fellow-passengers, one of the former speedily succumbed. The other two, together with the lady, suffered severely, and made imperfect recoveries, while outside the fort conditions were no less serious. The blanks so made in our numbers were sadly apparent, and yet the survivors from attacks, and those who had not been struck down, found in each successive death this rather ghastly consolation, that, as the *ratio* of mortality was "being made up," so did their chances of escape increase. All this while the few of us who were capable of the exertion took our walk morning and evening when the weather permitted, our one promenade that towards "the Salt Pond." As we did so, the melancholy sight presented itself, of a small number of newly arrived missionaries[1] gloomily pursuing the same route, "waiting," as we were

[1] Of the Wesleyans.

informed, "for their seasoning," before being sent inland to their respective stations. One after another was missed; it was announced that "he was down with his seasoning"; and then—the receipt of a black-edged envelope told the rest.

Meantime I retained my health to a degree that under the circumstances was remarkable. As a result of this happy exemption from sickness, various duties devolved upon me in addition to those within my proper sphere, among those extra responsibilities being professional work in the Colonial Hospital, and charge of the Commissariat Department for the troops—the latter altogether alien to my training or tastes. So conditions went on till July, a month which proved to be the most unhealthy and deadly of any throughout the year. It was then that, night after night, I was the solitary member of "our mess" who took his place at table. I made the acquaintance of, and speedily became on friendly terms with, some mice, whose place of residence was under the floor, but which freely communicated with the messroom by numerous apertures, and was in other respects dilapidated; nor did it take long before some of the little animals acquired sufficient confidence to scramble up my leg and so on to the table, partake of dinner with myself, thus calling to my mind the story of the Prisoner of Chillon. With the month of August came improved health conditions, and for the four or five succeeding months all was cheerful in that particular and important respect.

Among those who succumbed during the sickly months was Captain Maclean, husband of the poetess, L. E. L.—Letitia Elizabeth Landon, who died at Cape Coast Castle in 1838, under circumstances of great mystery. It was hoped that among his papers would be found some containing his own account of the sad occurrence, but that hope was not realized. From careful inquiries, however, I was led to the belief that her death was due to natural causes, and to them alone. Now the body of the deceased husband was laid in the grave close to that of the wife,[1] and both rest under the pavement of the castle quadrangle. The story of the gifted lady interested some of our number, as incidents connected with her short life on the Coast were related by Mr. Hutton and others who had enjoyed her acquaintance.

The occurrence of the "healthy season" was hailed as such event could only be in a locality where every man had to run the gauntlet for life during four to five out of the twelve months which make up the

[1] Some account of L. E. L. is given in my separate book, *Life on the Gold Coast*. I consider that the cause of her death was disease of the heart, with which she was known to have been affected several years.

year. Amusements of different kinds were instituted, short excursions taken in various directions along such roads or pathways as existed for purposes of communication along the coast and to places inland. In the absence of horses—for these most useful animals when brought to the coast rapidly pine away and die—our means of transport consisted, for the most part, of a chair so placed between two poles as to be thus carried by two or four Africans, according to the weight of the individual. There were a few small light carriages, in some respects like a Bath chair, in others like a victoria, drawn by Africans, who, to judge by their antics and shouts as they raced against each other, must have enjoyed the work immensely. Picnics became "the order of the day"; Saints' days, birthdays, and holidays were most "religiously" kept, and for the most part very enthusiastically celebrated. On one of these occasions we visited what at one time had been a coffee plantation in the near vicinity, but then deserted; the buildings reduced to ruin, the coffee bushes choked by the ordinary bush, the natural impression being that the owner had fallen a victim to his "seasoning," that he had no successors on his estate;[1] or, if he had, that they had also succumbed.

Pursuits relating to natural history became so many sources of pleasant and intellectual occupation. Ornithology was especially interesting, combining as it did observation of birds in their natural haunts and conditions. A large number of specimens were shot, one portion being subsequently given to the Natural History Museum of Edinburgh, another to Sir William Jardine, by whom notes taken at the time were published.[2] A song bird (*Drymoica mentalis*) that fell to my gun was for the first time, I believe, given as an illustration in that brochure; another illustration being that of a large and handsome swallow named after me, *Hirundo Gordoni.*

On one occasion, while combining ornithological study and "sport," I had an unpleasant experience with one of several kinds of poisonous snakes that here abound, frequenting chiefly prickly herbage in immediate proximity to such roads and pathways as then existed, as also the sedgy tract of open ground near the Salt Pond, a little way westward of the settlement. While traversing that tract I came suddenly face to face with a large black cobra. One barrel of my fowling-piece had been already discharged. The remaining shot—a mixture of Nos. 6 and 9—was fired, more as a result of instinctive action than steady aim, by me, but with good effect. The charge traversed the

[1] Still called "Napoleon."

[2] Under the title of *Contributions to Ornithology*.

body of the reptile as if it were a bullet, so close was it to me; then its writhings were such that I came within them, not a little to my own horror. In the emergency my Fantee "boy" speedily dispatched it by means of the heavy stick he carried for the purpose of beating the bush. The skin—considerably over six feet long—ornamented the wall of my barrack-room while I remained on the coast. Puff-adders are numerous, and from their sluggish movements are easily killed. On one occasion I killed six partially-grown individuals during a morning's walk on the Salt Pond road.

When, as already stated, administration of British settlements on the Gold Coast was taken over by the Colonial Office, it was made immediately subordinate to that of Sierra Leone. The inconvenience of that arrangement was soon made manifest. The force with which the oceanic current runs southward along the coast is sufficient during some months of the year to prevent sailing brigs from beating up against it; and as at the time alluded to a regular line of steamers had not been introduced, the outcome of that state of things was the inconvenient necessity of letters and dispatches for the headquarters of the Government and Command being sent *viâ* England, several months becoming thus necessary before answers could be received. Cape Coast Castle and its dependencies had a Governor and Colonial Secretary, both of whom were resident. Justice was administered by a court presided over by a British official designated Judicial Assessor, assisted by selected native chiefs. Of them, "King Aggary," then upwards of eighty years of age, was the most prominent and distinguished. As a young man he had served on board a British man-of-war, in accordance with the custom of the time, and so, according to his own manner of expression, he "had learned sense."

For a long time past native rulers whose "kingdoms" adjoined British settlements along the Gold Coast had voluntarily placed themselves under protection of our flag, and thus in a manner become British subjects. Their several laws and customs were retained, with the exception of human sacrifice, a practice abandoned many years ago. Succession to rank and property descended through the female line; that is, the eldest son of the eldest daughter became heir-apparent. In the kingdom of Akim the sovereign is a female, the succession being also in the female line.

A visit to Accra occupied two days, and a similar time to return. The path along which I travelled—for no road existed—led for the most part through the bush close to the beach; at times it was by the beach itself, so that only when the tide was low was it practicable to proceed at all. At intervals the occurrence of rugged promontories and heaps of boulders rendered it by no means an easy undertaking to get over them. Arriving at the river Sekoom, its borders were lined by mangrove trees (*Rhizophora*), the long tendril-like roots of which interlaced above the soft mud alternately covered and left exposed as the tide flows and ebbs. In some places the trunks of those trees were covered within tide mark by a small species of oyster, and presented the additional peculiarity of a few small fish—the climbing perch (*Anabas scandens*) laboriously ascending to the height of a couple of feet or so from the water level, there "holding on" for a little, then dropping into the muddy river after basking in the sun. At Accra, three forts, belonging respectively to England, Holland, and Denmark, were in close proximity to each other: the first occupied by some twenty black soldiers and half a dozen native militiamen, the guns old and useless, the fortress itself dilapidated; the second nothing more than a trading store of the Governor; the third, the strongest of the three, but noted for its extreme unhealthiness. Subsequently we learned that it was completely destroyed by an earthquake.

Several of the forts that had belonged to the former African Company were abandoned some years previous to the present date (1848); among others that of Amelycha, or Apollonia, about seventy miles to windward of Cape Coast Castle. For a time matters in the district so called progressed very well under the rule of a humane and otherwise good native chief named Yansu Acko; but having died in 1830, he was succeeded by Quako Acko, a man of cruel and tyrannical disposition, who, although he continued to fly the British flag, gradually became less and less loyal, and finally withdrew allegiance altogether. Meanwhile he was in a continual state of warfare with the States adjoining his own, extending his depredations to Asinee and Axim, respectively belonging to France and Holland. In 1835 his conduct had become so outrageous that a force from Cape Coast Castle was sent against him, and for his misconduct he was subjected to a fine of 300 ounces of gold dust. So little effect had this upon him, however, that in 1838 a second expedition was sent against him, and a further fine of 800 ounces inflicted upon him. From that time to the present he has persisted in annoying the adjoining States. Within his own "kingdom" his word was absolute, his great ambition apparently to surround his palace with festoons composed of skulls of enemies slain in battle or of captives butchered. With increasing boldness as time went on, he destroyed several villages within Dutch territory, and carried away some of their inhabitants. He maltreated officers and men belonging to French and British ships, who landed at his capital for purposes of trade. Finally, when remonstrated with by the Governor of Cape Coast,[1] he insulted and otherwise maltreated the members of the embassy sent to him, certain of whom he retained as captives. The Governor took action against the recalcitrant chief. Orders were issued directing the formation of a contingent force, some thousands strong, to consist of men pertaining to vassal tribes. A brig was chartered for the occasion; ammunition and stores of various kinds, including casks of fresh water, placed on board; for it was known that the scene of coming operations was destitute of that necessary element. Ammunition was issued to the "volunteer" contingent, to whom pay in advance was distributed. At this point the officer[2] named to command fell ill and speedily died of coast fever, and his place had to be taken by a lieutenant[3] of the 1st West India Regiment; the Commissariat officer[4] being non-effective from sickness, the duties pertaining to his office fell upon me in addition to my own.

The resources of the colony in respect to white men limited the number of those available for the present expedition to six only, the "regular" troops to no more than about half a company of the 1st West India Regiment. Four of us by ship;[5] two accompanied the levies proceeding by land, their forces increasing as they advanced. Arrived off Dixcove, we landed at that place, to witness the native ceremony, and excitement attending thereon, of "burying the peace-drum." The unusual noise and tumult connected with the ordeal seem to have attracted the notice of wild denizens of the adjoining forest, one of which, a baboon of large size, "assisted" with his presence on the occasion; he was declared to be "the great Fetish"; his advent to be a happy augury for the undertaking before us. Our next point was Axim, at that time Dutch, but now British. There we landed; there the entire force at our disposal assembled, and arrangements were completed to enter hostile territory. The small party of whites was accommodated within the fort, the native forces bivouacking in and around the town,—the town consisting chiefly of sheds or huts composed of palm branches inartistically tied together. In the open space or market place in its centre stood a pole to which were fixed portions of human skeletons, remains of freebooters from Apollonia, who having been caught were "disposed of" according to African fashion. In the vicinity roads were non-existent; some rugged pathways were all the thoroughfares with which the place was provided.

[1] Commander, afterwards Sir W. Winniett, R.N. He died on the Coast.

[2] Captain Losack.

[3] Lieutenant Bingham. He lost his health during the expedition, and shortly thereafter died in England.

[4] C. Swaine.

[5] The brig *Governor Maclean*.

Between Axim and the river Encobra stretched a sea beach two miles in extent, broken at intervals by irregular masses and boulders of primitive rocks; beyond it to a similar distance a belt of impenetrable forest, pathways through which, formerly existing, had for some years past become obliterated. Through that tract of bush we had to make a way, not only for ourselves, but also for our "forces." Armed with an axe and long knife such as bush men in this part of Africa use, we cut a path for ourselves to the summit of a promontory from which it was practicable to take bearings for further progress. Meanwhile, and all through the following night, large numbers of men were busy clearing a road by which the mass of our contingent could advance. At daybreak our strange body of irregulars was mustered, and what a sight it presented! War dresses, wild in character, grotesque in aspect; umbrellas of many colours, carried over particular chiefs; uncouth gesticulations in the performance of war dances; strange sounds from drums, horns, trumpets, and other "musical" instruments, the chief ornaments on which were jawbones and other fragments of human mortality, combined to impress us with the aspect of savagery so presented. At the head of one of the "companies," and in command, was a lady, who thus asserted her hereditary position as chief of her tribe.

In the early hours of a day in the first week of April (1848), our "army" began its march towards the left bank of the Encobra. By previous arrangement a number of canoes, sufficient to take the force across that river, were already outside the bar at its mouth, and these were quickly utilised for our purpose. A dense mass of natives crowded the opposite side of the river, its dimensions quickly increasing as others emerged from the bush. Our "artillery" consisted of two twelve-pounder rocket tubes, and two others of smaller calibre. In the absence of a "combatant" officer, I had been put in "command" of these, and having previously indulged in the necessary practice, was in a position to open fire upon the "enemy" as soon as the necessary order was given by the Governor, who was in supreme command. A few missiles were discharged; a few lanes ploughed among them, and then pell-mell the mass vanished in the forest. Having got across the river, we speedily reached an Apollonian village, deserted by its ordinary occupants, who in their haste had left behind their flocks and herds, both of which were quickly annexed by our "contingent." Continuing what proved to be an extremely fatiguing march along the sea beach,—often having to wade more than knee-deep in the rippling tide,—we passed on the border of the forest a succession of villages, from all of which their occupants had fled. Towards evening we reached a town of considerable size. Our day's march had been extremely exhausting, so that rest for the night was most welcome, especially to us white men.

In the course of the succeeding night, such snatches of sleep as we obtained were several times interrupted by the beating of tom-toms, braying of trumpets, the rushing hither and thither of considerable portions of our army. Now it was an alarm of night attack by "the enemy"; then the noisy return of a foraging party, bearing with them as trophies the heads of two Apollonians, which they cast before the Governor as tokens of their prowess. Resuming our march early the following morning, we arrived at the river Abimoosoo, across which we were floated by means of canoes that had so far followed by sea, keeping just outside the line of breakers. Shortly thereafter we were met by a messenger from "the king" against whom we were in progress; his office [to express the desire of his Majesty to know with what object the Governor had brought an army into his country. The reply was a ball cartridge (according to the custom of the coast), together with a reply that if the king surrendered, then "a palaver" would be held, but not till then. Meantime we pressed on, and in the early part of the afternoon entered the capital of the king, to find it completely abandoned. Never before had I felt so "done up" and exhausted as now. I was, moreover, ill, and had every reason to believe that an attack of the much-dreaded fever of the coast was upon me.

As if to celebrate the entry of our "army" into the royal city, arrangements were speedily made by the native leaders to have a grand procession. When it did take place, no more wild and "savage" display could well be imagined than that presented by it. All around us were ghastly relics of death and murder. The palace garnished with festoons of human skulls, of which I counted one hundred and eighty after the greater part of such ornaments had been torn from their places and kicked about as playthings by our "soldiers." The avenue leading to the palace was formed by palm-trees growing at short distances from each other along either side of the roadway. From time to time the king had disposed of a certain number of his enemies by living sepulture in a standing position; a cocoa nut placed on the head of each, the earth thrown in, and as in the progress of time the plume of palm grew higher and higher, each tree received the name of the particular enemy represented by it. At different points around, the larger trees were ornamented with various relics of humanity, skeleton hands and other fragments being nailed or otherwise attached to stems and branches.

During the few following days different portions of our contingent were variously employed. An expedition, led by two of our white associates,[1] started inland, with a view, if possible, to capture the fugitive king; another, consisting entirely of blacks, having started independently into the bush, returned in triumph, with "music," war dances, and much discordant noise, bearing with them gory heads of three Apollonians who had fallen into their power. A third party of our people, having proceeded on an independent expedition, came upon two men who had been made prisoners by order of that chief, each of them laden with three sets of heavy irons, which they had worn continuously during the two previous years. The manacles were removed after much labour; but their unhappy bearers, when relieved of them, were unable to stand erect. So long had they been kept in a sitting posture by sheer weight of their fetters, that the joints had become accommodated to it. Shortly afterwards eighty-eight other prisoners were discovered, their fetters similarly removed, but they themselves fixed in the sitting posture to which they had for longer or shorter periods been borne down by iron manacles.

Everywhere around the town the bush was impenetrable, for all communication with neighbouring tribes had been cut off for some years past, the pathways thus become obliterated by the forest. Attempts to cut new ones were but partially successful. Meanwhile serious difficulties beset us in respect to water, for the lagoons and rivers within available distance being brackish, they quickly ceased to be resorted to. A few casks of fresh water from our chartered ship thrown overboard were washed ashore, their contents carefully distributed among ourselves; but the fact became very evident that this supply being extremely limited, our "occupation" of the town must be short indeed, whether the object of our expedition was obtained or not.

Most fortunate for us there was treason in the king's camp. By reason of his cruelty and tyranny, he had rendered himself hated by and hateful to his subjects. Now their opportunity had arrived. Three of their chiefs having tendered their submission, so far imitated certain civilized nations as to negotiate for the surrender of their king—their terms by no means exorbitant, namely one hundred ounces of gold dust, and a flag to them respectively. And so the bargain was closed.

A few more days passed, during which "palavers" of all sorts took place, and parties dispatched in various directions, though seemingly without result. Evening approaches; there is unusual tumult among our contingent. Discordant noises, emitted from drums, horns, and

[1] Messrs. Brodie Cruickshank and Frank Swanzy.

human mouths, announce the approach of large bodies of men; they are the former subjects of the king,[1] whom they carry manacled and give over to the British leader. We feel relieved by the prospect of speedy ending of our privations and fatigues; for of our number, four are prostrate by sickness. So long as our prisoner, savage as he is, continued out of sight, we did our best to follow him up relentlessly. Now that he is in our presence, bound hand and foot, an object of abject misery, big tears rolling down his coarse black face, some of us were unable to smother a shade of sympathy for the man, monster of cruelty as he was.

Of atrocities committed by him the record of two will here suffice. He caused his mother to be secured to a stake at low-water mark when the tide was out, her eyelids to be cut off, her face turned towards the sun,—so left until overwhelmed by the returning flood, and her sufferings put an end to. His pregnant sister he caused to be cut open while alive, that he might see the position in her womb of the unborn infant, then directed that according to native custom her body should be buried within the palace.

In the room under the floor of which the remains were interred, bearing upon them her golden ornaments, the captive king was placed under guard, and so remained during the following night. With the return of daylight it was seen that the floor had been opened by the guard, the remains exhumed, all ornaments wrenched therefrom; the body itself, considerably advanced in decay, offensive to sight and smell, thrown back into the still open grave. Thus the king had spent the night side by side as it were with the remains of his murdered sister, witness to the acts of savagery to which they were subjected.

Our object attained, the return march began at midnight; our prisoner, several of his wives, together with other members of his family, being under the charge of a strong guard. The four sick white men, unable to take their proper places in the ranks, were carried, country fashion, in the long baskets already described, our bearers being subjects of the king whom we were carrying away prisoner. Again the beach, left dry by the receded tide, was our highway, and along it our "brave" men proceeded. How the sick fared is illustrated in my own experience. As the fierce tropical sun ascended in the heavens, the fever from which I suffered increased, headache was severe; fresh water there was none wherewith to moisten the parched mouth. In this plight, having by signs indicated my desire

[1] Quako Acko by name.

that my basket should be placed on the ground, I endeavoured to make my way to the ripples left by the recurring waves; but in so doing strength gave way, and I fell prostrate on the sand. Immediately I found myself being gently lifted back to the basket by my carriers. One of them climbing a cocoa-nut tree that grew in our immediate vicinity, cut off a large specimen of its fruit, which was speedily opened by a companion beside me, its "milk" emptied over my face and given me to drink. At the time and often since I have thought gratefully of that act by the wild African, and have contrasted it with its counterpart met with among "civilized" peoples.

Arrived at Axim, and the necessary arrangements completed, we re-embarked on the little brig that had already done good service in connection with our expedition. The captive chief, or "king" as he was called, was speedily on board, under the care of a guard, the anchor raised. Wind and current favoured us, and so we quickly arrived off Cape Coast. In the early hours of morning we landed. Our prisoner was securely placed in a cell of that fortress. The populace of the native town, on hearing the news, were in great commotion; our friends, merchants and others, from whom we had parted a month before, were full of congratulations. Then followed invitations to dinner, picnics, and so forth, until the rainy season, already threatening, fairly broke upon us and put a stop to all.

Among other characteristic incidents related to us was that, as soon as our expedition had marched away, the women of Cape Coast, omitting the slight costume usually worn by them, went about their ordinary occupations in a state of nudity. One of the oldest of the foreign residents, astonished at the circumstance, inquired as to the reason for such an extraordinary proceeding; he received as answer from the perambulating statue so addressed the Fantee equivalent of "What does it matter? All the *men* have started for the war," much emphasis being given to the word "men."

The work of paying up and disbanding the contingent portion of the force was quickly carried out. In the former, gold dust was the currency employed, of which the equivalent value of three-halfpence was the daily rate given, no allowance being required for food. Years passed away, and then I learned that the wretched king, having lost his reason in his confinement, pined away, and died a drivelling idiot in his prison. One by one our party of white men engaged in this small but extremely trying piece of service dropped away, and for many years before the time when the present notes are transferred to these pages I have been the sole survivor. The expedition was mentioned approvingly in the *Times* some months after it had become a thing of the past. Medals and decorations for similar services in West Africa were then in the future.

Fifteen months on the Gold Coast; then came the welcome news that a ship with "reliefs" on board was sighted. Great was the excitement as we watched her gradual approach; great the zest with which their arrival was welcomed; hospitable the reception accorded to them; great the marks of kindness in various ways shown to us by residents. It was long since news had reached us from England, for regular mail communication did not exist. Papers now received were eagerly read, for they were filled with details illustrative of a threatening political aspect in various kingdoms of Europe.

Taught by experience how treacherous and dangerous was the climate of Cape Coast, I determined to proceed by the first ship to sail, irrespective of immediate destination, the chief object being "to get away." The arrival of the transport *Baretto Junior*, with reliefs of West Indian soldiers and African recruits for regiments in the West Indies, afforded me the desired opportunity. On 24th of May we embarked, the ship dropped with the current to Accra, and then sailed for Barbados.

Glad and thankful to have successfully run the gauntlet as it were against the climate of Guinea, the clear sea air, notwithstanding its temperature of 83° F., had its usual beneficial effect on health impaired on the Coast. The transport in which we sailed had on board three hundred Africans, of whom about one-half were soldiers, the remainder recruits, that is, captured slaves, selected from among those in the Adjudication Yard[1] at Sierra Leone, and duly "enlisted" into West India regiments. A good many of the soldiers were accompanied by their wives and children. Among the "recruits" was a very strong athletic African named Kakungee, one of a cargo of slaves, the vessel conveying whom had recently been captured by a British man-of-war. A fellow-slave, but now "recruit," gave information of the violent and uncontrollable temper of Kakungee while on board the slave ship; that on two occasions he had suddenly attacked fellow-slaves, killing his victims before a rescue could be effected. With a view to guard against similar occurrences on board the *Baretto Junior*, he having speedily shown the violence of his disposition, he was secured to the deck by means of a cask—in one end of which was a hole sufficiently large to let through his head, but not his shoulders—being put over him and cleated down. In that manner he was kept during the early part of our voyage, food and liquids given to him, but his hands prevented

[1] Slave-ships captured by British men-of-war were taken to Sierra Leone, their cargoes there transferred to the establishment so-named.

from being made use of for either purpose. His imploring requests to be relieved, and promises of good behaviour, led to his release, and being allowed to mix with his fellow-countrymen. Suddenly and without provocation he attacked a comrade. A Yorruba man of great physical strength came to the rescue; dealt the assailant such a blow that he reeled to leeward, and striking his head against a stanchion, lay insensible in the scupper. For nine days he remained in that condition, notwithstanding means used for his restoration; at the end of that time he died—a victim to his own incorrigible violence.

Twenty-nine days from Accra, our ship lay at anchor in Carlisle Bay, Barbados.[1] Proceeding on shore to make the usual official reports to the military authorities, we gained particulars in regard to the widespread revolutionary spirit through the nations of Europe; that in London serious demonstrations were threatened. Unhappily we also learned that an outbreak of yellow fever had occurred among the troops occupying barracks on the Savannah; that among victims of the disease were some medical officers. The upshot was that I was ordered on shore for duty. That afternoon I "took over" the barrack-room assigned to me, vacated very shortly before through death of its occupant. Disinfection and other means of modern sanitation were little if at all thought of in those days; nor, up to the present, close upon half a century since the event, has the malady extended to me.

The general aspect of Barbados is at first sight very beautiful. Approaching the island from the northward, it appears as a mass of rich green vegetation, the border of sea grape trees,[2] like so many bearded men,—whence its name was taken,—becoming more distinct as we approach. Towards its interior a succession of hills rise to a height of eight hundred or a thousand feet, their sides mostly covered with turf, with here and there clumps of trees, the intervening valleys divided by different estates and lots upon which are grown sugar-cane and guinea-corn.[3] The houses have such a home-like look that the name of "Little Scotland," long since given to the island, seems appropriate, more especially when the landscape is viewed from the summit of one of those hills inland, to which in one of our excursions we proceeded. Unhappily a check—temporarily, it is hoped—has been brought upon the once flourishing sugar industry of the island. Since the emancipation of slaves took place, properties have altogether fallen in value, proprietors have been ruined, the universal complaint being that the freed slaves cannot be got to work. Geologically the chief component rocks of Barbados consist of coral limestone and coral. In

[1] On June 22, 1848. [2] *Coccoloba uvifera*. [3] *Sorghum vulgare*.

respect to its fauna, it has the peculiarity of possessing but a small proportion of venomous snakes as compared with the other islands of the West India group. The people who have been born on the island are known as "Bims." Their colour is a mixture of red and albinoid white; their special characteristic said to be pride.

Comparing the climate of Barbados with that of tropical India, the former has various advantages. To a certain extent it is bracing and exhilarating; the prevailing breeze, as it comes across the Savannah, pleasant to the sensations, so that officers and other persons ride out at all hours of the day, their faces ruddy, themselves to all appearance in robust health. At intervals of seven to eight years, epidemics of yellow fever occur, such as that which recently attacked the 66th and 72nd Regiments, and after a temporary decrease in its severity, recurred with more than usual intensity and mortality. With regard to physical conditions, geological and otherwise, there is to all appearance nothing of a kind to supply explanation, whether of the advent, increase, temporary cessation, sudden return with increased intensity, and final cessation; neither can explanation be drawn from those conditions for the lengthened duration of non-epidemic intervals, or of the cyclical return of the disease in pestilential form.

Embarked on board the *Prince Royal* transport, I sailed for England. During the homeward voyage only one incident deserving notice occurred. In a clear moonlit night we became aware that we were in collision with a vessel of no great size. As we rushed on deck, we were shocked to observe that the craft suddenly disappeared a short distance astern of us. No less to his own surprise than ours, a sailor belonging to her was found on our deck, cast upon us in a portion of her rigging that lay across it. He was carefully seen to by us, taken to Portsmouth, and there handed over to the Spanish Consul, for we had ascertained that the ship run down had sailed from Corunna.

Gravesend reached, we disembarked; in due time reported our arrival at Headquarters. The authorities granted the usual period of leave of absence in accordance with Regulations at the time in force. From them also I received a letter conveying the thanks of Earl Grey for services performed in Africa. A few days thereafter I learned that of our "reliefs," three in number, two had died within a month after landing at Cape Coast, one of them my own successor. Fortunate, therefore, was my resolve not to delay departure.

Often is the statement made, but nearly always by persons who live at home at ease, that deaths of British officers in Africa and other tropical countries are due to their irregularities and vices, not to combined conditions collectively constituting climate. The officers with whom I was associated on the Gold Coast were in their habits and general manner of life as nearly as possible like their contemporaries in England; nor did the few who at times exceeded somewhat appear to suffer in any respect more than did those of more temperate habits. It is the climate of Guinea, and it alone, that kills the white man, and in yet greater proportion the white woman.

An incident which occurred shortly after I had arrived in London was in its way illustrative of the state of public feeling at the time. It was while spending an evening in Portman Street Barracks,[1] then occupied by the Scots Fusilier Guards, that orders from the Horse Guards directed that the battalion should be kept within barracks and under arms; information at the same time circulated that on the previous day there had been a "rising" of the Chartists at Ashton, near Birmingham, and that a similar outbreak in London was intended. Subsequently we learned that the Duke of Wellington, then Commander-in-Chief, had made ample arrangements for such a contingency, though with so much secrecy and discretion that not a soldier was to be seen on the street. But the anticipated outbreak did not take place.

A portion of leave granted was devoted by me to the combined objects of restoring health and gaining knowledge. At the beginning of the winter session I re-entered at Edinburgh University to benefit by the lectures of Sir George Ballingall. Meanwhile, a friend [2] was interesting himself in appropriate quarters in view to my being released from further service on "the Coast."

[1] With my friend J. A. Bostock.

[2] General Sir Henry King, K.C.B.

CHAPTER VIII

1848-1851. *IRELAND*

57th Regiment—Enniskillen—War in Punjab—Weeding out—Routine—"Albuhera day"—Ballyshannon—Sligo—Monro of the Blues—Orange festival—General conditions—An execution—Surprise inspections—Married—March to Dublin—Clones—Kells—Trim—Dangan—Maynooth—Dublin—Duties, etc.—Civilities—Donnybrook—Medical staff and Order of the Bath—Kaffir War—Adieu to 57th.

GAZETTED[1] to the 57th, I joined that distinguished regiment at Enniskillen, receiving from members of the "Die-hards" much civility and courtesy as a new-comer among them. A few months passed, and newspapers contained details of victory over the Sikhs at Chilianwallah,[2] though at a British cost in killed and wounded of 89 officers and 2,268 soldiers. With a sense of relief, intelligence by the following mail was read that crushing defeat had been inflicted upon the enemy at Goojerat,[3] though with a loss to our forces of 29 officers and 778 men; the dispersion of the beaten army, the flight of their Affghan allies towards the Khyber Pass—for disaffection on the part of Dost Mahomed had not yet been completely appeased.

During winter the weekly route march, with its attendant little incidents, furnished about the only events of regimental life that need be alluded to. As an outcome of what was looked upon as a scheme of "economical" administration proposed for political reasons, a reduction in regimental strength was ordered, several soldiers weeded out of the ranks in accordance with orders received. Not long thereafter public attention was drawn to "The Defenceless State of Great Britain" by Sir Francis Head, to whose book, so named, credit was given for measures speedily taken to reverse the schemes of reductions in *personnel* and *matériel* alluded to.

With the return of summer the routine of regimental life became again pleasant as compared with the monotony incidental to the dreary months of winter. The leave season over, the process of preparing for

[1] December 22, 1848. [2] January 13, 1849. [3] February 21.

inspection seemed the only object for which the regiment existed, men and officers lived; for no sooner was the dreaded ordeal past and over, than the process was resumed for that which was to come six months later on. As so many interludes, entertainments given and received, games, and "matches" of various kinds became so frequent as to be looked upon as somewhat monotonous.

Exceptional in these respects was the anniversary, on May 16, of the battle of Albuhera in 1811, on which occasion the 57th Regiment earned the soubriquet of "The Die-hards,"[1] of which it is so justly proud, the *esprit de corps* maintained thereby as well as through anniversary celebration being among its most valuable heritages. Then came the birthday of Her Majesty; after it, the celebration of Waterloo, "the credit of the regiment" being fully maintained on these occasions.

Trips in various directions by water and land proved to be most enjoyable. Boating on the beautiful Loch Erne became a favourite pastime, picnics on some of the many islands with which it is dotted acquiring an interest of their own. Of those islands one has[2] a semi-sacred character; upon it stand ruins of an ancient church,[3] and, as believed, a still more ancient round tower. By road to Beleek[4] and Ballyshannon was no less pleasant and interesting. Around the promontory on which the first-named stands, the river Erne rushes as a magnificent torrent; the second noted on account of its "salmon leap," and legendary story connected with the islet[5] at a little distance seaward from the cataract. Extending our trip to Sligo, we visited the ecclesiastical ruins and buildings pertaining to that city. In proximity to one of them, several small heaps of human bones lay among the grass, exposed to wind and weather. Inquiry elicited that they were exhumed remains of dead prior to 1832, the great mortality by cholera in that year rendering it necessary thus to "make room" for interment of the numerous victims. But the necessity for leaving exposed the vestiges of mortality was not apparent to us at the time.

At Bundoran I made the acquaintance of Lieutenant Monro, late of the Blues, living in retirement, his prospects ruined as a result of the duel into which he was forced with his brother-in-law, Lieut.-Colonel Fawcett, 55th Regiment, whom he killed on that occasion. Coming

[1] Out of 570 officers and men who went into action at Albuhera, the commanding officer, 22 other officers, and more than 200 men were placed *hors de combat.* The "dead were found lying as they fought in ranks; every wound was in front."

[2] Davenish.

[3] Dedicated to St. Molash, who died A.D. 563.

[4] The manufacture of Beleek ware was then a thing of the future.

[5] See *Illustrated London News*, October 12, 1849.

as that duel did not long after the "meeting" between Hawkey and Seton, in which the latter received a wound that resulted in his death, public opinion became aroused against the practice. Within two years thereafter the Articles of War were so modified as to declare it to be a military offence on the part of an officer to fight a duel or fail to take measures to prevent one from taking place. For a considerable time past there had been a growing feeling in the army and in civil life against a system by which it was possible for the bully and the aggressor to have an advantage as a "professed duellist" over the less experienced adversary whom he might see fit to "call out."

The celebration of the victory of the Boyne, July 1, 1690, and that of Auchrim on 12th of the same month, 1691, was enthusiastically observed. Processions of men, bedecked with the distinctive colour of their party, led by bands of music and bearing with them a profusion of flags, paraded the streets of Enniskillen. From many windows orange flags and other party emblems were displayed; from the church steeple festoons of orange-coloured ribbons waved in the breeze. In other respects much of what was "demonstrative" in character took place, but the general impression produced upon strangers and uninterested spectators was not unlike that experienced as we looked in India upon "religious" festivals.

The visit of Her Majesty to Ireland, and the prospect of a Levée to take place in Dublin, attracted to that capital every officer whose duties and position admitted of his being temporarily absent from his regiment. The question of expediency of the Royal visit had for some time previous been subject of conversation, nor was there an absence of curiosity and anxiety in regard to the reception the Queen might meet with on the occasion of her traversing the streets. Everywhere it was enthusiastic, so much so that Her Majesty was much impressed. The following day the Levée was held; some two thousand presentations were made, and in the list of those who had that honour my name was included.

At this time the general state of things in our immediate neighbourhood was this:—The intensity of famine by reason of the potato blight of 1847–8 had to some degree become lessened; favourable summer weather had brought about an abundant crop of grain, relief works were in progress, the expenses of administration out of proportion to the meagre sums which actually reached the workers. All the while political and religious antipathies manifested themselves in violent forms; murders perpetrated in the close vicinity of our county town.

Some of the alleged perpetrators of those crimes underwent their trial at the County Assizes. Two were convicted and condemned to death. On the day of their execution a guard provided by the 57th was drawn up at a little distance from the main entrance of the prison, where the apparatus for carrying out the extreme sentence of the law was kept in readiness. Behind the soldiers the large open space then existing was crowded with interested spectators, the proportion of women being estimated as four to one of men. The dread ordeal over, one of our men was brought to the regimental hospital in a condition of delirious terror, his delusion that one of the men executed was dangling over his head. All means used to soothe or relieve him failed; his horrible delirium continued with little or no interruption through some few days and nights, only ceasing with his own existence, for the same terrible impression haunted him to the very last.

The system of "surprise inspections," at the time in force, applied to regiments and departments; inspecting officers were wont to appear without warning, such ordeals being over and above those held in ordinary course of routine. That the higher authorities saw good reasons for their action in this respect is not to be doubted. Those reasons, however, did not transpire; but among our soldiers the irritation caused by unusual proceeding went far to overbalance whatever good might have accrued from it.

On the 14th of March, 1850, the most sacred event of a man's life occurred in mine—that event, my marriage [1] to Annie, daughter of John Mackintosh, Esq., of Torrich. Time was pressing, for rumours were in the air that the regiment was well up the roster for foreign service. Leave of absence had accordingly to be curtailed; but, on rejoining the 57th with my young bride, she was received with the same kindness that had been shown to myself. Not many days thereafter, she proceeded to Dublin, where, pending the arrival of the regiment, including myself, she was most hospitably received by the family of a brother officer.[2]

Our progress to the Irish capital included several days' march; for, although railway communication could have been made use of for part of the distance, the authorities had decided that it should not be so. In our march, we passed through or were billeted for a night at places in relation to which history records a good deal of what is interesting. For example, Clones has an ecclesiastical history dating back to the sixth century; Kells, otherwise *Kenlis*, boasts of ruins of a monastery, said to have owed its foundation to St. Columba; in near proximity to Trim stands the rectory of Larour, the former residence of Dean Swift, and near it a fragment of what had been the house of

[1] The ceremony solemnized by the Rev. J. A. Grant, of Nairn.

[2] Major and Mrs. Shadforth.

Stella. The ruins of Dangan Castle in the near neighbourhood were interesting, in that in them was shown to us an apartment said to have been the actual birthplace of the Duke of Wellington—with what degree of truth it was not deemed necessary to inquire.[1]

The village of Maynooth, at the time of our march through it, was in appearance wretched and decayed, even as compared to others along our line of route. At its eastern end is the avenue that leads to Carton, seat of Ireland's only duke.[2] But the name of the village has become associated with its Roman Catholic College, which dates from 1795, and was endowed by Sir Robert Peel[3] with an income yearly of £30,000—a measure much discussed at the time of our visit, as indeed it has continued since to be.

Arrived in Dublin, the barracks assigned to the 57th were the Linen Hall—old, and long before then condemned as unfit for occupation; accommodation for all ranks insufficient. Thus my experience in searching for lodgings began. Some months elapsed; then the regiment was "broken up," small parties distributed among various barracks, to be, after another interval, collected in the Royal Barracks—large, spacious, and, at the time, looked upon as well adapted for their purpose.

Duty, relaxation, pleasure, as represented in Ireland's capital, succeeded each other among our officers. In accordance with rules then in force, much of my own time was taken up in connection with the more military functions of parades, drills, field days, and ceremonial "trooping the colours." Regimental entertainments, levées, and "receptions" at the Castle were so many interludes in our general routine.

In accordance also with the custom of the time, civility and attention in various ways by learned societies and institutions were extended to medical officers of the garrison, myself included. Access to lectures in the Colleges was placed at our disposal; so was admission to the Botanical and Zoological Gardens. Invitations to pic-nics and to boating excursions in the beautiful bay further helped to render pleasant our stay in Dublin.

The once famous Donnybrook Fair[4] had not then become a thing of the past, although its extinction was approaching. The assemblage of people on the occasion comprised the wild in aspect, dirty in person, squalid, imperfectly clothed, all more or less strongly smelling of whisky, some dancing to music of their pipes; but so far as we saw,

[1] Another statement is that his birth took place in Upper Merrion Street, Dublin; his baptism in St. Peter's Church.

[2] That was in 1850.

[3] Parliament, June, 1845.

[4] August 31, 1850.

without the mirth, laughter, and other signs of Irish life of which we had heard so much.

Through the advocacy of Sir De Lacy Evans, and almost by it alone, officers of the Medical and Commissariat Departments were admitted to the second and third grades of the Most Honourable Order of the Bath.[1] In battles connected with recent campaigns, surgeons of British regiments were exposed to fire of the enemy in a degree only second to that of combatants, the casualties in killed and wounded among them testifying to the risks ran by them in the performance of their duties on those occasions. Other circumstances of military life tell more against medical officers of regiments than those whose duties are merely "combatant." The combat over, the latter, if unscathed, takes his rest, such as it may be under the circumstances, but the most arduous duties of the former then begin. On marches incidental to campaigns, the halting ground reached, requirements of the sick and wounded must be attended to, often under great difficulties. In times of epidemics, the combatant runs risks common to all; the surgeon, in addition to them, is exposed to those incidental to close association with subjects of those epidemics, together with mental and physical wear and tear in the performance of professional duties. Hence arises the proportionately high rates of mortality that prevail among junior departmental ranks.

Some time thereafter, war was undertaken against the Kaffirs under Sandilli, their chief. Eight infantry regiments were hastily dispatched to take part in the coming campaign, and so the 57th was placed among the first to proceed to the same destination in the event of reinforcements becoming necessary. Married officers, therefore, lost no time in forecasting arrangements to be made by them respectively in the event of the anticipated contingency becoming a reality.

My personal arrangements in that respect became hastened by the birth to me of a son.[2] Anticipating such an event, I had already opened negotiations for exchange to a regiment serving in India, conscious that colonial rates of pay and allowances were inadequate to meet the needs of double establishments during war time. By-and-by the time arrived when connection had to be severed with a regiment to which I had become much attached, and of its traditions proud as any other of its members. A farewell dinner, by invitation of Colonel Goldie[3] and officers, and then adieu.

[1] *London Gazette*, August 12, 1850.

[2] Born on April 12, 1851.

[3] Killed at Inkerman.

CHAPTER IX

1851-1852. *DUBLIN TO WUZZEERABAD*

10th Foot—International Exhibition—Sail for India—Incidents—Battened down—Chinsurah again—Sunderbunds—Purbootpore—Kurumnassa—Incidents of the river trip—By Grand Trunk Road—Hospitable Brahmins—Louis Napoleon—Deobund — Saharunpore— Jugadree—Umballah—Noormahal — Loodianah — Ferozeshah—Ferozepore—Lahore—Googeranwallah—Arrive at regimental head-quarters.

AMONG regiments stationed throughout the Punjab, then but recently annexed, was the 10th Foot, to which, by exchange,[1] I was now appointed. Towards that province I accordingly started without delay. Arrived in London, we visited the great novelty of that day, the palace of glass situated in Hyde Park, in which was held the International Exhibition, progenitor of a long series as it was destined to be. No time was lost in completing arrangements for the coming sea voyage in so far as restricted pecuniary means permitted. Early in June we embarked on board the *Lord George Bentinck*, I in charge of troops; some hours thereafter the ship was under sail and away.

Among the incidents of our voyage these were recorded at the time of their occurrence; namely, some of our crew drunk and insubordinate, others impertinent; recruits undisciplined; junior officers unacquainted with duties required of them. In a quarrel between soldier and sailor the knife was used, fortunately without fatal result. The death-roll included one child, a soldier who in *delirium tremens* jumped overboard, another who accidentally fell into the sea during a squall at night,—his death-scream, as he fell, most painful to hear.

Far away in southern latitudes [2] we experienced a hurricane such as occur from time to time in those regions. Ten days and nights it continued to rage; hatchways battened down; men, women, and children confined 'tween decks, deprived to a great degree of light and air, their food and drink handed to and passed from each to other as best could be

[1] *London Gazette*, May 23, 1851. [2] 41° S.

under the circumstances; decks washed from stem to stern by heavy seas, the ship running before the wind; sky so thick that "sights" were impracticable, and so our exact position left conjectural for the time being. This, added to experiences already mentioned, was the kind of initiation into the rougher side of military life to which my wife was subjected; she herself in delicate health, our infant son severely ill, his "nurse" a young untrained woman, the wife of a recruit.

The sea voyage ended, our detachment was conveyed by steam-boat and flats to Chinsurah, as on a former occasion when transit was by means of country boats. Within a few days after arrival there, cholera attacked our young recruits, many of whom, as also the wives of some among them, fell victims. The sudden death of our child's nurse was the first shock and trying experience his mother had to face in India.

Starting on November 1, again by steamer and flats, our route was by the Sunderbunds to reach the main stream of the Ganges. A week previous that region was swept over by storm wave and hurricane, by which several ships, among them the steamer *Powerful*, were wrecked. Two days were occupied in passing along the narrow creeks that intersect the partially submerged forest tract, a thousand miles in superficial extent, to which the name of Sunderbunds is given. At the end of that time we are in the Ganges.

Time passed without special incident. Arrived at Purbootpore, a village on the left bank of the river,[1] the place was interesting only as being the locality where, on August 11, 1851, the Moolraj of Mooltan died, and was burned in accordance with Hindoo rites. He it was who instigated, in April, 1848, the murder of Vans Agnew and Anderson, and headed the revolt which led to the siege and capture of that fortress by British forces, and proved to be the first act in the second Sikh war of that year. The Moolraj was for upwards of two years detained as a political prisoner at Calcutta; his health having given way, Government sanctioned his transfer to Allahabad, and while on his way thither death overtook him.

Not far from Buxar we passed the point of junction between the river Kurumnassa and the Ganges. The former stream is by good Hindoos held accursed, so that to touch its water is to them pollution. This reputation, however, would seem to be of modern date,—namely, October 23, 1764, when the forces of Mir Cossim were defeated by those under Major Munro;[2] pursued by them to that river, in which many of them perished. It was a similar occurrence in 1826 on the part of the Ashantees at Acromanté that gave to that place in Guinea

[1] On the twenty-second day of our river journey.

[2] Afterwards Sir Hector.

the name of "accursed," by which it was known during my period of service there.

In some respects our river voyage was pleasant; the cool dry air, the incidents of each day including walks on shore, the peculiarities of village life along the banks, the "fleets" and single craft we met, became, in turn, sources of interest to us. As this the dry season advanced, the size of the once mighty stream diminished, shoals became numerous, boats ran aground, delay and other inconvenience the consequences. On one such occasion several recruits from the particular boat concerned, started away clandestinely in the shallow water to indulge in the luxury of a river bath. Suddenly a scream was heard; two of their number disappeared; whether engulphed in a quicksand, or carried away by a crocodile, no one could tell.

Our river journey ended at Allahabad. Thence our progress was to be by march along the Grand Trunk Road. A short halt was permitted to enable officers to purchase such camp equipment and stores as pecuniary means were equal to. Early in December we marched out of the—to me—familiar place. Nine days thereafter, arrived at Cawnpore, the terrible story in connection with which was in the not distant future. Here my wife had her first experience of one of those violent whirlwind storms whose distinctive name is taken from the locality;[1] her surprise great on seeing some tents, articles of clothing, etc., drawn up and disappearing in the meteor.

At Kullianpore I found my way into the enclosure of a Hindoo temple. Great was my surprise at the offer of hospitality by the priests connected with it, they being in the act of partaking of a meal as I entered, the particular dish called "phillouree." Of it accordingly I partook; but the incident seemed to indicate that then at least my hosts entertained no religious horror against the European.

Arrived at Meerut, the *Overland Express* brought news that "Louis Napoleon having the army on his side has carried all before him, dissolved the ministry and courts of law; has thrown himself on the people, and intimated his readiness to be designated by any title they may decide upon giving him." The next act in the drama so announced was soon to come.

Deobund was soon reached. There took place, in 1827, the last suttee permitted under public sanction. Since that date the practice has been officially suppressed, though it has been stated that isolated instances have clandestinely occurred. On the former suttee ground stood in its centre a temple; a series of small minarets of peculiar

[1] "Cawnpore devils."

device indicate spots on which immolation of widows had taken place. The priests readily admitted us to the threshold of the shrine, but, unlike their brethren already mentioned, offered no food. In the neighbouring grove, numerous baboons—representatives of Humayon, the monkey god—chattered and made grimaces at us.

At Saharunpore a visit was paid to the Botanic Gardens. The excellence of their arrangement and management seemed to merit the eulogies bestowed upon them, a centre as they are from which plants are distributed throughout India, and to various European countries. The process of acclimatization was particularly interesting; so also was the care with which plants of temperate climates were being arranged and packed for dispatch to hill sanatoria in the Himalayas, there to remain throughout the coming hot season. It was a somewhat strange thing to see a daisy being thus nursed.

At Jugadree the detachment, its stores and equipment, crossed the Jumna, there so divided by shoals and islands as in effect to be four different rivers. Across the first the men waded at an hour so early that dawn had not appeared; the second and third were passed by means of bridges of boats such as are common on Indian rivers; over the fourth a bridge had been erected, so elegant in construction as to claim general admiration. Through its arches rushed currents of sparkling water, in the eddies and shallower parts of which were seen fish rising to flies; along the banks grew willow, acacia, and wild fig trees, the adjoining fields rich with well-irrigated crops of wheat. In the far distance rose above the haze of morning the snowy peaks of Himalayah.

Arrived at Umballah, headquarters of the Sirhind Division, a short halt was made, according to the custom of the time, for the double purpose of repairing equipage and exchanging draught animals where necessary. According also to the custom of the time, some of our number were invited to partake of friendly hospitality by officers stationed there.

Continuing, northward from Umballah were seen ruined remains of pillars raised by order of Jehangir[1] to mark the halting places of Noor Jehan, otherwise Noor Mahal, on her journey from Delhi to Lahore. Those remains seemed to occur at intervals of six to eight miles, representing the length of each daily journey of that *Chère Reine.*

Loodianah had an interest in that, during a severe cyclone some years previous, portions of barracks occupied by the 50th Regiment were blown down, several men being killed in the catastrophe, besides many injured. In the first Punjab war the Sikhs made a rush upon the

[1] Jehangir, A.D. 1605–1627.

station, set fire to and destroyed various bungalows and other buildings within it. Further depredations by them were checked by their defeat at Aliwal [1] by Sir Harry Smith.

Arrived at Kool, the position occupied by the army of Tej Singh preparatory to the battle at Ferozeshah, we mounted elephants and so rode to the field of that disastrous victory of December 21 and 22, 1845. Our ride for five miles was across open flat country, covered here and there by acacia bushes, occasional patches of cultivation occurring as we proceeded, the crops consisting of wheat and grain (dolichos). The village of Ferozeshah, half concealed by groves, had yet some remains of entrenchments and batteries, behind and on which the Sikh guns were placed. Along the ground for a considerable distance in front of that position lay scattered and bleached by six years' exposure bones of gallant men, chiefly of the 62nd Regiment, for here it was that so many of them were swept away on the first of those eventful days. Of our small party there was one who had shared the risks and "glory" of that battle, and now pointed out the several positions occupied by the opposing forces.

Ferozepore, for many years the frontier station, ceased to be so when, after the battle of Sobraon,[2] British occupation of the Punjab took place. At one time a sandy plain, it had become beautified by ornamental trees and shrubs, and in other respects somewhat attractive in appearance.

Crossing in its near proximity the Sutlej—Hesudrus of the time of Alexander—we were within the territory of the Punjab—Panch-ab, or "Five Rivers." Five more marches and we encamped close to Lahore, capital city of that province; our camp pitched on ground where in former times had stood cantonments of troops in pay of Runjeet Singh. In near vicinity stood houses of British officials, some tombs and mosques, one of the latter transformed into an English church.

Arrived on the right bank of the Ravee (Hydraotis), our camp occupied ground close to the tomb of Jehangir, and not far from that of his empress Noor Jehan, "Light of the World," whose romantic history interested some of our number, if not all. Thence to Goojeranwallah, birthplace of Runjeet, "Lion of the Punjab," and anciently the Buddhistic capital of the province. In recent times the camp ground has obtained unpleasant notoriety, it being so infected with poisonous snakes that a new site for that purpose has been selected.

[1] January 28, 1846.

[2] February 10, 1846. Punjab annexed, by Proclamation, March 29, 1849.

Ten months' travel by sea and land, I joined the regiment into which, hoping thereby to advance my own prospects and position, it had cost me so much in means and personal trouble to exchange. Having done so, the occasion seemed opportune to take stock, as it were, of that position. At the date in question regimental appointments in India had their market value, according to their several kinds, and the period still unrun of service in that country. That of my own position was reckoned at £100 for each year so before us; thus my exchange cost six and a half times that amount, in addition to which the cost of passage, added to other unavoidable expenses, placed me on the debit side to the extent of £1,180, all of which, having had to be "raised" as best I could, was an incubus to be got rid of with the least practicable delay. [Although anticipating the order of this narrative, the fact may be stated in this place that, by the aid of my dear wife and her patient submission to curtailment of luxuries and even necessities, pecuniary obligations were cleared off within eighteen months. As we shall see, troubles of other kinds arrived against which it became most difficult to bear up.]

CHAPTER X

1852-1853. *WUZZEERABAD*

Wuzzeerabad cantonments — City — Flying column—Public conditions—The hot season—Rainy season—Sickness and death—Birth of a daughter—Australian gold fever—Struck by soldier—Assault and confession—The "Iron Duke"—Items of news—Snake-bite—Prowling animals—Routine life of a soldier—Attempt at improvement—Book club—The sick soldier—Illness of wife—Incident of travel—Traite — Murree—Murder of Mackeson — Its outcome — Hazarees attack Murree—Wife's adventure—Charitable hospital.

IMMEDIATELY after the decisive battle of Goojerat,[1] by which the Sikh army was completely overthrown, a position for troops was selected on an extensive plain stretching for many miles along and from the left bank of the Chenab.[2] That portion of the plain chosen as a site for what were to be cantonments was at the time under indigo cultivation; on it tents were pitched and "lines" drawn out in accordance with regulations bearing on the subject. With the approach of hot weather the tents were walled and covered in by mud, straw, and such other materials as under the circumstances were obtainable; then the tents were struck, partitions of mud "run up," and so houses or bungalows formed. By similar means "barracks" for the soldiers and their establishments were erected; the whole declared to be the station of Wuzzeerabad.

Six miles away stood the city of that name; in its centre the palace occupied by General Avitabile, in the service of Runjeet Singh, and under him Governor of Peshawur at the time of the first war against Affghanistan. Extending from the main entrance to the city, what in former days must have been an imposing avenue of trees is represented by dilapidated willow trunks; at intervals smaller towns and villages occur, all surrounded by richly cultivated fields. Across the river, said to attain a breadth of fourteen miles during the rainy season, is seen the town of Goojerat; towards our left the position

[1] February 20, 1849.
[2] Chenab-Acesines.

of Chilianwallah; in the far distance the Pir-Punjal and other peaks pertaining to the Cashmere range of the Himalayahs.

Our force, equipped as a "Flying Column," was so held prepared and ready, if need arose, for emergent service. Rumour had it that among the people the state of things incidental to recent annexation did not meet with universal acceptance; that the system of Thuggee had extended to their country from Bengal, where for some years previous it had been relentlessly hunted down by Colonels Sleeman and Graham. At the new station of Sealkote an English church was in course of being erected. In reference thereto the strange report circulated among the natives that their children were being kidnapped, to be there offered as sacrifices. Meanwhile two expeditions were in progress of formation: the one to Swat, under command of Sir Colin Campbell; the other to Burmah, under that of General Godwin.

The hot season was soon upon us. As it advanced we became painfully aware how unsuitable, under the circumstances, were the extemporised "houses" already mentioned. By the aid of tatties and thermantadotes,[1] it was possible to reduce temperature within doors to something like 112° F.; but such contrivances were themselves expensive, and in some instances beyond the means of individuals. The sense of oppression from the prevailing heat was greater during the night than in daytime; the stillness of the air, laden with impalpable dust, affected not alone people, but quadrupeds and birds, while over everything a yellow haze lay thick and heavy. Then would come a thunder burst; forked lightning threatened, and in some instances struck our houses; a downpour of rain would follow, and for a few days thereafter all would be comparatively agreeable. Later on hurricanes of dust burst upon us, their violence sufficient to unroof some houses and barracks, to be followed by storms of rain, and ultimately by the season so called. Early in September the hot season was at an end; the moist atmosphere became even more oppressive than it had been while dry heat prevailed, so that all of us looked forward anxiously to the advent of cold weather properly so called.

All belonging to the regiment suffered considerably in health; deaths of soldiers were numerous, the physical powers of all much depressed, a large proportion thus unfit to take the field in case of emergency. It was felt, however, that hospital *régime* was likely rather to increase their disability than benefit their condition; hence they were permitted to remain in barracks, though exempt from duty—a circumstance here

[1] Composed of roots of the scented grass *Andropogon muricatum*.

noted as indicating the insufficiency of mere statistics to represent conditions of physical fitness of troops.

Among the deaths was that of a young surgeon,[1] only a few months in India when attacked by climatic illness, to which he succumbed. For some time before life passed away, incapable of expression by voice, his look of terror told plainly his state of mind as he faced approaching death. The scene was most painful to witness.

On September 5, '52, a daughter was born to me. The event took place in early morning. Shortly after mid-day information reached my beloved wife, through tittle-tattle of servants, that a guest,[2] who occupied a tent in our compound, was dead by heat apoplexy. Several of our men were struck down by the same disease, so that absence from my own domestic sphere was unavoidable under the trying circumstances of the day.

Within a week from her date of birth, an attempt was made by her ayah to poison the infant, the reason for the intended crime neither then nor subsequently ascertained. The prostrate mother from her bed saw the native woman put "something" in the mouth of the babe, who was immediately thereafter seized with tetanic spasms; nor was it without much difficulty that her young life was saved.

The recent discovery of gold-fields in Australia led to a somewhat unpleasant state of unrest on the part of a few soldiers serving in India. Letters from friends and relatives in the colonies instigated them to endeavour by means, whether foul or fair, to get sent thither, where fortunes could very quickly be made. The result was the outbreak, as if epidemic, of crimes of assault on officers and non-commissioned officers, the idea being to get tried before a General Court-Martial and sentenced to transportation; after which, once in Australia, it would be an easy matter to find one's way to the gold-fields. This "gold fever" resulted in a Resolution by the Commander-in-Chief to put a stop to the assaults in question; in one instance—and it sufficed for the purpose in view—the death penalty awarded was carried out.[3]

On a morning in June, while examining a soldier who was about to appear before a Garrison Court-Martial on the charge of striking a sergeant, I received from the prisoner a somewhat severe blow on the forehead. Astonished at the occurrence, some little time was needed to collect my thoughts and decide upon the line of official action most suitable under the circumstances. In the interval I learned that the Garrison Court-Martial had been intentionally ordered to assemble for

[1] Jacob.

[2] The young man may be indicated by his initials, J. C. G.

[3] In a soldier of the 14th Hussars at Meerut.

the express purpose of defeating the object the man was known to have in view, and this being the case it was natural to assume that in assaulting me he had in view trial and sentence by the more important tribunal. Aware as I was that a sentence of death might be the possible award, and desiring to avert such a penalty, in making the official report of the assault I suggested that an inquiry should take place as to his mental condition at the time. Three months elapsed, and then the man appeared before that ordeal; he was found "not guilty" on the plea of "insanity." In due course he was sent to Calcutta, to be taken there into the Lunatic Asylum. At the end of a year he was discharged "cured" from that establishment, and while *en route* to rejoin the 10th he died of cholera. So ended that episode.

About the time I was struck a similar assault was committed upon the surgeon[1] of the 3rd Light Dragoons, occupying barracks also at Wuzzeerabad. He took steps to have an inquiry made into the mental condition of his assailant. On that inquiry I sat as president, and this is the substance of the story told me by the man. From the time when he first enlisted he had been haunted by visions of a murder committed by himself and his "pal" on Wandsworth Common in 1845; he made every endeavour to get killed while charging the Sikhs in battle; he had committed offences so that he might be taken to the guard room, and thence made pretended attempts to escape in the hope of being cut down by the sentry; but failing in all these he had struck the officer, in order that for so doing he might be tried, condemned, and shot. These particulars were duly entered in the report submitted to the authorities; meanwhile, the regiment to which he belonged received its orders for home, and left the station, taking with it as prisoner this unhappy man. It was not till long thereafter that the sequel of his story was heard of.

The death of the "Iron Duke" of Wellington, news of which was received early in November, was made the text of remark and discussion, the official acts and demeanour of His Grace towards officers and the army generally being looked at from different and at times directly opposite points of view,—the impression which seemed most generally to prevail being that although no one denied him the credit of great services performed in the first fifteen years of the century, yet for many years thereafter he had been "past his work"—a commentary which bears interpretation in more ways than one. It cannot be said that many signs of mourning for his loss were apparent.

Early in 1853 English papers brought news among other matters that Louis Napoleon had been recognised as Emperor by the Powers of

[1] Dr. Henderson.

Europe, though not with good grace, that a suspicion existed of a possible attempt at invasion was under consideration, an order for the concentration of troops of the regular army and militia at particular points being the outcome of that suspicion. Another item in those papers reads strangely while these notes are being transcribed, and conditions alluded to have developed in significance; namely, "The influence of the lower orders is fast on the increase, and altogether we seem to be on the eve of a crisis, the ultimate issue of which it is impossible to predict." Shortly thereafter came news of the Emperor's marriage to a Spanish lady,[1] his personal popularity in the army not enhanced thereby. According to Indian journals, overtures had been made to the British Resident at Moorshedabad by Sirdars of Affghanistan with a view to approach Government on the subject of taking over that kingdom. The truth or otherwise of the report did not transpire; but that the rumour was current was itself a suggestive circumstance.

As the hot season advanced, snakes, poisonous and otherwise, became numerous in cantonments. A sepoy while asleep was bitten by one of those reptiles. He soon became unconscious; blood oozed from two small punctures on the instep where he had been bitten, from his mouth, nostrils, and from under his finger-nails.[2] He was treated by means of large doses of ammonia and turpentine, and ultimately recovered.

Prowling beasts of prey made night hideous. On one occasion much alarm was occasioned by one of them becoming "rabid," rushing violently at and biting animals and people. Considerable numbers of both were so injured by the pariah dog; some of those bitten were treated, some not, but no specific results followed the injuries. In the bazaars within cantonments prowling jackals and wolves were so many dangers to infants asleep on charpoys at night; some instances occurred in which they were carried away and devoured by the larger animals mentioned.

The conditions of a soldier's life in India at the time alluded to were calculated rather to weary than enliven him. The climate ill suited for out-of-door exercise; many of the men unable to read, and disinclined to learn; their two resources the bazaar and the canteen; their tastes and pursuits animal; mind a blank; the body a ready prey to disease. Absolutely no good result was to be gained from official reports on these points, and suggestions for improvements. I addressed

[1] Eugenie de Montijo, Comtess de Téba.

[2] Indicating bite by Bungarus (Krite).

letters to the journals in the hope of enlisting attention in favour of station reading rooms, lecture rooms, etc., but with the result that little notice was taken of my representations.

In the 10th Regiment itself, through the action of two or three officers, some of the soldiers enrolled their names as members of a "Mutual Improvement Society." Meetings were held; tea and other light refreshments served in view to attracting men; lectures and demonstrations given on such subjects as Forts and Battles mentioned in the Bible,[1] Strata of the Earth's Surface, Uses of the Human Body; classes for reading and writing also set on foot. Not long thereafter, a General Officer,[2] by order of the Commander-in-Chief,[3] arrived at Wuzzeerabad "to put a stop to so dangerous an association." Military opinion was not then ripened for the innovation.

After some delay, and with considerable difficulty, a Book Club for the soldiers was launched in the regiment; the officers were already well provided in that respect. As with the one class, so with the other, works on "service" subjects were mostly read, but intellectual occupation was thus available whereby to pass the weary and exhausting days of the hot season. [Recollecting these endeavours made by a small number of us in 1853 to advance the intellectual condition of the British soldier in India, the few of us who still live attach suggestive significance to the extract now given from the most interesting work by Lord Roberts, entitled *Forty-one Years in India*.[4] Under the date 1887 he wrote: "My name appeared in the *Jubilee Gazette* as having been given the Grand Cross of the Indian Empire, but what I valued still more was the acceptance by the Government of India of my strong recommendation for the establishment of a Club or Institute in every British regiment and battery in India. Lord Dufferin's Government met my views in the most liberal spirit, and, with the sanction of Lord Cross, 'The Regimental Institute' became a recognised establishment."]

The second hot season of our residence at Wuzzeerabad proved even more severe than the first upon the health of our soldiers, large numbers of whom suffered from illness special to the climate and locality. Unfortunately for those so prostrated, the apathy and indifference of the native servants connected with the hospital were such that many lives were thus sacrificed which under more favourable circumstances

[1] These lectures were given respectively by the Chaplain (Rev. Cave Browne), Engineer Officer (Captain Davidson), and myself.

[2] The Honourable Thomas Ashburnham.

[3] Sir Charles Napier.

[4] Published in 1897. Vol. ii., p. 418.

would in all probability have been saved. For example :—A soldier in barracks, during the hottest hours of the day, is discovered by his comrades to be seized with heat apoplexy, or to be suffering from the scarcely less alarming symptoms of ardent fever. He is by them placed in a dooly and so dispatched to hospital. The bearers who carry him are indifferent to life and suffering among themselves, but if possible more so in respect to the white man, and so their pace is by no means rapid. They reach the "surgery"; but there, if they find no one present, they put their dooly down, while they themselves sit in the verandah to smoke, perhaps to sleep. After an interval more or less long, the presence of the sick—it may be unconscious—soldier is discovered; the circumstance, after another interval, comes, or is brought to the knowledge of the subordinate, who, just roused from his siesta, and considerably narcotised by his "hookah," takes time to collect his energies, and so be able to visit him. Even then the actual nature and severity of the attack is not always recognised and dealt with; so when the surgeon pays his evening visit, the patient is dead.

Among those struck down by severe illness was my dear wife, vitality brought to so low an ebb that only by holding a hand mirror to her lips and observing the slight moisture left thereon could the fact be realized that she still breathed. In this our time of trial, sympathy and aid came unexpectedly, but not from sources whence they were looked for as an outcome of services rendered. When her removal became practicable, she proceeded by dooly dâk towards Murree, then newly established as a hill station and sanatorium. Our cavalcade—for I was of the party—crossed the Chenab, partly by boat, partly by being carried through shallow water and marshy tracts. Arrived at Goojerat, the field of battle, at a little distance from the city, was found to be so overrun by vegetation as to be recognisable only by monuments to individual officers erected on spots where they had fallen. The day wore on; a messenger arrived, bringing, with "salaam from the Collector Sahib,"[1] soup and other delicacies suitable for an invalid and infants. He had heard casually that a lady, severely ill, was in the dâk bungalow; hence this outcome of kind thoughtfulness towards complete strangers to him, as we were.

Jhelum, on the river so named,[2] was the next stage of our anxious journey. Thence, next night to Pucka Serai. Arrived at the dâk bungalow, it was found that the building intended for travellers consisted of one room; in it a single bedstead, on which lay an elderly field

[1] Mr. Sapte, long since passed away to the majority.

[2] The Hydaspes of the ancients.

officer, who, in transit to the hills, had arrived shortly before us. Attendants were absent; supplies unobtainable; there was no alternative but to carry my sick wife from her dooly and place her alongside the sick officer. How the child and infant fared all day is not recorded. Resuming our weary way as the cool breezes of evening set in, early morning found us at Rawul Pindee, then as still a favoured military station. Thence, in evening, towards the foot of the hilly range towards which our journey was directed. Night had closed in before the actual ascent began. As yet there existed no road properly so called. Progress was slow: rocks and boulders in the way caused many difficulties; but these surmounted, the light of our torches showed that in our progress we had attained a region of precipices, rugged valleys, and rapidly running streams.

As morning dawned we were set down at Trait, a place the loveliness of which—surrounded by pine-covered hills; its rich green vegetation, the purling rivulets that traversed the valley, the coolness of the breeze that wafted over us—all these, delightful in themselves, exerted upon my wife an effect to be described as magical. Then it was that from her dooly the pale, emaciated form emerged. Enthusiastically she clutched a twig of pine tree I had just cut; its grateful resin scent brought to recollection associations of bygone days. From that moment her recovery began.

The further journey to Murree was continued, the cool air at the elevation of six to eight thousand feet, to which we had attained, enabling us to travel by day, instead of only by night as in the plains. A road was in course of being made, but as yet that by which we continued was little else than a rugged mountain path, leading upwards through forest composed of sycamore, pine, chestnut, and other trees familiar in our English woods; the altered conditions of temperature, scenery, and general surroundings were health-giving in their effect. Before many hours had passed we were welcomed and hospitably received by our friends, Dr. and Mrs. Banon.[1]

A few days elapsed, and through the station bazaar rumour circulated that on the 11th "a great earthquake would take place at Peshawur," "a native prophecy" having so declared. On the 13th information was received that on the 11th[2]—namely, the date indicated—Major Mackeson, Chief Political Officer at Peshawur, had been assassinated by an Affghan from Jallahabad; the murderer having delivered his thrust raised his hand to repeat the blow, when—so it was stated—a

[1] On September 1, 1853.

[2] Telegraphic communication did not then exist.

native rushed between them and received it. Subsequent information led to the belief that the murder of political officers at various other seats of local government had been intended, the existence of a conspiracy with that object well known among the native population.

Rejoining the 10th without delay, like every other officer who observed the signs of the times, I could not help seeing that as an immediate outcome of the Peshawur murder, the aspect of public affairs, not only on the North-Western frontier, but throughout India, rapidly became such as to cause anxiety to administrators, while it led officers and soldiers to speculate on the chances of active service. The prime mover in the murder of Major Mackeson was believed to be Sadhut Khan, chief of the Lalpoora State. Immediately on the occurrence of the murder British troops were moved onwards from Rawul Pindee, orders issued for others to march from other stations to take their place. These proceedings occupied several days, as all such movements had to be performed on foot. In the meantime the troops arriving at Peshawur were received with signs of disaffection by the Mahomedans of that city; while Rawul Pindee, left for the time being with a diminished garrison, was threatened with attack by a band of Hazara men under an impostor named Peshora Singh,[1] who pretended to be a son of Runjeet Singh. That attack did not take place, but a movement somewhat threatening in character was made towards Murree, at the time occupied by invalid soldiers and their families, wives of officers (mine included), and the small number of officials required for the inconsiderable dimensions it had then attained.

On the night of September 28, some hours after darkness had closed in, messengers sent round for that purpose spread the alarm throughout that station that the Hazarees were rapidly advancing up the hill towards it; orders at the same time issued by which all should forthwith repair to the residence of the Commissioner, leaving their houses "standing." A heavy thunderstorm prevailed at the time; lightning flashes at intervals lit up the miry pathways along which the ladies and children had perforce to walk, in some instances a distance of a couple of miles. My own dear wife, as yet unrecovered, and unequal to such an exertion, was carried, together with her two children, and so reached the general rendezvous, where earlier arrivals had barricaded themselves as best they could by means of tables, chairs, and other articles of furniture. Meanwhile the Commissioner[2] collected such officers, soldiers, and police as could be brought together in the emergency. Marching as best they could in the darkness, they came in

[1] Peshora Singh was drowned in the Indus.

[2] Mr. Thornton.

contact with the rebels at daylight, and after a smart skirmish dispersed them, the Commissioner being wounded in the *rencontre*.

By the middle of October my wife, though far from restored to health, was sufficiently well to return with her two children to the plains. Starting from Murree in the evening, her palanquin-bearers speedily showed themselves to be ill-disposed; while she, unprovided with a guard, as some other ladies had been, was rendered helpless in what proved to be a most painful position. Frequent halts, unnecessary delays, repeated demands for buxees (presents), and general disregard of her requests to keep the palanquins together, continued throughout the long dreary hours of darkness, and well on in the following day. It was afternoon before she was deposited at the dâk bungalow of Rawul Pindee; but the party conveying her infant was nowhere in sight, nor could tidings of it be obtained. Thus did several hours pass. Then it was that the arrival of an officer[1] enabled my wife to communicate to him her state of anxiety and alarm. Without delay he proceeded to the residence of General Breton, in command, with the result that a cavalry escort was dispatched in search of the missing ones. Another period of delay, fear, and anxiety, and the palanquin with the infant arrived. It appeared that her carriers had simply deposited her on the roadside in the jungle, and dispersed. What might have happened is painful to contemplate.

For some time past a charitable hospital for the benefit of the native population in and around cantonments had been maintained by subscriptions and other contributions from officers of our regiments, the professional duties connected therewith being performed by myself. Gratitude on the part of those who benefitted by that institution was never expressed verbally, and in many instances not at all; indeed, claims were in some made for pecuniary reward, on the plea that individuals had submitted themselves to be operated upon. In a few instances, however, active gratitude was expressed, even in a somewhat demonstrative manner. The use of chloroform was then in its very early stages. In the instance of a child, that anæsthetic was administered while it lay placidly in its mother's arms. When under the influence of the drug, the little patient was gently lifted, placed upon a table, operated upon,[2] then replaced in the position from which it had been taken, still apparently asleep, and placid. The surprise of the mother was very great; the whole thing declared by her to be *jadoo*—that is, witchcraft !

[1] Captain, afterwards General Sir William Payne, K.C.B.

[2] Lithotomy.

CHAPTER XI

1854-1856. *MEEAN MEER*

Meean Meer—Death of Brigadier—Unpleasant recollections—First telegraphic dispatch—A son—Simla—Canal—Uniform—Shalimar Gardens—Lahore—Sebastopol—Dost Mahomed—Troops to Crimea—Aspect of affairs—Santhal outbreak—Another survey—Journey to Simla—Severe illness—A weary journey—Death of infant—Sick leave—Oude annexed—A sad case—Sail for England—Our voyage—Arrive in England—Aberdeen.

AFTER a succession of orders and counter-orders, the 10th marched away[1] from Wuzzeerabad; on the eighth day thereafter entered the recently erected and spacious barracks of Meean Meer. On the extensive plain where they stand, the Khalsa army assembled in 1845, prior to the "invasion of India" by them, and prior to that date quarters there existed for the troops of Runjeet Singh. On the same plain in 1846, the victorious army under Lord Gough encamped, and so commanded Lahore, situated some six miles distant. The name of the locality is that of a saint, a native of Bukkur in Scinde, who flourished in the time of Jehangir,[2] and whose tomb still remains in tolerable repair.

Among those who died in the early part of 1854 was the Brigadier commanding,[3] an old officer whose service in India had extended over about fifty years. He represented a class, then somewhat numerous, of men who had proceeded to that country while as yet in their teens, and thenceforward spent the whole or greater part of their lives in it. The funeral was performed with full military honours; but what struck us as incongruous and out of place was the suddenness with which, after it had been completed, the strains of "The Dead March" were succeeded by those of what were described as "rollicking" airs. Surely, under such circumstances, it would be more appropriate were the troops marched back in silence to their barracks.

[1] On November 15, 1853; arrived on 23rd.

[2] A.D. 1605-1627.

[3] Sir James Tennant, K.C.B.

Unhappily a painful state of "tension" had for some time previous existed in relations between the officer in command and those immediately under him; confidence was seriously impaired among all grades; actions and "system" of the superior looked upon as capricious, influenced by personal feelings, and, in some instances, tyrannical. The outcome of all this was, in respect to those affected, a condition very difficult to be borne, an existence approaching the miserable in place of one of friendly communication after the manner of regiments in general. Among the ranks there was reason to believe that attempts had been made, and others contemplated, against the objectional life. The following incident was suggestive under the circumstances of the time. A soldier came to hospital; a man of good character, long service, and known never to shirk duty. To the usual question, "What is the matter with you?" he answered, "Nothing, sir." Then, "What brings you here?" "Because I am harassed and worried to death, and have come to ask if you can give me a day or two's rest." His request was acceded to, and so, in all probability, a serious crime averted.

In the middle of March a Lahore newspaper published what was the first telegraphic [1] intelligence ever received in this part of India. According to that intelligence, the Russian Ambassador to England had taken his departure from London; France and England were dispatching troops in view to joint action in support of Turkey, those from our own country comprising twenty-two battalions, and so leaving only eleven, exclusive of Household troops, in home garrisons. A month later came the further news that all the forces in the United Kingdom were under orders of readiness for service; that a powerful fleet had been mobilised; the army materially augmented, several regiments recalled from the West Indies, and the fleet dispatched to the Baltic.

On 30th of March a son [2] was born to me by my beloved wife, as I wrote at the time—another hostage to Fortune, and very material inducement for exertion on my part to earn, if possible, means whereby to maintain and educate my children in such a manner as is incumbent upon me. The state of her health required that with the least practicable delay she should proceed to the hills. A house was engaged at Simla for the season, and there she passed the greater part of the hot months.

My health having given way, I proceeded to that sanatorium somewhat later in the hot season. Forty miles from the plains, and 7,600 feet above sea level, the climate of Simla is agreeably cool, but rain

[1] Called by the natives "Bijlee ke dâk," or "Lightning Mail."

[2] Baptized on April 24, 1854.

so heavy that during the three months of summer the fall amounts to 100 inches. In the faces of declivities from rocks and mountain spurs grew deodars and rhododendrons, intermingled with wild apple, cherry, holly, walnut, etc.; orchids, ferns, ivy, and woodbine. Small but rapid streams pursue their tortuous course over their rocky beds in each narrow valley, and at a distance of some two or three miles are two cascades of some 70 and 120 feet in height. Away in the distance the magnificence of the snowy range, consisting of what seems like an interminable succession of white glistening peaks, fixes the mind in wonder and admiration; while in a clear day it is possible to see the plains, together with the windings of the river Sutlej.

The "inauguration"—otherwise commencement—of what was to be the great canal uniting the Ganges and the Jumna was duly celebrated. The subject of that canal was discussed in the public papers from different points of view; the channel, while intended to irrigate many tracts that stand in need of being so fertilised, would be used in places where such aid to agriculture was not required, and in certain localities "malaria" would appear where none now exists. It may be curious to compare those predictions with the results of experience.

Somewhat later in the year a Cheap Postage Act came into operation in India, according to the system adopted in England since 1841. Another matter noted at the time had reference solely to the army; namely, that an entire change took place in the uniform of soldiers and officers, one item relating to which was that thenceforward the infantry were directed to leave the upper lip unshaven,—in other words, to grow moustachios.[1]

In the middle of October my wife and children arrived from the hills. With health restored she was able to enjoy rides and other excursions around our station, the crisp morning air of the Punjab restoring to her cheeks, as to those of others that had become pallid, the rosy tinge natural to them. The frequency with which field-days and other great military displays took place—for our force numbered 13,000 fighting men—gave her, with other ladies, opportunities of being present on such occasions, and entertainments of sorts furnished us with an object or excuse to visit what were then the well-kept and ornamental gardens of Shalimar, the original planning of which is credited to Sultan Beg, an "Admiral of the Fleet" to Shah Jehan.

Occasional visits had to be made to Lahore, the history of which city presenting many points of interest, a few particulars relating thereto may be interpolated in this place. Surrounded by a line of

[1] By orders dated Horse Guards, October 7, 1854.

ramparts now dismantled and rapidly going to decay, sufficient remains to indicate the great strength of the original fortifications. At regular intervals there are gateways, at each of which a strong guard was formerly posted for defence. Through one such gate we entered, and were immediately in a labyrinth of narrow and crowded streets. The houses, built partly of brick, partly of sandstone, are three and four stories in height, their fronts more or less elaborately ornamented by carvings of different kinds, but all such devices presenting evidence of decay. What formerly was the palace of Dyhan Singh is now a pay office for British troops. The Shish Mahal, or Glass Palace, is much defaced; the precious stones of its mosaic work taken away, the spaces at one time occupied by them giving to the whole an aspect of dilapidation even beyond what has actually taken place. What was the audience hall, however, remains in good repair, the walls and roof ornamented by mirrors of various sizes, some set in silver frames, others in those of gold, the whole interspersed with paintings done in the most gorgeous colours. But how changed the style of occupants now from that which in days gone by harmonized with such surroundings! As we entered, there sat upon the marble floor a motley crowd of Sikhs, men and women, old and young, their costumes betokening that they were of the labouring classes; the mission that brought them hither to receive, at the hands of representatives of the great Company Bahadur, pensions for sons, husbands, or fathers who fell in battle against that wonderful and mysterious abstraction known to "the masses" of India only by that designation. In close vicinity to the Shish Mahal was a large mosque, very similar in style and appearance to the Jumna Musjid at Delhi; it was now occupied as a magazine. Thence we proceeded to the gateway where a few years ago Rajah Nao Nehal Singh lost his life,—whether by accident or design is still by some few persons considered doubtful. Adjoining that gate stands the tomb of Runjeet Singh, on entering which we found two priests ready to give whatever aid the Feringhee might stand in need of. Under a coverlet of green cloth the Grunth, or Holy Book of the Sikhs, was carefully preserved; but the cloth was raised for us, so that we might look upon the sacred volume. In a shrine under an unfinished dome within the temple or tomb, the ashes of Runjeet were preserved, the shrine itself concealed under a green cloth; the walls of the mausoleum covered with paintings and other representations of Sikh mythology. In another building, though of less artistic appearance than that mentioned, were preserved the ashes of Nao Nehal Singh and of Soochet Singh; between the two shrines containing them lay covered as before the Grunth.

In the last week of October came news that the Russian camp before Sebastopol had been forced, but with a loss to the allied forces of 2,500 in killed and wounded. Many of us, besides the interest natural to the important events then taking place in the Crimea, had personal acquaintances among the actors in the drama of war there in progress, and were moreover conscious of an existing possibility that we also might be transferred to that sphere of action—a possibility looked at from various points of view, according to circumstances, pecuniary and matrimonial, of individual officers.

The Indian papers of the day gave currency to a report that our quondam ally and prisoner Dost Mahomed had been making endeavours, by means of vakeels, to sound the Indian Government in regard to an alliance, offensive and defensive; intimating at the same time the possibility of his coming to terms with Russia, should his proposal be rejected. But according to the views expressed at the time, little danger was apprehended in the North-West,—that is, from Russia,—on account of the natural mountain barrier that serves as a defence in that direction.

Early in 1855 news reached us that Inkerman had been won[1] by our troops, though at a cost to those engaged of 2,600 in killed and wounded out of 6,000, the 57th being among the heaviest sufferers. Several regiments[2] had already been sent direct from India to the Crimea; the 10th expecting to follow to the same destination, officers and soldiers composing it held themselves prepared for such an emergency, which however did not occur. Among ourselves the chances of service nearer at hand were freely discussed, as were possible risks that might attend the further withdrawal of troops from India. That a state of unrest existed was declared from day to day in the columns of the local papers, and was evident to all who chose to pay attention to palpable indications. Few, if any, of us at the time gave a thought to the conditions to which that unrest was due, nor to the outbreak in which it was so soon to culminate.

All ranks and grades pertaining to regiments were interested in the varying phases of public affairs, their personal comfort, convenience, and possible prospects being likely to be affected thereby. For some time past Persia had treated British representatives with growing marks of disrespect, and now the circumstance led to the withdrawal from Teheran of the Commissioner of Her Majesty at that capital. There were, moreover, suspicions of an intended movement on Herat, in accordance, as believed, with Russian instigation; consequently,

[1] November 5, 1854.

[2] Namely, 22nd, 96th, and 98th Regiments, 10th Hussars, and 12th Lancers.

the early dispatch of an expedition was looked upon as a probable contingency,—the object, according to one set of views, to "assist" the Shah; according to another, to coerce him. Speculation was indulged in as to the regiments most likely to be so employed, "ours" being considered one of the most likely to be so. Our arrangements were made accordingly; but a year had to elapse before war was actually declared.

In the month of July (1855) came the unexpected news that the Santhals had broken out in rebellion. We asked each other, Who are the Santhals? They were a half-savage tribe inhabiting the Rajmahal Hills; nor was it possible at the time to ascertain the ostensible cause of their outbreak. The troops sent against them consisted of a local corps,[1] composed of their own tribesmen, the natural result being that they fraternised with the rebels. The next "force" dispatched to quell the outbreak was a body of sepoys of the 7th N.I.,[2] and they, it was reported, fired over the heads of the rebels, their officers using their fists upon the men who did so.[3] Meanwhile the rebellion spread; depredations and murders were committed wholesale. Martial law was proclaimed in the disturbed districts; troops were employed during seven months against men armed to a great extent with bows and arrows; at last the guerilla warfare was brought to a close. The inaction of the sepoys on the occasion alluded to became significant some time thereafter when the great mutiny occurred.

The death of the Czar and accession to the Russian throne of Alexander were the most important items of intelligence brought by the mail arriving early in April; another, his expressed determination to continue the war with vigour. Other items of intelligence noted at the time as having more or less important bearings upon affairs in India, included the withdrawal of Lord Aberdeen from the Ministry and the appointment of Lord Palmerston as his successor; the death of Joseph Hume, who, it was remembered, had begun his career in the Burmese war of 1824–26; and lastly, the cross-fire between Admiral Sir Charles Napier, on his return from Cronstadt, and Sir James Graham, the First Lord of the Admiralty. Then came details of the attacks on the Mamelon and Malakoff Towers, and of the losses incurred by our troops, more especially by the 57th. Following thereon, intelligence arrived of the outbreak of cholera among the allies in the Crimea, and of the death thereby of Lord Raglan.

[1] Bhaugulpore Hill Rangers.

[2] Together with 8th and 40th N.I., mutinied at Dinapore in 1857.

[3] *Delhi Gazette.*

In the early days of September, the serious illness of my wife at Simla rendered it necessary that I should proceed thither without delay. On the journey all went well, till on arriving at the river Beas—the Hyphasis of the ancients—the palkee in which I was being conveyed across, by means of a boat, was by some mischance permitted to fall into the stream, after which accident, time so pressed that without interruption I continued my journey. Arrived at the foot of the hills, I mounted a horse, and, lantern in hand,—for night had now closed in,—I proceeded along the rough footpath which then was the only representative of a road. Soon the darkness was absolute; the roughness of the pathway had increased; the thick jungle was close to me on either side. Then it was that my steed stumbled and fell; myself and lantern were on the ground; my light extinguished. In this condition of things I perforce remained a considerable time, until a party of pedestrians, having at their head a torch-bearer, came upon me. I was glad to return with them to the nearest staging bungalow, and there remain till morning. Next day I resumed my journey. I reached my destination tired and feeling much indisposed.

Five days thereafter I was seized with what proved to be a most serious illness. One day of intense headache, another of shivering, then prostration, then delirium, after which a blank of more than a couple of weeks. Such were the results of this untoward journey. During those days and nights of delirium, a succession of very horrible dreams, hallucinations or mental wanderings haunted me, one of the most painful being that everything in my room—bed, tables, chairs, etc. —was alive, and that I myself was double; at the same time I was haunted with an intensely strong desire to die. In the third week of my illness my state was so far improved that I was able to sit up in bed, but only for a few minutes in the day. During this trying and anxious time to my dear wife, she had to tend me, not only by day, but also at night; her servant, the wife of a soldier, assisting her. It was in these circumstances that she gave birth to a son on October 7.

Weak in body, and ill as I was, my wife far from recovered, with the additional charge of a baby to that of a sick husband, we left Simla on October 26; in due time arrived at Umballah, and on November 4 joined my regiment there, it being *en route* to Dinapore. The following day I underwent the ordeal of having the uvula cut off, that organ having become so elongated during the severity of my illness as by constantly irritating the throat to add to the severe cough and lung complication which formed part of my illness.

Much of our march was by road already traversed. Our usual hour of starting ranged from three to four in the morning; we had to rise at least an hour before that time, and I well remember how on such occasions my dear wife, herself very ill-fitted by reason of the weak state of her health, prepared for me a cup of egg-flip, and so enabled me to bear removal from my camp bed to the dooly in which I travelled. But as we marched from day to day, health so far recovered that I became able to walk some little distance at a time by means of a stick. My left lower limb was much the weaker of the two, but at first I failed to perceive that it was to some degree paralysed.

On Christmas Day our young infant was observed to be somewhat ill. With great rapidity his symptoms increased in severity, and on the last day of the year death came as a relief to his sufferings. As soon as practicable after the severity of his illness declared itself, we hurried on from camp to the dâk bungalow at Barode, and there the dear innocent babe passed away to his rest. The thought of leaving the remains of our loved one in the jungle was horrible; we accordingly procured such a coffin as could be roughly put together by the bazaar carpenter, and with our melancholy burthen pushed on to Benares, where we arrived at 1 a.m. on New Year's Day. It was not, however, until sunset of the same day that arrangements for the interment were completed, and the remains reverently committed to earth in the Military Cemetery.

Four months elapsed, illness still prostrated me. Recovery was little likely to occur while I remained in India; consequently there was no alternative but to proceed on sick leave to England. On arriving at Calcutta, much difficulty was experienced on obtaining temporary accommodation, the hotels and other establishments being full. After some delay quarters in Fort William were assigned to me; furniture and equipment obtained on hire, and so I waited until official routine had been gone through, and authority granted for my departure.

For some time past the contemplated annexation of Oude was known throughout the military stations of India. The carrying out of that intention was naturally looked forward to as likely to result in a force being assembled, and perhaps engaged on active service. My own incapacity to take part in any such service was a severe disappointment. When, added to my physical condition, the fact that pecuniary affairs had not yet emerged from a state of difficulty, and that prospects were far from bright as to health being ever restored sufficiently to enable me to meet responsibilities attached to me as "bread-winner," the general survey of the position in which I stood was decidedly depressing. In one respect it was a relief to me to learn that all chances of service had been averted; that Oude had been annexed without the necessity for sacrificing life—at that time at least.

In the suite of rooms adjoining ours in Fort William an officer was suddenly seized with cholera, the attack rapidly progressing to his death. After that event his young wife, who had been constant in her attentions to him, observed his fingers move spasmodically, as often happens in such cases; thereupon she rushed to the medical officer in attendance, exclaiming frantically, "He lives, he lives; why say you that he is dead?" Nor was it easy to convince her that her hopes were vain,—that he had gone to his rest. The scene was altogether a very painful one to witness, though one by no means uncommon in India.

Suffering as I was from physical weakness, and conscious of the possibilities that might happen to those dependent upon me, in the probable contingency which now presented itself vividly to my mind, the fact that for some days I became prostrated under the influences then prevailing was no surprise to myself. On the 5th of March the *Marlborough*, in which we had embarked the previous afternoon, started in tow of a steamer; but what between breakdowns and other mishaps, it was not until the 17th—St. Patrick's Day—that our homeward voyage really began.

The voyage was by no means propitious, for, as noted at the time various causes of discomfort and inconvenience were at work. Scarcely had we got to sea before the woman engaged to attend our children became ill, and so gave up her work; mumps and whooping-cough affected nearly every child on board; my eldest had a tedious attack of fever; my wife became ill, partly from arduous attendance on the children, partly from the unwholesome conditions on board. Gradually there had become perceptible a stench, which in its intensity affected seriously the health of the people on board, and rendered discoloured the white-lead paint throughout the vessel, the plated dishes, and articles in personal wear. Pumps were set to work and kept continually in use; myriads of maggots were thus taken up with the bilge-water, proving the existence in the depths of the vessel of animal matter in a state of decomposition. A formal representation by the officer[1] commanding the invalids on board and myself to the captain was made on the subject, with a request that he would put in at Delagoa Bay. That representation was ignored; and so the remaining portion of the voyage had to be got over, the conditions just mentioned having, as expressed, "to wear themselves out."

On the 1st of July we passed the Azores at so short a distance from

[1] Colonel Blachford, 24th Regiment.

them that we were able to enjoy the view of those beautiful islands. Nearing Plymouth, our ship was boarded by a venerable pilot, who, though seventy years of age, was actively employed in his responsible and arduous vocation. On the 14th of that month we reached Gravesend, and there disembarked; my wife infirm in health, two of our children unrecovered from their attacks of illness while on board, myself with one limb disabled, my physical condition to a great extent wrecked. In due course the ordeal of a Medical Board was gone through; the members of that body were able to appraise the significance of that condition, but in accordance with "the system" of the day were unable to recommend leave of absence for any longer period than three months—a period obviously insufficient for restoration to health and activity.

A few weeks were spent in travelling in search of health. The fact being evident that further leave must be applied for in due time, the climate of Aberdeen was selected as one suited to my then condition; in that city, accordingly, we remained for several successive months, with result as anticipated, that the bracing winter air proved to be health-restoring and invigorating, though the period during which I was permitted to enjoy it was insufficient for its full benefit being obtained. In various ways civility was shown to us by residents. On the winter "session" at Marischal College being opened, a kind invitation was sent to me by Dr. Pirie to attend his lectures. Little thought I at the time how soon some of the valuable teaching communicated in those lectures was to be practically applied.

CHAPTER XII

1857. *ABERDEEN. DINAPORE. OUTBREAK OF SEPOY MUTINY*

An unpropitious New Year—Depart for India—A quotation—Distilling water—First news of Sepoy mutiny — Madras — Conditions at Calcutta — The *Soorma* — Terrible tales — Berhampore — Rajmahal — Bhaugulpore — Monghyr—Delhi and Agra cut off—Rejoin the 10th.

THE year 1857 began with me inauspiciously. Unrecovered from illness, it was necessary that I should proceed to the metropolis, there to appear before a Medical Board. A short extension of leave being granted by that tribunal, the fact was communicated in a manner personally offensive, with the intimation superadded that if at the expiration of the period I was still unfit to join my regiment, I must make way for a more efficient officer.

The aspect of affairs, so far as I was concerned, was gloomy. On the one hand I had the prospect of half-pay for an indefinite time, on a rate[1] quite insufficient to meet the ordinary needs of myself and family; on the other, to return to India in the state of physical illness in which I then was. Taking an estimate of my worldly means, the circumstance came out that from insurance, and small amount of investments as they then stood, comparing the result with income on half-pay, the receipts of my wife as a widow would exceed by a trifling amount that to which I should be entitled in the alternative first named. Thereupon decision was quickly made; a solicitor prepared my "last will and testament." I placed the document in the writing portfolio of my wife; took leave of her as she lay weak and ill in bed;[2] started away to rejoin my regiment, the children clapping their little hands as I did so, and shouting, "Papa's gone away for toys."

Embarking[3] at Gravesend, the earlier part of our voyage was without special incident. The excellent selection of books sent on board for the use of the troops—for a considerable number were being conveyed to India—enabled those who so desired to get through a good deal of

[1] Of 8*s*. per day. [2] A son born on March 14, 1857.
[3] The *Palmyra*.

reading. A passage in one of those works seemed so appropriate at the time to personal conditions that it was duly noted; namely, "The evil we suffer is often a counter-check which restrains us from greater evil, or a spur to stimulate us to good. We should therefore consider everything, not according to present sensation of pain, or the present loss or injury it occasions, but according to its more general, remote, and permanent effects and bearings—whether our higher faculties are not brought more into play, and our mental powers more invigorated by the meditation and experiments necessary to secure ourselves."[1]

A considerable part of the voyage passed without special incident. Some "heavy" weather was experienced, but in that respect nothing unusual or of a kind likely to do harm to ship or stores. Great, therefore, was the consternation with which we learnt that water casks and tanks had so suffered that the sea water had got into and rendered their contents unusable. At the time we were in the latitude of the Mauritius, and about twelve hundred miles east of that island. What was to be done? The chief officer and myself devised a distilling apparatus, constructed with kettles, boilers, gun-barrels, and leaden pipes of *sorts*. Our success was considerable; some twenty gallons of "fresh" water were thus obtained throughout the day, and so on during twenty-two that had to pass before land was reached, though from some of our lady passengers comments were not wanting as to the "nasty" taste of the product. Meanwhile fuel ran short; bulkheads and spars had to be utilised; our ship reduced to skeleton state. In that condition we arrived off Madras and anchored.

The news we there received was at the moment astounding, as it was unexpected. The greater part of the Bengal army in open mutiny; sepoys murdering their officers, together with their wives and children; widespread disaffection among the native troops of both the other Presidencies. As written at the time, and when the intelligence was fresh: "It appears that the ostensible cause of the outbreak was the issue of cartridges greased with animal fat. But for a long time past a deep-rooted determination has existed among the natives to throw off a foreign yoke, and to raise for themselves a king of the Delhi line of succession. Large numbers of mutineers are said to have fled to the imperial city; many officers and their families have been massacred."

At Madras the state of things indicated that something very serious and unusual was in progress. European residents enrolled as volunteers; Fort St. George in process of being manned and provisioned;

[1] *Entomology*, Kirby and Spence.

ammunition got ready for immediate use; at each post where stood a native sentry there was also placed a British soldier, or pensioner, the latter "embodied" and armed for the occasion. The regiment[1] in the fort was held ready for emergencies; so were the artillery at St. Thomas' Mount. The Mahomedan inhabitants of Triplicane, a suburb of Madras, were declared to be in open revolt.

At the mouth of the Hooghly the arrival of the pilot on board was eagerly looked for, his recital of news listened to with painful interest. In that recital particulars were given of murder and atrocities[2] committed by mutineers on women and children, the names of the victims at the same time given. Disembarking at Calcutta early in August, unusual military turmoil was in progress. At short intervals throughout the city parties of extemporised volunteers were posted; Fort William was in course of reinforcement; the streets were patrolled by armed parties of Europeans, while everywhere an air of unrest seemed to prevail. At Government House sentries of the Body Guard were on duty, their arms the ramrods of their carbines. An impression existed that as the date was that of the Mahomedan festival, the Buckra-eed,[3] the occasion was likely to be celebrated by an attack on the capital—a belief which derived support from the fact that a spy from the King of Oude, then at Garden Reach, had been captured while conveying a traitorous letter, his trial and execution following thereupon without much delay. Other preparations in progress indicated the conditions of the time; accommodation, stores of food and clothing, as well as other requirements, were being got ready in anticipation of women and children, survivors from deeds of blood at up-country stations, who were known to be on their way hither. Comments were very freely made on the energy displayed by commanders in some instances, in contrast with pusillanimity in others.

A passage order obtained, I embarked as deck passenger—for there was no spare cabin—on board the river flat *Soorma*, proceeding with a body of Sikh troops and their officers, Sir James Outram and staff being in the steamer to which the *Soorma* was connected. On the day of our departure we met in the Hooghly a steamer and its flat, both crowded with ladies and children who had succeeded in effecting their escape, but whose husbands, fathers, or other relations had for the most part fallen victims at their respective stations.

Very terrible were the tales some of the "refugees," as they were called, told of atrocities committed within their own knowledge, or of which

[1] The 43rd Light Infantry.

[2] Hosea xiii. 16.

[3] Buckra-eed. In commemoration of the sacrifice by Abraham, according to the Koran, of Ishmael, child of his bondswoman.

they had received what in their estimate was authentic information. A few examples must suffice:—Two young ladies [1] stripped naked, tied to hackeries, and so driven through the streets, then dishonoured by sweepers and barbarously murdered. A lady tied up in her own house, and so forced to witness the murder of her husband. An officer, to save his wife and child from dishonour and abuse, shot them both, before being himself cut down. The massacre at Cawnpore perpetrated by bazaar butchers employed for the purpose. A young lady with her own hand killing five of her assailants, then throwing herself upon her sword rather than fall into the hands of their fellows. A lady, with her husband and child, while endeavouring to escape on horseback; her husband dying in the jungle as a result of exposure; she forced to abandon his corpse, and with her child continue their flight. And so on.

At Berhampore, the 11th Irregular Cavalry and 63rd N.I. had recently been disarmed; their horses and arms collected around the military hospital; that building put into a state of defence; houses in its vicinity in process of destruction; guns and other arms being sent into the station by the Nawab of Moorshedabad.

At Rajmahal news received that mutineers besieging Arrah had been dispersed; that "something" had happened to a party of the 10th. Havelock's force, in its advance on Lucknow, severely seized by cholera; losses by death,[2] and inefficiency by sickness so great that he was under the necessity of returning to Cawnpore, there to dispose of sick, and obtain reinforcements preparatory to resuming his advance. Sorties by the rebels in Delhi repulsed with heavy loss to them; Lord Elgin arrived at Calcutta, accompanied by some marines and artillery; other reinforcements expected to arrive in a few days.

At Bhaugulpore the display of the Union Jack from a Mahomedan mosque indicated the fact that the edifice was occupied by British troops.[3] We learned also that a portion of the 5th Irregular Cavalry, suspected of mutinous intentions, were about to be disbanded by the 90th Regiment in progress up country; that a few days previous men of the former corps, occupying a station in near vicinity of this place, murdered Sir Norman Leslie, one of their officers, and wounded several others; that, notwithstanding these circumstances, the officer in command urged his confidence in the loyalty of his men, as a reason that they should be spared from the disgrace of being disarmed. His

[1] Names of these and other victims to be mentioned are in my possession.

[2] Five officers died in one day.

[3] A detachment of 5th Fusiliers.

prayer was acceded to. That night the men deserted their officers, rode off with their horses to join the 32nd N.I., at Deoghur.

Monghyr was in a state of panic; a small body of the Northumberland Fusiliers, aided by residents, doing their best to put the dilapidated fort in a state of defence, and making other preparations against possible emergency.

Communication with Agra and Delhi only practicable *viâ* Bombay; all direct telegraph wires destroyed; military and residents at the first-named place, secure within the fort, declaring themselves able "to hold out" for a long time, notwithstanding that in a *sortie* against the rebels they had suffered severely; at Delhi offensive measures against mutineers languishing by reason of heavy sickness and mortality among our troops besieging that city.

Rejoining the 10th[1] at Dinapore, that station was seen to be without sepoy troops; the barracks formerly occupied by them deserted; the barrack square filled with refugees from neighbouring places. Next day the 90th Regiment, in progress up country, was temporarily detained, as attack by mutineers was anticipated and had to be guarded against; a considerable number of the men fallen sick, had on that account to be landed, for they also were being conveyed by river. A few days thereafter a detachment of the 10th arrived from Jugdispore, at which place they inflicted considerable loss upon the mutineers, who had taken part in the disaster to be presently noticed as having befallen a portion of the regiment at Arrah. But continuity demands some particulars relating to events which led up to the disaster and expedition so alluded to.

[1] August 18.

CHAPTER XIII

1857. *EARLY MONTHS OF SEPOY MUTINY*

Mutiny and disaster—Major Eyre at Arrah—Outbreak at Patna—A dastardly proceeding—Progress of events—Further reports—The regimental hospital—Soldiers' wives to be armed—Madras regiments—English reinforcements—Meean Meer—Shannon Brigade—Victims of mutiny—Women and children—Details of Cawnpore—A lady refugee—Mortality in 5th—Extension of mutiny—Current events—Action and contrast—Delhi and Lucknow—Successes—Bankers—Reinforcements—English opinion—Active proceedings—Ghastly evidences—Sir Colin Campbell—"Clemency"—Active work—Blown from a gun—More active work.

THE force stationed at Dinapore consisted of two troops of European Artillery, 10th Foot, a portion of the 37th British, the 7th, 8th, and 40th Native Regiments. Among the three last named signs of disaffection had for some time past been apparent to their officers, though unhappily ignored by the general,[1] an old, infirm, and irresolute man. On the 25th of July he was so far moved to action as to direct that percussion caps should be taken away from their magazines of arms, and from the men themselves. A parade for the latter purpose was ordered; thereupon the sepoys became openly mutinous, fired upon and otherwise threatened their officers; they finally broke away, taking their arms with them. Meanwhile, the white troops were not permitted by the general to open fire upon or pursue the mutineers, who, taking the direction of Arrah, soon placed themselves under the leadership of the powerful chief Koer Singh. Arrived at that place, they laid siege to the house of Mr. Boyle, in which the few residents of the small station had collected, and, to some extent, fortified the building. On the 27th a party consisting of men of the 10th and 37th proceeded by steamer, in view to relief of those besieged; but the vessel ran aground, and so their object was frustrated. On the 29th a second steamer having been procured, the combined party proceeded in her; in due time arrived at Beharee Ghat on the river Sone; there landed, and began their march towards Arrah. Un-

[1] Lloyd.

happily, a night advance was determined upon. After much toil, not acquainted with the ground, not knowing their way, having to cross a deep ravine or nullah, and to surmount other difficulties, they entered the town about midnight, and after the moon had set. A heavy fire was thereupon opened on them. Men and officers were unable to see each other. Captain Dunbar, the officer in command, fell dead; confusion was the immediate result. A certain number found their way back to the open country; but so heavy were the losses, so great the disorganization of the whole, that the expedition not only failed in its intended object, but met with serious disaster. The remnants were brought back to Dinapore, where they arrived on 30th of July; it was then found that out of 415 officers and men who had started on that service, 170 were killed and 120 wounded, making a total of 290.[1] The wounded who were rescued were more in number than could be accommodated in hospital; supplementary buildings had accordingly to be utilised for them. Throughout the regiment chagrin and disappointment were general; stories circulated that acts of atrocity had been perpetrated on some of the wounded. Soldiers were loud in their imprecations against the rebels, declaring their determination "to pay them off for it."

Major Eyre, hearing of the disaster that had befallen the troops under Captain Dunbar, advanced by forced marches from Buxar; on August 2 he attacked and dispersed the besieging rebels at Arrah, who thereupon fled towards Jugdispore. On the 8th a party of the 10th under Captain Patterson, together with some other troops, arrived at Arrah from Dinapore. On the 11th, in conjunction with those of Major Eyre, it started in pursuit of the sepoys; they had taken up a position at a village named Jota Narainpore. There they were attacked by the men of the 10th, who rushed upon them with a shout, killing numbers and dispersing those who escaped their bayonets.

At Dinapore, Sir James Outram inspected the 10th, and having issued orders with regard to further proceedings continued his journey southwards, taking with him some officers belonging to the mutinous native corps. The arrival of Sir Colin Campbell at Calcutta to assume supreme command was followed by the departure of Sir Patrick Grant to resume his own proper command at Madras. At Patna a partial outbreak by the Mahomedans had recently taken place, Dr. Lyell being killed during it. A recurrence of that disturbance being threatened, a detachment of the 10th was sent to Bankipore as a personal guard to the Commissioner of Behar, whose residence was at that place.

[1] Out of fifteen officers, twelve were killed or wounded.

When the great body of the sepoys at Dinapore mutinied and fled, certain of their number were employed on various duties within the barrack ranges occupied by the British troops. Unable like their brethren to effect their escape, they laid down their arms, declaring themselves to be loyal, or "staunch," according to the phrase of the day; tents were issued for their use, and a neat little encampment established on a space of open ground between the barracks and adjoining river bank. In the course of the following night screams issued from that encampment; in due time some soldiers, with their officers, proceeded with lights to the tents, to find several of the sepoys dead, others more or less severely wounded by bayonet thrusts, but without any clue to their assailants. Whether or not, as asserted at the time, the men of the 10th were implicated in this dastardly outrage, remained uncleared up by the official inquiry which followed in due course.

In rapid succession news reached us of events at different places within the sphere of mutiny. The investment of Delhi more closely pressed by the combined British and Sikh besieging forces. From Agra that the rebels had withdrawn therefrom. From Oude that Havelock had resumed his advance towards Lucknow, inflicting *en route* severe defeat upon the opposing rebels. From Calcutta that reinforcements were being daily dispatched inland by bullock trains; but as the rate of progress of those animals did not exceed two and a half miles per hour, considerable time must elapse before the troops so sent can be brought into actual use. Other items of intelligence were, that a body of Ghoorkas sent by Jung Bahadur as an auxiliary force had been attacked by the rebels, upon whom they inflicted defeat with heavy loss. The river steamer *Jumna* in its progress upwards beyond Allahabad was so heavily fired upon by the mutineers, at the same time the water of the Ganges becoming so shallow, that it had to abandon further attempts to proceed; there was therefore no alternative but to withdraw.

In the city of Patna the condition of things, already unsatisfactory, became still more so, the intention of the Mahomedans therein declared to be an attack on the "Kaffirs" on their great festival day of the Mohurrum,[1] falling this year on 31st of August. As a precautionary measure, therefore, a line of defences was rapidly thrown up between the city and cantonments. Next came a report that the 9th Irregular Cavalry, after doing good service at Delhi, had fraternised with the rebels; with them made a dash at a besieging battery protected by

[1] Mohurrum. The first ten days of the Mahomedan New Year are dedicated to the festival so called.

Sikhs, their attempt defeated by the 75th Regiment. Then sad accounts of sickness and mortality by disease in addition to casualties in battle among the besiegers; for example, the 1st Battalion 60th Rifles, 400 strong when it first took up its position, had not in its ranks now 200 effectives. From Allahabad the statement came that some of the "staunch" gun lascars were detected in an attempt to load their guns with bricks and mortar.

The state of things in our regimental hospital, characteristic of the time, was this:—In the months of July and August deaths included two officers and seventy men. The long corridor-like wards of the building, together with its verandah, were filled partly with wounded men, remnants of the unfortunate Arrah expedition, partly by those affected with diseases special to the season of the year. The requirements of the wounded demanded much manual attention. What, therefore, between handling wounded tissues and their dressings, finger-tips became sodden like those of a washerwoman, and tender to the touch; the stooping attitude necessary while performing dressings and operations so fatigued the muscles of the back as to make it painful to be in, or again to change that attitude; at the same time the moist heat prevailing made such exertions particularly exhausting. The hospital had already been fortified, arms issued, and so arranged that in case ot necessity they could be made use of by some of the patients; sandbags were arranged for purposes of defence on the roof, the walls loopholed; indeed, the only shots at the escaping sepoys of the 40th N.I. were from it.

Rumours circulated that a combined line of action by the disaffected in Patna and mutinous sepoys under Koer Singh, one of the Nana's lieutenants, was contemplated against Dinapore, garrisoned as the station by only a portion of the 10th Foot. To meet such a contingency, it was proposed to arm the women belonging to the regiment; nor had those of us who had some knowledge of their general style and prowess any doubt as to the result, should they come in conflict with such adversaries. Indeed, there was every reason to believe that already a mutineer had lost his life by the hand of one of our Amazons armed with a bayonet.

The arrival of a Madras infantry regiment, in the ranks of which were some Hindostanees, gave rise to some little speculation as to possible events, should they be brought against their rebel countrymen. At the same time news circulated that a mutinous spirit had been shown in one of the cavalry regiments[1] of that presidency, and in at least two of infantry[2] in that of Bombay.

[1] 8th. [2] 21st and 27th.

Under the circumstances of the time, welcome was intelligence by English mail that a powerful force was in progress of dispatch to India; its numerical strength 25,000 men, including Royal Artillery, then to be employed in Hindostan for the first time. Now also came the first faint rumour that the transfer of Indian administration directly to the Government of Her Majesty was intended.

From Meean Meer came news of successful action against intended "rising" on the part of native troops at that station, the attending circumstances of that action being in some respects like those of the historical ball[1] at Brussels on the eve of Quatre Bras. Among the regiments disarmed, as an outcome of that action, was the 26th N.I. For some time thereafter the sepoys belonging to it remained "loyal" and "contrite." Suddenly, under the shelter of night,[2] they fled, having first murdered one of their officers. At break of day troops were sent in pursuit; the fugitives overtaken on the left bank of the Ravee. Of their number fully 100 were shot down, 150 or so drowned in their endeavour to swim across that river, the remaining 200 ultimately captured, brought back to their station, and executed. It was of the concluding act of the drama that news now reached us.

In the afternoon of September 4, the *River Bird* arrived from Calcutta, having on board the "Shannon Naval Brigade," under Captain—soon to become Sir William Peel. No sooner were they disembarked than all paraded for drill. Lookers-on rapidly collected to witness the novel proceedings, the wild rollicking manner in which the bluejackets pulled about and worked their ship's guns of large calibre. That evening the officers were our guests at the regimental mess. Our next meeting was to be under circumstances even more stirring than those now taking place.

From time to time the papers of the day gave what statistics were available in regard to lives sacrificed, directly and indirectly, by the present outbreak of the sepoys. According to one paper,[3] those numbers were as follows, soldiers, officers, women, and children being included in the totals; namely, Meerut, 29; Loodianah, 3; Sealkote, 8; Fyzabad, 7; Gwalior, 15; Rohnee, 1; Jounpore, 1; Jhelum, 1; Allahabad, 15; Mehidpore, 7; Mosuffernuggar, 1; Bareilly, 70; Delhi—on the outbreak of the mutiny, 82,—killed or died by exposure subsequently, 40; Hissar, 9; Shahjehanpore, 1; Cawnpore, 19 (exclusive of those to be subsequently enumerated); Meean Meer, 2; Mhow, 34; Sooltanpore, 3; Saugur, 1; Neemuch, 4; Indore, 2; Patna, 1; Moradabad,

[1] At Meean Meer the ball by the 81st Regiment took place on May 12.
[2] July 30.
[3] *Phœnix*, September 28, 1857.

4; Darjeeling, 1; Futtehpore, 1; Lucknow, 22; Benares, 5; Agra, 16; Jhansi, 43; Jullundhur, 4; Ferozepore, 3; Raneegunge, 3; Indore, 15; making in all a total of 494. These numbers do not include the many instances in which lives were sacrificed by exposure and hardship, nor the numerous young soldiers who succumbed while being conveyed along the Grand Trunk Road.

With regard to the most terrible of all episodes,—namely, that of June 27, at Cawnpore,—an account by one of the very few survivors was published in the *Friend of India*;[1] namely, "Those who in the boats survived from the artillery fire directed upon them were taken back to Cawnpore; the men secured by cords, and with the ladies brought before the Nana, who thereupon gave orders for their destruction. The ladies were placed on one side, the men, bound as they were, drawn up in line, and his troops ordered to fire upon them. Some of the ladies broke away, and rushing to their husbands, clasped them in despair, determined to die with them. A chaplain who was of the doomed number begged that a few minutes might be granted them to prepare to meet their God—a favour which was granted; others called upon their executioners to finish their bloody work. A volley of musketry; the victims reeled and fell, some dead, others still alive, though wounded; their murderers rush upon them with tulwars;[2] they deal death around, nor do they cease their work when life is extinct, but continue to mutilate the bodies of the dead. The women and children, numbering one hundred and fifty-nine persons, were retained till July 15, and then destroyed by butchers employed for that diabolical purpose. Two days thereafter, but too late to avert the catastrophe the forces led by Havelock entered Cawnpore." At a somewhat later date further particulars appeared[3] with reference to the same sad episode. According to them the list of persons whose lives were sacrificed there, whether in the entrenchments between June 5 to 27, in the boats on the latter date, or on July 15, when the last remnant was butchered, as just related, was as follows; namely, Honourable Company's Artillery, 61; H.M.'s 32nd Regiment, 84; 1st European Fusiliers, 15; H.M.'s 84th Regiment, 50; officers of regiments and staff, 100; merchants, writers, and others, 100; drummers, etc., 40; women and children of soldiers, about 160; of writers merchants, and drummers, 120; ladies and children of officers, 50; servants (after many had absconded early in the outbreak), 100; sepoys and native officers sick in hospital, 20; total, 900. But there

[1] Of September 3, 1857. [2] Native swords.
[3] *Calcutta Englishman*, October 15, 1857.

is every reason to believe that these figures are approximate rather than actually exact.

Orders were received and quickly carried into effect, whereby the wives and children of men and officers of the 10th were dispatched by steamer to Berhampore, at the time considered a place of safety. A company of our regiment marched towards Gya, then threatened by the mutinous 5th Irregulars, and defended only by a small body ot Rattray's Sikhs. The withdrawal of the Treasury from that station resulted in the official ruin of the civilian concerned; but under the circumstances of the time the verdict of opinion among those on the spot was that his action was justified.

Among the refugees proceeding by steamer down country was Mrs. Mills, whose husband, Major Mills, of the Bengal Artillery, had been shot by his mutinous men while endeavouring to escape from Fyzabad, by swimming the Gogra. This unfortunate lady had been wandering in the jungle for nearly three months. She now was ill from hardships and starvation; one child, an infant, had died, the remaining two were ill with cholera; she herself nearly devoid of clothing, without servant or other help, almost completely broken down; nor was it until a few days ago that she learned the fate of her husband. A brother officer of Major Mills, Captain Alexander, placed a suite of rooms in his house at her disposal. In due time she and her children were so far restored in health, and provided with clothing, that they continued their journey towards Calcutta.

For some time past a detachment of the 5th Fusiliers occupied a building connected with the Opium Stores in Patna, the rate of sickness and mortality among the men composing it being so great as to equal 90 per cent. of deaths per 100 strength per annum. A visit to the place by Colonel Fenwick and myself revealed the fact that the quarters assigned to them were in all respects unsuited; while, therefore, the remaining portion of the men were withdrawn, their place taken by men of the 10th, steps were taken, and successfully, to avert similar casualties among the latter.

Still there came news of mutiny from stations far apart: from Assam on the one hand, to Ferozepore on the other; while of regiments of the Bombay Presidency, a similar spirit had extended to at least four of their number. Indeed, so general had mutiny become that scarcely a remark was made as the news of some fresh outbreak circulated; but among officers and men of our regiment the desire was loudly expressed to "get fairly at them in the field," little if any account being taken of relative numbers.

At this time my own physical state gave way under the weight of arduous duties; several brother officers also were rendered temporarily incapable of work; but at the earliest possible date we returned to our respective spheres, determined to "put the shoulder to the wheel." The good news reached us that a further defeat had been inflicted upon the Arrah mutineers by Major Eyre. The arrival of reinforcements by ship from England had begun to cause wonder and some consternation among the rebels. For reasons the nature of which did not transpire, certain newspapers were temporarily suppressed. The immediate result of that measure was that private letters took the place of the journals so dealt with; groups of men assembled at the post office on the occasion of morning delivery, news was interchanged, and thus a tolerable knowledge maintained of events in progress at different stations.

From Azimghur came information that there the rebels had been attacked and defeated by the Ghoorka troops of Jung Bahadur.[1] It was said that a force consisting of 3,000 Cashmere troops, sent by Goolab Singh, was approaching Delhi, in aid of the British, by whom the siege of that city was being vigorously pressed on. Then came news that on September 16 an entrance had been effected by the Cashmere Gate; 125 guns captured, though with a loss to our troops engaged of between forty and fifty officers and 650 men killed and wounded. From Nagpore, that the mutinous 50th N.I. had been attacked, and to a great extent destroyed by the column advancing from Madras. From the Punjab, that some fifty men of the 10th Cavalry and a number of mutineers of the 55th N.I. had been executed by order of Sir John Lawrence. In contrast with these energetic measures were Proclamations by Government, full of sympathic expressions with regard to "the poor misguided men," as applied to the perpetrators of deeds already alluded to.

A few days passed, and then came information that very stirring events were in progress; that Delhi was completely in the hands of our troops, the king a prisoner, two royal princes shot by the hand of Hodson.[2] The forces under Havelock and Outram had effected[3] an entrance into the Residency of Lucknow, and so "relieved" the besieged garrison of that city. The story of that "relief" was everywhere related with pride. But the fact was deplored that the "relieving" force, as a result of the losses sustained, had itself to add its numbers to the besieged. Among the latter, casualties by shot and disease had, up to the date of "relief," included fifty-seven women

[1] At Manduri, ten miles from that station.

[2] On September 21, 1857. [3] On September 25, 1857.

and children. On the following Sunday, collections were made in cantonment churches, for the purposes of a fund being raised wherewith to aid sufferers by the present rebellion.

Thereafter news of successes at different points against the rebels came in rapidly. Thus from Delhi a force had gone in pursuit of one party of them; in Central India the 52nd N.I. was broken up by the Madras column; near Sherghotty the Ramghur Battalion annihilated; in the vicinity of Mirzapore a body of mutineers defeated by a small force comprising the 5th Fusiliers and 17th Madras N.I. At this time the "Pearl" Brigade, under command of Captain Sotheby, arrived at Dinapore; two companies of the 10th, under Major Longden, started towards Benares, there to be ready for emergencies. At intervals disaffection occurred in portions of the 32nd N.I., occupying various positions in neighbouring districts. Now came news that the last fragment of that corps had broken into mutiny and fled; their object to unite with the rebel force beyond the Soane, commanded by Koer Singh.

Information was received that a body of mutineers 4,000 strong, with twelve guns, was in progress from Oude to make an attack on the Treasury at Chupra, and afterwards to threaten our small body of effectives at Dinapore. Then we learned that Rajah Maun Singh, of Gorruckpore, hitherto believed to be "loyal,"—he having given protection to some ladies whose husbands had been murdered by the sepoys, —had joined the rebels with a force of 9,000 men. As a counterpoise to such items, the troops under Colonel Greathead, descending by the Grand Trunk Road, had defeated the sepoys, inflicting heavy loss upon them, subsequently possessing himself of Alighur, together with its guns and stores. A significant indication of the tendency now being assumed by bazaar opinion was that native bankers, who in the first outbreak of the mutiny sent their treasure to Calcutta, are having it brought back to their places of business.

We were at this time in a position to estimate the strength of reinforcements already sent, and in process of being dispatched from England, to re-establish authority in India. These comprised eleven regiments of Light Cavalry; fifty-five battalions of Infantry; four troops of Horse Artillery; eleven companies of Foot Artillery; seven Field Batteries; four companies of Engineers, equal to a total of 87,000 men. With these there were fourteen medical officers, over and above those pertaining to regiments and other bodies.

As each successive body of troops arrived, officers belonging to them were invited to our mess; thus we gathered something in regard to the tenor of opinion in England in reference to events in progress around us. Very different was the impression so conveyed, of views entertained at home, from what under the actual circumstances of the time was to be expected. From the long distance, the sepoy was looked upon as mild and harmless in disposition, but driven to revolt by acts of oppression to which he had been long subjected,—those acts, however, not definitely stated; Sir John Lawrence and General Neil were said to be cruel and otherwise objectionable persons; the policy of "clemency" all that was estimable, and to be desired. The contrast between the views so expressed, and actual occurrences such as have been already mentioned, taking place almost before our very eyes, gave rise to comments, some of them more expressive than sympathetic.

Meanwhile the progress of events went on. A body of mutinous sepoys had found their way from Delhi to Bithoor, the residence of the Nana. There they were attacked by a force sent for the purpose from Cawnpore, under the command of Colonel Wilson, their stronghold destroyed, guns, ammunition, and other stores contained in it captured. At Raneegunge the Headquarter portion of the 32nd N.I.[1] was disarmed by Colonel Burney, their commanding officer, to whom was given up also the treasonable correspondence being carried on by the sepoys belonging to it. At Agra the camp was attacked by a body of rebel cavalry, estimated at 1,500 strong. The picquet of the 9th Lancers, comprising not more than twenty-four troopers, under command of Captain French and Lieutenant Jones, charged and cut its way through them; but in so doing the first-named officer was killed, the second wounded. The station of Chupra in our near vicinity being threatened, the "Pearl" Brigade, under Captain Sotheby, R.N., was ordered by the Civil Commissioner of Patna to proceed for its protection—a new experience for a naval officer to be ordered by a civilian. At our own station reinforcements, comprising a portion of the 82nd Regiment, were a welcome addition to our weak garrison. Particulars were published of the cost in casualties at which the troops under Havelock attained the relief of the Lucknow garrison; namely, sixteen officers killed and forty-five wounded; of soldiers, 400 killed and 700 wounded, equal to nearly one-third of the force engaged. No wonder that in their turn the remnants became part of the besieged garrison.

The party of the 10th already at Benares was held in readiness to enter Oude, and there act as occasion might require against assemblages of mutineers. At Jounpore, a body of rebels were attacked by the Ghoorkas, who severely defeated them, killing or disabling some 250 out of 1,200 of their strength. Some ghastly

[1] From Deoghur.

indications of events in progress were furnished by floating bodies in the Ganges, these being seen during several successive days, as with vultures or other foul birds perched upon and tearing their flesh they were carried past our station. Among them were six white bodies, lashed together by ropes, suggesting the means by which the victims had been destroyed.

By the end of October, Sir Colin Campbell started from Calcutta to assume direct command of the troops actively engaged against the enemy. Travelling by "dâk," and having with him an escort of inconsiderable strength, he narrowly escaped capture by the mutineers of the 32nd N.I., who lay in wait in the vicinity of the Soane, his escape being due to the fleetness of his "gharry" horses. After that incident the same party of mutineers doubled back and endeavoured to enter Oude by crossing the Ganges near Patna, but were defeated in their attempt by the armed river steamer *Koladyne.*[1]

In bitterly sarcastic terms the policy of "clemency" towards and sympathy expressed for the "misguided" sepoy found utterance after this manner in the *Friend of India*: [2]—

"Pity the sorrows of a mild Hindoo, whose tottering steps have brought him to your door,
To murder you he did what man could do, and can you blame him that he did no more?
Ripped from the body of your outraged wife, he tossed your unborn babe upon his pike!
Yearns not your heart to save and sooth the life of one who thirsts again to do the like?

---

[1] Forty years thereafter,—namely, in 1897,—Lord Roberts, bearing in mind the events of 1857, writes:—In reply to the question, "Is there any chance of a mutiny occurring again?" With reference to that question he remarks after this manner: "I would say that the best way of guarding against such a calamity is—By never allowing the present proportion of British to native soldiers to be diminished or the discipline and efficiency of the native army to become slack.

"By taking care that men are selected for the higher civil and military posts whose self-reliance, activity, and resolution are not impaired by age, and who possess a knowledge of the country and the habits of the peoples.

"By recognising and guarding against the dogmatism of theorists and the dangers of centralization.

"By rendering our administration on the one hand firm and strong, on the other hand tolerant and sympathetic; and last, but not least, by doing all in our power to gain the confidence of the various races, and by convincing them that we have not only the determination, but the ability to maintain our supremacy in India against all assailants.

"If these cardinal points are never lost sight of, there is, I believe, little chance of any fresh outbreak disturbing the stability of our rule in India, or neutralizing our efforts to render that country prosperous, contented, and thoroughly loyal to the British Crown." (Vol. I., p. 449.)

[2] Of November 5, 1857.

You do not kill the serpent in your path, you do not crush the bug when you have caught him;
And why bear malice 'gainst one who hath but turned on you the arms whose use you've taught him.
Those arms at present I have flung away, finding that somehow we miscalculated;
And that we should have picked a luckier day to glut us with the blood we hated.
And now I stand expectant at your gate, trusting for pardon and fraternal love:
Of serpent wisdom you have shown of late not much; show me the softness of the dove.
And then I promise you, as time shall suit, the rich reward you'll have deserved to share,
The untiring hate of a remorseless brute, the poison of the reptile that you spare."

While Peel's "Shannon" Brigade, so recently with us, was in progress from Allahabad to Cawnpore, it became united to the 53rd and a party of the 93rd Regiments. The combined force was seriously engaged at Futtehpore with a strong body of mutineers, and although successful in defeating them severely, after a conflict of two hours' duration, the victory was at the cost of many lives, among them Colonel Powell, formerly a brother officer in the 57th. The mutineers of the 32nd N.I., unable to cross into Oude, had again taken up a position on the Soane; there they were attacked and defeated by Rattray's Sikhs, though not without severe proportional loss among the latter. The party of the 10th from Benares came in contact with and routed a body of the Oude rebels at Atrowlea. Meanwhile the forces under Sir Colin Campbell were fighting their way from Cawnpore towards Lucknow.

Martial law had for some time past existed at Dinapore. In accordance with that effective code a Court-Martial was ordered to assemble for the trial of a sepoy of 14th N.I., on the charge of taking part in the massacre of our men at Arrah, as already mentioned. Before that tribunal the man was duly tried; by it convicted and sentenced to suffer death by being blown from a gun. Early in the day following a strong guard of the 10th took charge of the doomed man, to whom, in the usual way, the sentence of the court was read. He was immediately marched to the rear of the barracks, where preparations were complete for carrying into effect the dreadful penalty. His step was firm, though his countenance expressed despair and terror; his hands quivered, lips moved as if in prayer. While being secured in the fatal position, he seemed dazed; the heart-beat reduced to a mere flutter; a bandage tied over his eyes, he faintly said, "*Hummara kussoor nahin hye*"—it is not my fault. The officiating assistant stood aside, the hand of the Provost Marshal was raised, there was a loud report, and shreds of humanity flew in various directions. A scene to be witnessed only under compunction of circumstances. Mutineer prisoners brought to the station for that purpose had in all cases fair and open trial.

Welcome was the news that during the night between November 22 and 23 the besieged garrison of Lucknow had been withdrawn therefrom by the force under Sir Colin Campbell, and was being escorted towards Cawnpore. At the same time accounts reached us of the attack by the Gwalior contingent on the last-named station; of their temporary success by reason of numbers, and of their defeat with heavy loss in men and guns by the Commander-in-Chief. Worn out by fatigue,—for he was physically a delicate man,—General Havelock fell a victim to cholera shortly after reaching the outskirts of Lucknow. In the vicinity of Jounpore a small British force came in contact with the Oude rebels. On that occasion our Ghoorka allies were said to have expressed a wish not to fight any more, and to have shown their reluctance accordingly. Then came information that a large number of ladies and children from those besieged, together with a considerable body of sick and wounded soldiers, had arrived safely at Allahabad from Cawnpore, *en route* to Calcutta.

CHAPTER XIV

1857-1858. *THE JOUNPORE FIELD FORCE*

The 10th ordered on service—The start—More defeats of rebels—The Jounpore field force—Preparing for work—Action at Chanda — Hummeerpore — Forced marches—Sooltanpore—Captured relics—Reinforcements—Rebel messengers—An attack—A wounded officer—Arrive at Lucknow.

ORDERS to take the field had been expected, and preparations made accordingly in the 10th, so that when they did arrive all was in readiness to carry them out immediately. Uncertainty for some time prevailed with respect to the 73rd N.I., professedly and somewhat demonstratively "loyal," but known to be in a dangerous state of disaffection, ready to sweep over the indigo-yielding places in Tirhoot, some of the planters from which, abandoning houses and factories, had betaken themselves to Dinapore for safety. A report spread that a body of rebels had crossed the river Gogra and threatened the "Pearl" Brigade at Sewan; a steamer accordingly started to Benares, conveying detachments of the 10th and 37th Regiments, to be in readiness to act from that base as circumstances might require. Reports at the same time told that the 11th Irregulars had broken away from Berhampore; that they had been severely handled by the 5th Fusiliers, but that they were making their way towards Tirhoot.

By daylight on December 23, a detachment of our men and officers was in progress of embarking on board a steamer for conveyance towards Chuprah, at and from which place they were intended to act in concert with bodies of Ghoorka troops for the assistance of threatened stations in Tirhoot. Equally early on the 24th our headquarters marched away from barracks. Arriving in due time at the point where the Ganges was to be crossed, much delay resulted from the incompleteness of arrangements made for the purpose. Evening had far advanced when we arrived on our camping-ground; tents were far behind; so were the messing arrangements. From such "reserves" as our haversacks supplied our first meal was taken, after which we bivouacked "on the cold ground," under shelter of a mango grove. Next day being Christmas Day, equipment and arrangements were got into working order and ready for eventualities. On the 26th the sound of firing, as if at Sewan, indicated that the arrival of the 10th was none too soon, and shortly thereafter news came in that an attack, not determined in character, by the mutineers had been repulsed. In the course of the next few days the Nepaulese contingent captured a considerable number of mutineers belonging to the 11th Irregulars, but those of the 5th Irregulars succeeded in joining the body of rebels assembled under Koer Singh.

New Year's Day brought the welcome news that the rebels had been severely beaten at Alumbagh by Sir James Outram, great loss inflicted upon them, and four of their guns captured; also that Colonel Seton had defeated a body of mutineers at Futtyghur. Having moved our camp to a position north-westward of the town, we discovered a saltpetre manufactory for the use of the rebels. Firing was again heard in our near vicinity, indicative, as we soon learned, that our Nepaulese allies had attacked a rebel village, which they captured and destroyed.

The 10th were ordered to advance towards Azimghur, to be joined *en route* by other regiments, the combined force to be named the Jounpore Field Force, commanded by Brigadier-General Franks. On the second day of our progress, at a place called Muttyala, the first active signs of disaffection were shown by some of the villagers; it was quickly suppressed, however, by the simple method of handing over to the Provost Marshal those who had so acted, and having them flogged. No further trouble with natives was experienced; and so, without adventure, on the fourth day of our march we crossed the river Gogra, and entered the district of Azimghur. Thence to the provincial city our progress was cautious and wary; villages through which our route lay were seen to be deserted by their ordinary inhabitants, except the old and very young, by women and the infirm.

At Azimghur—once a pretty and otherwise favoured station—the public buildings, including the church, had been reduced to charred and roofless walls, gardens wasted and disfigured; a series of huts in course of being erected for the faithless sepoys at the time, when on June 3 the 17th N.I. broke into mutiny, left standing as they then were; the gaol strongly fortified, everything destructible bearing an aspect of ruin. Within the intrenched position at the gaol a small force of Ghoorkas kept at defiance the rebel sepoys who had already made two unsuccessful attacks, with considerable loss in life and of two of their guns. Resuming our progress, the 10th reached Aroul on

January 26. There the various portions[1] of the force of which we were to form a part united, and was organized for its prospective duties. A halt of three days sufficed. On the 29th a march of twenty-three miles was performed by our little army, the minimum quantity of equipment and transport accompanying it. Several houses in ruins, belonging to planters, were passed in our progress to the river Goomtee; that river was crossed, and about midnight we bivouacked on Oude territory. By break of day our force was again in motion towards its objective point, now known to be Lucknow. That day's march was uneventful, except that the water in the roadside wells was rendered unpalatable by branches of neem tree (*Melia Azadirachta*) thrown into them by the rebels.

A short halt was made at Singramow, during which preparation was made for eventualities. Intimation was there received that the rebels were collecting their forces at Chanda, about a dozen miles in front of us, and that their pickets had advanced to within four or five miles of our camp. On February 19 our force was under arms at daylight, and then began its advance towards the enemy. About nine o'clock a halt was ordered; men and officers partook of such "breakfast" as under the circumstances they could get, while staff officers rode to the front to reconnoitre. A long line of rebels was seen to occupy a somewhat elevated position at a little distance from us. Our guns immediately advanced, opened fire upon them, their fire being for a short time returned. The 10th—Colonel Fenwick at their head—threw out their skirmishers, and thus covered, advanced at steady pace towards the point where the rebels seemed thickest. They, however, did not long stand their ground; before our men came within striking distance the sepoys gave way and took to flight. Pursuit was impossible, by reason of want of cavalry; but the small band of mounted infantry, recently extemporised from the 10th, managed to come up, with some of the enemy, of whom, in the language of the day, they "gave a good account." We subsequently learned that the forces against whom we had been engaged comprised 8,000 men, commanded by Bunda Hussun, a lieutenant of Mendhee Hussun.

It was intended that our force should encamp on the field whence the rebels had fled. While halting for that purpose, it was found that a second engagement was to take place; that the enemy had taken up a position at Hummeerpore, a little distance from their former, and

[1] Our force consisted of the 10th, 20th, and 97th British regiments; six battalions of Nepaulese troops, under the command of General Pulwan Singh; two Field Batteries, and some thirty to forty mounted men of the 10th. By virtue of seniority I assumed medical charge.

under shelter of a wood. From there their guns soon opened fire upon us. Ours quickly replied; a few casualties in our ranks were the result, when darkness having put an end to the duel we bivouacked on our ground. When morning dawned, it was seen that the position they had occupied was abandoned; our camp was accordingly pitched, and so we remained, prepared for the next move.

Resuming our advance towards Lucknow, two successive marches of great length, and consequently fatiguing, were performed, considerable numbers of our transport animals completely breaking down, and so being the cause of much inconvenience to our force.

On the 23rd, about 10 a.m., our skirmishers drew upon them fire from a position taken up by the rebels at Sooltanpore. That position was attacked, and from a direction unexpected by them; thus disconcerted, their fire was comparatively little destructive in our ranks, nor was it long before—having discharged upon us a volley of grape—they abandoned their artillery and fled, leaving fourteen guns, besides stores and a large quantity of equipment, in our possession, also much ammunition and loot. Again the mounted men of the 10th[1] did good service in pursuit of the fugitives; some of our artillery followed, and it was said destroyed large numbers of them, the loss to our troops engaged being again comparatively small. Thus were the forces of Mendhee Hussun defeated, though numbering 6,000 regular sepoys and 6,000 matchlock men; the station of Sooltanpore recovered after being held by the rebels since the previous month of June.

After some delay our camp was pitched on the ground our men had won, and we halted for a day. A party dispatched to destroy a manufactory of gun carriages deserted by the rebels came upon various relics, with which doubtless were connected sad and painful associations; these included what had been an elegant barouche, a palkee garree, and a metal toy—the whole pertaining to victims of the first outburst of mutiny among the troops there stationed. Near our camp the artillery were occupied in bursting the guns deserted by the enemy.

On the 25th our force resumed its march at daylight, and so continued till late in the afternoon, making one short halt to allow the troops to draw water from some village wells, a second to cook and distribute food. Shortly after we had started a very hideous object presented itself to view; it was the body of a native suspended by the feet from a branch of a tree, his arms dangling in mid-air, and so doubtless indicating the cruel manner of his death. Arrived at

[1] Under Captain Bartholomew.

Mosufferkhan, where it was arranged that our camp should be pitched, we found awaiting to join us a reinforcement of Sikh and Pathan Horse, together with some mounted men comprising half-castes and Christians who had belonged to mutinied or disbanded regiments all of whom had been sent by forced marches to our aid. Some stray mutineers were discovered in near proximity to camp by our scouts, and by them duly "disposed of."

A long and arduous march through difficult country; the villages along our route deserted by their inhabitants, the fields destitute of labourers. On arrival at our camping ground near Jugdispore, it was ascertained that our advance guard had fallen in with and captured two messengers conveying a purwana, or order, from the Ranee of Lucknow to the zemindars of the district just traversed by us, intimating to them the advance of a small body of English, and calling upon them to destroy the intruders at Sooltanpore; also to send without delay provisions for the rebel troops holding Lucknow. A day's halt and much-needed rest for man and animal. On 28th a long march, in the course of which we passed through some villages strongly fortified and loopholed, but deserted by inhabitants. Reinforced as we now were by cavalry, they scoured the vicinity of our route, in the course of their proceedings coming upon seventeen rebels, some wearing the uniform of their former regiments, all of whom they killed.

With rain and boisterous weather the month of March began; it was therefore somewhat late in the morning of the 1st when our advance was resumed. As we proceeded, the discovery was made by our scouts that a considerable body of rebels occupied a point at some little distance on our flank. The main body of our force was accordingly halted, while a portion was sent against the mutineers, the result being that in the attack upon them the latter had sixty of their numbers killed or wounded, and lost two of their guns. Resuming progress, we traversed a number of towns and villages, all strongly fortified, but sparsely occupied. Night had closed in when we reached our halting-place. While tents were being pitched, lurid flames at intervals in our near vicinity told the fate of villages and isolated houses.

During the attack just mentioned several hand-to-hand conflicts took place between the Sikh troopers and the rebels. In one of these an officer received a tulwar cut which severed an artery. By-and-by I came upon him, prostrate on the ground, alone, and bleeding to death. A ligature was applied to the divided vessel; he was placed in a dooly, and so carried to my tent, where he remained during the following night. While there he was visited by some of his men, who laid before him various articles of loot—some valuable—of which they had possessed themselves, and now presented to him. In contrast with an incident shortly to be related, and also in its way characteristic of a class, the fact made an impression upon me that under the particular circumstances of time and place, the officer alluded to [1] offered to me—who in all likelihood had been the means of saving his life—not one thing of the many laid out for display on the floor rug of my tent.

Early on March 3 the sound of heavy guns from the direction of Lucknow told that active work was in progress there. Later in the day a staff officer, escorted by a squadron of the 9th Lancers and two Horse Artillery guns, arrived in camp as bearer of dispatches. These contained orders that on the morrow our force should advance and take up the position assigned to it in relation to the contemplated attack on that capital. They informed us that already the Dilkhosha had been captured. On the following day our force was accordingly in motion towards Lucknow. It had not proceeded far when information was received that a small body of rebels occupied the inconsiderable fort of Dowraha, situated at the distance of a mile or so from our line of route. A body, unfortunately, as events proved, too small for its intended purpose, was detached with the object of effecting its capture; but with the loss of one officer killed and several casualties among the rank and file, the position had to be left untaken, while our force continued its march. In the afternoon we took up the position assigned to us on an extensive plain between Dilkhosha and Bebeepore, and so merged into the general force under the Commander-in-Chief.

[1] For his gallantry in the attack mentioned he was awarded the Victoria Cross.

CHAPTER XV

1858. *CAPTURE OF LUCKNOW*

Rifles against cannon—The sailors' battery—The circle narrows—The 10th in Lucknow—The Moulvie's house—Ladies rescued—Surgeon's place in battle—Soldiers' gratitude—Martinière—Wrecks of victory—The city—The Residency—Isolated casualties—Flight of sepoys—Columns in pursuit.

THROUGHOUT March 5 heavy bombardment continued, the batteries of rebels within Lucknow replying actively to those outside the city. On the 6th, Captain Graham's company of the 10th occupied an intrenched position at an angle of the Mohamed Bagh, where during the night temporary defences had been thrown up, the task assigned to, and successfully performed, being by their rifle fire to keep down that from rebel guns of a battery close to Begum Serai. It became an exciting sight to watch the enemy as they moved their guns into the several embrasures of their battery preparatory to discharging them upon our position, and then the effect of the volley poured into those embrasures by our men; then the burst of flame—our soldiers instantly throwing themselves prone on the ground; the thud of round shot upon our protecting rampart; our soldiers starting to their feet, pouring volley after volley as before into the embrasures, while the guns were being lowered therefrom to be reloaded. Thus the seemingly unequal duel went on. After a time the rebel fire from that particular point began to slacken, then ceased. The men of the 10th had done their work right well. Other portions of our general force were engaged elsewhere, preparatory to the grand attack about to be delivered.

Steadily during the next two days the circle of fire narrowed around the city. On the 9th a more than usual heavy artillery fire took place between our forces and the enemy. The sailors' battery of 68-pounders was engaged against large bodies of the rebels assembled among a range of ruined buildings at the western end of the Martinière, the men who worked the guns taking affairs with such coolness that, in the intervals between firing, cleaning, and loading their respective pieces, they squatted in parties of four on the ground, and proceeded with games of cards, in which they seemed to take as much interest as in the effect produced by their fire. About 2 p.m., to an increased rapidity of fire from sailors and artillery guns was added more active *pings* of rifles, and somewhat later on the position of the Martinière was in the possession of our force.

Two more days of arduous work by all ranks, the rebels gradually but steadily being pressed in from their advanced positions; the siege guns opening heavily upon the city; bodies of rebels in their endeavours at flight falling into the hands of our troops, many of their own numbers being killed. Our force increased by the arrival of reinforcements from Cawnpore, and by that of 10,000 Ghoorkas under Jung Bahadur, the advent of the latter causing some interest, and not a little amusement, dirty and untidy, flat-faced, small-sized as they were, their guns drawn by men instead of horses, their whole aspect more suited to dramatic effect than for such work as was then in progress.

On March 11 the Begum Kotee was stormed and captured by a combined force of 93rd Highlanders, 4th Sikhs, and Ghoorkas, the losses sustained by the assailants being on the occasion very heavy in both men and officers. In the afternoon of next day, the 10th, led by Colonel Fenwick, occupied the position thus so gallantly won. Everywhere around signs indicated the deadly nature of the struggle that had taken place during its assault. Bodies of defenders, bleeding and mangled, lay in heaps; some were being thrown pell-mell into a V-shaped ditch, down, then up the sides of which our troops had in the first instance to scramble, while exposed to terrific fire by the defenders. As we entered, our artillery hastened to prepare for its further work of bombarding at close quarters. During the night we bivouacked within the city. On the 13th, the 10th forced its way against severe opposition directly through the city towards the Kaiser Bagh, while other portions of the troops were similarly at work from other directions. Again, as night closed in after a day of most arduous work and heavy list of casualties among our numbers, the 10th bivouacked in streets and gardens wrested from their sepoy occupants. On the 14th the regiment went on with its work of conquest, heavy fire from roofs and loopholes bringing to earth, now one, then another, and another of our men as we continued to advance. At last the Kaiser Bagh was reached; it was quickly entered by Captain Annesly at the head of his company, by means of a gateway first detected by Havelock, then adjutant of the 10th; thus the central point within the city, held by the rebels, was now in the hands of our troops.

At a short distance from that position, and partly hidden by other buildings, were the ruins of what had until the previous day been the residence of the notorious Moulvie,[1] by whose orders, in the earlier days of the mutiny, several of our countrymen and countrywomen who had fallen into the hands of the rebels were put to death. As our troops now entered the enclosure within which those ruins stood, they came upon two gory heads of British soldiers, who had during recent operations been captured by the rebels. The Moulvie had, however, escaped, but was known to be in the still unsubdued part of the city, whence he exerted command over the rebels yet actively engaged against our forces.

A communication of romantic and pathetic interest now reached the more advanced portion of our force. It detailed the fact that two ladies[2] were in the hands of the rebels, their lives threatened, their position in other respects one of serious danger; it urged those into whose hands it might fall to press onwards to their rescue. As subsequently transpired, those ladies were held prisoners by Wajid Ali, and by him treated with some degree of consideration, so much so that suspicion was brought upon him in respect to his fidelity to the rebel cause. He it was also who sent, by the hand of his brother, to the nearest British officer, the letter alluded to. Instantly on receipt of it, Captain McNeil and Lieutenant Bogle, at the head of a rescue party of Ghoorkas, started under the guidance of the bearer of the letter. The house in which the ladies were was quickly reached; the two captives were placed in doolies, and together with their protector escorted, notwithout much difficulty and risk, to the camp of General Macgregor.

While these operations were in progress, one or other regimental surgeon was constantly with the fighting line, rendering what aid was practicable to those struck down; and here it is well to mention that whenever officer or soldier felt himself wounded, his first call was "for the doctor." Nor is it to be questioned that the moral effect of our presence was very considerable; the presence of a hand to succour imparted confidence.

As soon as practicable, the wounded were withdrawn to our hospital tents, and there their injuries more particularly attended to. While work in front was in progress, and as a consequence that in hospital was most active, I was on an occasion occupied during twilight in so affording

[1] The Moulvie of Fyzabad, known by the name of Ahmed Alee Shah (also called Ahmed Oola Shah), was a native of Arcot, in the Madras Presidency. He was said to understand English and to have been a man of acumen and boldness. He was ultimately killed at Powayne.

[2] Mrs. Orr and Miss Jackson.

aid to a wounded soldier just brought in, myself on my knees on the ground and leaning over him. A touch on my shoulder, and then in a soldier's voice, "Here, sir, put that in your haversack," the action accompanying the word, and the man passed on his way, my attention too much occupied to observe his appearance. When work was done and I returned to my tent, I examined my haversack; I found therein a brick of silver, of sufficient size to make, as subsequently it did, a tea and coffee service, the donor remaining unknown. The circumstance is noted, as in contrast to that already mentioned, in which an officer was concerned.

A visit to the Martinière revealed the effects of recent operations against that building; statues and other works of art dilapidated, broken, and in ruins; doors and other woodwork torn and split, walls, ceilings, corridors injured in every possible way, large masses of *débris* at particular places indicating those upon which shot and shell had been most heavily directed. From the summit of the building we traced the route by which, in the previous October, the relieving force had effected its advance, together with some of the buildings historically associated with that gallant feat, including the Yellow House, Secundra Bagh, Mess House, and Motee Mahal.

In our field hospital the wreck of our "glorious victory" was to be seen in plenty; officers and soldiers, wounded, maimed, or in various instances terribly burnt and disfigured by explosions; many groaning in their agony, others placidly bearing their sufferings, a few unconscious to pain, the death-rattle in their throats—all arranged on pallets, and far less comfortably seen to than were their comrades fortunate enough to be taken into their own regimental hospitals.

The streets along which the 10th had so recently forced its way to the Kaiser Bagh presented a scene of utter devastation: walls blackened, loopholed, shattered with shot-holes of various sizes, the buildings roofless and tenantless except by dead bodies gashed or torn by bullets, their cotton-wadded clothing burning, sickening odours therefrom contaminating the air; heaps of *débris* everywhere, furniture, utensils and dead bodies, all mixed up together; breaches made by heavy guns to make way for advancing infantry, round shot by which they had been effected; domes, at one time gilded and otherwise ornamental, but now dilapidated and charred; costly furniture, oil paintings once of great value, ornamental glass and china strewed about, and everywhere to be seen; ornamental garden lakes black from gunpowder cast into them; the gardens trodden down, mosaic work of cisterns broken into fragments. At Secundra Bagh, where on November 16 some two thousand sepoys perished at the hands of the 53rd and 93rd Regiments, the bones of the slain, now, four months after the event, lay in heaps, a heavy odour of decomposition pervading the enclosure.

At the Residency a deep irregular-shaped pit immediately outside the Bailee Guard marked the spot where, in the latter days of the memorable siege, the rebels had prepared their mine against the defenders of that position ; inside and close to the same entrance were the remains of the countermine by which the operations connected with the former were detected, and itself sprung upon the besiegers. The door of that gateway, penetrated and torn by bullets ; buildings roofless and bespattered with shot-marks, including that where ladies and children spent the eighty-five days to which the siege extended, and that in which Sir Henry Lawrence received his death-wound,—the whole presenting an epitome of what war implies, not to be forgotten.

For some time after Lucknow was virtually in the power of our force desultory fights continued to occur at places in and around the city. In the portions actually held by our troops, isolated men occasionally fell by a rebel bullet. Among other casualties, two officers had the misfortune to fall into the hands of the sepoys, by whom they were put to death, and their heads, so report said, borne away as trophies.

No sooner had the principal positions held by the rebels been captured from them than their flight from the city began, at first in small bodies, but rapidly increasing in numbers as channels of egress became known among them. Although without artillery, considerable numbers carried their small arms, while others were content to abandon everything, and seek only their own safety. One armed body of the fugitives, while endeavouring to get away in the direction of the Alumbagh, was fallen upon by our troops and severely dealt with ; in other directions, however, the fact became known that large bodies effected their escape without being attacked, in places where no special difficulties intervened,—nor did explanation of the circumstance transpire.

Several field columns were immediately organized and dispatched along different routes known or believed to have been taken by the escaped rebels. Years afterwards the gallant services performed by one of those columns [1] were detailed in a published Biography. Other bodies found their way to the neighbourhood of Azimghur and there united with a considerable force of their brethren, which had on March 21 defeated a small body of British troops at Atrowlea, obliging it to retire within entrenchments at the first-named city.

[1] Sir Hope Grant, K.C.B.

CHAPTER XVI

1858. *THE AZIMGHUR FIELD FORCE*

The force extemporised—Jounpore—Tigra—Azimghur—Prestige—Casualties—Pursuing column — Mr. Venables — Night march — Painful news — Ghazepore—Recross the Ganges—Arrah—Preparations—Beheea—Jugdispore—Resting—Jungle fight—Chitowrah—Heat and exhaustion—Work under difficulties—Our commissariat lost—Peroo—Bivouac—Return to camp—Threatened attack—Village destroyed—Our physical condition—Dhuleeppore—Preparing for attack—Guns recaptured—A sad duty performed—Sick and wounded—Messenger mutilated—Keishwa—Slaughter—Force to Buxar—Non-effectives—The force ceases to exist—General orders, thanks, and batta.

THE task of the 10th was looked upon as finished; the regiment had been sixteen years in India, the entire period continuously in the plains. With an expression of glee on the part of the men was the order received to commence our homeward march,—that is, to proceed towards Calcutta, there to embark for England. On the 28th of March the regiment turned its back on Lucknow; after several hours of weary progress it reached its camping ground. About midnight we were roused from slumber by the arrival of a cavalry escort and Staff Officer, with orders that the regiment should march forthwith towards Goorsagunge, there to form part of a field force under command of Brigadier-General Lugard, its object to raise what had become the siege of Azimghur by the combined rebel forces just mentioned. Before ten o'clock on the 29th our soldiers, to use their own expression, had "done twenty-eight miles of road, heel and toe," disappointed at the unexpected change in destination, but also, in their own phrase, "ready for the new work cut out for them." Other portions of what was to be the Azimghur Field Force[1] quickly reached the appointed rendezvous, and the process of organization was complete. Then we learned that the combined rebel force under Koer Singh surrounded Azimghur; that a body of British, while *en route* thither from Benares,

[1] It comprised 10th, 34th, and 84th Regiments, 1,700 Sikh cavalry, a portion of military train as cavalry, and three batteries of artillery. I was principal medical officer, also in charge of the Staff, in addition to my regimental duties.

had suffered severely while in conflict with them; that therefore the rapid advance of that under General Lugard was urgently called for.

Continuing our march from day to day, we traversed much of the route by which our advance upon Lucknow had recently lain, it being marked by whitened bones of men slain, ruins of villages, and huts destroyed by fire; otherwise no event worth notice occurred until the 9th of April, by which date we had reached Budlapore. On the morning of that day our force marched from its camp at 2 a.m., proceeding thence direct to Jounpore, a distance of twenty miles. There information was received that the rebel troops around Azimghur were commanded by Mendhee Hussun, Koer Singh being present with them.

Men and animals, tired out by fatiguing marches, were equally constrained to make one day's halt. On the morning of the 11th information led General Lugard to deviate from the regular route and proceed towards Tigra, situated on our left, adjoining the left side of the river Goomtee, the rebels under Gholam Hussun being reported to have there taken up a position. A reconnoitring party speedily discovered the point taken up by about 500 rebels with two guns; they were at once attacked by our irregular cavalry, eighty of their number killed, the remainder dispersed, though this small affair lost the life of Lieutenant Havelock, cousin of our Adjutant.

Another day's halt to rest our men and animals; the heat already severe, 102° F. in our tents. Resuming our progress, our force arrived within striking distance of Azimghur after darkness of the night had closed in, and bivouacked on the position assigned to us, the rebels for some time disturbing our rest by their bullets that kept dropping among our ranks. With dawn on the 15th the several members of our body militant were at their posts, prepared for the work before them. As the 10th moved forward past a strip of dense jungle that skirts the river Tonse, a smart fire was opened upon us from the thicket, as also from a grove at some distance across that stream. The first of these positions was at once attacked by our artillery, the infantry rapidly following; by means of a dilapidated bridge hastily repaired, some cavalry and artillery got across and so attacked the second. Other portions of our force were engaged with similar activity at the points assigned to them respectively, the result being, that after losing considerably in their numbers, the rebels fled pell-mell, and as we entered the city only some of their killed and wounded were anywhere met with. It was subsequently found that they had lost some guns, much equipage and stores, and that, under command of Koer Singh, they were in full flight towards the Ganges.

When, as already mentioned, the rebels from their position in the jungle opened fire upon the 10th, the demeanour of our men, hardened as they were by long service in India, and accustomed to the work of war, was such as vividly to illustrate the advantages of having old soldiers under such circumstances. Although taken by surprise, our men wavered not; with equanimity our Colonel,[1] as he turned towards them, said, "Steady, men, steady." There was a sharp fire of musketry into the brushwood, instantly followed by a charge with the bayonet; native voices were heard as the sepoys recognised the soldiers they had to deal with, calling to their comrades, "*Bhago, bhago bhai, dus pultan aya*" (Run, brothers, run; the 10th have come). A minute more, and those who escaped bayonet thrusts by our men were in rapid flight.

Resulting from the day's encounter a considerable number of dead had to be interred, and wounded attended to. For the latter accommodation had to be procured, as well as for our sick, whose numbers had been rendered considerable by the great fatigue and exposure undergone during our recent long and arduous marches. As a guard to those so provided for, as well as to hold the city now in our power against further attack, and leave our force unencumbered for further action, the 34th was detailed to fulfil both duties.

A column under command of Brigadier Douglas started in pursuit of the body of rebels directly under Koer Singh. They having made a stand against Douglas as soon as the first panic of defeat had somewhat subsided, the pursuing column was on 17th reinforced by additional artillery, cavalry, and part of the 84th. Within a few hours thereafter the sound of active firing told us what was taking place; then the arrival of wounded men declared that serious work was being done. In due time we learned that the rebels had been defeated, a hundred of their number killed, and one of their guns captured.

Among the wounded so brought in was Mr. Venables, an indigo planter, a typical representative of the rough, ready, and energetic men who collectively become the makers of Greater Britain. Mr. Venables had, by his own force of character, prevented open revolt in the district of Azimghur after the 17th N.I. had mutinied, and, by means of levies raised and commanded by himself, repelled an attack by the latter; subsequently on various occasions he was in actual conflict against the rebels. Gangrene of the wounded shoulder took place, and within a very short time his death occurred, much to the sorrow and regret of those of us with whom he had been associated. After his death it was discovered that he wore upon his bosom the wedding ring of his deceased wife.

[1] William Fenwick, than whom a more upright man could not be named.

She had died at Azimghur, and now his body was laid in a grave close to the remains of her for whom his affection was manifest in tangible form.

On the 23rd General Lugard learned that notwithstanding their recent defeat the rebels under Koer Singh were advancing, as if to threaten Ghazepore. At 9 p.m. our force was in motion towards them. The night march was long and trying; for some hours our way was enlivened by the clear moonlight, but the air was hot and sultry. Occasional halts were necessary to enable the men to rest for a little, and refresh themselves with draughts of water. Arrived at Mohumdee next morning, several hours elapsed before camp equipage arrived and tents were pitched, for as on various previous occasions our men outmarched their transport train. There news reached camp that Koer Singh had so far succeeded that nearly all the men commanded by him had got across the Ganges; but that Douglas, having arrived and opened fire upon them from the left bank, their chief had been severely wounded,[1] and of themselves many put *hors de combat.*

Later in the day the painful news circulated in camp that a small force, composed of men of 35th, the Naval Brigade, and some Sikhs, sent from Arrah to intercept the rebels then in rapid flight from the Ganges to Jugdispore, had met with disaster at their hands. The force referred to was that under the command of Captain Le Grand, 35th Regiment.

Two successive marches during the hottest period of each day, and we were at Ghazepore. Officers and men, forced by reason of seasonal temperature to dispense with outer uniform, wore only *khakee* trousers and woollen shirts, the sleeves turned up for sake of comfort. Thus equipped, dusty, and grimy, our aspect presented a sorry contrast to the neat and in some instances elegant turn-out of men and women who rode out from cantonments to see our force march into camp.

Resuming the march next morning, the occurrence of a rain storm drenched us, but even that was an agreeable relief in the great heat and dust heretofore prevailing. No halt took place, but throughout that day and following night our wearied men continued what was indeed their forced march. By daylight on May 2 we arrived at Synhee Ghat. There, by means of steamers ready for the purpose, the work of crossing the Ganges rapidly proceeded, and by 9 a.m. we were in the Arrah district. We were now reunited to the column which under Douglas had been recently sent on from Azimghur, it having succeeded

[1] Of that wound Koer Singh soon thereafter died. The command of his forces then fell to Umeer Singh.

in preventing Koer Singh's men from falling upon Arrah after inflicting on a small body of our troops the disaster already mentioned.

Not until the 4th were all our stores and equipment transferred to the right side of the river, and our force in readiness for further work. The following morning our camp was pitched at Arrah,[1] and thus an opportunity afforded us to visit places in and around that station with which some recent painful events were associated. A building occupied a few months past by a civil servant now presented the appearance of a star-shaped fort from the embrasures of which the muzzles of guns projected; masses of ruins told where other bungalows had been. There stood the small fortified house, its walls loopholed and battered by rebel bullets, a memorial of the gallant defence made by Herwald Wake and his few comrades until relieved by Major Eyre. At a little distance eastward from the city is the scene of the great disaster ot July 30, already alluded to more than once; the road by which our men had marched, bordered on either side by isolated houses, at one spot by a clump of "toddy" palms, at another by a tope of mango trees; there the Hindoo temples at which, it was said, certain of our men on that occasion were offered as sacrifices to Kali; there the trees on which others were hung, though, as expressed by those on the spot, the events referred to are as far as possible "hushed up."

Information reached General Lugard that the rebels in considerable force had taken up a position at Jugdispore. He resolved to march upon and attack them without unnecessary delay. All extra establishment and equipment was left to be retained in store; sick and men otherwise non-effective eliminated; commissariat and transport suited for service on which we were about to enter, alone set apart for the purpose; mobility and efficiency the two qualities held in view.

In the lightest possible marching order our advance began on May 27. While it was yet dark, thirteen miles of road were got over; two more after daybreak, we then arrived at our intended camping ground; our only incident the capture of a spy,[2] in the act of counting the numbers and noting the composition of our column. The rebels had determined to oppose us *en route*. For that purpose they took up a position in a tract of jungle through which the road extended near Beheea; there our artillery opened fire upon them, and thence they were quickly expelled. The aspect of the sky portended a dust storm; it was now upon us with all the usual violence of such meteors, the air so laden with dust that for a time all was dark. Then came a deluge of rain, soaking us

[1] Here we received Government General Orders relating to the late Jounpore Field Force, my name in the list of those "mentioned."

[2] Captured by myself and duly handed over.

completely, converting the hitherto parched ground into a swamp, but reducing the temperature from 100° to 85°. As the sky became clear, a strong body of rebels were observed advancing towards us. At once a party was dispatched against them; brisk fire by the artillery, then our cavalry dashed in among them; they broke up and soon disappeared in the jungle. All through next night the camp was on the alert; pickets patrolled in all directions. In early morning of the 9th our advance was resumed.

During the march parties of rebels hovered on either flank, but at a safe distance from our column. As we neared the town of Jugdispore the enemy advanced upon us from front and flanks. When they came within striking distance, our column, already prepared for such an emergency, took the initiative; our men, to use their own expression, "went at them with a will." Before sunset that town, together with the palace of Koer Singh, were in our possession.

The 10th was a day of comparative quiet; men had to rest after their arduous work; those prostrated by heat and fatigue be attended to, information obtained regarding movements of the fugitive enemy, and arrangements made for further action against them. While our force was thus enjoying comparative quiet, news reached our commander that the rebels had taken up a position at Chitowrah, situated deep in a dense jungle, some seven miles distant from our present camp; that a column comprising the 6th Regiment was in a position near Peroo to co-operate with us; that the column under Sir Hugh Rose was steadily closing around Jhansi; and that in Rohilcund our troops had obtained several important successes.

In the forenoon of the 11th a sufficient guard for its protection being left in camp, a strong body[1] of our force marched to attack the rebel position at Chitowrah. It had not proceeded more than three miles when an earthwork across the road for a short time interrupted progress; that obstacle overcome, a heavy fire from the dense jungle on our flanks and front opened upon us. As a reply our artillery opened with grape, after which skirmishers dashed into the thick forest, with the result that they carried all before them; but pursuit was impossible by reason of its density.

The heat of the day, great as it was in the open ground, was overpowering while we traversed the forest already mentioned. It was fortunate for all of us that this contingency had been foreseen and provided for by General Lugard; skins full of water, carried by elephants, camels, and bullocks, forming part of our equipment on the

[1] Comprising 10th Foot, Military Train Madras Artillery, Madras Rifles.

occasion. At short intervals of time and distance, soldiers and officers indiscriminately placed themselves under the open mouths of those skins, had their heads and clothing drenched; then continuing their march until the hot wind effected complete evaporation, they again and again underwent a similar ordeal. Nevertheless, many staggered, some fell from heat and exhaustion, others gasped for breath. Considerable numbers had to be brought along in doolies; among those so prostrated was Colonel Fenwick.[1] Exhausted as we were, it was fortunate for us that our enemies were wanting in resolution to take advantage of our condition.

Wearied and fatigued as were men and officers, little in the way of food was needed. Tea—that ever-agreeable beverage under such circumstances—was about the only thing obtainable at the time. Rest was out of the question during the night. Impressions of the day's work, repeated *pings* of musketry from the adjoining jungle, the thud ot bullets on the ruined walls among which we lay, the occasional arrival of wounded men,—all combined to banish sleep; while to those engaged in looking after sick and wounded, whose numbers had become considerable, their work left them worn out and exhausted.

Daylight of the 12th revealed to us the scene of action. In jungle recesses mangled corpses; in the ruins, now utilised as "barracks" for effectives, and hospital for those struck down, whether by wounds or sickness, heavy moans of the suffering were intermingled with coarse jests of their more fortunate comrades. The unpleasant fact transpired that our commissariat supplies had fallen into the hands of the rebels, while the force was engaged against them in the jungle as already mentioned. Breakfast for men and officers became a meal more nominal than real; orders were issued for the march to be resumed southward, so that our force might the more effectively co-operate with another making its way from that direction.

Early in the afternoon our force was on its march towards Peroo, with a view to effect that junction. As we advanced, the forest became less and less dense; emerging therefrom into open country, the burnt remains of huts and villages were passed. Some stray shots reached us from small concealed bodies of the enemy, but these were quickly silenced by parties of our men detached for that purpose. Without opposition in more serious form we arrived, while it was still daylight, at a mango tope, in which we bivouacked for the night, all necessary precautions being first taken against surprise. During that night a

[1] An honourable man, considerate and straightforward in official as in private relations, he had effected much during the time he held command to restore to their normal state things already alluded to.

thunderstorm burst over us; this was followed by heavy downpour of rain, which soaked us to a degree that made sorry objects of us, situated as we then were, and at the same time reduced the ground that formed our beds to the condition of a marsh.

A raid was made upon cattle and rice, both of which were found among some ruined huts; the former were shot, and with the latter cooked, thus meal thus provided being savoury or otherwise according to whether individuals had or had not in their haversacks a small reserve of salt. At dawn next morning a strong party was detached to bring in supplies sent on to us from camp. It was not long before that escort was engaged with the rebels by whom it was attacked *en route*, and having defeated them, proceeded to obtain the needed supplies, with which in due time it returned to us. As a part of that escort were some young soldiers of the 6th Foot, recently arrived from the Cape of Good Hope. On their arrival back from that duty they were in so exhausted a condition that when time arrived to break up our bivouac they had to be removed by means of bullock-carts, elephants, and gun-carriages; the older soldiers of the same party, though much exhausted, were able to resume the march with their respective companies.

In the great heat now prevailing, the distance of nineteen miles that separated us from our standing camp was got over by ten o'clock that day; many so exhausted that, unable to keep up with the column, they followed as best they could, arriving as so many stragglers, but fortunately for them, unmolested and undiscovered by the rebels. During the absence of our column, our camp, left under protection of the 84th, was threatened by the rebels, who, however, were easily beaten off.

An attempt, made by men engaged for the purpose, to burn down the jungle—work in which had already cost us the lives of many men—was but partially successful. While at one point this was in progress, from another came indications of attack by a considerable body of well-armed rebels. The 10th were quickly in movement towards them, a few of their bullets telling among our ranks. Soon, however, the enemy disappeared in the dense forest, our men returning to the comparative quiet and "comfort" of their tents.

Short was the rest enjoyed by them. On the third day an attack from our side was directed upon two villages occupied by the rebels in our near vicinity. Similar attacks on other villages succeeded each other; a convoy with supplies from our base at Arrah arrived; attempts on a larger scale than heretofore to burn down the forest were made, but unsuccessfully; and so, with the hot season upon us, did all concerned try their best to carry out the general work we had to do.

Some idea of the physical condition of our troops may best be gathered from the particulars now to be given. Soon after the middle of May fevers and bowel disorders had become very prevalent among them ; in other ways they suffered severely from the prevailing heat and fatigue. As to myself, according to my diary, "from the time I became attacked at Azimghur, I have found it impossible to throw off my illness, and now am exhausted and debilitated to a great degree by the continued heat. Were it not my duty to hold out for the benefit of my wife and children, I would certainly apply for sick leave." By that time, although our force had been only ten days in the field and jungle near Jugdispore, the number of non-effectives was so great as to seriously impair its efficiency and mobility; as many of these as could be so disposed of were accordingly sent under strong cavalry escort to Arrah. Cases of sunstroke were of occasional occurrence, though far less so than we had expected. Our transport suffered scarcely, if at all, in a less degree than our men, thus still further adding to the daily increasing difficulties under which we were expected to act as an efficient force. Another phase of our difficulties arose from the want of vegetables as part of our food. From the day when we first took the field supplies in this respect have been absent, the result being that men and officers are more or less suffering from land scurvy.

On the 20th our force made an attack on the village of Dhuleeppore, recently destroyed, but in the ruins of which a body of rebels had assembled. The result of that attack was discomfiture to them, though, unhappily, unusually heavy loss to the assailants.

Then followed a few days of comparative rest to our men ; but meanwhile the rebels re-occupied the position from which so recently they had been driven. Arrangements were accordingly made for a renewed attack on that place.

At daylight on the 20th our force was in motion: one portion by a road just within the skirt of jungle, a second along the plain on which the affair of a few days before took place. As they drew close upon the rebel position, fire was opened from two howitzers captured on the occasion of the disaster to the party under Captain Le Grand already mentioned. Three rounds were fired before the 10th and 84th were able "to get at" the rebels. Once among them, the guns were quickly recaptured, many of the gunners killed, the rebels in flight. Our men returned to their tents.

Our camp ground had become so offensive, and otherwise objectionable, that, leaving for a time a body of our force sufficiently strong to hold its own in case of emergency, the larger portion, under orders by General Lugard, proceeded to take up a fresh position. The move involved a march of four miles and upwards. While *en route* we traversed the scene of Le Grand's disaster. Isolated bones, some partly gnawed, lay scattered about; fragments of utensils of sorts strewed the surface,—sad relics, in their several ways, of the episode referred to. A halt was made; the fragments of what had been gallant men carefully collected and most reverently interred. We then resumed our way.

The numbers of sick and wounded had now exceeded the capacity of our transport; it became a matter of necessity to get rid of them, so that the force might be left ready prepared for further action. Being provided with a strong cavalry escort, I started with a full convoy of such non-effectives. We traversed a piece of country directly in front of the rebels, halting under the shelter of a mango tope during the hottest hours of daylight; resumed the journey at nightfall, and reached Arrah before daybreak. There the sick and wounded were disposed of in hospital; our return journey quickly resumed, and without adventure we were again with our force in time for further work.

A few days prior to the date now reached, a messenger had been sent with dispatches from General Lugard to the officer in command of a column co-operating with his own. The man presented a sorry plight as he returned to camp; his nose cut off, his right hand severed at the wrist, his face and other parts of his person besmeared with blood, himself faint, bewildered, and dazed. After a time he related the story of his capture. He had reached his destination without mishap, had delivered the dispatches of which he was bearer, received those in reply, and started on his return journey with them. While passing through a rebel village on his way he was arrested, his papers taken from him, he himself ordered for execution, as traitor and spy. On the plea that in the state of mutilation inflicted upon him his appearance would be more deterrent among possible waverers in the rebel cause than would be the fact of his being put to death, the extreme penalty was commuted.

A body of rebels having destroyed an indigo factory and taken up a position at Kishwa, our force started at 3 a.m. on the 2nd of June towards that point. As we approached it, a heavy though happily ineffectual fire was opened against our ranks. The 10th marched steadily onwards. The rebels did not long remain to permit our men to close with them; pell-mell they fled, the Madras guns sending several charges of grape-shot after them, the cavalry then taking up the pursuit. We afterwards bivouacked in the open.

Driven thence, the rebels returned to their former position at Chitowrah. By daylight on the 4th of June our force advanced upon them in two separate columns: the one along the narrow jungle road already mentioned; the other, under the command of Brigadier Douglas, by the southern border of the same jungle. As we neared the densest part of forest, in the heart of which lay that hunting seat of Koer Singh, we suddenly found ourselves exposed in a semi-circle of fire in front and both our flanks; fortunately without much damage to our numbers. There was a momentary halt, then a cheer, and into the forest dashed the 10th, trusting to their bayonets rather than their rifle fire. The rebels fled, at first through and from the thicket whence their attack had been made, our men following close upon them; next, through ruins of houses and enclosures; through a cactus hedge, across an open plain, our soldiers gaining upon them in the race, the result being a loss to our enemies of ninety-four, fallen by bayonet thrust of our regiment alone. Wearied and exhausted, a short rest had to be allowed to men and officers. In our return journey towards camp we again traversed the ground over which the running fight described had taken place; the rebels killed in the early part of the day were represented by so many masses of skeletons, blood covered, some few shreds of flesh still adhering, thus telling what had been the work done in the interval by jackals, dogs, and vultures.

The immediate result of the rebel defeat at Chitowrah was that their force divided itself into small parties, each of which seemed to proceed on its own initiative, some as marauders, others with the apparent object of making for Buxar, and thence across the Ganges. With a view to act against the latter, a portion of our force, reduced as it now was by casualties and sickness, was placed under command of Brigadier Douglas, and proceeded on the duty assigned to it.

To the regret of all associated with him, General Lugard completely broke down in health; several of the officers were ill or had been invalided; the numbers of our soldiers who had become non-effective was very large. Under the circumstances in which we were thus placed, the fact became evident that unless it was intended by the responsible authorities that our force should be permitted to melt away and so cease to exist, a speedy return to cantonments was necessary to preserve that portion which still existed of its component elements.

Great, therefore, was the relief with which, in obedience to orders to return to cantonments, we marched away from Jugdispore on June 15. Our first day's march was no more than six miles long. Our men, however, had no longer the stimulus of expected fight to brace them up; many fell out *en route*, to come in as stragglers during the day. Continuing our journey, we once again passed through Arrah, then crossed the Soane, marching into quarters at Dinapore on the 19th of that month. The Azimghur Field Force had done the work assigned to it, and now ceased to exist as such.

The arrival of General Orders,[1] in which were contained the official dispatches relating to work performed by the force of which we had so recently formed a part, became naturally enough an event of importance to most of us, gratification to some, disappointment to others. Much praise was accorded to the 10th Regiment, as a whole, for arduous work efficiently done, and special reference made to individual officers whose services were "mentioned" in those dispatches. Paragraph 19 of the Orders in question gave the report by Sir Edward Lugard thus: "I beg most especially to recommend to His Excellency's notice —— [myself], Surgeon of the 10th Foot and Senior Medical Officer in charge of this force; his exertions have been untiring; though at times suffering from sickness, he never quitted his post, but continued his valuable superintendence. I feel more indebted to him than I can express." With reference to which the entry made in my diary at the time was: "I am thankful to God for having enabled me to fufil my duties satisfactorily, and, for the sake of my dear wife and children, hope advancement may speedily follow so handsome an acknowledgment of services performed." A few days afterwards we had the further gratification of reading "Orders" awarding to each of us six months' batta.

[1] Government General Oders, dated Allahabad, June 16, 1858.

CHAPTER XVII

1858-1859. *DINAPORE. PLYMOUTH*

Record of events—Various—Proclamation—Parliamentary debates—Sikhs—Ghoorka "allies"—Rainy season—Last of H.E.I.C.—Rebel forces—Native comments—Warrant for A.M.D.—Subjects of talk—The drama ended—Personal chagrin—Farewell service—March away—Parisnath—Raneegunge—Embark and sail—Order by Government—On board ship—England.

A PERIOD of rest in cantonments had become a matter of necessity to restore physical efficiency to our regiment, worn out as men and officers were by service in the field. The ordinary duties incidental to barrack existence in India were performed by all, our spare time devoted to current records of events announced from day to day by the newspapers. A few examples now follow.

No sooner had our force departed from Jugdispore than the rebels returned to their former positions in the extensive jungle by which that place is surrounded. Among the proceedings taking place elsewhere was the defeat, by Sir Hope Grant, of a strong rebel force at Nawabgunge. In the vicinity of Shahjehanpore, the Moulvie already mention was killed by the troops of a Rajah[1] who had risen against his authority. Gwalior had been re-captured; the Ranee of Jhansi killed while leading her troops at that place against the Central India Force. Reports of disaffection in certain Bombay regiments. In our own near neighbourhood, a threatened outbreak by the prisoners in Patna gaol led to the dispatch thither of two companies of the 10th. The rebels had collected in a body of considerable strength at Chuprah, from which position they were committing depredations on trading boats on the Ganges; a portion of the 35th was accordingly dispatched against them. Another party of rebels threatening Bulliah, a detachment of the 10th proceeded by steamer towards that place. Various lines

[1] Namely, Juggernath Singh, Rajah of Powayne, a man who, in the early days of the mutiny, had acted in a very unfeeling manner towards such fugitives as fell into his hands.

of communication were kept open by parties of troops placed at suitable points along them. The position at Arrah was so strengthened as to be secure against attack. The arrival of a small kind of gunboat intended for use on rivers was in its way important, as indicating the introduction of a new means of attack.

At this time the issue of certain Proclamations by Government seemed to attract much attention among the rebels still in the field; the tenor of the one an invitation to them to lay down their arms, the other in effect confiscating the property of landowners in Oude, with a few exceptions. "It is all very well," said they, "to invite us to come in, lay down our arms, and accept forgiveness; but why make the offer if you have the power to subdue us?" "Hitherto, if we committed murder, robbery, or burnt houses, we were hanged, imprisoned, or put on the roads for life; now we have done all these things, and we are invited to accept forgiveness. Truly this is a great raj; may it live for ever! . . ." Adverting to the first of those Proclamations, Lord Canning had expressed himself: "It is impossible that the justice, charity, and kindliness, as well as the true wisdom which mark these words, should not be appreciated." That is the way they were so. The second was at once called "the Confiscation Proclamation"; its almost immediate effect, an outbreak of hostility among chiefs who were otherwise more or less ready to remain passive if not actually favourable to existing law. At a subsequent date it was cancelled.

The debates in Parliament on these dispatches and many other comments on them were daily perused with great interest, not only by ourselves, but, as we learnt, by the rebels still in arms, the several views expressed by them somehow reaching cantonments.

The publication of orders, in which it was considered that services performed by the Sikhs were referred to in exaggerated terms as compared with the purely British, produced for the time being one effect to which allusion may here be made. "Why," said a very intelligent officer of that nationality, who was well known to most of us in cantonments, "you admit yourselves that we saved India for you; if we can do that for you foreigners, why should we not take the country for ourselves?" At the very time he spoke there were 82,000 Sikh troops in British employ. It was therefore not altogether subject of surprise to learn, as we did, that a mutinous plot had been discovered in the 10th Sikh Infantry at the distant station of Dhera Ishmail Khan.

Nor were matters satisfactory on the part of the Ghoorkhas, recently our "allies." The circumstance transpired that correspondence had been discovered between some of the higher authorities of Nepaul and the Royal family of Oude; that Jung Bahadur had expressed himself dissatisfied with degree of acknowledgment awarded by the Indian Government for services rendered by himself and by his troops.

With the advance of the rainy season sickness and death made sad havoc among our ranks. Meanwhile a state of unrest among the general population became more and more apparent, fanned as it was by reports circulated among them that large reinforcements from England would speedily arrive. Nor was that unrest confined to the non-military sections; some of the remaining sepoys believed to be "staunch" were said to have been detected in treasonable correspondence with their brethren in open rebellion; that representatives of mutineers had taken service in the ranks of the police force.

The 1st of November, 1858, began an era memorable in the history of India. On that day was read at every military station throughout the country the Proclamation by the Queen, declaring the transference to Her Majesty of the governing power hitherto exercised by the Honourable East India Company, the 10th Regiment and other troops occupying our present station being paraded at the civil station of Bankipore to impart additional splendour to an otherwise imposing ceremony. The Proclamation was read by the Commissioner of the district, an immense concourse of natives being present on the occasion.

With reference to the portions of that Proclamation in which, under certain specified conditions, pardon and amnesty are offered to rebels, the *Punjabee* newspaper of October 30 publishes a return of the army still opposed to us in Oude alone, comprising, according to figures there given, 79 chiefs, with an aggregate of 271 guns, 11,660 cavalry, 242,100 infantry, or 253,760 men in all; an imposing force indeed, considering that the suppression of the outbreak is declared to have been accomplished.

From the rebels still in the field, various comments on the terms so offered reached our cantonments. They considered that for crimes committed the sepoys deserved punishment by death, nor could they understand the exemption to that penalty now expressed. "As an earthquake"—according to their "prophets"—"has three waves, so will there be three shocks to British power in India: one we have just had; a second will occur a few years hence; the last after a longer interval, when the British position in India will vanish."

The arrival of papers with a new warrant [1] for the Medical Department of the Army naturally enough was of considerable interest to

[1] Of October 1, 1858.

those of us who belonged to that branch of the military service. As expressed in my diary at the time: "Most liberal it is, wiping away at one swoop the grievances under which the Department has laboured, and making it, as it ought to be, one of the best, if not the very best, in the Army." The great importance of the duties pertaining to that department in relation to individual needs and general military efficiency of a force was then prominently in my view from actual experience.

Shortly after the Proclamation by Her Majesty was read, a counter document of similar nature was issued by the Begum of Lucknow; but the latter produced little if any effect upon the rebels or their chiefs, numbers of both "coming in" one after another to make their submission. An attempt was made by a leading journal [1] to ascertain the number of persons who, being convicted of crimes against the State, had suffered the penalty of death. They were, according to that paper, as follows, from the outbreak of the Mutiny, namely:—By military tribunal, executed by hanging, 86; by civil tribunal, 300; the number shot by musketry, 628; blown from guns, 1,370; making a total of 2,384. The deposed King of Delhi recently passed our station by steamer, *en route* to Calcutta, and finally to Rangoon, there to spend the remaining portion of his life. The event gave rise to comment in respect to the action of the old king against the Indian Government, including his correspondence with the Shah of Persia in 1856; his reputed sanction of atrocities at Delhi in May, '57; his correspondence with Lucknow, etc. Another subject of talk was the reported escape of the Nana, the truth of which was soon thereafter confirmed. Lastly, the publication of correspondence between Colonel Edwards, Sir John Lawrence, and the Viceroy,[2] in respect to that portion of the Proclamation which related to native customs, religious and otherwise, afforded ample subject to discuss in our social coteries.

In the early days of 1859 came the welcome orders that all detached parties of the 10th should rejoin Headquarters, for the purpose of volunteering preparatory to the departure of the regiment for England. Other orders directed various reductions to be made in military establishments now in India; among them the withdrawal of several time-expired regiments, and the return to their respective ships of the Naval Brigades temporarily employed; that regiments still in the field should proceed to quarters; brigadiers commanding columns cease to hold appointments as such—thus declaring in effect that the campaign

[1] *Friend of India*, December 2, 1858.

[2] Afterwards noticed in Chambers' *History of the Revolt*, page 607.

connected with the great Mutiny was ended. But the facts were well known that bodies of rebels and mutineers were in the field, special forces actually employed against them; that bodies of disaffected had taken refuge in Nepaul. These and various other incidents were looked upon as so many supplements to the great drama at the end of which official orders declared that we had arrived.

Now there occurred an event the outcome of which to several men who, like myself, had held distinct charges of troops on active service, was much chagrin and disappointment; namely, our supersession in promotion by four officers, personally good, but who, though in the Crimea, had neither there nor elsewhere held equivalent positions. Some little time thereafter there appeared in a service journal[1] a leading article "On the partiality and injustice to the Department exhibited in the late promotions." This was the first outcome of a warrant regarding which first impressions were as already recorded.

At last came orders for the 10th to prepare for an early march towards the port of embarkation for England, and that meantime volunteering should be open to soldiers desiring to prolong their service in India. All such orders were obeyed with the greatest possible alacrity. The usual formalities on similar occasions being attended to, 141 of our men availed themselves of the option thus given them, and so ceased to belong to the corps in which they had performed much excellent work under very trying circumstances. On an intervening Sunday a farewell sermon[2] was preached to the regiment in our garrison church, and as I noted at the time, "strange as it seems, some of the soldiers were visibly affected thereby"; but as I have had numerous opportunities of seeing, soldiers of the period now referred to, notwithstanding the undoubted roughness of the great majority, had in their numbers many men keenly sensitive to the finer impulses of our common human nature.

Before daylight on February 10, our regiment began its march, "played out" of Dinapore by the band of the 19th Foot. Eight days thereafter we encamped in near vicinity of Gyah, a place sacred to Buddhists, and interesting in other ways. Two days more and we were on the Grand Trunk Road. Soon at the hot wells of Burkutta, the water of which, clear and having a slight odour of sulphur, is said to have many medicinal virtues.

In observing the necessary custom on a march, of halting on the seventh day, an opportunity was afforded those of us interested in such

[1] *Naval and Military Gazette*, January 8, 1859.

[2] Colossians iii. 15: "And let the peace of God rule in your hearts, to the which also ye are called in one body; and be ye thankful."

matters, to ascend the hill of Parisnath. Occupying the eastern table-land of the Vindyha range, itself 4,449 feet in height, like Mount Aboo on the west of the same range, its summit is covered with small Jain temples. Its sides are clothed with dense forests of sal (*Vateria indica*).

In the course of our march, several trains of camels or kafilats, with their Cabulee drivers, were met, as they were on their return journey from Calcutta to Affghanistan. In accordance with the custom of the time, they had begun their journey from Cabul eight months previous, and hoped to return at the end of four more, thus completing it in one year. These kafilats brought with them for sale in India, and Calcutta more especially, fruit of different kinds, spices, skins, asafœtida, and salep;[1] with the proceeds of the sale of which they purchased and carried back with them bales of cotton goods, and others of European manufacture. These caravans, including camels, drivers, and "followers," presented a picturesque and patriarchal scene, as in long lines they seemed to glide along the road. Arrived at Raneegunge, our camp was pitched for the last time. There a delay of several days took place, while arrangements were in progress for embarkation; hurried journeys by rail to and from Calcutta being made by those of us whose duty it was to carry those arrangements into effect. A series of coal-mines situated not far from our camp were being worked; but the industry was, comparatively speaking, in its infancy.

In the early morning of St. Patrick's Day, the regiment, stepping out cheerfully to the familiar music appropriate to the occasion, and dear to Irish soldiers, marched away from camp to railway station; thence proceeded by train to Howrah, then by river steamer to the ship *King Philip*, and so embarked. On the second day thereafter our ship, taken in tow by a river tug, began her homeward voyage. As we glided past Fort William, a Royal salute, fired from its ramparts, was a gratifying compliment paid by order of Government to the departing regiment for services performed by it during a most eventful episode in India's history. Wearied and worn out as our men were as a result of those services, no cheer was raised in response to the unusual compliment being paid to them.

The order by Government so alluded to was in these terms:—"*The Calcutta Gazette Extraordinary*, Friday, March 18, 1859. No. 360 of 1859. Notification. Fort William, Military Department. The 18th March, 1859.—Her Majesty's 10th Regiment of Foot is about to embark for England. His Excellency the Governor-General cannot allow

[1] Root of *Orchis mascula*.

this regiment to pass through Calcutta without thanking the officers and men for all the good service which they have rendered in the last two eventful years: first, in the outbreaks at Benares and Dinapore; next, as a part of the Column under their former Commander, Brigadier-General Franks; and more lately in the harassing operations conducted by Brigadier-General Sir E. Lugard and Brigadier Douglas on either bank of the Ganges. The Governor-General in Council desires, in taking leave of the 10th Regiment, to place on record his cordial appreciation of their valuable services. The regiment will be saluted by the guns of Fort William on leaving Calcutta. By order of his Excellency the Viceroy and Governor-General of India in Council.—R. J. H. Birch, Major-General, Secretary to the Government of India."

[Subsequently the officers of the 10th, including myself, received among us nine promotions and honorary distinctions for the services above alluded to.]

During the homeward voyage several deaths occurred among our men, exhausted as so many of them were by fatigue and exposure on service. Perhaps it was that the incidents of that service had to some extent affected the feelings heretofore so often manifested by soldiers in presence of death among their comrades; at any rate, it became a source of regret to some of our numbers to observe now the indifference shown on such occasions; indeed, scarcely was the solemnity of committing a body to the deep finished than games, songs, music, or dancing were resumed by parties of the men. The long rest afforded by the voyage did much to restore health to men and officers, and in other ways was beneficial to us all.

As we neared England a pilot boarded our ship. He had with him a bundle of papers, from which we learned, among other matters, of the occurrence of war in the Quadrilateral, full details being given of the great battles of Magenta and Solferino. In the accounts contained in the same papers of the state of public affairs preceding that campaign, a probable explanation was afforded of the suddenness with which active measures against the mutineers had ceased, and considerable forces withdrawn from India. At Gravesend, on July 13, the regiment transhipped to the *Himalayah*, and so was conveyed to Plymouth, there to be quartered in the Citadel. A few days thereafter,[1] I had the happiness of being with my beloved wife and children, grateful in spirit to Providence that life was preserved through the arduous ordeal now relegated to the past.

[1] July 24.

CHAPTER XVIII

1859-1860. *PLYMOUTH. DEVONPORT*

First incident—Our men—Disaster at Taku—Wrecks—A launch—Phrenology—Aspect of affairs—Warships to China—Militia and Volunteers—Improved conditions—Regimental schools—Female hospital — Windsor—Most Honourable Order of the Bath—Preparations—Mines—Cheesewring—Affairs—Decade—Mutiny medals.

SOON after our arrival I became the possessor of a horse and carriage, both purchased from "a friend." With pleasant anticipations I started on our first drive, accompanied by my wife and her lady friend. We had not proceeded far along the country road before the animal bolted clean away; after wildly rushing for some considerable distance, the carriage came in contact with the embankment, was upset and broken to pieces, the two ladies severely injured. The accident happened at the entrance to a country house; the ladies were admitted thereto for a little, a glass of wine given to each; they were driven home, after which no inquiry was made regarding them. This first experience of "hospitality" impressed us at the time, and now is noted as in its way characteristic. We had not been "introduced" to the family.

Unfortunately it so happened that among the men of the 10th there were some who used not wisely the balance of "batta" still remaining unspent by them. The result was that they brought obloquy upon themselves, and to some extent upon their more steady and well-behaved comrades who were altogether undeserving of it. So it happens on other occasions; the actual number of men in a regiment who commit crimes may be small, though their offences may be statistically considerable.[1]

In September attention was painfully drawn to the unfortunate failure at Taku of the war vessels conveying the British and French ambassadors to the Peiho *en route* to Pekin, that failure involving the loss of

[1] The 10th Regiment was composed of the following, according to religious denomination; namely, Episcopalians, 29 officers and 236 men; Presbyterians, 8 and 28; Roman Catholics, 5 and 301. It may be taken as an example of an "English" regiment.

three gunboats and 464 men belonging to them. From that moment it became evident that troops and ships must prepare for service in the Far East, and although, as the 10th had so recently landed, it was unlikely that the regiment would as a whole be concerned, it was probable that some individual officers might be so; several of us accordingly took an opportunity of making ourselves acquainted with the current of events in China from the date of the *Arrow* affair in October, 1856, to that of the Taku incident alluded to.

Following close upon the news of that disaster came the wreck of the *Royal Charter*, involving the loss of 470 lives, near Bangor, during one of those autumn storms so frequent on English coasts. Public sympathy was much aroused by these events, quickly following each other as they did. Unhappily the last named was not at the time isolated of its kind, though in its details not exceeded in painful accompaniments by any.

A new war vessel—the *Narcissus* frigate of fifty guns—being to be launched, the ceremony proved not only interesting but impressive, in respect to sentiments it evolved. An immense assembly met by invitation in Devonport Dockyard to witness the event; as the hour of four struck, the beautiful ship glided amidst a round of cheers into what thenceforward was to be her proper element; her career in the future in that respect like the career of the new-born infant—uncertain, beset by risks.

Very different in character was another "function" at which I "assisted"; namely, a lecture with demonstrations on phrenology, the "correctness" of that "science" being illustrated by the lecturer by references to the characteristics of the Hindoo in respect to mildness, gentleness, and tractability. To those of us recently returned from scenes already described, his remarks and demonstrations seemed outcomes of misapplied knowledge. Yet, such as they were, they "went down" with the enlightened British public, as represented by that particular audience.

Various circumstances, domestic and foreign, combined to render regimental life one of uncertainty, at the particular time now referred to. In India more than one column of our forces were actively engaged against the rebels who declined the terms of the gracious Proclamation already mentioned. The recently enlisted men for so-called "European" regiments of the late East India Company had combined in what was called "The White Mutiny"; they were shipped to England, there to be discharged the service.[1] Dis-

[1] Of their number a few enlisted into the 10th, and soon attempted to disseminate their particular doctrines. But Barrack-room Courts-Martial and sharp punishments

affection had appeared in two native cavalry regiments stationed at Hyderabad.[1] With regard to Europe, the condition of affairs in and relating to Italy was disturbed and uncertain. In France, the effusions of certain Colonels, added to other indications hostile to England, seemed to have an unpleasant significance, more especially that in which an appeal was made to the Emperor "to give the word, and the infamous haunt in which machinations so infernal are planned"—namely, London—"should be destroyed for ever."

A strong fleet of combined English and French warships proceeded to China. Extensive stores and supplies of all kinds were shipped for that destination, magazines were replenished; appearances indicated that important operations were in the near future. Uncertainty and speculation regarding probable events pervaded all ranks pertaining to regiments now available for emergent service; all held themselves prepared accordingly.

Various Militia regiments, embodied during the Crimean War, still occupied barracks throughout England; at Devonport and Plymouth the Warwickshire and Dublin Regiments, together with the Forfar Militia Artillery, being quartered. Second battalions were in progress of being added to the twenty-five first of the line. Now also, for the first time since the Revolutionary War, regiments of Volunteers were being rapidly formed. So important was the occasion considered to be that special invitations were issued to witness in the Town Hall the first parade of the Volunteers belonging to what were called "The Three Towns," and to inaugurate the formation of the regiment so constituted. The building was well filled by officials and others; great was the enthusiasm with which the ceremony passed off, the numbers of Volunteers in the ranks of the new regiment being ninety-three.

Some changes, having for their object the improved condition of the soldier, were now in course of introduction. Thus orders were issued on the subject of corporal punishment, the infliction of which was reduced to a minimum. In other respects the stringent methods heretofore considered necessary for the maintenance of discipline were so relaxed that old officers were wont to predict a number of evil consequences as sooner or later sure to follow.

With the introduction of the national system of education into regimental schools, the reading of the Holy Bible in them was looked upon as seriously menaced in the present and threatened with prohibition in the near future. According to orders issued on the subject,

—by means of belts—quickly convinced them that they were—so much matter in the wrong place.

[1] 5th and 6th Madras.

"the Bible is only to be read, and religious instruction of any kind given, during one hour per week, and then in the presence of the Roman Catholic priest." Many among us looked with dread and apprehension to the probable outcome of the changes so begun.

That in the large garrison of Plymouth and Devonport there existed no regular hospital for the wives and children of soldiers seemed to most of us a very anomalous circumstance. Correspondence on the subject between myself and the Divisional authorities was without practical result. Taking advantage of the popularity and influence of Miss Nightingale at the War Office, I addressed myself to that lady. In a marvellously short space of time orders were received to set on foot such an establishment; they were quickly carried out, very much to the benefit of the classes for whom it was intended.

On January 15, 1860, I received a letter from the Registrar of the Bath, directing me to hold myself in readiness to proceed to Windsor, there to receive the Insignia of that Order, to which I had some months previously been gazetted.[1] Two days thereafter—namely, on the 17th—a further letter ordering my attendance at Windsor Castle, at quarter before 3 p.m. precisely, on the 19th. On the 18th I proceeded, taking my dear wife with me, to that Royal burgh. The early part of the forenoon of the 19th was occupied in visiting some of the points of interest connected with the Castle, more especially the Round Tower and St. George's Chapel, the latter containing that most beautiful work of art, the cenotaph to the Princess Charlotte.

Punctually at the hour appointed, those of us who were to be similarly honoured drove to the Castle. We were shown into the Oak Room, and there, taking count of each other, discovered that our party numbered fourteen. Luncheon over, a messenger announced that Her Majesty was ready to begin the ceremony of investiture. The Lancaster Herald,[2] who had meantime very courteously initiated some of us in the formalities to be observed, then mustered us in our order. He led the way, we following, into the great corridor, at a door opening into which we were halted, to be called in our turn to the Royal presence. The first to enter was an officer upon whom the honour of knighthood was to be conferred. Each Companion was summoned in his order of seniority as such. The cross with which we were severally to be invested was by the Lancashire Herald carried upon a cushion of crimson velvet. The door being opened, we separately entered a small apartment, at the further end of which stood

[1] *London Gazette*, May 14, 1859.

[2] Mr. (afterwards Sir Albert) Woods.

the Queen; at her right side the Prince Consort. Our names announced, we advanced, making obeisance as we did so, knelt upon the right knee; the cross was attached over to the left breast by Her Majesty; we kissed hands, retired backwards, profoundly bowing the while. Thus we emerged, and the ceremony was over.[1]

Preparations on a large scale for the expedition to China were in rapid progess, the military forces to be sent thither comprising regiments direct from England, others, British and native, from India. Public attention and a good deal of adverse criticism were directed to what was looked upon as excessive naval and military estimates in a so-called time of profound peace. At important military and naval stations, fortifications were much extended, and newly armed with Armstrong guns; for, although there was much of what was ludicrous in the "boastings of the French Colonels," the fact was apparent that their expressions were not altogether unnoticed by our authorities.

Excursions in various directions were taken; some with the object of seeing places of historical interest, some to take note of the early spring flora, others to examine geological features of the neighbouring country. One such visit was to copper mines near Liskeard, there to see for the first time the beautiful "peacock" ore brought from the depths of earth and displayed to our gaze by means of a hammer wielded by the sturdy arms of "Captain Jane,"—for the superintendent of the mine was a woman so named.

At a little distance from the Canadian and Phœnix mines rises the Cheesewring, a granite hill some 1,200 feet in height, the rocks on its summit so piled upon each other as to thus give rise to its particular name. On some of those rocks were marks of boulder action, also tracings that bore distinct resemblance of vessels in ordinary use by Hindoos at their worship on the banks of the Hooghly, and now attributed to the Druids, one of whose places of sacrifice this *tor* may perhaps have been.

More and more did the state of uncertainty and unrest in which regimental officers had to perform their duties increase during the early months of the year, by the condition of affairs in Continental Europe. With regard to items of the general complication then noted, the following extract from my diary, written at the time, reads somewhat strangely to-day, namely: "France resolved upon the annexation of Savoy, notwithstanding the strongly expressed opposition of England against that measure; the threatened occupation of Tetuan by Spain,

[1] I was the first regimental surgeon invested by Her Majesty with the Cross of the Bath.

opposed by England, as being against the terms on which England remained neutral between that country and Morocco."

The first decade of wedded life completed,[1] the following reference to the occasion was written at the time: "Notwithstanding all that I have undergone since that event, sufficient of my early romance remains to enter in this place the motto which on that occasion surrounded the bon-bon broken by my bride and myself at our wedding luncheon—'My hopes are in the bud; bid them bloom.'" As the paragraph is being transcribed, the fifth decade is not far from completion. With affection chastened and sanctified by trial and affliction, I express to the Almighty humble gratitude that from bud my hopes have indeed advanced to bloom—holy and refined.

Towards the end of April, soldiers and officers of the 10th received their medals awarded for the campaign connected with the Indian Mutiny. No pomp and circumstance of military display took place on the occasion of their doing so. On the contrary, from the manner in which the distribution took place, all such accompaniments were intentionally avoided. It was while walking on the public thoroughfare in Devonport, that by accident, as it were, I met a sergeant in whose hand was a packet of little card-case boxes; one of these he presented to me—it contained my medal. I then continued on my way!

[1] March 14.

CHAPTER XIX

1860. *DEVONPORT. HONG-KONG*

Ordered to China—Embark—"Overland" route—Alexandria—Cairo—Desert—Suez—Red Sea—Aden—Galle—Across the Bay—Penang—Baron Gros and Lord Elgin—Hong-Kong.

ON April 26 I had the unlooked-for surprise to receive a demi-official letter from the Departmental Office, warning me for service in China on promotion. The note of the circumstance recorded in my diary at the time was this: "Bitter has been my disappointment on being superseded. In my turn I am now to supersede others; but the system is not the less cruel to those who suffer by it." The promotion so indicated implied that I was about to pass over an entire grade,[1] including its members, all of whom are my seniors in the service.

Short was the time allowed to make arrangements for my dear wife and children, from all of whom I took leave on May 2. On the following day I received further orders in London, and proceeded to Southampton; on 4th embarked on board the P. and O. steamer *Ripon*; by 2 p.m. we were on our voyage.

The "Overland" route was now before us, its attractions and incidents new to me. The bold coast scenery of Portugal, towns, forts, and convents succeeded each other at short intervals; Mondego Bay; Mafra, near to which the "lines" of Torres Vedras were begun, by England's great commander. Then the Spanish coast with its vineyards and olive groves, villages and hamlets; Tarifa, at the siege of which by the French, in 1811–12, the 87th Regiment gained distinction by repelling the assailants under General Laval,[2] the old Moorish walls of that town being clearly seen by us. Now came into view, on our right, Ceuta, far away behind which rose peaks of the Atlas range; the great rock and fortress of Gibraltar, between it and Africa the "gut" some twelve miles broad; then we are in the comparatively wide ex-

[1] Namely, that of Surgeon-Major.
[2] January 4, 1812.

panse of the "blue Mediterranean." Rising to a height of 11,000 feet, the Sierra Nevada, white with snow and magnificent in outline on our left, the chilly breezes from which now swept across our track. Next, passing close by the Cane rocks, where since the previous January a lighthouse was established; then the sight of the Gulf of Tunis carried historical associations back to Carthage and its wars. The island of Pantellaria, pretty to view from the distance, but as a penal settlement for Sicilian convicts, it is in all probability less agreeable as a place of residence. Then, on our right, Gozo, the cultivated terraces on which could be distinctly seen through our binoculars; otherwise the island looked treeless and bare, the most prominent objects upon it a succession of fortifications, for it is garrisoned by British troops. Yet, bare as it seems, Gozo is said to be a "garden" whence fruit and vegetables are chiefly supplied to Malta. Now we approach that island, the densely crowded town of Valetta comes in sight; we enter the harbour, ramparts and bastions on either side of us, the monotony of the town buildings interrupted by spires and pinnacles; every building dazzling white. As the anchor drops, we know that our stay is to be brief; a hasty run ashore, a visit to St. John's Cathedral, the Armoury, one or two other places of interest, then we resume our journey eastward.

Alexandria was our next point of interest. As in the early hours of morning we approached that historical port and city, the lighthouse, the numerous windmills along the shore line, were the distinctive objects first seen; as we entered the harbour, the Lazaretto, seraglio and palace of the Sultan were on our left. Ships of all nations, but the majority British, swing at anchor in our near proximity. A steamer conveyed us to the railway station, whence by train to Cairo, passing on our way an extensive line of ruins of the ancient aqueduct of Alexandria, destroyed by Diocletian, A.D. 296; the station of Meyrout, the name indicating Mæotis, the lake or reservoir so named being indicated by a succession of shallow pools, on some of which "sportsmen" were engaged in shooting water-birds of sorts; then the windings of the Mahmoodieh Canal to our left; fields of bearded wheat and barley ready for the sickle, while in some few places "thrashing floors" were extemporised, oxen unmuzzled engaged on them, as in the days of the patriarchs. Crossing the Nile at Kafr ez Zajyat, the first glimpse of that sacred stream was obtained; then the Pyramids of Ghizeh came in view, recalling to our minds many associations connected with their wonderful history; then early in the afternoon we were at Cairo.

El Kahira, "the Beautiful"! Under the guidance of a dragoman from the hotel where a brief stay was made, we started to explore the city.

Winding our way through narrow streets, named respectively the Turkish, French, and Greek Bazaars, opportunity was given to observe the manners and strange variety of persons and costumes in those places. Having visited various smaller mosques, we ascended to the Citadel, the work of Saladin, A.D. 1176, but interesting not so much in itself as for the famous mosque of alabaster contained within it, that edifice erected by Mahomed Ali, and now forming his tomb. The portion of the citadel wall whence, on the occasion of the massacre of the Mamelukes by order of that monarch in March, 1811, Emir Bey leaped his horse to a depth of 60 to 80 feet, then succeeded in effecting his escape, was carefully scanned. At a little distance from it we stood in the palace yard in which 700 doomed Beys, having been treacherously invited to a pretended marriage, were shot down from loopholes around, while in a window pointed out to us the Pasha sat looking on, and quietly enjoying his chebouk. From the walls we readily followed by the eye the Nile, winding and flowing smoothly on as in the days of the Pharaohs. Green with vegetation was the island of Rhodda, upon which, B.C. 1517, the infant Moses was found by Thermuthis, the king's daughter;[1] in the distance the plain of Bussateen, upon which tradition records that the Israelites encamped in the first day of their flight. Further away were the Pyramids of Sakarah and Dahshur. Beyond them the haze seemed to blend with the desert.

Next day the passengers *via* Marseilles arrived, and the whole party of us resumed our journey. It was not long until our train had entered the desert, extending far as the eye could reach; in some places varied by sandhills of different sizes, in others flat, but everywhere destitute of vegetation save a few stunted bushes. In the bright sunshine the mirage glittered deceptively, presenting the appearance of sea and islands, to vanish in their turn as we approached them. A few short halts at stations, and we detrain at Suez, to resume our journey by sea; we have completed the "overland" portion of it.

Suez, supposed to be the ancient Arsinoe, was interesting for the reason that in our approach thereto we had an opportunity of observing the line of retreat assigned by tradition to the Israelites in their flight from their oppressors. But now our movements were hurried; we were quickly on board the *Colombo*, ready waiting for us in the gulf, and so away we steamed towards the Red Sea.

Our progress was uneventful during the five days occupied in traversing that much-dreaded track. The temperature of air and sea rose to a higher point than we had yet experienced; the numerous islands,

[1] Exodus ii. 5, 6; see also Josephus.

the greater number destitute of lighthouses, were material proofs of dangers to navigation by night—a danger rendered the more significant as we steamed close past a rock on which a P. and O. vessel [1] had shortly before been wrecked. As we passed the position of Mocha, binoculars revealed to us the white houses, minarets, pillars, and balconies of that Arabian town.

The rock of Aden, bare, rugged and unattractive in appearance, rose before us; in due time we were at anchor in the bay. The usual rush ashore was not indulged in, because of the great heat prevailing, nor did we look with envy upon the few residents who took their afternoon drive along the strand, our own amusement consisting in throwing small coins into the sea, and seeing the great agility of young Arabs as they dived after and caught them.

In the early morning of June 4, our ship arrived in Galle harbour, the view as we entered rich and beautiful, the hills on either side and in front thickly covered with palms and under vegetation, but the heavy hot atmosphere causing a sense of great oppression. The south-west monsoon was at full strength, the sea beating in heavy breakers over some rocks at the harbour. As we entered we came close to the wreck of the *Malabar*; that vessel, while starting from her anchorage a few days previous, having on board the English and French Plenipotentiaries to China, was driven upon a rock, and wrecked by the heavy weather prevailing. Here we had to tranship to the *Pekin*, to continue by that vessel our voyage eastward. While so delayed, we indulged in the usual drives to places in the neighbourhood, everywhere through dense forests of palms, alternated with those of other tropical forms, the atmosphere hot, damp, and oppressive. The Cinnamon Gardens, so named from what was formerly a principal product of the island, were in a state of neglect and decay; the cinnamon industry a thing of the past, like that of the nutmeg, at one time prosperous while as yet Ceylon was Dutch property; nor was the cultivation of coffee a success by British planters, the shrub which yields that berry being attacked by insect and vegetable blights, the general result being ruin to nearly all interested in its cultivation.

The accident referred to led to the rescued passengers from the *Malabar* being sent on board the *Pekin*, and our ship was crowded to a degree that speedily became unpleasant. As we steamed across the Bay of Bengal in heavy monsoon weather, the ports had to be closed. Then it was that, in addition to the sweltering atmosphere "below," emanations from opium, that drug being the chief portion of the ship's cargo, affected

[1] The *Alma*.

us unpleasantly, first by the sense of taste, then by exerting to some extent its narcotising influence; it was therefore a most welcome relief to us, as we approached Sumatra, to get into clear weather, to have everything thrown open, and so enjoy the delightful change that had taken place in our condition.

Our next point was the high and thickly wooded island of Penang. Our ship having dropped anchor, several of our party started to "explore" that very lovely island. We drove along well-made roads, on either side bordered with bamboo hedges, through which flowering creepers stretched or hung in festoons. Bungalows, each in its well-kept garden, in which grew palms, tropical fruit trees, and flowers, were thickly dotted about; an extensive field of "pawn" pepper, then groves of nutmeg trees were passed, and we arrived at the object of our excursion, the cascade, 140 to 160 feet high. Here, for the first time, we indulged in that delicious fruit the mangosteen.

Arrived at Singapore,[1] the busy aspect of the town, with its population of 70,000, chiefly Chinese, impressed us. We noted with interest the numerous temples connected with the sects into which that population is divided. In the course of a ramble taken for purposes of discovery we were accosted by a Chinaman. He addressed us rudely; laughing and gesticulating as he spoke, he said, "Plenty English going to China; they will soon be all shot;" thus expressing his own views and probably also his desire in regard to the issue of the war. Among a great variety of articles publicly exposed for sale were two small pieces of ordnance; nor could the sale of such weapons be interfered with, as no Declaration of War had so far been made. While our ship, the *Pekin*, remained in harbour, some of our number paid their respects to His Excellency the Governor—namely, to Colonel Cavanagh—whose story at Maharajpore has already been recorded.

On various occasions during this part of our voyage, opportunity brought us in contact with the representatives of France and England, our fellow-passengers. Baron Gros was generally reserved in manner; Lord Elgin, on the contrary, frank and open. The latter expressed his views that an advance on Pekin had become a matter of necessity; in his negotiations with the Chinese, he meant to ask only for what is reasonable and just, and having done so to obtain it; but not to take advantage of one concession to base upon it a demand for another. He was of opinion that the season was too far advanced to permit of further proceedings than the capture of the Tientsin forts, as a base of operations for the ensuing spring; some of the islands in the Gulf of Pehchili being

[1] Lat. 1° N.

taken possession of to serve as sanatoria. He observed, with reference to the existence of the Taiping rebellion, that if on the one hand the influence of the Court at Pekin were to be seriously weakened, the schemes of the rebel party would be thereby assisted; while on the other hand severe chastisement was necessary as retribution for treacherous action against our ambassadors and their ships at Taku. Therefore, the difficulty to be overcome was to punish and yet not seriously injure the Imperial power. But events were to outrun the anticipations so expressed.

Hong-Kong was reached on Midsummer Day. As the town of Victoria came in sight, the general aspect presented by it produced a favourable impression upon us; the light and airy style of houses rising in tiers above each other upwards along the precipitous mountain face, that mountain culminating in a peak some 1,500 feet above sea level, presented a panorama different altogether in character from anything we had hitherto seen. The circumstance that the town and the roads where the shipping lay were completely sheltered from the south-west monsoon then prevailing furnished full explanation for the oppressive damp heat to which we were at once introduced.[1] It became my painful duty to announce myself to the officer, who, by the fact of my arrival, was superseded in his position, with whom in his disappointment and chagrin I much sympathised.[2] Indeed, so greatly did he feel what he looked upon as the disgrace into which he had departmentally fallen, that his subsequent career was unfortunate; nor did he ever return to England.

[1] In 1841 the island of Hong-Kong, considered by the Chinese as "only a barren rock," was ceded to the British. Within the short period of nineteen years, the surprising transformation above indicated took place.

[2] The date of my rank as Deputy Inspector-General, May 11, 1860.

CHAPTER XX

1860. *HONG-KONG. TIENTSIN*

Expeditionary force—An incident—The island—Different bodies of troops—Certain difficulties—Red tape—Canton—"Sing-song" boats—Honan—Beggars—The city shops—Temple of Five Hundred Worthies—Buddhist temple—News from the north—Pekin occupied—Hong-Kong to Shanghai—Taiping rebels—Treaty—The city—Vicinity—H.M.S. *Roebuck*—Taku—Tientsin.

THE expeditionary force had already sailed northward, its equipment and appliances on a scale of completeness unknown prior to the recent Royal Commission. Before that expedition started, all non-effectives, whether by sickness or other causes, were eliminated; what was called a Provisional Battalion was organized for their reception, as well as for that of newly arrived reinforcements from home to fill expected "waste" among those actively engaged. The ordinary barrack accommodation at Hong-Kong being insufficient, huts were erected at various points, among others on the peak called Victoria; a large vessel in harbour fitted up for hospital purposes, and vessels engaged, as necessity arose, for the transport of invalids to the Cape of Good Hope and England.

Among the non-effectives left by the —st Regiment was an officer now indicated by the initial M——. At his request I visited him, in company with his medical attendant. It was evident at a glance that he was extremely ill, his life rapidly ebbing away. He addressed me after this manner: "I have asked you to see me that you might tell me what you think of my state." To my inquiry, "Are you prepared to receive my answer?" he replied, in impatient tones: "If I were not, I would not have asked the question." "I am sorry, then, to believe that you have but a very short time to live," was my remark. "I thought as much. Do you see that packet on my chest of drawers? I want you to take it away with you; as soon as I am dead, to burn it unopened in your own room." Such was his request, and so far I acceded to it. The following morning M—— was dead; his packet burnt as he had desired. A sequel to this incident will be mentioned hereafter.

In the words of a newspaper correspondent,[1] the island of Hong-Kong may be compared to a beautiful woman with a notoriously bad temper,—to be admired from a distance, but not become intimately acquainted with. At the date of our arrival the midday heat, as gauged by our sensations, was great; the sky cloudless, exercise or duty out of doors very trying, a sensation of sickness experienced in a way altogether different from what was felt in India. Early in July the rainy season began. Quickly a series of waterfalls poured over rocky promontories; Victoria Peak was enveloped in mist; temperature moderated, the general conditions became bearable. So they continued till September; intervals of rain and sunshine alternated with each other. Unhappily endemic forms of disease went on steadily increasing in prevalence and rates of mortality. A favourable change took place in all these conditions as the last-named month advanced, and progressed till the cold season fairly set in.

The portion of the force with which I was immediately concerned included British and native Indian troops, the latter belonging to the three several presidencies of that Dependency. Each of these bodies had its own code of Regulations, in accordance with which routine duties were conducted, while all of them seemed unwilling to accept those of the Imperial service, under which alone administration of the expeditionary force had of necessity to be conducted.

Another difficulty in which I was personally affected seemed to arise from the circumstance that some of the instructions under which my duties in relation to shipping had to be conducted were special, while those under which the naval authority on the spot conducted his department were general. Unhappily a good deal of friction was the outcome of this state of things, all of which might have been possibly avoided had mutual explanation been given in respect to the particular orders under which we were severally acting. It seems to me, also, while I refer to what was very unpleasant at the time of its occurrence, that in many circumstances connected with public duties where misunderstandings arise, they would be most readily prevented by means of elucidation of the points of view from which divergent action is taken, or the interpretation of orders from which it is adopted.

As an example of the system of "red tape" under which duties of very ordinary description had to be carried on, the following may be mentioned:—A water-pipe connected with the military hospital went wrong; the supply through it had to be cut off, to the very great inconvenience of the sick. I at once reported the circumstance to the

[1] Wingrove Cook.

Officer in command of the garrison, such being the routine directed by Regulations, requesting at the same time that immediate steps should be taken to make the required repairs. My letter was by the Commanding Officer transmitted to the Engineer Officer, who forwarded it to the Clerk of the Works, who came and inspected the defect in the pipe, then wrote a report about it to the Engineer Officer, who sent the report to the Commanding Officer, who sent to the Town Major, who sent it to me. Meanwhile, the hot season being at its height, and nothing actually done to remedy the defect complained of, I was constrained to again start the correspondence by observing that what was urgently required was, not reports, but that the damaged pipe should be repaired. Doubtless my letter to that effect had, like its predecessor, to be transmitted through the series of "channels" so enumerated. I quite forget at this distance of time whether the pipe was ever repaired or not.

The circumstance that a portion of our force occupied quarters at Canton led me to visit that important city. The steamer by which the trip thither along the Pearl River was performed bore the romantic name *The White Cloud.* We passed the Bocca Tigris or Bogue forts,[1] continued our journey through a district thickly interspersed with villages and hamlets, but destitute of pasture land, though otherwise richly cultivated, the rice fields profusely irrigated. Whampoa was mean-looking, the greater number of its houses erected on piles so as to overhang the river; the stream crowded with ships and vessels of sorts belonging to various nations. The foreign population lived in "chops" or hulks of Chinese junks; others were utilised as offices and merchants' stores. Docks were being established, and other improvements effected which, in later years, have made that place the actual port of the southern capital.

Arrived at Canton, landing was effected by means of one of the thousands of sampans or passenger boats that lay along either bank and crowded the river,—these boats "manned" by women, who kept up a chorus of laughing and talking, their cheery and, for the most part, well-looking faces indicating that cares, as understood in the West, pressed upon them but lightly, if at all. "Sing-song," or Flower-boats,[2] gorgeously painted and otherwise ornamented, lay in tiers, and towered high above the humble sampan. The particular race of natives by whom, through many generations, they have been occupied, are looked upon as descendants of the *kin* who held Northern China, A.D. 1100,

[1] Captured by the British, February 25, 1842.

[2] In the early part of 1894 hundreds of these boats were destroyed by fire.

supplemented by those of traitors who aided the Japanese in their descent upon Cheh-kiang, A.D. 1555–1563. Having landed, the "carriage" by which our further trip was taken consisted of "chairs" made of bamboo work, carried on the shoulders of three brawny Chinamen, namely, two in front and one behind, their strong muscles thrown in bold relief on their uncovered chests and limbs as they carried us at rapid pace along. Such were the conditions in 1860.

The island of Honan was occupied by various important *hongs*, or places of business belonging to native Chinese merchants. One of them, the property of Houqua, whose name at that time was familiar in England, was devoted to the cleaning and preparation of teas for the market. The large and well-aired hall within was occupied by a series of tables placed at convenient distances from each other. At each sat a man or woman—for the sexes worked together—who from a basket at hand picked the coarser fragments, and so left the finer description of the tea to be dealt with again. In another hall stood a couple of fanners;[1] through them the tea was passed, the finer portions being separated in the process from the coarser. This apartment was ornamented with flowers and shrubs in pots; a delicious flavour of "the fragrant leaf" pervaded the air. All around was scrupulously clean and tidy, the *employés* neat in person, well-clothed, apparently well fed, and, to judge by their smiles and good humour, very happy.

Everywhere in the streets blind beggars abounded, each armed with two flat discs of bamboo; the sound produced by constantly beating them against each other became decidedly unpleasant by their very numbers, rendering conversation impossible. Whether a great part of their blindness was due to disease or to artificial means, we had no means of ascertaining.

The Tartar suburb or quarter of Canton comprised narrow streets paved with flag stones, intersected by narrow canals, spanned at intervals by bridges after the style of the "willow pattern plate"; the houses of no more than one storey high, for the reason that in China it is considered pretentious for a man to raise himself above his fellows. The odours that everywhere prevailed exceeded, in variety and intensity, all that had heretofore been experienced. The people, old and young, male and female, poor in circumstances as many of them appeared to be, looked physically hale, strong, and healthy. Traversing the breadth of the city, we arrived at "The Heights," on the slope of which stood the Yamen of the notorious Yeh; near thereto, "The Five-Storied Pagoda," now occupied by French troops, and above it waved the Tricolour; while in a series of bell tents were the men of the 87th

[1] *Phoong quei*, or wind-box.

Royal Irish Fusiliers—the conjunction not altogether a happy one, seeing that the 87th wear on their shakos a French eagle, in commemoration of that captured by them at Barossa. Various temples and other public buildings were visited in the course of our interesting excursion; one of the latter a native prison, ricketty, tottering, and foul, its unhappy inmates lying upon the damp floor, chained, or with *cangs* on their necks, their existence dependent upon food supplied from without, their naked bodies besmeared with filth and presenting many ulcers. Many of them were not accused of crimes committed by themselves, but were undergoing punishment for the reason that their relatives had joined the ranks of the Taiping rebels. We intentionally refrained from a visit to "the Potter's field," or execution ground, immediately adjacent to the prison.

Everywhere along the streets were signs of activity and industry; shops containing all sorts of clothing materials, strangely ornamented umbrellas and lanterns; others devoted to old curiosities, jewelry, or watch-making, a good many to lacquer ware; nor could we withhold admiration of the elegant patterns and workmanship of such articles as cabinets, tables, screens, fans, etc., exposed for sale. But here, as in countries more advanced in certain phases of civilization, signs of superstition are apparent. Above the door of such establishments a horse's hoof is nailed, and so Satanic influences guarded against. In the enlightened West, a horse's shoe fulfils the same purpose.

The Temple of the Five Hundred Gods or worthies, then deemed one of the most characteristic sights of Canton, well repaid our visit to it. Among objects within that edifice is a miniature pagoda of eight stages, the whole consisting of beautifully cut marble, its total height twenty-five feet. The figures of the gods or heroes are all life-size. They represent various nationalities, one of their number in feature and dress like an Englishman. According to legend, the person so commemorated was a sailor, cast ashore wrecked on the coast of China. His life being spared, he ultimately rose to high position, and finally was, in effigy, honoured with a place in this Walhalla.

Another portion of the building was devoted to the purposes of a Buddhist temple, in which, at the time of our visit, "service" was being performed, or "celebrated." The scene within comprised an altar, plain, without idols or other decoration; situated in an open space, bare-headed and shaven priests, some wearing robes of blue, others of grey cloth, all with a yellow-coloured surplice thrown over the left shoulder and brought loosely under the right arm. As they knelt at various distances from the altar, in seeming accordance with their rank, their hands in attitude of supplication, they joined in chanting what, in its intonation, resembled the Litany of our Western Churches; at intervals a small bell being gently struck, as in the Roman Catholic service. A congregation of men was present, but manifestly destitute of reverence or devotion. A few days were thus pleasantly spent; I then returned to duty at Hong-Kong. At the time referred to, that island was noted for the hospitality of residents, and the scale of magnificence upon which it was carried on. It was my good fortune to enjoy much of it, and of friendliness in other ways; among others, from representatives of the great houses of Jardine, Dent, and others, and from Mr. Campbell, then of the Oriental Bank.

Towards the end of August, a French Express boat brought intelligence that the English and French combined forces had landed at Pehtang; that, while advancing thence to Taku, our cavalry had been charged by the Tartar horse, with results disastrous to the latter. A few days more, news reached us that a somewhat sharp action had taken place, with somewhat severe loss to the allies, but leaving in their hands Taku and neighbouring forts; that the whole disposable force was in rapid motion towards Tientsin, in view to carrying out the intention of Lord Elgin to push on to the capital. A short interval passed, when attempts at negotiation at Tientsin having failed, the army continued its onward march. At Tungchow, a very sad occurrence befell it. By treachery, a body of Chinese, headed by the Prince Tsai, captured several officials, officers, and others; namely, Mr. Parkes, Mr. Bowlby (of the *Times*), Mr. Loch, Mr. De Normann, Lieutenant Anderson, Captain Brabazon, and several troopers belonging to Fane's Horse. The Chinese army, under San ko Lin Sin, was, however, completely beaten; the road to Pekin left clear. Lord Elgin at once sent a communication to the Emperor, that, in the event of a hair of the head of one of the prisoners being touched, the combined forces would burn the Imperial palace to the ground.

A few days more, and on October 13 the allied army was in possession of the Chinese quarter of Pekin; the palace outside and north of the city given up to loot; the Emperor fled; the Summer Palace in ruins; the Chinese army vanished! Unhappily, news at the same time reached us that, although Mr. Parkes and Mr. Loch had been given up by the Chinese, they had been subject to various indignities before being so; but that others of the prisoners had succumbed under the barbarities to which they were subjected, among them Mr. Bowlby.[1]

[1] In 1841, a brother of Mr. Bowlby was appointed to the Army Medical Department, and ordered to the West Indies. From the first, he expressed a foreboding of death by yellow fever, an event which happened shortly after his arrival there. Nor s his a singular instance of the same kind; several have been met with in India.

Early in November, information reached us that a treaty of peace had been signed in the Imperial capital by Prince Kung and Lord Elgin. In accordance with its conditions, in addition to a war indemnity to be paid by the Chinese, a special sum was to be given for the families of the captives who had been killed or died in captivity. Thus, the object of the expedition had been obtained more speedily than Lord Elgin expected. The forces began their return march from Pekin towards Taku, there to embark, a brigade being detailed to occupy Tientsin until the indemnity should be paid.

In obedience to orders to join "the Army of Occupation"[1] at Tientsin, as the brigade left at that place was now officially called, I left Hong-Kong by the steamer *Formosa*, on November 28. Next day, we passed the mouth of the river Han, on the western bank of which stands Shah-tew, or, as pronounced in English, Swatow; the day following, traversed the channel that separates the island of Formosa from the city of Amoy on the mainland. Already the temperature was pleasantly cool, sky clear, wind and sea rather high, the effect of these conditions bracing and exhilarating, as compared with that produced by the trying and unpleasant climate we had left behind us. The general aspect of the coast wherever visible, as we advanced on our voyage, was bare and inhospitable. In our course, islands were numerous, the majority apparently uninhabited even by birds, and otherwise uninviting to look upon. As we approached the Yangtse, vegetation covered more and more thickly the islands passed by us; sea-birds were increasingly numerous, the water thick with mud. We arrived at Shanghai on December 3.

In the latter days of August, Shanghai had been seriously attacked by the Taiping rebels. On both occasions, the Imperialists fled before the enemy; but a foreign contingent of British, Indian, and French troops, with a body of volunteers composed of the foreign residents, repulsed the rebels, on whom they inflicted severe loss. During the attacks in question, several buildings had been destroyed or seriously damaged, the ruins being prominent objects in our view. So also were the remains of barricades and other extemporised defences. On the day of our arrival, the Indian Navy vessel, the *Feroze*, having on board Lord Elgin and suite, steamed up the Woosung River and anchored alongside us. The following day the *Grenada* arrived, with Sir Hope Grant, his staff, and various senior officers of the expedition, whose allotted task was completed in that the object of the expedition had been attained. But a new phase was about to be assumed by public

[1] In the official position of P.M.O.

affairs; arrangements had to be made for events, the shadow, as well as substance, of which affected the immediate vicinity of Shanghai, and extended over a great part of China. Whereas, diplomatic and military action had been directed heretofore against the Imperial power, both were now to be devoted to the support of that power, and against insurrectionary movements,[1] the real object of which was the overthrow of the ruling dynasty. Various bands of marauders, taking advantage of existing disturbances, were devastating the neighbourhood. Piratical bands, in which were enrolled escaped sailors and vagabonds of sorts, were giving so much trouble on the Yangtse, that it was necessary at once to dispatch a small river force for their suppression.

Copies of the Treaty[2] signed at Pekin on October 24 were immediately affixed to the walls throughout the native city of Shanghai. Crowds of Chinese assembled at various places to read the unwonted documents, printed as they were in their own language. An English version was at the same time published, for the benefit of foreigners, the nine articles comprised in it being to the effect that—(1) The Emperor expresses his deep regret for the affair at Taku; (2) Her Majesty's representative shall reside permanently, or occasionally, as she may wish, at Pekin; (3) Eight millions of taels (£2,000,000) to be paid in instalments (as indemnity); (4) Tientsin to be opened for trade; (5) Emigration of Chinese to British colonies to be permitted; (6) Kowloon to be ceded; (7) The Treaty of 1858 shall come at once into operation; (8) That Treaty shall be published in Pekin and in the provinces; (9) On the Convention being signed, Chusan to be restored to Chinese (from occupation by the British), the British forces to commence their march from Pekin to Tientsin; that, if necessary, Taku, the north coast of Shantung, and Canton shall be occupied until the indemnity is paid. The morning after that Proclamation had been affixed to the walls, it was found in tatters and defaced!

A visit to the native city and its immediate surroundings introduced us to scenes characteristic of Chinese habits and of the particular circumstances of the time. Within the city and fosse a succession of narrow dirty streets, low-built houses, canals spanned by "willow pattern" bridges, cook shops, vegetable stalls, fur and "curio" shops. Adjoining one such street, a wretched shed, the damp earthen floor partly covered with straw, partly with refuse of very filthy kind. On

[1] Chiefly the Taipings.

[2] That is, the Treaty of Tientsin, dated 1858, was ratified, and, together with a Convention of Peace, signed by Lord Elgin and Prince Kung.

the floor three human dead bodies, emaciated from starvation; a woman almost devoid of clothing, wasted to an extreme degree, wailing piteously over one of the three; another, still alive, but to all appearance in the last extreme from long-continued want of food. This we were informed is *the* place to which the miserably poor, and those who give up the battle of life, resort to die. Among the establishments visited were numerous fur shops, an extensive store of china or porcelain ware, a factory in which is woven the beautiful gold embroidery for which Shanghai is famous,—the embroidery being for the most part on blue cloth, its own most characteristic pattern the Imperial dragon, distinguished by having five toes, whereas the more plebeian emblems of the same survival of the pterodactyl has but four. What had been until recently ornamental "Tea" gardens were now occupied by French troops; once highly ornamented buildings within such enclosures converted into barracks for our allies. Uprooted shrubs and valuable plants lay about decayed and withered; rockwork, including fanciful-shaped miniature bridges, cast like so much rubbish into what had been artificial lakes and streams peopled by fish and water-plants. The glory of the place was indeed gone—desecrated, as the Chinese could not inappropriately say, by Western "barbarians."

To a distance of several miles inland from the city the aspect of the country is more or less that of a continuous burial ground, interspersed with coffins left as they were placed, upon rather than under the surface of the ground, many of them broken and so exposing to view their ghastly contents. Here and there patches of ground were devoted to the cultivation of vegetables, in the midst of graves and coffins; while continuing our walk we met isolated coolies carrying at each end of an elastic piece of bamboo, supported on the shoulder at its middle, a jar containing the bones of their "ancestors," being so borne away, doubtless, to be reverently disposed of elsewhere. Everywhere the district was intersected by canals and water-courses, raised and narrow pathways across the intervening fields; we seemed to be wandering in the "city of the silent." Alongside the several canals and pathways were avenues of trees and ornamental shrubs.[1] The presence of the magpie, jackdaw, wagtail, and sandpiper carried our associations away to the "insignificant island in the Western sea." Game birds were abundant, as we had an opportunity of witnessing in the city market; but since that date we learn that villas, gardens, and ornamental grounds have grown up, and so completely transformed the

[1] Chiefly privet (*Ligusticum*) and lycium. Among the representatives of British plants were the dock, dandelion, and ivy-leaved veronica.

landscape as seen by us. Almost at every turn we met French soldiers off duty, or in considerable bodies marching from Woosung, at which place reinforcements were being landed from transports; in fact, there was little in the aspect of Shanghai to indicate that it was an English settlement. These and some other excursions were taken in company of Mr. Lamond, to whom I was much indebted for hospitality.

H.M.S. *Roebuck*, by which I was ordered to proceed northward, left Shanghai on December 11. Three days afterwards we were off the promontory of Shantung; the weather propitious, sky clear, breeze moderate, temperature on deck 48° F. to 44° F., sea smooth. But a rapid change took place. During the night of the 14th, darkness became so intense that Captain Martin, deeming it unsafe to proceed in a region little known and imperfectly surveyed, determined to cast anchor. By midnight we were in a heavy wind storm; it having cleared off by daylight, the ship resumed progress and was speedily among the Meatao Islands; a few hours more and we were in Hope Sound, otherwise a sheltered position in the concavity of the larger island of that group, called Chang Shang, where we found the British fleet collected, that of the French being off Chefoo, not far from our own. The *Roebuck* was ordered to await dispatches. While so doing, a number of rough-looking natives, brown in hue, Tartar in feature, their clothing partly consisting of wadded cotton, but in addition abundance of furs, came alongside in their boats, bringing with them rolls of bread, vegetables and fruits, similar to those we are accustomed to see at home. The presence of numbers of the common gull, the colder weather, the rougher sea, combined still further to recall the shores of England.

Arrived off Taku,[1] so thick was the haze and mist by which that place and the sea to some distance from it were concealed, that for several hours neither the forts nor coast were visible, nor was it till the following day that we were able to land. The little gunboat the *Clown* having taken us on board, we were quickly in sight of the forts, some of them very formidable in appearance; in the shallow discoloured water stakes still stood in lines where they had opposed the approach of Admiral Hope's gunboats, and we were able to estimate the further difficulties on that occasion presented by the long stretch of mud which at low tide separated us from the forts. As evening was closing in, we entered the mouth of the Peiho; in due time were within the southern fort, above which floated the Union Jack, the northern being similarly distinguished by the Tricolour. The great extent of its mud ramparts

[1] On December 16.

was seen as we passed the inner gateway; huts in rows that had been occupied by its defenders were now used as barracks by officers and men of the detachment temporarily stationed here, or by military stores. In all directions old gun carriages, broken wheels, furniture, and *débris* of sorts lay about in a state of confusion. I was under the very unpleasant necessity of *begging* a night's accommodation from an officer, a charity which he kindly accorded me.

Mounted on a borrowed horse, without guard or guide, I started next day *en route* to my destination, the distance to be travelled not less than thirty miles. A midday halt to rest my steed; a solitary ride along an ill-made road, through a flat, uninteresting tract of country, and final arrival without misadventure at Tientsin, completed the day's proceedings. Already the cold had become severe; the wind, strong from east, swept over the plain; patches of water and canals were covered by ice; thus the journey has left on memory not a very agreeable impression. On arrival, however, I was kindly received by a brother officer.[1]

[1] Dr. Galbraith.

CHAPTER XXI

1860-1861 *TIENTSIN*

Arrangements for troops—The city—Absence of Tartar soldiers—Rides—Dogs and birds—Agriculture—Grain-stores—Winter—Great cold—Moderating—Spring—Temples—Chinese "sport"—New Year's Day—Public baths—Ice-house—Foundling hospital—Story of Roman Catholic bishop—Hospital for Chinese—The "golden lily"—Gratitude—Wounded Tartars—Chinese Christian—Tortured Sikhs—French hospitals—Death of General Collineau—Sickness among the troops.

ARRANGEMENTS rapidly advanced in regard to accommodation, food supplies, and medical care of the troops. *Yamens—i.e.*, residences of wealthy inhabitants—were hired for temporary conversion into barracks. Markets and shops presented ample supplies of food, clothing, and articles of convenience, their owners showing much eagerness to do business with us. A tendency to pilfer, and other petty crimes, manifested itself on the part of some Asiatic followers and others, but was quickly suppressed by the Provost Marshal and his staff, after which discipline and order reigned among all classes pertaining to our force. Our French allies occupied quarters provided for them in the part of the city on the left side of the Peiho, the British and Indian being on the right of that river.

The city was of great commercial importance, its population some 800,000; streets narrow and filthy, houses low and dilapidated; in extent stretching away to and embracing the point of junction between the Imperial Canal and Peiho, thus covering a space of at least four miles by three. Merchandise from Corea and the south of China arrived abundantly as at a general depôt. Around the city proper a high wall extends, the crowded portion outside being called "suburbs," but in no other respect different from the intra-mural city. In the Peiho was a Russian gunboat; in the city a small colony of Russian merchants, peacefully carrying on their business, and apparently on the most friendly terms with the people. A few Tartar traders, some leading their strong shaggy ponies, others Bactrian camels, all laden with merchandise, were met with. As we pursued our way through the mazes of the city, the people simply ignored our presence, taking not the slightest notice of us, although by the caricatures of Europeans we frequently came across in shops and elsewhere it was evident that we were by no means welcome guests. In an open space a modeller was occupied in making, with great ease and rapidity, a series of figures in clay, representing, though with droll exaggeration, the Sikh and British soldiers. Women were conspicuous by their absence; virtue in the sex was honoured and commemorated by memorial arches at certain points throughout the city. Everywhere in the crowded, narrow, and extremely dirty streets, foot-passengers jostled each other; the diseased, of whom many suffering from loathsome affections, coming in contact with those better-to-do, and to all appearance healthy. At intervals a puppet show, the prototype of Punch and Judy, or more pretentious "show" attracted crowds; itinerant "doctors," their carts decorated with exaggerated illustrations of diseases and accidents, remedies for which were vociferously lauded and offered for sale. On either side pawnshops and restaurants; at the doors of the latter customers gambling whether they should pay double or quits for refreshments or foods served to them.

In vain we looked for representatives of Tartar troops, who were said to form the ordinary garrison force of Tientsin. We learned that, for the period of occupation by the foreigners, steps had been taken "to keep them out of sight."

A series of rides into the country in the vicinity of the city presented a great variety of interesting objects and incidents. On the left bank of the Peiho, a short distance down the course of that river, numerous large stacks of table salt attracted attention, as similar stacks on the same spot did that of Lord Macartney's mission nearly seventy years before. The arrival of the first trading ship under the recent treaty was an event not without interest; it was a small schooner, the property of a very eminent firm[1] at Hong-Kong, and as it immediately became ice-bound, it was to be a familiar object to us throughout the succeeding winter. Although so recently at war with the Chinese, we from the first walked or rode into the country without molestation, receiving invitations by signs to enter houses and huts that lay in our way; tea and cakes of various kinds being invariably pressed upon us on such occasions. In certain directions it seemed as if there was one continuous burial ground; coffins in all stages of decay strewed the surface; at intervals bodies of children sewn up in mats were seen, while

[1] Messrs. Dent.

on one occasion we saw the revolting spectacle of a dog in the act of carrying away the dead body of an infant.

In every village there were great numbers of dogs, fierce towards us foreigners; some by no means unlike "collies," others terriers, of which a very handsome variety obtains its special title from Shantung, to which district it more especially pertains. There were also the mandarin or "sleeve dogs," so named from the fact that as pets the smaller varieties are carried in the wide sleeves of the outer garments worn by the wealthy classes. There was the Canton or "chow-chow" dog, a large animal with a very thick coating of hair, the tail curling from its root; the head triangular, broad at the base, rapidly tapering to the muzzle; the eyes far forward, as if looking upward, something like those of the lemur. Pet birds were kept by many people, songsters being the greatest favourites. Of those observed were a large species of skylark, canaries, thrushes, linnets, a species here called the wamee, like the Shamah [1] of India.

It became an object of interest to note the progress of agriculture, and the phenomena of nature generally, from the first opening of mild weather, onwards till autumn. On the 1st of March wheat sowing began, the fields having been prepared during the previous few days for that operation; five days thereafter—namely, on the 6th—the first indication was evident that buds were about to open, a species of poplar being the tree to take the lead in this respect. The operation of ploughing the fields then began; the implement used was of light construction, drawn by one man, while another guided it. Fields then began to be cleaned, manure to be spread, seed of various kinds for grain and vegetables sown, preparations for irrigation carried out; and as the surface ground thawed, and so became the more easily dealt with, ploughs of heavier kinds were used, mules, bullocks, and men promiscuously used and yoked together in draught. In other places women and girls were employed in field work. By the 15th signs of verdure began to show themselves near the irrigation canals, partly in the first leaf of autumn-sown wheat, partly of some culinary vegetable. On the 20th, wheat sown on the 1st had "shot," and was in tolerable leaf; after this its progress was rapid, for by the 9th of June the fact was noted that "some fields of wheat were turning yellow the crop nearly ready to be cut"; pease, full in the pod.

At the distance of about four miles from Tientsin, on the left bank of the Peiho, we came upon a series of buildings, the purpose of which the storage of grain against famine. Sixteen such buildings, arranged

[1] *Copsychus saularis.*

in two rows of eight, constitute the group devoted to that purpose; each building some 300 feet in length, 45 to 50 in breadth, its walls 30 in height, the whole raised on a plinth from the ground. By Imperial edict cultivators are obliged to deposit in these and kindred stores elsewhere a certain proportion of grain every year: an arrangement which has come down from ancient times, and on that account is now mentioned.

Very rapid was the increase of winter cold to its point of culmination. Situated in the latitude of Lisbon, the temperature of 5·5° F. during the night preceding the shortest day was to us a new and unlooked-for experience, yet next day active outdoor exercise was indulged in; the sensations soon ceased to indicate the actual degree of cold prevailing. Already the Peiho was closed in by ice, boats had given place to sledges, and they, pushed on by means of poles, were used in great numbers for transport of merchandise. A detachment of troops had just arrived by *White Star* at Taku. The officer in command landed with his men, his intention being to make arrangements for their march from that place, and then return to the ship for his wife. But meanwhile ice had formed so rapidly on the shallow bay that communication between the vessel and shore was impossible, the result that the *White Star* had to return to Hong-Kong, nor did the officer[1] alluded to see his wife or kit until next spring had well advanced. According to the Royal Chinese Almanack, published at Pekin, the winter season is divided into nine periods of nine days each. The first begins on December 20, the third on January 8, it ends on 17th of that month, and is considered to be that of the greatest cold; the last of the series is considered to end on March 2.

Communication with ships in the northern part of the Gulf of Pe chili being cut off, letters had to be dispatched by land to Chefoo, two hundred miles to the southward, there to be put on board. Now a cold north wind set in; the temperature in our rooms sank at night to 3° F. As we awoke in the morning small icicles clung to moustaches, and during the day the sensation of cold became unpleasant. In the provision shops, fish and game frozen; some of the latter, especially deer, in artistic or picturesque attitudes, were exposed for sale. Men were engaged in cutting blocks of ice from that which covered the river, to be kept in pits and ice-houses for use during the heat of next summer. Through the openings so made small nets were let down for the capture of fish that happened to resort to those air-holes. Within our quarters water for cooking purposes and for the morning bath had to be obtained by breaking blocks of ice and placing the fragments to

[1] Colonel Muter.

be liquefied in a vessel on the fire. Out of doors the unusual sight might be witnessed of soldiers carrying in sacks on their backs the blocks of ice into which the daily allowance of beer or porter had been congealed. As winter advanced sensation of cold naturally enough increased; northerly winds came over the long tract of flat country, several degrees in extent, that lay between us and Mongolia. Now it was that in our quarters we utilised the Chinese heated platform as a bed, to which is given the name of *kang*, not only for sleeping thereon, but for sitting or reclining during the day. Fireplaces according to advanced Western principles had been constructed, under the superintendence of the Royal Engineers; in them was burnt a liberal allowance of fuel, consisting of Manchurian coal and Pe chili mud in about equal proportions; but, as expressed by our Chinese servants, the arrangement was more calculated to carry the warmth clean away up the chimney than to diffuse it in our apartments.

On February 19 there were signs that the intensity of winter was about to cease; the mid-day sunshine had in it some genial warmth; intensely cold winds that had for some time prevailed now did so no longer; the haze in which city and district had been concealed was to some extent gone, and yet the reading of the thermometer was a minimum at night of 8° F., at nine a.m. 19·8° F. Snow that had shortly before fallen began to melt as day advanced, and the thick coating of ice on the Peiho became wet and sloppy. The few succeeding days, increasingly mild and genial, well illustrated the regularity and rapidity with which seasonal changes here take place. On March 3 winter was considered to be ended, spring to have began according to the Chinese estimate already mentioned, though at night the thermometer indicated 30° F., and at nine a.m. 33° F., snow meanwhile falling gently.

On 5th of that month a state of great electric tension in air was indicated by our registers. As in India, that condition heralded change in weather, its seasonal recurrence so regular that it is reckoned on to a day. The crews of a Russian gunboat and of an English schooner, frozen up through the winter, at once began the work of preparation for sea. On the 11th the ice suddenly broke up; in massive blocks grating against and rolling over each other, it floated along the stream. Next day, bridges of boats were re-established, ordinary traffic by boat resumed; within a few hours all traces of ice had disappeared. On the 14th the gunboat *Drake* arrived from Taku, bringing for us thirteen weeks' letters from home, none having been received while cut off from the world as we had been for so long. Orders were at the same time received directing Mr. Bruce to proceed to Pekin, and our force to remain at Tientsin, pending the manner of reception given to His Excellency at the Imperial capital. By April 6 the temperature rendered the exercise of walking unpleasant. By the middle of June, in the absence of tatties and other Indian appliances, resource was had to large blocks of ice supported over a tub in our apartments; close to and half embracing these we sat, in the airiest of costume, in our endeavours to keep ourselves cool under the circumstances.

Everywhere in and around the city, steps were taken to maintain due observance of respect towards buildings dedicated to purposes of "religion" or philosophy. In the early days of occupation, some of the Asiatics with us treated a few of those buildings in a manner that they would have violently resented if directed against their own in India; but the employment of stringent measures put an end to such demonstrations. In one of those temples, namely that dedicated to "Oceanic Influences," at a short distance beyond the city walls, the Treaty of Tientsin of 1859 was signed, the ratification of that deed being the actual cause of the present war.

Invited to a Chinese hunting and hawking party, the "meet" to take place at a distance of a few miles from the city, we proceeded to the appointed rendezvous under guidance of men sent for the purpose by our hosts. In early morning of a bitterly cold day in January we started, our steeds, shaggy, unkempt-looking Tartar ponies. Arrived at the appointed ground, several falconers, all on foot, each bearing on his wrist a peregrine, hooded, awaited us; the hounds of the kind known in India as the rampore, all under charge of a mounted whipper-in. All around us a dead flat plain extended, to all appearance interminably, all crops removed, the surface frozen hard, but without snow. Soon the pack was scouring the plain in full chase of an unfortunate hare, the hounds being slipped as the quarry started; the falcons, unhooded, take wing. Away went our ponies at full speed, their pace a run, not a gallop. First one falcon and then another swooped down upon and rolled over the hunted animal; the dogs fast gain upon her; she disappears, for in this forestless region holes in the earth and burrows are so taken advantage of by ground game. A huntsman bares his arm; he reaches into one such opening; the hare is drawn out, crying in its terror like a child; it is dispatched by a blow on the nape. This we are told is "sport." To some of us it would be more appropriately called barbarous and unmanly cruelty. Further details of what proved to be "a successful day" need not be related.

New Year's Eve,[1] according to the Chinese Calendar, was celebrated

[1] On February 9.

by the discharge of thousands of crackers and other fireworks, that being their manner of announcing to the world that the ceremony of propitiating their household gods had begun; the object in view, absolution for equivocal acts committed during the past twelve months. For several previous days the city was *en fête*; establishments closed; caricatures distributed as so many valentines; visits of friendship and of ceremony exchanged; family and other misunderstandings arranged; much feasting and carousing indulged in; houses swept and garnished in token that all things unpleasant, whether physical or ethical, had been cast out. The fronts of houses were decorated with strips of vermilion-coloured paper containing expressions of good-will and congratulation; ornamental lanterns were everywhere on sale, for purposes of illuminations, their shapes various and often grotesque, as fishes, frogs, dragons, and monsters of various forms. Buddhist temples had on their altars a series of gigantic candles, all "dyed red," bearing designs of dragons and other mythical creatures, before which people knelt with every appearance of devotion.

It became a source of interest to a few of us to visit places and institutions of purely Chinese origin or character. Of such places, a public bathing establishment was one, the interior well lighted, spacious, pervaded by steam from water heated by a furnace, the fuel of which consisted of reeds and straw. A series of troughs, and at one end a plunge bath, were being used by considerable numbers of men at a time, the charge for each being about a farthing. Here then were public baths existing as a Chinese institution, though even yet their introduction generally into England remains rather in the initiative than accomplished stage.

Very different in kind was an ice pit, otherwise a large underground room, one part of which was devoted to the preservation of that substance, another having a series of shelves crowded with vegetables and fruit of different kinds. As we descend into that pit, the sensation we experienced was that of comparative *warmth*, so bitterly cold had the wind outside become.

The Chinese Foundling Hospital, situated in the suburbs of the city, was a large and substantial building; its chief ornament a tablet, the characters on which intimated that the door over which it was placed was the entrance to "The Hall for Cherishing Children." At the time of our visit the institution contained eighty foundlings; to each of those still in infancy was assigned a wet nurse. One portion of the establishment was occupied by children, and some grown-up persons affected with various infirmities, as the blind, the deaf, and the idiotic, together with their respective attendants. Being invited by the superintendent to visit his own quarters, a tablet over the entrance door thereto displayed the characters, "We beseech thee to rescue the naked"; on the walls of the reception hall a series of tablets with names of patrons and donors of considerable sums; others with items of regulations relating to the administration of the institution. The children, if in good health, are disposed of at fourteen years of age—some adopted, some become servants, others apprenticed to trades. To the girls who marry, a dowry of the equivalent value of £5 is given.

At the end of March a visit by the Roman Catholic bishop of Pekin gave us the opportunity of hearing from himself his strange story. In 1834 the cathedral erected in Pekin by the Jesuits in the seventeenth century was closed during an outbreak of the populace against that mission, several of its members put to death, others "disappearing," to be no more heard of. Among the latter was for many years the bishop. Taken from the power of the rioters by some of the Catholic converts, he was concealed by them in the capital, and protected for the long period of twenty-seven years, he meanwhile carrying on his special work among them. The arrival at Pekin of the allied army was quickly followed by the re-opening of the cathedral and celebration of Grand Mass therein. On that occasion, as the procession of priests attached to the forces, and their acolytes, advanced toward the altar, the bishop, wearing ordinary Chinese costume, emerged from the throng, and took his place at its head. The Emperor of the French being made acquainted with the story, desired to see the bishop at the Tuileries to hear it from himself. While on his way through Tientsin the bishop remained with us several days. To inquiries on the subject, he remarked that his *first* endeavour with the Chinese was to teach them the practical results of Christianity, rather than inculcate doctrines, the significance of which were beyond their train of thought.

As early as practicable, measures were taken to establish a charitable hospital for the sick poor of Tientsin. For that purpose £100 was given by Admiral Sir James Hope, and subscriptions established among the officers of the force; applications to the rich natives being unproductive. At last, a building capable of accommodating twenty patients was engaged and fitted up for its purpose; professional work being undertaken by Dr. Lamprey, 67th Regiment. Under him its reputation rapidly spread, so much so that applications for admission exceeded our means of reception. In those days the use of chloroform was still in its infancy; very wonderful in the idea of the patients did its effect appear, exceeding, as they expressed themselves, "the power of the Dragon." The majority, however, looked upon the drug with suspicion, preferring to undergo operations—even of great severity—without it or any other anæsthetic. Their apparent indifference to pain under such circumstance was to us subject of amazement.

Duties connected with this hospital gave me an opportunity of seeing the contracted foot, otherwise "golden lily," of a Chinese woman. The foot had been deformed by the method of cramping usually followed for that purpose; the four smaller toes pressed under the sole, the natural arch raised to an altogether abnormal degree, the points of support limited to the heel and tip of the great-toe. The process of contraction takes place in early youth; it is conducted by means of bandages "artistically" applied, and is said to be painless. The aspect of the foot is thus made hideous, while the natural contour of the calf being destroyed, the appearance of the limb below the knee is—to Western eyes—ungraceful.

Neither by word or manner was the slightest gratitude expressed for benefits thus conferred upon them. But in one respect their demeanour drew from us a measure of appreciation; namely, in the care and assistance shown to each other by male patients. Contrasted therewith, however, their want of thoughtful care for sick women was no less remarkable; the more suitable of the two wards having been given up to the latter, the arrangement was protested against in no "gallant" terms by the men.

For a short time an idea seemed to prevail that an object with which the hospital was set on foot was, that in it attempts would be made upon sick inmates to press upon them what they called "the Western philosophy." Their minds were set at rest on this point; but among the patients there was a Christian convert, around whom other inmates in increasing numbers came to listen, while he read and expounded from a Chinese version of the Scriptures of which he was the possessor.

In our regular military hospital were several Tartar soldiers, some of them severely wounded, who had been picked up on the field of battle by our establishments, and now treated like our own men. In due time they recovered from their injuries as far as art could effect their restoration; they came to appreciate the *comforts* of their position so much that among their numbers no anxiety was expressed to be discharged. Application was made to the Chinese local authorities to receive them. The reply by them was to the effect that "the men having fallen in battle, they were officially dead; there being no precedent of dead men coming to life again, they could in no way recognise or acknowledge them." A liberal sum of money was subscribed by us for them; it was distributed among them; they were then, with military formalities, handed over to the local authorities, to be by them sent on to the care of the British Representative at Pekin. Before being so disposed of, they were seen by the bishop already mentioned. To his question, "What do you now think of the Barbarian doctors?" the answer given by one was that he could no longer fight as an infantry soldier, but he might do so as a cavalry man; by a second, that "he had been left upon the field dead, his wife a widow, his children orphans. By the care shown to him, he had been lifted up from death, fitted to return to and work for those dependent upon him; nor had he breath in his chest sufficient to express his gratitude for it all."

Among the inmates of the hospitals pertaining to our force were some of the Sikhs who, during the advance of the army on Pekin, had the misfortune to be taken prisoners, and subsequently subjected to cruelties as already mentioned. Their wrists bore large cicatrices, marking the position of the cords with which they had been so tightly bound that ulcers in which maggots crawled were results, the agony so great that several of their companions in misery had become delirious, and died under it. On September 18, a party of eighteen, including an officer, all of Fane's Horse, were taken prisoners; of them the officer and eight sowars succumbed under the atrocious cruelties to which they were subjected, the remaining nine being now in hospital.[1] But it would serve no good purpose to give particulars in regard to these sad occurrences.

Our French allies suffered in health during the period of greatest cold to an extent even greater than did our own men, the circumstance being readily accounted for by the fact that the former were insufficiently provided with warm clothing; indeed, many of them were dressed as when on board the transport ship in which several months previous they had been brought, *via* the Red Sea, to China. Whereas with us, every honour was shown at the burial of such soldiers as succumbed to the circumstances of our position, no such formality was seen by any of us in the quarter occupied by the French; but as day by day the black wooden crosses increased in number in their cemetery, these silent tokens told that they too had the hand of death among them. A temple had been converted by the French into a military hospital; the sick accommodated therein well cared for, its administration altogether under the Intendance, the duties of medical officers limited to professional attendance on the patients. Among the latter was a soldier who bore marks precisely like those of our own men already alluded to as having been made prisoners and tortured, he having been of their party.

[1] Details are given in my book *China from a Medical Point of View*, p. 437.

While the winter cold was most intense an epidemic of small-pox raged among the native Chinese, and to a less degree among both the British and French portions of our combined force. In the latter, General Collineau, its commanding officer, was an early victim. As he expressed himself before he lost consciousness, it was hard that after having escaped the dangers of various campaigns, including thirty battles, he should come to Tientsin to die of such a disease. He entered the army as a private soldier, obtained each succeeding step for services in the field, culminating in that of general officer for the Italian campaign.

Our British soldiers suffered severely in health, and, what was remarkable, to a greater extent than did the Sikhs, although the latter paid less attention to warm clothing and care of their persons in other respects than the British soldier. Our officers were affected variously; the younger, and those who had not undergone tropical service, enjoyed the cold weather immensely; but with those of us who had but recently undergone the wear and tear incidental to the Mutiny campaign, things were very different, the severity of the winter cold inducing among us serious illness.

CHAPTER XXII

1861. *TIENTSIN. CHEFOO. NAGASAKI. DEVONPORT*

Fraternity of beggars—Relief fund—A Buddhist nunnery—A Buddhist temple—Ancestral worship—A pantheistic mosque—A Chinese dinner—An opium den—A missionary plan—Postal arrangements—Remittances—Vegetation—Birds—Mr. Bruce proceeds to Pekin—Camp formed—The Spirit of Fire—French "ideas"—"Sheep grows its own wool"—Taipings—Sir John Mitchell—Sickness among troops—Emperor dies—Trip to Chefoo—Town and vicinity—Taoist temple—Resume duty—The force breaking up—Nagasaki—Places visited—Embark—Homeward bound—Aden—Cairo and Alexandria—Death of Prince Consort—Devonport.

THE Fraternity of Beggars constitutes one of the institutions peculiar to Tientsin, the numbers of mendicants to be met with being very great indeed, comprising old and young, fat and lean, the healthy, the deformed, and the diseased. One particular class are to be seen almost devoid of clothing on the upper part of their persons, even in the coldest weather, when the thermometer ranges from zero to a few degrees above; the use of thick clothing and furs by most people considered indispensable; yet that their health in no way suffered from such exposure was evident by their appearance. Another notable class represent to some degree the order Flagellants, their appeals for charity emphasized by a series of self-inflicted blows on their bodies by means of a piece of wood or a brick-bat. These several classes live in communities, one of which I visited. In a wretched hut, in coldest winter, destitute of fire, thirty-five men, all in a state of nudity, were huddled together, having a cubic space per head of 57 feet. The atmosphere was foul and offensive, the inmates for the most part strong, and to all appearance healthy. Here, as in China generally, the rule that "once a beggar, always a beggar," has few, if indeed any, exceptions.

An attempt was made to relieve some of the poverty and distress which were so prominently before our eyes. For this purpose a fund was established, a sum of eight hundred dollars being collected among the officers of the force; the subject was brought to the notice of the

Chinese officials and wealthier classes in the city, the result being that they not only refused to aid the work, but opposed it in various ways. Finally, notices were issued that the sum collected would be distributed at the house used as a "church" by our troops; a guard of soldiers was mounted to preserve order, and at the hour appointed seven thousand applicants for relief had collected. Unhappily the crush speedily became greater than the guard was capable of resisting; in the pressure of the crowd a number of persons, chiefly women and children, were trodden under foot, several crushed to death, and of those less severely injured fifteen were carried into hospital.

As winter advanced, sickness among our troops increased to such a degree that various *yamens* or other buildings had in succession to be hired for that purpose. On such occasions, in addition to the officers specially concerned in making the selection, some representative city (Chinese) officials, the whole party under the protection of our own military police, made an inspection of the buildings most suitable for our purpose, after which an application was duly made for the particular one fixed upon. On an occasion of this kind, Captain C. E. Gordon, R.E., who shortly afterwards was to become so prominent a character in Chinese, and subsequently in Egyptian, war-history, formed, as usual, one of the party alluded to. In the course of our excursion we came to what from the outside appeared to be an eligible enclosure for our purpose. A series of loud knocks at the outer door brought to it a neatly attired and rather good-looking *boy*, as we at first supposed, whose manner of receiving us was the very reverse of polite. *He* was quickly brushed aside; our party was in act of entering, when our Chinese escort intimated the fact —up till that moment unexpressed—that we were forcing our way into a Buddhist nunnery, against the expressed objection of a nun. Our regret was real; explanations were exchanged; we were informed that the community within adopted male costume as an indication that they not only renounced the world, but with it the emblems of their sex. We were "received" by the Lady Superior, tea and cakes offered to and partaken of by us; we were then permitted to visit the "private chapel," and finally we parted from the *religieuses* on the best of terms. Needless to say, their establishment from that time forward was by us held sacred.

A visit was made to "The Temple of Future Punishments." That temple comprises a series of buildings, the entrance to the general enclosure in which they are situated having on either side a stone figure of a dog, probably the Buddhistic ideal Cerberus. Within the several buildings well-executed clay *figures* represented the subjects of departed spirits, undergoing all the forms and degrees of punishment to which evil Buddhists were condemned, the whole reminding us, on the one hand, of those described in "The Vision of Meerza," and, on the other, of illustrations contained in at least one publication by the Roman Catholic Church. Among the various forms of punishment so illustrated was that of crucifixion; another illustration included the humpless bullock, as if relating to the worship of Isis and Osiris; a third presented the rites of the Indian Chukkur Poojah, and so on.

On visiting an old Buddhist temple on the left bank of the Peiho, our reception by the priests belonging to it was most friendly and hospitable. On the principal shrine were the orthodox representations of "the three Buddhas,"—namely, past, present, and to come. In other portions of the same sacred edifice were figures, doubtless of saints; before each a joss stick smouldered, while our venerable entertainers talked and smiled, even in presence of their gods. This portion of our visit over, we were invited by the priest to enter the house of one of the brethren. Having done so, tea in small cups, and cakes, steamed instead of baked, were served to us.

Arrived at a dwelling-house, in which various members of the family were engaged in the ceremonies connected with ancestral worship, we were permitted to be spectators of that ritual. A small shrine, erected for the occasion, had upon it two figures, probably Confucian, for they were without any characteristics of Buddhism. It was further decorated with flags and other ornaments. Offerings of apples were arranged upon the shrine; a vessel containing joss sticks, otherwise incense rods, one of which was taken by each worshipper in his turn and lighted; there were also piles of tinsel paper, from which pieces were successively taken and set on fire, the belief of the worshippers, all of whom were grave and orderly in demeanour, that messages were by that means conveyed to their departed relatives. But there were no women present at the ceremony. On either side of an enclosed passage, communicating with the ancestral hall, a series of tablets, roughly estimated at two hundred, were arranged, the impression conveyed to us being that each ancestor has his particular day on which his worship is celebrated.

We were at first unprepared, on visiting a principal mosque, to learn that several others of less magnitude existed for the considerable Mahomedan population in the city. The mosque alluded to was to a great extent Chinese in external style, but within had all the usual characteristics of such edifices; superadded to these, however, there was, on the middle of the floor, a tablet of Confucius, around which was entwined in bold relief the Taoist dragon! The moolahs were Chinese in feature and costume, and wore the Mongolian *queue* or pigtail. As we entered we found them deeply engaged in the study of the Koran, written in Arabic, which language they spoke fluently.

Having had the honour of being invited to dinner by a Chinese gentleman, the occasion was taken advantage of to observe the phase of native life so presented. As guest of the evening, I was received with much ceremony by Chang, for such was the name of the host; there was much bowing, "chin-chin"-ing, and hand-shaking, each person for himself shaking his own hands as he held them clasped upon his breast. Then followed a respectful inquiry as to my honourable years,—otherwise, how old I was,—and it by a desire to be informed as to how many children had the honour to call me father, a bow and expressive gesture indicating that sons only were to be counted in the enumeration. All this took place in an outer apartment; the party was then invited to proceed to the dining-hall, separated from that in which we at first stood by a series of apartments, all handsomely furnished and ornamented. In each corner of these rooms stood an ornamental lantern, having in it a red-coloured taper, in token of rejoicing; on the wall directly facing the door, a tablet upon which, in Chinese characters, was the moral maxim, "Not to covet is a virtue," otherwise a compressed epitome of the tenth commandment. In the dining-room we took the chairs assigned to us. On the table, arranged with much taste, were dishes containing fruit, fresh and preserved; a dish on which were some neatly cut slices of what looked like ham; on another a pyramid of eggs that had been first boiled hard, then permitted to remain buried in the ground for a year. These delicacies partaken of (and the eggs referred to were by no means nasty), our host filled the tiny cup at the side of each guest with hot sham-shu,—*i.e.*, a spirit distilled from millet,—bowed to each of us in succession, and returned to his seat. The course which followed was mainly composed of the root of water lily (*Nelumbum*); it again by one of sharks' fins; then olives preserved in syrup, or perhaps rather jujubes;[1] more fruits of sorts, variously preserved; sea-weed, sea-slugs[2], and other delicacies. Although chop-sticks were arranged for each of us, knives, forks, and spoons—all of silver, but the last-named of Chinese pattern—were also placed for our use. Several courses of this kind having succeeded each other, the more *material* part of the banquet was introduced, in the shape of portions of fowl and duck, served *à la Russe*; then a repetition of preserves as before; winding up with a portion of rice—the sign that dinner was over.

[1] *Zysiphus jujuba.* [2] *Holothuria.*

Dessert was laid in another room; thither we repaired, and with toasts, talk, and a good deal of festivity the evening passed away.

A visit to an "opium den," and inquiries to which that visit led, induced me to make, at the time, an entry in my diary thus: "I have witnessed much wretchedness and want among the victims of this vice (namely, opium-smoking); but neither in a greater degree nor among so large a proportion of the people as are debased in the United Kingdom through the evil consequences of indulgence in spirits." The institution of such establishments was at the time looked upon as among the first fruits arising from the treaty, in accordance with which Tientsin, as a port, has been opened to foreign shipping.

The visit alluded to was made in company with an American missionary.[1] His plan for obtaining influence over the frequenters of such places was to point out to them the evils present and prospective of the vice in which they were indulging, and so endeavour to wean them from it. By seeking for, and assisting in various ways, outcasts and the neglected,—by reconciling, when possible, those between whom misunderstandings had arisen, and in other kindred methods of proceeding, rather than in direct attempts at religious conversion, he had succeeded in making for himself a sphere of great usefulness and influence.

The postal arrangements in connection with our portion of the force were so imperfect that only by means of Chinese messengers employed at high rates of pay, which had to be made up at our individual cost, our letters were conveyed to Chefoo, to be put on board a steamer. The French, on the other hand, had with them two officers from the Post Office in Paris, under them a party of sailors, for the purpose, without expense to individuals, of keeping up postal communication between Tientsin and the same port.

With regard also to the transmission of family remittances, a similar contrast existed; it was impossible for us to send such remittances otherwise than through a bank or mercantile house in Hong-Kong, at the same time that the greatest difficulty and inconvenience existed in sending money to that island. The French, on the contrary, have with them special officers sent from the Paris Treasury for the purpose of transacting business of this kind. If, therefore, our arrangements are in most respects superior to those of our allies, these are examples of the few in reference to which we are comparatively at a disadvantage.

In the early days of April a great advance was apparent in the aspect of vegetation; long red catkins of poplar trees hung pendulous

[1] Mr. Blodgett.

to a length of several inches; plants, numerous in their variety, rapidly came into blossom, many being species familiar to us in England, the progress made by all of them astonishing. Vines that had been buried deep in long trenches, and so protected against the cold of winter, were disinterred, laid along the surface of the ground as if to dry, then secured upon trellis-work erected for the purpose, after which the succession of bud, leaf, flower, and fruit was very rapid. In the near vicinity of irrigation canals, peach trees presented lovely displays of pink blossom; at intervals the "white cloud" of cherry flowers gave contrast to the whole.

From this point onwards interest increased in observing the successive aspects of Nature. On March 17 temperature was sufficiently mild to bring into activity a few winged insects; a perceptible change in the aspect of the fields was apparent; tender shoots of green cereal leaves were rising from the ground, and tree buds began to manifest coming activity. Migratory birds were now in flight northward in their course, wild swans being the first to start on such a journey, and to suffer at the hands of the snarer. Early in April the swallow,[1] so well known in England, made its appearance; and thenceforward, with White's "Selborne" in hand, note was taken of the order in which various species made their appearance—an order which coincided to a remarkable degree with what happens at home.

The departure of Mr. Bruce[2] to take up his position as British Representative at Pekin marked the opening of a new era in the relations between our own and the Imperial Governments. The Emperor[3] was still at Jehol, whither he had fled on the approach to his capital of the allied army; it was known that his chief adviser, the Prince Tsai, was inimical to foreigners; that the details of government were conducted by Prince Kung in conjunction with the Manchu Prince Wan siang; moreover, that the Taiping rebels were carrying their conquest rapidly northward, and so threatening the existence of the reigning dynasty; hence it was that our force was held ready prepared for eventualities. Happily the reception accorded to the British Minister, if not all that could be desired, was not of a kind to call for actual protest.

By way of occupation to our soldiers a camp was pitched and temporarily occupied by them at a little distance from the city; parades and drills became frequent, the general routine of duty much like that in an English garrison. Men who had suffered in health during the winter, and those time expired, were got ready for dispatch

[1] 9th. *Cypsilis affinis.* [2] On March 22, 1861. [3] Hienfung.

homewards, being conveyed by military train waggons to Taku, and thence by steamer to Hong-Kong *en route*. Of time-expired men the greater number were in the best of health and vigour, inured to military life, and in all respects desirable as soldiers, so that their departure was a serious loss to the efficiency of our force.

With a view to facilitate access to the recently established camp, the somewhat forcible measure was taken of cutting through the city wall. That an objection should be raised by the citizens was a matter of course; a deputation accordingly waited upon our Brigadier to protest against the dilapidation, the reason assigned by them being that "the Spirit of Fire" enters from the south, and danger to the city was thus to be apprehended.

Intercommunication between the French and British officers was friendly, if not exactly intimate, the former being invited to entertainments of different kinds given by the latter. On one such occasion conversation turned upon the nature of the influence being exerted upon the Chinese mind by our presence respectively: "Yes," observed our neighbour, "we have a great mission to perform: you to benefit them by your commerce; we (the French) by our ideas!" One morning news reached us that a considerable portion of the French contingent had been dispatched for service in Saigon.

On the subject of commerce the Chinese had already their own views in relation to the indemnity to be paid to "the Barbarian." Double import duty was imposed on all foreign goods landed at the port; one moiety to be paid before leaving the ship, the other prior to actual landing. By this simple method, according to the expression used, "the sheep would grow its own wool." Not that the price to the Chinese receiver would increase; the dues must fall upon the exporter.

Meanwhile the Taipings were steadily advancing in their progress of devastation and murder; the atrocities reported as committed by them horrible in their details. Towards the end of April, Admiral Hope and Brigadier Staveley proceeded to Pekin, at the request of Prince Kung, who desired to consult with them relative to a plan initiated by himself, of dispatching a body of British troops to aid the Imperial forces against the rebels in question. The circumstance sufficed to put all concerned on the *qui vive*; our field arrangements were overhauled and seen to; all preparations made for contingencies. Shortly afterwards news spread that a considerable body of Tartar cavalry had been sent from Tientsin against them; that the British were to be withdrawn from Canton, and thus a force 2,000 strong left available for service against the rebels.

Our Ambassador, finding it well to consult personally the general officer commanding the troops in China respecting the somewhat important question at this juncture, of retaining our force intact or diminishing it, that officer was summoned to the capital. It was while he was *en route* towards Pekin that I had the pleasure of making his acquaintance, and of adverting to an incident already mentioned with reference to the battle of Maharajpore. In the interval of seventeen years which has meanwhile elapsed, Captain Mitchell, of the 6th Foot, had become Major-General Sir John Mitchell, K.C.B. I asked him whether he had ever received the watch sent to him from the field by request of General Churchill. He seemed surprised to learn that I had been the sender; and taking it from his watch-pocket exclaimed, as he showed it to me: "There it is, and it goes as well as ever." The expletives which accompanied the action are here omitted.

As in the severity of winter the health of the troops suffered greatly, so it did, though in a different way, when late in July and early in August summer heat was at its highest. During the latter period heat apoplexy, cholera, and a very virulent form of small-pox prevailed to such an extent and with such mortality that a veritable panic spread among them. Fortunately these terrible maladies continued but for a short time, a change to temperate in the state of the atmosphere seeming to put a sudden and complete check to them. While they continued they affected only the foreigner; the Chinese enjoyed their ordinary health; but they deviated altogether from the method, so general in India, of protecting their heads from the heat of the sun by means of thick turbans; on the contrary, they freely exposed themselves to the fiercest sun with no covering whatever on their shaven heads. According to them, the cause of this sudden outbreak of illness was *the* comet. An immense and brilliant comet had shortly previous appeared in the heavens—a strikingly grand object to gaze at, and wonder; but in the eyes of many a portent of evil.

Various rumours circulated with reference to the state of health of the Emperor: that he was ill; that he was in perfect health; that he was dead; that he had been murdered; that he was neither, and so on. After a time authentic news of his death was received; that, as expressed by the Chinese, "he had ascended upon the dragon to be a guest on high"; that his son Chesiang had been named as his successor, under the name or title of Tung-che, or "Felicitous omen," otherwise "Union of law and order"; that a Board of Regency had been appointed for the conduct of government; that its chief members, including the Empress-Dowager, were persons of anti-foreign proclivities, the Prince Kung retaining his position as a kind of Secretary of State for Foreign Affairs. At the date of his accession the young Emperor was no more than eight years of age; but a truly Chinese method of adding to them was adopted: his Council *bestowed* upon him three years—namely, one from heaven, one from earth, and one from themselves; his age, moreover, was calculated as having been nine months at the date of his birth.

A trip to Chefoo having been arranged, in company with our Brigadier-General, Sir Charles Staveley, I proceeded by H.M. gunboat *Woodcock* to Taku; thence by H.M.S. *Simoom.* Like many others at Tientsin we had suffered considerably in health, first from the great cold of winter, then from the no less trying heat of summer, with the outbreak of epidemic disease already mentioned. Soon, however, the open sea, with its clear air, added to complete relief from official responsibilities and duties, had an effect for good upon us. But we were not a little surprised to observe that while those actually ill among the ship's company amounted to the large proportion of 15 per cent., those who remained "efficient" were pale and sickly, a circumstance attributed by their officers to their exposure to land-winds, while cruising or at anchor in the Gulf of Pe chili.

Arrived at Chefoo, we landed by a roughly-built jetty, on which in large letters was painted the word *Odins*, thus indicating the crew by whom the work had recently been effected. We were hospitably received by Mr. Morrison, the Consul, son of the eminent Chinese scholar. He having provided us with horses, we were speedily away, enjoying a ride through a tract of country remarkable for its loveliness; the open spaces covered with brilliant flowers, while along each side of narrow thoroughfares fruit trees at short intervals afforded us the treat of being able to stand up in our stirrups and pluck ripening pears as we proceeded. A second ride took us to the highest point of a range of low hills that separates the town from the inland districts. Thence we looked down upon a richly cultivated valley, along which ran a stream of considerable size, itself dotted with clumps of wood, in which were seen villages and isolated houses of agriculturists; the sides of the valley formed for the most part of gneiss-like hills, torn at intervals into deep and rugged ravines. In the distance inland the view was bounded by a serrated line of mountain peaks.

A visit to a Taoist temple was an interesting episode in an otherwise enjoyable excursion. The priest, apparently over seventy years of age, received us graciously; he "chin-chinned," shook hands—with himself, after the national custom; felt our arms, our legs, our feet; examined our saddles, girths, and bridles; inquired our several ages, proffered us glasses of water, patted the necks of our steeds; as we rode away, chin-chinned and shook hands with himself as on our arrival. His temple, situated on the summit of a small hill, was erected in honour of the North star. Near it stood two marble monuments in memory of ladies who, though left widows while yet young, refused to re-marry; at a little distance was a graveyard, the headstones in which were by no means very different in style from what may be seen at home. The faces of adjoining hills present a succession of terraces bearing abundant crops, and watered by *levadas*, as may be seen on the island of Madeira.

A few days most pleasantly spent, and with health considerably improved, we proceeded on our return journey; first by the French steamer *Feilung*, or Flying Dragon, to the mouth of the Peiho, thence by the French gunboat *l'Etoile* to Tientsin to resume official duties.

Great was the pleasure with which, early in August, we received intimation that our "army of occupation" was to be gradually broken up, the regiments and batteries composing it to be disposed of between England, India, and the south of China; great the satisfaction personally with which I received the welcome information that my connection therewith would cease. Towards the end of September embarkation began, detachments taken on board flats, and these towed down the river by gunboats, each party while marching from barracks being escorted by a band, to the strains of which—"Auld Lang Syne" and "The Old Folks at Home"—they went cheerily on board, and away from what to most of us had been a station devoid of attraction. In this way did the second 60th embark for England, having during its ten years of foreign service buried 300 of its members, 94 of whom in China during the past eighteen months. This is but an example of what "service" meant in the days referred to.

Next came my own turn to embark. Gladly did I proceed by H.M. gunboat *Slaney* to the *Vulcan* at anchor off Taku, embarking Indian troops. Captain Strode, in command, having received orders to proceed in the first instance to Nagasaki, an unexpected opportunity thus offered of seeing that port and city in Japan. The arm of the sea by which the harbour is approached extends inland to a distance of six miles, with a breadth of nearly two. On either side rises a range of hills interrupted by valleys, the whole covered with rich forest, or with cultivated fields, a succession of batteries being so placed as to command the channel. To the south of us rose the island of Pappenberg; the cliffs, 800 to 900 feet in height, are those over which, A.D. 1622, the Roman Catholic "Christians" were hurled. We next arrived at Desima, now grown into a large town, but to which locality in former times the Dutch traders were confined by gates and narrow ways, though now containing various houses built and in course of erection according to European models.

Among the places visited was the steam factory. There, under the direction of Dutch engineers, Japanese workmen were actively employed in the manufacture of machinery. In an adjoining dock a small steamer was having placed in her engines, that had been thus made and turned out; while in the harbour lay moored a steamer, the *Scotland*, manned entirely by Japanese officers and sailors. The town of Nagasaki was clean and tidy; very different in these respects from that whence we had arrived. There appeared to be at least some agreeable aspects of domestic life, inasmuch as men and women were seen partaking of their meals together; the people were polite and civil to us foreigners, and to myself, personally, the proprietors of a shop which I entered to purchase various articles were so civil as to take me through several parts of their dwelling-house, then into a neatly arranged garden attached thereto, and in parting to beg my acceptance of a packet of their tea, I having presented to some of the younger members a few new silver coins, to be made by them into studs. All the while we were being carefully watched by officials, though we were ignorant of the fact. [How little at that time did we anticipate the amazing strides Japan was to take during the succeeding five-and-thirty years!]

Arrived at Hong-Kong, my stay of a few days there was made the more pleasant by the receipt of orders to proceed to England by the first available opportunity, added to hospitable civility by friends whose acquaintance I had made while stationed there the previous year. Preparations for continuing my journey were speedily made; on November 15 I was on board the P. and O. steamer *Emeu*, from over the stern of which, without a tinge of regret, I waved what I hoped, and proved to be a final adieu to China.

Our journey was thence along the same track, but in a reverse direction to that over which I had passed twenty months previous. Arrived at Galle, we had, as before, to tranship, this time to the *Simla*, by which we traversed the Indian Ocean. The season of the year permitting us to "explore" some of the sights of Aden, we took advantage of the opportunity afforded by the brief delay of our ship at the anchorage. Driving through the narrow cut in the hard lava rock,—that had in distant time formed the wall of an active volcano,—we were at the cantonments, situated in the ancient crater; thence to the reservoirs, originally erected *in* the face of perpendicular rock, their design and construction due to Persian engineers, dating from A.D. 600. Our drive was next through a narrow gorge, opening towards the south, admitting the only breeze that can directly reach cantonments. From its outer limit a view was obtained of the open sea, and of the small island upon which, according to Arab tradition, Cain was forced to reside after his murder of Abel. Continuing our excursion, we arrived at the fortification known as "The Turkish Wall," that protects and defends the isthmus connecting "the rock" with the mainland. The shops on the beach were visited, and purchases made at some of them; among such purchases, ostrich feathers, here so common as to be used to decorate the heads of donkeys driven by Arab boys.

The people met with comprised Parsees, Somalis, Jews, and Egyptians. The Jews and Egyptians said to be descendants of those who fled to Egypt on the invasion of Palestine and Egypt by Nebuchadnezzar;[1] the Somalis supposed to be descended from former Abyssinian possessors of "Yemen," or that part of Arabia to which Aden belongs, or rather did belong. Other historical items relating to Aden include its early importance as an *entrepôt* of commerce between the Roman Empire and the East; in recent times the capture of the position by the British in January, 1839, it being the first military conquest effected in the reign of Her Majesty Queen Victoria.

To most of us the news we received on arriving at Suez was a surprise; namely, that which speedily became known as the *Trent* affair. Some particulars reached us also regarding the action present and intended of the English Government and War Office, the immediate effect being to lead us to anticipate active service within a very short time. Here we were quickly landed, distributed in railway carriages, and so sent on to Cairo, at which place another brief detention awaited us. I accordingly reverted under the guidance of my former dragoman, Hadji Selim, to the excursions previously interrupted by my departure eastward; visiting, among other places of interest, the ancient Coptic Church, erected, according to tradition, upon the cave in which, during their flight into Egypt, Mary and the infant Saviour took shelter one night. Thence, continuing our railway journey, we reached Alexandria, arriving there in a storm of such violence that to embark was impossible; consequently another halt was unavoidable. I took advantage of the occasion, in defiance of wind and rain, to visit some of the places of historical interest pertaining to this very interesting city, including the site of the ancient Pharos, Pompey's Pillar, and "Cleopatra's" Needle,[2] the latter prostrate in and almost covered by the sand; also, what was indicated as "St. Mark's pulpit." Time did not admit of a visit to the ruined aqueduct, of which, however, we obtained a glance while nearing the city.

Here the unexpected news reached us that the Prince Consort had

[1] Ezekiel xxvii. 23; xxix. 19.

[2] The same that now stands on the Thames Embankment.

succumbed to fever; that national sympathy was felt for the Queen under her bereavement, as well as sorrow and regret at the event, more particularly at a time when political matters throughout Europe, and in reference to America, were in a very disturbed condition.

From Alexandria the journey was performed by the *Ceylon*, comfortably, and without adventure. At Malta we learned that the American Congress had expressed approval of the Southern minister being captured on board a British steamer;[1] that troops were being prepared in England for immediate embarkation; that war appeared imminent and inevitable. On reaching Gibraltar we found in the bay the Mediterranean fleet, in which it was said all necessary preparations were being made for active service. Our entrance to the Bay of Biscay was duly announced by the ship's band with the well-known air so called. Warlike news greeted us on arrival at Southampton. Then followed, in quick succession, disembarkation, personal report at Headquarters, London, appointment to Devonport, and happy reunion to wife and children there.

[1] The *Trent*.

CHAPTER XXIII

1862-1864. *DEVONPORT. CALCUTTA*

Paris — Versailles—Champ de Mars—An incident—Rouen—Proceed to India—Calcutta—A *mélange* of subjects—Continued—A painful incident—State trial—Sea transport—General events — 43rd Regiment — More "news"— Scenes revisited—A rough journey—Hill coolies — Darjeeling—Sinchal—Nunsook—Rungeet—Pilgrims—Locusts—A happy event—Death of Lord Elgin—Agricultural Exhibition—Sittana—Spring sickness—Sanitary Commission formed—General news—Indigo—Cyclone—History of "Masterly inactivity."

ADMINISTRATIVE duties in the Western Military District of England, of which Devonport was, and still is, the Headquarters, were peaceful, and so contrasted with events during the past few years, as already recorded. In due time—the first for several years—I applied for and obtained the usual two months' leave accorded annually to officers serving at home. With my wife I proceeded to Paris, where time passed agreeably and profitably in visiting places of historical, artistic, and scientific interest, and in exploring public buildings and monuments with which that very beautiful city abounds.

On that occasion the French capital was *en fête*, the King of Holland being on a visit to Napoleon the Third; military displays on a grand scale the order of the day. One such display being arranged to take place at Versailles, we joined the crowds proceeding thither from St. Lazare. Having visited the château and its surroundings, we had the opportunity, while in the latter, of meeting the young Prince Imperial, then little more than seven years old, as he rode a small pony, accompanied and guarded by a group of attendants. Within the château we visited the various salons open to the public, among them the Salon de la Guerre and Grande Galerie des Glaces, little thinking as we did so that they were to be revisited under very different circumstances.

An important "function," at which we "assisted," was a grand review at the Champ de Mars, where 40,000 troops paraded for the purpose, accompanied by an imposing military train, and an efficient-looking pontoon train. The precision with which the various battalions and other bodies of troops took up their assigned positions was striking, giving to a looker-on the impression of a high state of efficiency. With the Champ de Mars I was to become unpleasantly acquainted eight years subsequently.

During our visit an incident took place which may be mentioned in these notes. While at the *table d'hôte*[1] one morning I got into conversation with a lady whose seat adjoined my own. In the course of talk the subject of the late expedition to China being alluded to, she mentioned the name of the officer whose death at Hong-Kong has been already recorded. I related to her some of the particulars already given, among others his request that I should destroy the mysterious parcel, and the fulfilment by me of that his dying request. As I did so, the lady seemed surprised; she informed me that her daughter, then seated at her left side, had been engaged to Captain M——, and she doubted not that the parcel in question contained the letters of the fair *fiancée*, whose health had given way, and on whose account both were now travelling.

A short but very pleasant visit over, I took leave of the fascinating capital, little thinking of the conditions under which my acquaintance with it was to become more intimate a few years thereafter. On our homeward journey a short stay was made at Rouen. To us that city had several points of interest, including its traditional association with the closing scene in the life of Joan of Arc, with its attendant barbarities; and as the capital whence William started on his conquest of England, the Caserne de Bonnes Nouvelles now occupying the site of the palace where Matilda received "the good news" of that conquest. Interesting also in that its cathedral contains the heart of Richard Cœur de Lion, together with a monument to that monarch. But the edifice which seemed to us the architectural gem was the church of St. Ouen, dating, it was said, from A.D. 533, and in its present form from 1318; with its numerous windows of stained glass, its western portal and arcade, its sculptured vase, from the surface of the "holy" water contained in which a reflected view is seen of the roof through its entire extent, including the exquisite workmanship of its ornamentation.

Returned to duty at Devonport, an intimation soon reached me that I was again to proceed on foreign service. A few days sufficed to make the necessary arrangements for my dear wife, who, with the children, must be left behind. Then came in quick succession orders to embark for Calcutta; then the very painful ordeal of leave-taking; then em-

[1] At the former Hôtel de Lille et d'Albion, now Hôtel St. James.

barkation at Southampton on board the P. and O. ss. *Ripon*, September 4, 1862, and away from England for a sixth tour abroad.

Arrived at Calcutta, I was appointed to administrative charge of the Presidency and Benares divisions, the duties connected with the former including charge of the office of Inspector-General, and inspections of all ships arriving or departing with troops, all those combined functions being of a much more arduous nature than at the time I was able to appreciate.

The cold season had set in, and with its advent the usual influx of higher officials to the Indian capital. Lord Elgin, recently appointed Governor-General, carried with him sympathetic feeling towards those who had lately served in China, and in this spirit extended his civility to myself, as to some others who had but lately arrived. It was while partaking of Viceregal hospitality that I met Admiral Sir James Hope, who had given such material help to the hospital for Chinese we had established at Tientsin. With him I discussed the question mooted in China of establishing at Nagasaki a sanatorium for invalid soldiers and sailors employed at various places on, and in vessels off, the coast; but, as I think unfortunately for both those classes, the proposal never came to anything.

The unusual *mélange* of subjects which gave rise to comment in Calcutta at the same time was in its way remarkable. The ex-King of Delhi had very recently died at Rangoon. The King of Greece was reported to have abdicated, and together with his queen fled from his kingdom. A crisis had occurred in Prussia. The Emperor of Austria was about to be crowned as King of Hungary. In America, a Proclamation had declared the emancipation of the slaves, various reports reaching us of threatened risings and other complications as outcomes of that measure. In the columns of some English journals, strong comments with regard to British policy in China in taking military action against the Taiping rebels. In Japan, a revolution, the city of Yedo destroyed by the insurgents. In the Straits of Corea, the Russians induced to abandon the island, of which they had quietly taken possession during the earlier stages of the Anglo-French expedition against China. Garibaldi wounded; a consultation of surgeons as to whether the bullet was in the wound or not—one would think, not a very difficult enigma to solve by men of experience in the field. The coming of age of the Prince of Wales, together with the honours and promotions announced on that auspicious occasion. The nomination of Prince Alfred to the throne of Greece. The proposed mediation by France between the Northern and Southern States of America, and failure of that attempt. The endeavours made to diminish as far as possible difficulties into which Lancashire weavers had fallen. Such are a few of the outside matters to which conversation in Calcutta was directed.

Among those more nearly connected with India was the report contained in the home papers of the Court-Martial—at the time notorious—having reference to the circumstances under which the death took place of the Sergeant-Major of the 6th Dragoons at Mhow. A very unpleasant incident at a Service Club was the subject of comment; the action taken with regard to it by the officer in chief command being discussed in terms more energetic than flattering. Towards the end of the cold season the ceremony took place of consecrating the well at Cawnpore into which were thrown the victims of the saddest of all sad episodes connected with the Mutiny of 1857.

There seemed to be a lull in the current of events in India; but not in those relating to various European nations, and to America. The insurrection which for some time past has been in progress in Poland was said to have assumed increased proportions. In England, the approaching marriage of the Prince of Wales was the subject of loyal excitement throughout the country. In America renewed endeavours to bring about cessation of the Civil War had so far proved futile.

With the advance of the hot season came the usual influx of sick officers from the interior, on their way home if possible, or to be treated in the hospital provided for their care by the Indian Government. Among them the story of one was very sad, and at the same time illustrative of that of many others. Brought to a hotel, together with his wife, a girl in age, he was found, when first seen by a medical officer, to be dying, consciousness all but gone; his wife unaware of his actual condition; both without friend or even acquaintance in Calcutta. There was no time for delay or ceremony. I accordingly informed her at once how desperate was his state, asking at the same time if she knew what was the position of his worldly affairs. Her reply: "Not more than the child unborn." I led her to the couch of the expiring man, and asked directly, "Where is your will?" He muttered rather than intelligibly expressed a reply, which seemed, however, to give his young wife the requisite indication. Within an hour thereafter he was dead. The widow and her infant had to be left for the time being in the apartment immediately adjoining that in which lay the corpse of her husband, until, with the Indian hospitality of that day, a resident family were communicated with, and sent their carriage for her and her infant; both of whom were cared for until arrangements were completed, and the bereaved ones some weeks thereafter sailed for England.

A good deal of talk was current in reference to two noted State trials of chiefs who had taken an active part in murders and other atrocities committed in connection with the Mutiny, but who had only recently come within the clutches of the law, notably at Lucknow and Bombay. At this time emissaries of the Nana were believed to be actively at work, the general impression being that he was alive and in Nepaul, whence he continued to issue instructions to sympathisers.

The near prospect of the canal across the Isthmus of Suez being completed, as well as some other considerations, led to a reconsideration by the authorities of the general question relating to the transport of troops between England and India, and *vice versâ*. Experience had recently shown the inconvenience and military objections against the long sea route *via* the Cape, including the long period during which to all intents and purposes troops in transit are non-effective. Statistics had so far been unfavourable in regard to the results obtained by sending to hill "sanatoria" soldiers suffering from organic illness. These circumstances were deemed of sufficient importance to justify inquiry into the whole matter, the outcome of the investigation being a scheme in accordance with which a line of Indian troopships was some time thereafter established.

Several circumstances combined to occupy public as well as official attention. The death of Dost Mahomed was followed by fratricidal wars between his sons; these conflicts were to continue during the next few years, and become historically interesting because of the policy of "masterly inactivity" observed towards the contending parties. Relations between England and Russia were in a strained condition; with Japan so unsatisfactory that the dispatch thither of a military force was contemplated. A certain amount of excitement was kept alive by rumours, more or less plausible, that the Nana was alive and active; first one suspect and then another was captured, but only to be set at liberty by judicial authority.

The dispatch of the 43rd Light Infantry for service in New Zealand was in Calcutta looked upon as quite an important event; arrangements for transport presented no difficulty whatever, but it was impossible to provide the regiment with equipment of a kind suitable for the service on which they were proceeding, for however well adapted for the circumstances of India is that authorized by regulations of the country, it is ill adapted for others in which camels and elephants as beasts of burthen are unobtainable.

From different parts of India came reports of disaffection, while from some, including Sittana, came accounts of actual outbreaks—*fanatical*, they were called. Early in October information reached us that under Admiral Kuper the British fleet had opened fire upon and destroyed the forts at Kagosima, though not without heavy loss to his own officers and men. Orders had been issued in England for the dispatch of reinforcements thither, and instructions to the same effect have been received by the Government of India.

In course of duty I visited the several stations within the divisions already named at which British troops were quartered, renewing acquaintance with places formerly well known, and connected with which were various associations, pleasant and otherwise. Of such places were the jungle road leading from Arrah to Jugdispore, so familiar in connection with service there; Beehea, where our force was suddenly attacked by Koer Singh's rebel sepoys; Jounpore, through the streets of which city in dead of night our field force marched towards what proved to be a somewhat severe action at Teegra, listening as we proceeded to the sound of "grinders" at their "mills," by which alone silence was broken; Azimghur, with the compound in which under fire from sepoy rifles we bivouacked, the line of march, and scene of action by our force against the besieging mutineers.

On that tour of inspection duty the journey from Dinapore to Darjeeling was attended by incidents of which the following are examples:—A hitch and consequent delay in regard to transit arrangements; several hours by railway train; a night spent in a wattle-and-daub hut called a dâk bungalow; twenty odd miles by steamer on the Ganges; starting by palanqueen; a break-down; return on foot several miles to the place whence I had so proceeded; delay and trouble in obtaining another conveyance of the same kind; another start; a short rest in the house of a hospitable civil servant; then on by raised causeway through a long tract of swampy ground; rowed across a broad nullah, and then the land journey resumed. After a little the discovery was made that the carrier of the luggage had dropped out of sight, nor could his whereabouts be discovered. On arriving at the "stage" where a relay of bearers was expected, there were none in waiting; the old ones heavily bribed continued, but at a slow pace, with many intervals to rest and indulge in smoking. Two more stages had to be got over in much the same manner, and then on reaching the rest house at the foot of the ascent towards Darjeeling, no provision whatever had been made for progress onward. Starting on foot, some four or five miles were got over, when meeting a native leading a small horse, or tat, bare backed, without halter or other substitute than a rope around its neck, I mounted the animal, but unable to guide it, had to resume walking, and so in time got over twenty out of the thirty miles that separate Punkabaree from the popular hill station. Railway transit between Calcutta and Darjeeling was in the far future.

In the near vicinity of Darjeeling numerous hillmen were employed improving and remodelling the road along which my walk lay. The general aspect presented by them was miserable and unpleasant. Tartar in feature and costume, the majority distinguished by *queue* or "pigtail"; many affected with goitre, others with large foul ulcers on legs or feet, unprotected by dressing of any kind,—the ulcers said to result from wounds inflicted by a poisonous fly abundantly met with here and hereabout.

In the early hours of the following morning a magnificent view of the snowy range, including the peaks of Mount Everest and Kinchinjunga was obtained, all reflecting brilliantly the first rays of sunlight, but later on becoming obscured by mist.

An experimental station for troops had some few years previously been established at Sinchal, situated on a mountain spur about a thousand feet higher than Darjeeling itself. Thither I went in course of duty, but only to learn how hateful the place was to officers and men quartered there, isolated, and for the most part concealed in cloud or mist as it was, the atmosphere damp, cold, and chilly. That the experiment was a failure was evident, but some time had yet to elapse before it was so acknowledged officially, and abandoned.

Situated in a deep valley, ten or twelve miles from Darjeeling, and at a level of four thousand feet below that station, are the mineral wells of Nunsook; the intervening spurs and ranges for the most part under cultivation with tea, coffee, or cinchona. Between us and the wells the Rungnoo River rushed in curling foam along its rocky bed, leaping as it went, as a cascade of considerable height and volume. Crossing that stream by a wooden bridge, then ascending among the rocks to a little distance, we reached the object of our journey. So deep and narrow is the mountain rent in which the chalybeate spring issues from the rock, that sunlight reaches it during no more than two hours daily. In its immediate neighbourhood was a hut in which a few British soldiers were accommodated, also "experimentally" to test the beneficial qualities of the spring. No wonder that they wished themselves with their regiment, or anywhere except at the well of Nunsook.

Another excursion was to the valley of the Rungeet River, some fourteen miles distant from Darjeeling, and forming the boundary between British India and Sikkim. The descent is steep; as we proceeded we met numbers of hillmen toiling upwards, bearing heavy loads in *kalbas* or baskets upon their backs—women were similarly engaged—the goods so carried consisting in a great part of borax, spices, and other "fragrant" substances, including asafœtida,—some of the people so fair that a rosy tint was on their faces. As we descended into the deep and narrow valley the snowy range, at first so prominent an object, became lost to view, precipices shut us in on either side, trees of great size rising from ledges or projecting from crevices. The Rungeet rushed as a large green-coloured stream along its rugged bed, at short intervals curling in white foam as it eddied around rocks or leaped in cascades over ledges; at a short distance from where we now were it joins the Rungnoo, the united stream so formed being the Teesta, which finally discharges itself into the Brahmapootra. Crossing the Rungeet by what seemed a very frail and unsteady bridge of cane,[1] we arrived in Sikkim, the span of the construction by which we did so being two hundred feet, the roaring torrent rushing beneath us. Such was the character of one part of the sphere in which in 1861 military operations had to be conducted against that region, including the transport of guns and supplies.

The return journey from Darjeeling was in some respects little less unpleasant than that to it had been. Arrived at Raneegunge, it became necessary to proceed towards the station of Hazarabagh, and for that purpose to take "garry" along some part of the Grand Trunk Road, by which in 1859 I had marched with the 10th Foot when *en route* for England. In the course of that journey crowds of pilgrims were encountered, each bearing upon his forehead the distinctive mark of the Hindoo sect to which he belonged, and carrying the pilgrim's gourd so familiar to us in mediæval pictures; all were devout in aspect and manner; some performing penance by crawling on hands and knees—a mode of progression by which the distance daily got over by them was said to be about one mile. And yet the majority of them had come from Ajudiah (Fyzabad), and were on their way to Juggurnath.

Two days thereafter I traversed a flight of locusts. Seen from a distance the mass looked somewhat like a snow shower in a clear sunshiny day, the apparent breadth of the flight over a mile, its length six or eight; the road and bare soil on either side completely covered by those that had fallen or alighted; the sound made by those still on the wing distinct and rustling. The conditions alluded to in this and the preceding paragraph illustrate those which existed while railways were in their early stages.

The arrival of my beloved wife on December 13 was an event to be chronicled, though for the time being a boarding-house was the substitute for the *home* to which I could take her. Like so many other ladies similarly situated, she had to place her children at school as best

[1] Something like its counterpart exists at Carrick-a-reed, near the Giant's Causeway, Ireland.

she could, and then take leave of them to join her husband in India. The necessity of so parting with one's children is one of the greatest drawbacks of service in India, or indeed anywhere in the tropics; it is lamented by all who are affected by it, and by none more than by ourselves. And yet it is unavoidable. Various instances illustrative of unsatisfactory results arising out of this necessity occur to the mind of most men of experience, not the least being that sons and daughters are thrown more or less at haphazard upon those whose method and manner of training is destined to determine the style of their own lives and the relations in which they are to stand with their parents.

The somewhat sudden death of Lord Elgin, while on tour, was followed by very general expression of sympathy; among those who had been associated with him in China, and so had opportunities of estimating his amiable and upright character, the sentiment was one of regret and esteem. But in India, as elsewhere—*le Roi est mort; Vive le Roi.* Sir John Lawrence arrived from England ere many weeks were over; was received by a guard of honor; duly sworn in, and matters official proceeded in their ordinary course.

For the first time, and as an experiment, an Agricultural Exhibition was organized and took place. The variety of animals brought from all parts of British India was great; so was that of native contributors and visitors; but there was reason to believe that lively interest on the part of the latter was sadly lacking; they thought of the entire proceeding in the light of a mere *tomashah*, or "hubbub," and nothing more.

In the further north,—namely, on the Sittana frontier,—the "rising" among some tribes of that region had just been suppressed; that favourable end attained in part by means of a military expedition, in part by persuasion, otherwise diplomacy.

Experience had long taught residents in Lower Bengal that the period of early spring is that when cholera is most to be dreaded, alike in respect to the suddenness of its attack and its fatality. The 55th Regiment, recently arrived and temporarily encamped at Raneegunge, became somewhat severely attacked by that scourge. Various instances of sudden death occurred from the same cause among old Calcutta residents, and the health of others began to droop; among them my wife.

Soon after the direct government of India had been assumed by the Crown, a Royal Commission was appointed to inquire into sanitary questions relating chiefly to the British troops in that dependency, and also to the native population, whether in cities, villages, or rural districts; their deliberations were necessarily protracted. In due course their report was published, and now the new Governor-General issued the necessary orders for the appointment, in Calcutta, of a Commission to give effect to their recommendations, familiarly referred to as the Thirty-nine Articles, that being their number. On that Commission I was appointed to serve.[1] It began its labours with enthusiasm, in the belief that by measures to be recommended by it the havoc by sickness and death to which our troops had been subject during the long period of our hold on India were to be materially lessened, their condition generally improved. At this date the number of soldiers required to fill the vacancies so caused amounted to 240 per week, and this we hoped to reduce considerably.

Among the Wahabees[2] of India there existed wide-spread spirit of disaffection, Patna and Dacca being two important centres of its propagation. From Europe came news of war between Denmark on the one hand, Austria and Prussia on the other; the combined armies being in occupation of Schleswig. That America had claimed from England indemnity for losses inflicted by the *Alabama*[3] on the plea that as "290" she was built in a British dockyard. The request of the Pekin Government for British officers to act against the Taipings being acceded to, the list of those so "lent" included the name of Major C. G. Gordon, R.E., whose remarkable career had thus its starting point. From New Zealand came, unhappily, news of misfortune to the regiment recently dispatched from Calcutta to take part against the Maoris.

On the invitation of a friend[4] we proceeded to his indigo factory, and so had an opportunity of obtaining some interesting particulars with regard to that industry, the actual origin of which in India, seems to have been due to civil servants of the East India Company. South America is the region to which the growth and manufacture of the plant and dye originally pertained. When introduced into India, the cultivators grew it simply at the request of the civilian in his particular district, and for the profit of the latter; after a time overseers were employed, but as in those days the presence of "interlopers" was discouraged by the local government, the class of persons employed was not such as to exert upon the natives that moral influence which would have been beneficial as it was desirable. This state of things after a time gave place to a better; the presence of adventurers, as

[1] Receiving a monthly allowance of 300 Rs.

[2] Named after Mahomed ibn Abd-el Wahab, born 1691; a puritanical sect of Mahomedans.

[3] Subsequently destroyed by the *Kerseage*, off Cherbourg.

[4] Mr. Eddis, of Hazalabut.

all who belonged not to the Indian service were called, had to be recognised, and so the indigo industry fell into the hands of men belonging to the middle class of British society. Then came what has ever since been looked upon as class legislation, the effect of which is considered to have been friction and disaccord between cultivators and planters.

One of the most severe hurricanes recorded in this part of India occurred on the night of October 7; the devastation caused by it on land, at sea, and in the river Hooghly, being great and extensive. Off Calcutta ships were driven from their moorings and wrecked; in some instances in tiers. So high did the storm-wave rise that the river overflowed the high embankment, carrying with it one or two vessels, one of which was left stranded near the Botanic Gardens; many houses were damaged, some completely destroyed; trees in all directions were prostrated, among them the once famous "duelling tree," under the shade of which in early morning "meetings" took place in days not long past, and "honour" was satisfied—at the distance of twelve paces.

Regarding hurricanes, the first of which definite record is available swept over Calcutta in 1737. An extremely violent one happened in 1821, on which occasion the storm-wave covered Saugor Island, destroying immense numbers of people, cattle, and wild animals. Another took place in 1842, then in 1851, and now in 1864, indicating something like a cycle, varying from eleven to thirteen years between their occurrence.

The significance of some among the public events alluded to in the preceding notes transpired in years subsequent to their actual occurrence; the following brief summary relating to the chief performers in that drama is accordingly given here. From the death of Dost Mahomed,[1] in June, 1863, till September, 1868, his third son, Sheer Ali Khan, who, with the sanction of the Government of India, succeeded him on the throne of Affghanistan, passed through a very stormy time. His two elder brothers, Afzul and Azim, and his nephew, Abdur Rahman (the present ruler), were in revolt against him. His

[1] At the time of his death sixteen sons of Dost Mahomed (Mahomed Akbar and Ghulam Hyder, the two heirs-designate in succession, died before their father) were alive, of whom the following are named in relation to the events above alluded to, namely: (1) Mahomed Afzul Khan; (2) Mahomed Azim Khan: these by a wife not of Royal blood. (3) Sheer Ali Khan; (4) Mahomed Amir Khan; (5) Mahomed Sharif Khan: these by a favourite Popalzai wife. (6) Wali Mahomed Khan; (7) Faiz Mahomed Khan: these by a third wife. Afzul Khan had a son Abdur Raman Khan, the present Amir of Affghanistan, and Sheer Ali had five sons —Ali Khan, Yakub Khan, Ibrahim Khan, Ayub Khan, and Abdul Jan.

favourite son and heir-apparent, Ali Khan, was killed in action in 1865. In 1866 he was defeated near Ghazni by Abdar Rahman, who released his father, Afzul, from prison, into which he had been cast by Sheer Ali, led him in triumph to Cabul, and proclaimed him Amir of Affghanistan. Afzul at once wrote to the Government of India, expressing a hope that as such the friendship of the British would be extended to him. He was informed in reply that the Government of Sir John Lawrence recognised him only as Ruler of Cabul; that as Sheer Ali held Kandahar and Herat, existing engagements with the latter could not be broken off. Afzul and Azim thereupon directed the Waziri chiefs in attendance at Court, together with the envoy, who had come from Swat to pay respects to the new Amir, to set on foot a holy war against the English, while an emissary was sent on a secret mission to Russia. In 1867 Sheer Ali was again defeated near Khelat-i-Ghilsie, and lost Kandahar. On this fact being communicated to the Government of India, Afzul Khan was in his turn recognised as Amir of Cabul and Kandahar, Sir John Lawrence at the same time informing him that the British Government intended to maintain a strict neutrality between the contending parties in Affghanistan. This policy on the part of the Governor-General was at the time called, often in sarcastic terms, "masterly inactivity."[1] Under the circumstances of the time, such public opinion as found expression in Calcutta approved of the policy in question. But neither to Afzul nor Azim was that policy satisfactory. They sent a copy of the letter conveying the decision of Sir John Lawrence to the Russian Governor of Tashkend, who was informed by Afzul that he had no confidence in the "Lord Sahib's" fine professions of friendship; that he was disgusted with the British Government for the ingratitude and ill-treatment shown towards his brother Azim, who, it was asserted, had encouraged his father, Dost Mahomed Khan, not to disturb the Peshawurfrontier during the Mutiny.

[1] See *Forty-one Years in India*, by Lord Roberts, vol. ii., pp. 41–43.

CHAPTER XXIV

1865-1868. *CALCUTTA. PORTSMOUTH*

Ahmed oola Khan—Seeta Khoond—Experimental sanatorium—Parisnath—India in Greece—Bhootan—Electric telegraph—Sickly season—My illness—Ootacamund—Todas—Climatic notes—Bangalore—Fort—Health unrestored—Benares—Temples—Sitala—Sarnath—Infants' grave—Sanitary Commission ceased—Again on sick leave—Cinchona Inquiry—A railway journey—Bank failure—Events—The Buffs arrive—Sanitary works—Expedition to Abyssinia—The struggle for existence—The *Jumna*—The *Euphrates*—Hurricane—Departure—Trincomalee—Aden—Suez—Docks "created"—Egyptian troops—Grand Shaloof—Gardens—Freshwater Canal—Ancient baths—Moses' Wells—Pyramids of Ghizeh—Sphynx—Temple—Desert cold—Portsmouth.

VISITING Patna in the course of duty, I was present in the court of the magistrate while Ahmed oola Khan, the suspected originator of the Sittana rebellion, was undergoing preliminary examination on a charge of sedition. For thirty years he had been suspected; yet he held a high position under the Indian Government, at one time as a member of the Board of Instruction, then a member of the Municipal Commission, and lastly a Commissioner of the Income Tax. During the Mutiny the Local Commissioner had reason to doubt his fidelity, and reported to Government the grounds upon which his suspicions were founded, the only result as stated at the time being censure for having given expression to them.

An official visit to Monghyr gave me the opportunity of driving to Seeta Khoond, in the near vicinity of that place. The spring so named has a temperature of 180° F., and is one of several in this part of India; but chiefly interesting in that the high priest of the temple connected therewith repeated to us its legendary association with the story of Rama and Seeta,[1] in terms very similar to what a few days before I had read in a compressed edition of the *Ramayana*. Here then is the record transmitted traditionally through many

[1] Referred to B.C. 1400—about.

generations of a more or less mythical event, the date of which considerably preceded that of Homer.

As an experiment, barracks for a small number of British soldiers were erected on the summit of Parisnath, in the hope that its elevation of 4,530 feet above sea level might exert a favourable influence on their health. A narrow pathway had recently been cut through the forest[1] by which the hill is covered. Ascending by it we traverse several precipitous ridges, between which deep and thickly wooded valleys intervene. Voices of many birds are heard as we proceed; among them the crow of jungle cock and scream of the coel;[2] black squirrels and lungoors dash rapidly from branch to branch, downwards into the forest beneath us.

Parisnath is the Sinai of the Jains.[3] On its summit are twenty-two temples pertaining to that sect, the largest consecrated to their chief deity, Parisnath, whence the name of the hill. Numerous pilgrims visit the shrines, more especially in the month of *Poos*, or November.

There are those who believe—with what measure of authority I know not—that an immigrant tribe from the vicinity of the hill in question having settled in ancient Greece, transferred the name of their sacred mountain to "Parnassus."[4] The legend may be on a par with that in accordance with which the name of Sevastopol is made to signify "The Place of Śiva."

For some time past unpleasantness had been breeding with regard to Bhootan; endeavours were made to come to a peaceful understanding with the chiefs concerned, but these having ended in failure, the dispatch thither of a military expedition was resolved on.[5] In the early part of the cold season a combined force of British and native troops was equipped, and proceeded on service to that territory, a chief reason for sending white troops being a report that considerable misconduct on the part of sepoys at Dewangiri had reached the authorities, the circumstance furnishing a suggestive commentary on action recently taken to materially increase the native army.

On March 4 an event occurred which, in its importance to India, should be mentioned: the first direct telegraphic message from Lon-

[1] Chiefly of Sâl. *Vateria*, interspersed with Bauhinia.

[2] *Eudynemus*.

[3] The Jain sect deny the divine origin and infallibility of the Vedas. It dates from the sixth or seventh century A.D.; culminated in the eleventh, and declined in the twelfth.

[4] See *India in Greece*, by Pocock.

[5] Under command of Sir Henry Tombs.

don was delivered in Calcutta, it having taken three days to reach its destination. As a painful coincidence, Colonel Stewart, to whom the public are indebted for the completion of that undertaking, died just as the work had been finished. Hitherto the telegrams received came through several lines.

The hot season this year set in unusually early; it was severe and protracted, sickness and death making havoc among all classes of foreigners, more especially our soldiers. Medical officers, like others, were prostrated in great numbers, the result being that those who remained fit for duty had much extra work thrown upon them. The establishment in India being so closely kept down so as to meet only ordinary requirements, it is inadequate when the demands become considerable, whether on account of epidemic or field service.

In July duty took me to Hazarabagh. The rains were on, the roads soft, and in many places submerged. On my return journey, detention for several hours at night in dense jungle was occasioned by the Siranee River being in flood, and impassable. The result of that exposure was a severe attack of illness, by which for two months I was prostrated and altogether incapacitated for work. Having hitherto avoided making an application for privilege leave, I now submitted such a request, but with the unlooked-for result that it met with a refusal—the fact that it did so illustrating the attitude of departmental seniors towards their juniors in those days. With reluctance I felt under the necessity of applying for a medical certificate, on which, as a matter of course, I obtained leave of absence.

At the time referred to, the Neilgherry hills were more get-at-able from Calcutta than were the Himalayahs; our[1] means of transit, by steamer to Madras, train thence to Coimbatore, bullock bandy or cart to Metapollium, hammock or pony to Ootacamund. The ascent of the ghat presents a succession of strikingly beautiful views, precipitous cliffs, mountain ascents clothed by dense forest, deep valley and shola thickly wooded, rushing streams and small cascades. Arrived at Coonoor, 6,000 feet above sea level, the temperature becomes mild; hedges chiefly composed of geraniums and roses; fruit trees, orchards, and gardens, all in full bearing, meet the eye. In front of us a succession of grass-covered "downs" appear, their general aspect completely different from that presented by Himalayan sanatoria. In due time "Ooty" is reached, but a severe attack of ague while riding up the ghat rendered the latter part of the journey the reverse of pleasant.

In the immediate vicinity of this place, and scattered about among

[1] My wife and Miss Dickson with me.

the higher points of the hills, the aboriginal tribe of Todas have their settlements, consisting of their peculiar-shaped huts, crowded together as if for mutual defence. Of their original history, not a trace, not even tradition remains; but other native hill races look upon them as the original owners of the soil, and pay them in its produce, for the Todas neither cultivate nor perform manual labour of any other kind, except that certain members of each village community have the duties assigned to them of milking their kine, and preparing their ghee, or clarified butter. They practice polyandry.[1] Infanticide was frequent among them until suppressed under the action of Government.

Very charming as a health resort was "the Southern Sanatorium" found to be. Temperature moderate in degree and range, relatively cooler than that of England in summer, warmer in winter, it possesses greater advantages in these respects than corresponding places in the Himalayan range. Thus, the mean shade temperature is—in January, 53° F.; February, 56°; March, 62°; April, 63°; May, 62°; June, 60°; July, 58°; August, 58°; September, 56°; October, 58°; November, 56°; December, 53°. Annual rainfall, 48 inches; rainy days, 19; with occasional showers, 81; cloudy, 28; clear and fine, 238 = 365. In the month of January, with a shade temperature of 53° F., that in the sun was 118° F.

A visit to Bangalore presented several items of interest. One was the peculiar method by which native workmen split off flakes of the sienite rock that there abounds; the process comprising the application of long-continued heat to the surface, after which the use of chisel, hammer, and percussion so applied as to produce the effect desired. A good deal of comment was the outcome of a visit paid to a "condemned" barrack building, in which was accommodated the band of an infantry regiment—the walls of the edifice in so tumble-down a condition that practice was prohibited lest the vibration caused by the musical instruments should shake the remainder to pieces.

The old fort well repaid a visit to it. In 1791 it was captured by the forces under Lord Cornwallis, the breaches then effected being still traceable by the soft material with which they were filled up, while the broad deep ditch around the fortress remains to a great extent in its original condition. Among the dungeons in which Tippoo Sultan was wont to imprison his captives that of Sir David Baird was indicated to us; as also the wheel to which the captives were put for the double purpose of raising water for palace use, and amusing thereby the ladies of the zenana.

[1] So do some of the tribes in the Himalayahs. So did the ancient Spartans.

With health unrestored, but rather deteriorated, duty had to be resumed. An important item connected therewith was the inspection of ships arriving with troops, or engaged for the conveyance of others homewards, considerable exposure and fatigue necessarily undergone in its performance. That risk to life was run in persisting to remain at my post, instead of leaving India, was sufficiently clear to myself; but circumstances determined me to run that risk.

Early in 1866 duty[1] took me to Benares. An excursion through the narrow streets and to the shrines within that ancient city was interesting, as a similar visit had been on a previous occasion. The aspect of those streets, the style of dress of the people, their modes of buying and selling, their religious observances, at the present day unchanged since a date six centuries B.C., when, as history records, Kasi was a flourishing city. The temple of Bisheshwar, "the poison god"—a personification of Siva, the special deity of Benares, the object of pilgrimage to thousands of Hindoos—has within it the shrine in the shape of a black stone, ever kept wet by Ganges water, before which their special acts of devotion are performed. The minarets and tapering summit of the temple still resplendent with gold gilding, with which they were last decorated at the expense of Runjeet Singh, of the Punjab. In close vicinity is the Gyan Kup, or "Well of Knowledge," in which Siva is believed by her worshippers to dwell, but from which arises offensive odours from decomposing floral offerings. In the "golden temple" itself is a figure representing the Kutwal, or judicial officer of Bisheshwar, in his hand a club, at his feet two dogs of stone—Orion and Canes venatici.

Numerous other temples stand in the near vicinity of this the largest and most important of all. Of these, one of small dimensions is sacred to Sanichar, otherwise Saturn, the face of the deity being of a blue or leaden hue. A second is dedicated to the goddess Anpoorna, of whom it is related that when Benares was first established as a city, a famine having occurred she supplied grain, Gunga, or the river Ganges, giving water, and so the people were fed; the custom then established of giving a daily allowance of grain and water being still continued, as witnesssed by ourselves. A third temple visited was dedicated to the Sun. Within it is a painting in which the great luminary is represented in a chariot drawn by seven horses, clearly the prototype of Phœbus and his car. A fourth, dedicated to Sukreshwar, or Venus, is much frequented by women ambitious to become mothers of handsome sons. To the courtesy and kindness of Dr. J. A. Dunbar, whose historical

[1] A severe epidemic of cholera among the British troops.

knowledge of these and other places visited was great, I was indebted for a most pleasant and interesting excursion.

Close to the river edge stood a temple to Sitala, goddess of small-pox, the deity being a stone much worn; before it three female devotees made poojah in hopes of thereby obtaining immunity against or cure of the disease for themselves and relations—a practice adopted also and in like manner by the Chinese. Nangrah, or the temple of the seven planets, after which are named the days of the week, was old and dilapidated, not having been "restored" from the time of the Mahomedan conquest, A.D. 1017, when, like many others, it was much injured. A small, square-shaped tank, the Nand Kunka, is said to be the point of junction between the Ganges, Jumna, and "sacred" Suruswattee; but inasmuch as a similar union is assigned to Prague, *i.e.* Allahabad, tradition seems to be at fault somewhere. Hindoos believe that those who bathe in that Pool of Siloam at Benares attain immortality. An object of different kind visited by us was the Man Mundee, or old observatory erected by Rajah Jey Singh, A.D. 1693, at the same time as that at Delhi, and, like it, now ruined. On the way to cantonments is the house in which dwelt Warren Hastings, 1773–1781; at a little distance that in which, in 1799, Mr. Davis repelled single-handed the attack by followers of Wazir Ali,[1] after the latter had been deposed from the throne of Oude by Sir John Shore, at that time Governor-General.

At a distance of a few miles, on a plain anciently known as the Deer Park, are the ruins of Sarnath, a city said to date from the fourth century B.C., to have been the place where Sakya Muni first publicly preached the doctrines of Buddhism, and to have been destroyed by fire in the seventh century A.D. On a mound formed by ruins stood a pillar like that of the Birs Nimroud. A second pillar had on it carvings and scrolls peculiar to the Buddhists, whose style of architecture was subsequently adopted by the Hindoos, to be reproduced in their temples.

A sad and to me affecting visit was to the grave of my dear infant. As I wrote at the time of his deplored death, so now, many years thereafter, the impression of the loved child comes vividly upon me.[2]

The Sanitary Commission already mentioned ceased to exist, and a Commissioner appointed to take over the duties it had performed. Great were the expectation of benefits to come, in respect to public health and decrease of mortality which were to result from the labours

[1] The son of Mr. Davis became Governor of Hong-Kong, and author of an extremely interesting history of China.

[2] St. Luke xviii. 16.

of our Commission; great also the individual confidence of members in the realization of such hopes. In the literary inquiries connected with my position on that Commission material was gathered for a work on Army Hygiene, then published by me.

As the hot season advanced, my health, already much impaired, suffered more severely than it had done while the heat of climate remained somewhat moderate. Privilege leave was therefore applied, and, after some delay, obtained. I accordingly made my way, for the second time, to Madras and Ootacamund, accompanied by my dear wife. Almost from the day of arrival my health improved; a series of excursions, rides, and walks adding to beneficial influence of the climate of that favourite place.

I had lately been appointed member of a Committee to examine and report upon the relative medicinal values of the various alkaloids obtained from cinchona. My attention thus drawn to the cultivation of the plant or tree, I visited the extensive plantation which then existed in the neighbouring hills, taking advantage to observe the various methods of cultivation adopted with a view to increasing to the utmost the deposit of quinine. But impressions were by no means enthusiastic in regard to the probable pecuniary success of this industry, or the permanent reliance of medical men upon its special alkaloid, the use of which had already become considerably less than it was a few years ago.

As the period of my leave drew to its close, and I began my return journey, some of the experiences attending upon Indian travelling in the hot season befell me. In the midst of storm and heavy rain, at 2 a.m., I arrived at Coimbatore, then the railway terminus, got into one of the carriages drawn up at the platform and there made myself at home till 4.45 a.m., at which hour the train started. As the day advanced, so did the strength of hot wind; the sky was lurid with dust, while I, suffering severe pain, could neither recline nor sit with anything approaching comfort. It was close upon midnight when I reached the hotel at Madras, at which I had arranged to alight.

With next morning came the newspapers of the day, containing the very unwelcome intelligence that the Agra Bank had suspended payment. Like many others in India, such small savings as I had been able to effect were deposited in that concern; so now, my health impaired, the rainy season before me, my wife left behind, my money store for the time being in a precarious position, circumstances wore an aspect by no means bright.

Returning to duty at Calcutta, the attention of public authorities was found to be occupied by the condition of matters in India, and that existing elsewhere, the latter having indirect relation to the country itself. From several places on the coast line, more especially Orissa, came sad reports of famine and of destructive pestilence, all of which in due time extended to inland districts, even to the upper provinces of Hindostan. To mitigate and relieve the suffering thus occasioned, Sir John Lawrence initiated a variety of measures which were destined in subsequent years to be systematized, and so meet the occurrence of similar occurrences throughout the country. Beyond our frontier, Sheer Ali, whose accession at Cabul had but lately been recognised, was strengthening his position. Russia engaged in subjugating Bokhara. In America there was talk about a Fenian invasion of Canada, almost immediately followed by the collapse of such a plan, if indeed it ever assumed shape. In Europe the unparalleled successes of "the seven days' war"; the surrender by Austria of Venetia to Italy. Another event of importance was the laying of the Atlantic Telegraph Cable, a scientific triumph in some respects more important than the military occurrences just alluded to.

Early in the cold season, the arrival of the *Nile*, having on board the Headquarters of the Buffs, gave me an opportunity of seeing once again my first regiment with which, twenty-one years ago, I sailed from the place where we now are for England. In the interval one or more generations, in a regimental sense, had come and gone; so that to "my first love" I was a stranger; officers and men unknown to me, I unknown to them.

In pursuance of suggestions by the late Sanitary Commission, a series of camp grounds were selected, to which in times of cholera troops might conditionally be sent. At military stations, barracks were to be erected in accordance with plans drawn out by the same body. In these respects, impaired as health was, inspection of stations, added to ordinary official routine, became an arduous duty.

Arrangements had to be made with reference to an expedition about to be dispatched against the King of Abyssinia. In calculating the probable requirements for which preparations had to be made, casualties by climate were looked upon as likely to exceed those in battle; supplies on a large scale were accordingly provided.

From bed to duty, from duty to bed: such in brief was the manner in which were passed the three last months in Calcutta. In one respect Fortune "smiled,"—namely, that hospitality of a friend [1] supplied all that need, or even luxury, required. The presence, moreover, of my

[1] George Dickson.

wife was a solace to me, though the condition of illness to which I was reduced must have been the cause of much anxiety to her.

The first of the new transport ships to arrive was the *Jumna*. Being sighted from Saugor at the end of September, a party of officials, of which I was one, was speedily on board the river steamer *Koladyne*, and away towards Diamond Harbour. The "trooper" soon loomed high on the horizon, her general shape unusual, and being painted white, her aspect differed from that of ships familiar to us. Coming to anchor at the last-named place, the 7th Dragoon Guards and 2nd Battalion Rifle Brigade were within a few days thereafter conveyed on board, and away the ship steamed towards Suez.

At the end of October the second of the Indian transports, the *Euphrates*, arrived at Calcutta, having on board the 2nd Battalion 60th Rifles, with which, six years ago, I had come down the Peiho from Tientsin to Taku, when that battalion and myself were homeward bound from China.

November was ushered in by the occurrence of a hurricane of extreme violence, an example of the most severe of those meteors to which this part of India is at intervals liable, the damage to shipping and on shore being a counterpart of what has already been related regarding another cyclone. On this occasion the *Euphrates* was forced ashore at Diamond Harbour, where, during several hours, she remained in a perilous position, but fortunately without damage, so that as the storm abated she was restored to her anchorage. In due course the ship arrived off Prinsep's Ghat, the first of her kind to come up the river so far. There the troops on board were landed, the hull carefully examined by divers, and being declared to be uninjured, preparations were made for the embarkation of the troops proceeding by her to England.

The 27th, or Enniskillen Regiment, having embarked, I went on board, together with my wife, on November 13. On the following day enjoyed the often-talked-of, long-hoped-for gratification of viewing Calcutta from over the stern of a homeward-bound vessel, at the same time conscious of a protecting Providence to whom, under a series of trying and otherwise unpleasant circumstances, my life had been so far prolonged, and I enabled to meet the necessities of those dependent upon me.

In due time we entered the remarkably beautiful harbour of Trincomalee. Dotted with numerous islands, all thickly covered with rich vegetation, the background filled up with a series of low forest-clad hills, the general scene—tropical in character—could scarcely be exceeded in loveliness. But the hot, damp atmosphere, as we landed and drove through the town of the same name, was such that we experienced no desire to prolong our stay.

Arrived at Aden, orders awaited the Commander to proceed at once to Suez, which he accordingly did; but the circumstance caused a good deal of excitement in the gallant Enniskillings, among whom the wish was father to the belief that they were *sure* to be landed and sent to Abyssinia.

Several vessels connected with the Abyssinian expedition were anchored in the Gulf of Suez as the *Euphrates* entered it. The canal across the isthmus had recently been begun, the troops arriving at either end having still to be conveyed by rail and then re-embarked. Here we speedily learned by telegraph that our corresponding transport from Alexandria had met with a mishap so serious in kind that delay of not less than three weeks was inevitable before we could proceed.

Extensive docks were then in progress near to our anchorage. They were formed from material raised from the sea-bed by dredgers and other mechanical means; the masonry supplied from the neighbouring Akaba range of hills. It was an unpleasant sight, as it was suggestive, to see in the ooze so raised, considerable numbers of human bones, confirming to some degree the evil repute assigned to Suez boatmen, chiefly Greeks and Italians.

A considerable number of Egyptian troops were encamped on the heights behind the city. The men, strong and active in appearance, had, it was said, been slaves, captured by the Bedouins in the Soudan and sold to agents of the Viceroy; they were dressed *à la Zouaves*, and armed with swords and matchlocks.

A trip being organized for the purpose, we proceeded by boat drawn by a couple of mules along the Freshwater canal; at the end of about five miles arriving at Little Shaloof, where arrangements were in progress so that by means of locks a junction between the two waterways should take place. From there we proceeded as before, some six miles more, to Grand Shaloof, where it was said the works in progress could be best examined. At that place the depth of the channel in course of excavation was 30 feet, the breadth 150. Crowds of workmen, including French, Italian, Maltese, and Greeks, were employed as navvies, the soil being carried up the sides by small rails, and deposited on either side to form embankments. In the successive layers of gravel, sand, and clay in which the workmen were engaged, organic remains existed in considerable abundance; among them oyster shells, encrinites, bones assigned to mastodon, and gigantic teeth of the carcharodon. The canal is in working order from Port

Said to Ismaliah, where, in Lake Timsah, it is joined by the ancient canal from Bulak.

At Shaloof a considerable village has sprung up in the midst of the desert; the houses consist of wooden huts, the population being employés on the canal. Around some of those huts little gardens had been made, peas, beans, greens, asparagus, artichokes, jerusalem artichokes, and spinach being among the vegetables grown in them; the plants of larger growth within and surrounding them in the form of incipient hedges included palma Christi, Eschynomene (or jait), thuja, and willow.

The Freshwater Canal, by which we returned to Suez, had an average depth of 5 to 6 feet, a breadth of 40 to 50. Its water, though originally no doubt *sweet* and fresh, was now brackish, but on that account not unsuited to the nourishment of particular kinds of plants, as along its sides grew in abundance tamarisk, reed grass, rushes, and bulrushes. A good deal of traffic was in progress along it; but otherwise the region on either side was desert, destitute of man, house, or tree, the only living things to be seen being a vulture in the distance, and in close vicinity a drymoica or reed warbler of some kind. According to history the portion of this canal which extends from Lake Timsah to Bulak was made under Sesostris;[1] a continuation of it extended to Suez,—namely, that by which we travelled. The original channel has several times fallen into decay, and been again repaired, the last occasion on which it was so being under Mehemet Ali.

The population of Suez was said to comprise the scourings of all nations. The place itself is not without points of historical interest. It is considered to occupy the site, or very near the site, of Pihahiroth, or simply Hira, Kolsim, and Arsinoe, the latter founded by Ptolemy Philadelphus.[2] At a short distance from its north-east gate is a mound on which stands a villa for the use of the Viceroy; at the base of that mound is a thick layer of asphalte,[3] believed to indicate the site of ancient baths. The modern town contains the house, now a telegraph office, in which Napoleon the First once had his headquarters. Discretion induced us, when visiting the town of evil repute, to go in sufficiently large party to hold our own if necessary.

An excursion to Ayûn Musa, or Moses' Wells, occupied pleasantly an entire day. Proceeding by steam launch to Quarantine Harbour, we there found mules and ponies, sent on the previous day. So mounted, we scampered over the five or six miles of desert that

[1] B.C. 1400–1200.

[2] B.C. 286–247.

[3] Believed to have been brought from Babylon.

separated that place from the objects of our trip. As we neared the wells, groves of date and other palms became more and more distinct; the groves were seen to surround each of the twelve wells that form the group, each moreover to be surrounded by walls, the garden so enclosed well irrigated from its particular well, and yielding produce abundantly. The largest well of the series is that to which tradition assigns the halting-place of the Israelites on the third day of their wandering in the wilderness of Etham after crossing "the Sea of Reeds," in the near vicinity of what is now Lake Timsah.[1] As then, so at the present time, the water of Marah is "bitter," otherwise brackish and undrinkable, though used for purposes of irrigation; that of the well in question gushed from the earth abundantly, bubbling as it did so from several apertures. From it we went on to examine the other springs that make up the group, on our way noting the style of tree and under vegetation, and searching, as we did unsuccessfully, for the "quails" (*Pterocles*, or sand-grouse) mentioned with reference to the temporary halt at this place made by the Israelites; three hours were so spent. On returning to the spring whence we had started, we found it partly empty; it thus told its own story—that it was tidal in character. The surrounding gardens, amply irrigated as they were from this well, yielded abundant crops of vegetables, including spinach, radishes, chives, onions, and tomatoes. Among the trees within the same enclosure were date, tamarisk, pomegranate, rose, fig, parkinsonia, cirrus, lawsonia (the mendhee or hennah of India), myrtle, and mulberry. Along the sides of the watercourses or irrigation channels a rich green carpet of digitaria (or dhoop grass of India) grew. We saw no such tree as had the property of rendering brackish water palatable to the taste; not even the moringa aptera, the pods of which, when masticated, are credited with that of rendering such water "sweet to the palate." On our return on board, we referred to Josephus,[2] and from his account have no doubt that Moses recognised the wells which now bear his name as in their nature tidal.

A very delightful excursion was that to Cairo, performed by rail across the desert. From that most oriental city we drove to the Nile, near to the island of Rodda; crossed the river by boat, passing close to the Nilometer while we were in transit; landed at Ghizeh; mounted donkeys; thence continued our journey over seven miles of road, consisting of a dilapidated raised pathway through alluvial fields and swamps dotted thickly with aquatic birds. Thus did we reach the

[1] Numbers xxxiii. 8; Exodus xv. 25. See also *The Bible ana Modern Discovery*, p. 89.

[2] *Antiquities of the Jews*, Book III. chap. i. sec. 2.

famous and very remarkable Pyramids of Ghizeh. The largest of these, namely, that of Cheops—B.C. 2400 about—was the special object of our excursion. In ascending one of its sides we had the aid of powerful Arabs, whose demonstrative methods of assistance were by no means appreciated by the ladies of our party. The massive stones that formed the stair-like ascent of this most ancient monument in the world had a thickness ranging from two to three feet; they consisted of two kinds, the one set of nummulite, the other of chalky clay, but the coating and outer layer that in ancient times completely covered them has long ceased to exist. The summit is flat; the view from it extensive: it includes Cairo, the Libyan hills, pyramids of Sakkara and of Dashur, the position of "the Battle of the Pyramids," the two smaller pyramids of Cephrenes and Mycerenes respectively, the Sphynx, and numerous tombs. On our left were the pits in which it is believed the mortar for the larger pyramid was mixed; the small mud pyramid, supposed to be that of Cheops' daughter; then in the distance heaps composed of materials raised from pillaged tombs.

The descent proved more difficult than the ascent. After a short rest we proceeded to explore the interior of the huge pile. From the entrance we descended, by a narrow passage not more than four feet in height, a distance of 106 feet, then ascended by another passage, at an angle of 27°, to "the Queen's Chamber." Returning to the point from which branches upward the great gallery, we ascended by it to "the King's Chamber," passing in our progress through the supposed position of four ancient portcullises. Returning to, and glad to be in, the open air, we passed on to Campbell's Tomb,[1] in which, at a depth of sixty feet from the surface, lies exposed the sarcophagus of porphyry described in books of travel. Thence to the Sphynx, now mutilated, yet whose intensely grave, placid expression struck us with awe, as it has affected other travellers who have visited it during the thousands of years included in its history.

Near the Sphynx is a temple excavated in the solid rock. Huge blocks, some seventeen feet long, of red granite are in it so arranged as to form passages and doorways; others of alabaster, of scarcely smaller dimensions, being interspersed among them. So far, information is wanting with regard to the history of this temple; but to us it is no less wonderful in its way than any of the other objects and buildings we visited.

At last the time came for the troops on board the *Euphrates* to resume their homeward voyage. It was with regret that we took leave of Captain Dunn and officers, and proceeded to the train by which the

[1] Referred to the period of the XXVIth Dynasty, B.C. 666–528.

transit across the desert was to be made. It was now late in December; the *sensation* of cold experienced by us during the night of our journey very severe, far beyond what readings of the thermometer indicated.

By afternoon of 28th we were on board the *Crocodile*, and away from Alexandria. On New Year's Day anchored in the Grand Harbour of Malta, in which as companions our transport had British ironclads, and vessels of all sorts belonging to various nationalities. Resuming our voyage on the 3rd, we passed Gibraltar on the 6th; thence homeward the passage was short but boisterous. On the 12th we landed at Portsmouth, our leave-taking very different in kind from that on quitting the *Euphrates*.

CHAPTER XXV

1868-1870. PORTSMOUTH

Duties—Geology—Societies formed—Portland prison—Parkhurst—Garrison prisons Gymnastics—Arrival of 33rd and 101st Regiments—Man of 3rd Light Dragoons —Sale of decorations—Illness—Discharging soldiers—Comments.

APPOINTED to the Southern District,[1] the duties connected with departmental administration were entered upon without delay. Within the garrison of Portsmouth, headquarters of the district, they included work relating to embarking and disembarking troops, in addition to ordinary routine; through the district, inspections ot military establishments and places with which I was already familiar.

In visiting establishments on the Isle of Wight some pleasant excursions were taken in company with a kindred spirit [2] in regard to natural things. With geological map in hand,[3] we walked from point to point comparing the strata as we proceeded with the several illustrative sketches there presented. So also official visits to the Isle of Portland gave opportunity of studying the history presented by its rocks and strata, with regard to its alternating elevations and submergences in geological periods. The operations in progress at Spithead in connection with forts intended to be built there supplied with ample material in different shapes those among us whose tastes led us to take interest in them.

Among our numbers were several men devoted to different branches of natural history; others whose tastes and pursuits were in more purely professional subjects. By means of a happy combination between the two a society [4] was set on foot, a room with fuel and light assigned to its use by the War Office, and an excellent library collected. Papers were read at its meetings, abstracts being published in the London professional journals. So great was the success which attended

[1] Of England. [2] Dr. Maunsell.
[3] *Journal of the Geological Society*, vol. x.
[4] The Army Medical Society.

our efforts that a society of allied kind was established by scientific and professional residents of Portsmouth and its vicinity.

The then governor of Portland convict prison had previously held a similar position at Norfolk Island, to which at that time the worst and most desperate criminals were sent from New South Wales. The men he had there to deal with were the most desperate and reckless of their class; but some of the accounts Mr. Clifton gave regarding his method towards them were most interesting, some even pathetic, the keynote of his system having been, on suitable occasions, to appeal to their human nature. With evident gusto we were invited to enter what he called his museum of implements with which from time to time attempts on his life had been made by convicts under his charge; and very miscellaneous were they as they lay upon their shelves, duly labelled and arranged. Among the convicts were some who had in their day occupied high social position, one of them in particular. Passing them as we did, our gaze was averted as we did so, but it was not in us to withhold from them a thought of pity.

At Parkhurst the "governor" of the convict prison was a lady, the convicts being women. It was the boast of Mrs. Gibson that, in maintaining discipline and administering justice for offences, no barrier of any kind separated her from the offender brought before her, and yet, unlike the experience already mentioned, with the exception of one occasion, violence had never been offered her. "Unless," said she, "I have sufficient moral power to maintain order, my influence would be gone." Her daughter had been carefully tended from infancy to womanhood by a life convict. But among her prisoners were some whose disposition was most desperate; there were others who, when they "felt a fit of passion coming on," made request to their "governor" that, as a favour, she would allow them to "go to the pump," so that by the violent exertion there required of them they might "work it off." A short time previous there had been under her charge as life convict a young lady, the story of whose "crime" and conviction occupied public attention to a more than usual degree, the question of her guilt being no less discussed than were the circumstances under which her confession had been obtained, the reality of that confession, and the relation of "confessors" to the individual on the one hand, and to law on the other.

The periodical inspection of Garrison prisoners came within the ordinary routine of duty. As a matter of information, inquiries on such occasions were directed to the effect, if any, of punishments undergone by soldiers in deterring them from subsequent crime, the usual reply received being that "the same men come here over and over again." Past experience in regiments had been to the same effect in regard to offences, and to a considerable extent also to men coming "on the sick report" to hospital, the numbers of the latter depending greatly upon the kind of duty, parades, drills, and so on, that was about to take place. Regimental surgeons understood all such moves on the part of the men, and for the most part were able to estimate at its approximate value the statements made by individuals.

While visiting a military gymnasium, attention was drawn to performances by the non-commissioned officer in charge, a noted gymnast, some of whose feats on the trapeze and otherwise were remarkable as showing high proficiency in his art. At the time of their performance his appearance indicated advanced phthisis, and within a month thereafter he succumbed to that condition. Other instances more or less similar to his have come under notice, indicating that the ability to perform feats of "strength" and agility is not a constant indication of robust health, although it may be of "knack" acquired by practice.

Duty brought me in contact from time to time with regiments with which on previous occasions I had been associated; for example, the 34th at Azimghur, 35th at Dinapore, 97th at Sooltanpore, and 67th at Tientsin. The arrival of the 33rd from Abyssinia was made an occasion to do honour to the gallant "West Ridings" for its services in that campaign. That of the 101st on its first tour of home service was attended by various incidents, some amusing in their way, showing how new to the men were the conditions in which they found themselves Fortunately for them "comrades" in garrison gave them willing help in landing baggage, carrying coals, filling straw beds, and so on.

Visiting the barracks at Chichester, I learned some particulars with reference to the sequel of the incident connected with a soldier of the 3rd Light Dragoons at Wuzzeerabad in 1853. That regiment now occupied those barracks preparatory to going on foreign service, but so numerous had been the changes during the interval that with difficulty was one man found who remembered it. According to his account the particulars given by the man then alluded to, in regard to his part in the murder on Wandsworth Common, the disposal of watch and chain of his victim, were confirmed by subsequent inquiries. The man himself was condemned to a lunatic asylum, and there he died.

While walking along High Street on one occasion, attention was attracted to two medals exposed for sale in the window of a well-known silversmith of that day. To them was attached a short printed notice relating that they were the identical decorations presented to the two men most distinguished for gallantry in the battle of Waterloo. In default of heirs they had come to be among the contents of an old curiosity shop. They had respectively been bestowed upon Colonel Macdonell and Sergeant Graham, both of the Coldstream Guards, for their defence of Hougomont against the combined forces under Jerome Bonaparte, Foy, and Bâchelu. On subsequent occasions, orders and decorations for the Mutiny campaign were, for lack of heirs, sold by public auction; a commentary on the passing value of such things, highly prized though they are by those on whom, for services rendered, they were conferred in the first instance.

In the spring of 1870 I experienced in person what in many other instances is a sequence of continued attacks of malarious illness, in that they seemed to culminate in one of great severity, even after nearly a year and a half of English climate. To the great care and skill of two army surgeons [1] I owe my recovery—indeed, my life.

Restoration to full activity was slow. Meantime, a duty devolved upon me the nature of which was unpleasant, as it seemed to me invidious. A scheme of Army retrenchment was to be enforced. In accordance therewith reductions in the numbers of men borne on their rolls were ordered to be carried out in regiments in our particular district as in others; the instructions under which officers concerned were obliged to act leaving to them little, if any, discretionary power.

The classes of men to be selected for discharge, and so make room or recruits to be enlisted under the short service system, comprised—(1) the sickly and weak; (2) those of bad character; (3) those who for reasons of their own were desirous of obtaining discharge. It was felt that, of the first, the greater number would be cast adrift, incapable of earning a livelihood, and so be thrown upon parish relief; that by the second, a number of incorrigible characters would be let loose on the public, to prey upon it either by begging or by crime, to be further a burthen to the taxpayer in respect to expenses of prosecution, and of maintenance in prison while undergoing punishment for crimes committed. The third class was composed of those who, having become trained soldiers, inured to discipline, were lost to the service when their individual value was at its greatest. Some of us felt strongly then that such numerical reductions as were deemed necessary, on account of public reasons, might have been carried out by the more gradual and less objectionable method of ceasing to recruit for a few weeks or months.

[1] Leach, 46th Regiment; O'Leary, Royal Artillery.

CHAPTER XXVI

1870. *JULY–SEPTEMBER. FRANCO-PRUSSIAN WAR. SIEGE OF PARIS*

Franco-Prussian War—Appointed to the French—German successes—Arrive in Paris—Rumours—Aspect—Ministry of War—Champ de Mars—Captured as a Prussian spy—Rumours and facts—A disturbed night—Revolution of September 4—Escape of the Empress—Vinoy arrives from Mezières—After the Revolution—The outlook—Arming the masses—Approach of the enemy—*Levée en masse*—Aspect of the city—Versailles "honourably" capitulated—Provisioning—Present and prospective evils—City gates closed—Preparations for the defence—Police in abeyance—Paris encircled—Some ambassadors quit—Conditions within—Arrangements for wounded.

IN the middle of July (1870) the morning papers recorded the incident at Ems, soon to become famous, between Benedetti and the King of Prussia, its effect in Paris a demand for war, and by the populace shouts of "*À Berlin!*" Events rapidly developed; the Powers concerned prepared for war; proffered mediation by England rejected by France. On the 21st of that month war was declared by the King of Prussia; on the 23rd by the Emperor of the French; on August 2 the young Prince Imperial received his *baptême de feu*;[1] war had begun.

A few days thereafter I was warned for service with the French in the capacity of Medical Commissioner, to report to the War Office on certain specified points relating to military organization in the field. Aware of the importance of duties before me, preparations were quickly made for entering upon them, including the payment of heavy extra premium to an insurance office.

From that time onwards my attention was directed to the remarkable development of military events by which those declarations were followed. In the first instance there was the small success of the French at Saarbruck on August 2, followed on the 4th by their severe defeat at Weissenburg, after which one defeat after another followed in quick succession; namely, Woerth and Spicheren on the 6th; Forbachen on

[1] At Saarbruck.

the 7th; St. Avold on the 9th, when the partial investment of Metz began; Strasburg invested on the 10th; the battle of Courcelles or Longville, near Penge, on the 14th; the battles of Mars la Tour, Gravelotte, and St. Privat, 16th to 18th, both inclusive, leading to the complete investment of Metz. The aspect of affairs had been so affected by those events that preparations for the defence of Paris began on the 23rd. The Germans following up their victories by that of Beaumont, near the Belgian frontier, on the 30th, forced MacMahon to fall back upon Sedan, after sustaining very severe losses in men, guns, and stores. In other directions, during the same period, one success after another continued to attend the advance of the invaders.

The 1st of September was with me a busy day; among its incidents, receiving instructions from the War Office, special passport from the Foreign Office, letter of credit and necessary cash from agents, and lastly, taking leave of my beloved wife. Leaving Charing Cross by the 8.45 p.m. train, I arrived in Paris early the following morning. Later in the day, in obedience to orders, I reported my arrival to the British Embassy, presenting at the same time my official credentials. I was informed that an application would be made to the Ministry of War for a *sauf conduit*, to enable me to proceed and join the "Army of the Rhine" under Marshal MacMahon, at that time "somewhere between Verdun and Mezières, on the left side of the Meuse."

An impression was "in the air" that all was not well with that army, but beyond rumours more or less vague nothing seemed to indicate knowledge of actual events of the previous day, still in progress at, and in the vicinity of Sedan. Afternoon and evening brought more definite particulars; telegrams from Mezières announced that MacMahon was wounded, fugitives inundating that town, all communication with Sedan "interrupted"; but to inquiries made in official quarters there was silence.

We had observed that near the Gare du Nord large numbers of workmen were engaged on the fortifications in that direction. Within the walls bodies of armed men, some in uniform, many not, marched along the thoroughfares or were undergoing drill. As day advanced crowds assembled at corners; pedestrians increased in number; kiosks and windows presented caricatures, in execrable taste, of Prussians from king to peasant. The Champs Elysées was comparatively deserted; already it had an unkept appearance. Here and there a small group gazed at the performances of Punchinello; a few equipages drove along its centre way. Agencies of various Sociétés des Secours aux Blessés had taken up positions in large buildings or open spaces; from many windows and over entrances floated Red Cross flags.

At an early hour on the 3rd, Colonel Claremont, Military Secretary to the British Embassy, conducted me to the several offices, from one or other of which he expected that the necessary orders would be issued to enable me to carry out the mission assigned to me. Failing to obtain those orders at one and all so visited, he made direct application to the Minister for War, but with no other result than an intimation that "the correspondence on the subject must pass through the ordinary routine, and in the meantime I must wait." It was evident that something very unusual had taken place or was in progress; the demeanour of the officials with whom we came in contact indicated the fact with sufficient clearness. Colonel Claremont was in all probability made acquainted with the nature of the events in question, for as we separated, each to proceed his own way, his parting remark was, "I don't expect now that you will go much beyond Paris."

The Champ de Mars forms a huge camp ground; *tentes abri*, guns, waggons, tumbrils, horses, and men crowd the space so named. Infantry of the line there are in battalions, many of them undergoing the earlier stages of military drill, their style and general aspect far from realizing the British idea of what is soldier-like. The arrangement of the camp itself, including tents, *matériel*, conveniences and necessities, slovenly and untidy.

In its immediate vicinity the Seine was a washtub for the troops, many of whom were occupied in beating, scrubbing, and otherwise cleansing articles of their clothing in the edge of the stream. I lean over the parapet and observe the process. I am grasped by a soldier;[1] others hurry to his aid; I am captured, a prisoner. The spy mania is rampant. I am marched off as such, first to one "post," then to another; passport and other official documents taken from me; my escort increasing as we proceeded. It comprises cavalry, infantry, and *gamins*, the latter becoming more and more "demonstrative" in their behaviour as we went, now shouting, "*À bas le Prussien!*" "*À bas Bismarck!*" now laying hands roughly upon me, until it looks as if in their excitement things might fare badly with me. Arrived at a police station in the Rue Grenelle, I found myself deposited in the company of a very miscellaneous assortment of *prisonniers*, and there spent some two or three hours as best I could. At the end of that time my credentials were flung at, rather than given back to me; the official of the place pointed to the door, and without deigning a look at me said, "*Voilà! Allez*," and so we parted. Naturally enough I was indignant, and on reaching my hotel declared my intention to report to our Representa-

[1] Of the 10th Infantry, corresponding to my old regiment.

tive the episode through which I had passed; but was quietly informed by others better acquainted than I then was with the state of affairs, that I need not trouble myself; he would do nothing in the matter.

As evening wore on, rumours of the morning assumed the aspect of facts, terrible in their nature as they were unlooked for and unexpected: the French had been hopelessly defeated at Sedan; MacMahon wounded and a prisoner; the Emperor a prisoner; 40,000 men[1] of his army prisoners; no obstacle to delay, far less prevent, the advance of the Prussians upon Paris. All was excitement along the streets and boulevards; shouts were heard of "*Déchéance!*" and "*Vive la République!*" Doubts and fears were expressed as to what on the morrow the fate of the Empress, who was still in the Tuileries, might possibly be.

All through the following night there were sounds of movement in the streets: the tread of troops on the march, the heavy roll of guns, tumbrils, and waggons. In the Chamber of Deputies transactions were in progress the nature of which did not transpire till long afterwards, though the results were to be seen within the space of a few hours. Men, who till then had been ministers and other officials of the Emperor, declared shortly after midnight the Imperial regime had ceased;[2] they elected from among themselves what was intended to be a "Governing Commission," and so discounted the events of the morrow. No wonder that such a self-chosen body failed to receive general acceptance, as indeed was scarcely to be looked for considering the many discordant political elements existing within the capital.

From early morning of Sunday, the 4th, a dense and tumultuous crowd filled the Place de la Concorde; in the Rue Royale and Faubourg St. Honoré workmen were hauling down Imperial eagles and "N's," by which various public buildings were distinguished and ornamented, the mob cheering them as they proceeded with their self-imposed work. The gates of the Tuileries gardens were open, the gardens of the palace filled with people; down the Rue de Rivoli, and upwards towards the Arc de Triomphe, the Champs Elysées, streams of people were in motion. Across the entrance to the bridge leading to the palace of the Corps Législatif, a body of regular troops was drawn up with bayonets fixed. Down along the Champs Elysées marched in cadence to beat of drum and note of bugle an imposing force of National Guards. Nearer and nearer they came; greater and greater was the excitement in the crowd, including the small body of foreigners

[1] In reality 80,000 men prisoners, and 200 guns lost.

[2] The Resolution on the subject was proposed in the Corps Legislatif by M. Jules Favre.

who, like myself, were irresistibly drawn to, and by curiosity held in the scene. A moment more and the two sets of forces must have been in actual collision with each other—with what consequences who could predict? Then were raised upon bayonet points the képis of the regulars, as from their ranks the shout burst forth, "*Vive la Garde Nationale!*" The latter instantly followed suit; the shout of "*Vive la Ligne!*" told us that fraternization was complete. The hall of the Legislature was immediately occupied by the bourgeois; half an hour later the Government of the Defence was proclaimed in the Hôtel de Ville. Armed men in blouses took the place of sentries of the Guard at the Tuileries; the tricolour still waved above the central dome of the palace. The sympathy of us foreigners who mingled in the crowd was with the Empress, as we expressed to each other in subdued tones, our wonder as to the means by which her escape would be effected, or whether she was to fall into the hands of the masses, now wild with excitement as they yelled out "*Déchéance!*" "*Vive la Nation!*" "*Vive la Réqublique!*" interspersed with still more threatening ejaculations. That a Revolution had taken place, the Empire given place to the Republic, was evident; the apparent ease with which that great change had been effected was matter of surprise to onlookers, and to the people by whom it was effected. In the Place de la Concorde the sergeants de ville were roughly handled, old scores paid off, in some few instances their lives taken; the statues of Strasbourg and other cities were draped in crimson cloth; then came along the quays bodies of infantry, cavalry, and artillery, not to open fire upon the revolutionary crowds, but in progress to the outskirts of the city.

Long after the occurrence of the events just related, the circumstance transpired that arrangements had in anticipation been made to ensure the safety of the Empress. The passages of the palace and inner gates were occupied and otherwise protected by a considerable force of the Imperial Guard, so that as in their haste the crowd rushed in from the direction of the Place de la Concorde, they were moved on and on until they emerged from the palace into the Cour de Carrousel, where, finding themselves so far outmanœuvred, they stood irresolute. It was then that, taking advantage of their confusion, the escape of the Empress was effected by the aid of Prince Metternich and Madame La Breton Bourbaki; whether with that of M. F. de Lesseps or not seems to be questioned.

Vinoy at the head of the 13th Army Corps arrives from Mezières, his retreat therefrom, in face of the Germans flushed by victory at Sedan, looked upon as the most masterly performance yet achieved. His forces occupy camp in the Avenue de la Grande Armée, and thither crowds resort to see the men who had performed so successful a feat; the order and regularity in all that concerns them indicating their training and discipline in strong contrast to what was so recently experienced in the Champ de Mars. But chiefly was attention directed to certain mysterious objects carefully concealed by canvas coverings, but with an outline like that of artillery guns. These were *mitrailleuses*, from which great results were anticipated.

To walls of houses and enclosures were affixed announcements that the Republic had been declared, and giving the names of those who now constituted the Provisional Government. Other notices similarly displayed contained appeals to patriotism on the part of the National Guards, and manhood of the capital, that they should rally to the rescue of *La Patrie en Danger*. Troops of the line marched in various directions, the object of the movements not apparent. Groups of men stood at intervals along the streets, the *képi* as yet the only item of uniform worn by them.

The tone of the press moderated from what had lately been; it was evident that grave events threatened, the possible nature of which caused thinking people some anxiety. Cafés usually brilliantly lighted and crowded with customers became less so; uniforms took the place of civilian costume at the small tables within and without. Outside the ramparts, houses and other buildings were in course of demolition. On the defences the work of repair and strengthening was in progress. Railway stations were crowded by people,—some endeavouring to get away, together with their removable belongings; others to get all such property inside for comparative safety.

Preparations for defence went on apace. Private carriages disappeared, except such as were retained by special permission; public conveyances decreased in number, the horses belonging to them being requisitioned for public purposes. Women pedestrians were few; scarcely a man to be seen on the streets, in shops, offices, and other establishments, but those who wore more or less complete uniform; those on the streets carrying rifles, side arms, or both. At night, and throughout the day, the sound of drum and bugle was incessant; here and there varied by the Marseillaise sung in stentorian voice. In the Place de la Concorde successive bodies of armed men paid homage before the statue of Strasbourg, gesticulating and vociferating as they did so, that emblem becoming concealed under the wreaths deposited upon it. Meanwhile, to prevent the Prussians from obtaining the game hitherto preserved for Imperial purposes, a public battue to take place at Compiègne was proclaimed.

Men, to whom in the emergency arms were issued, increased

numerically faster than did the means of providing them with uniform. Already did the circumstance suggest itself to many that by placing in the hands of the masses such means of offence, a source of possible danger to public safety was thereby created. That idea was speedily fostered by the occurrence of scenes of disorder in some localities by the men so armed; by others no less suggestive, in which men "fraternized" with troops of the line over absinthe in cabarets.

By the 10th of the month the Prussian forces, 300,000 strong, were at Ligny, not more than twenty-five miles from the capital. The terms in which by certain journals appeals were made to the invaders were questionable in respect to dignity: on the one hand, if as "friends," offering friendship; on the other, if as enemies, barricades and sewers transformed into mines to be exploded under them. M. Balbi proposed that *portable* fortresses, each of a strength equal to one hundred thousand men, should be sent against them; other proposals for annihilation of the advancing armies were submitted to the authorities, and declared impracticable.

During next few days information as to transactions was received with increasing vagueness, such items as seemed reliable only through English papers, and that not for long. Some of the classes, who in more peaceful times had willingly served in the ranks when "drawn," now expressed a desire to serve by substitute, if they could. Mobiles in great number arrived in Paris from the provinces. Public announcements declared that so great was the devotion of the people to the Defence that the *Levée en Masse* would leave the proportion of men at their homes as one to twenty-eight women. According to some published statements, the men already enrolled were more formidable in numbers than in quality; the withdrawals from the city of those liable to service so numerous that special measures against them were proposed in respect to their civil rights and property. A report circulated to the effect that cartridges and other ammunition contained in ordnance stores had been seriously tampered with.

It is Sunday. Fashionable resorts, including the Champs Elysées and Gardens of the Tuileries, are crowded with men and women. Cafés partially deserted a few days ago are now crowded. Booths of Punchinello are surrounded by knot of amused spectators, the style and demeanour of the people generally by no means such as might be looked for under the circumstances present and prospective. Mobiles recently collected from the provinces rush about irregularly wherever the crowds are thickest; their rifles at the "trail"; their bayonets fixed,—sources of danger to everybody. Streets and roadways show signs of neglect. News circulates that the Canal de l'Ourque and some other conduits have been "cut" by the Germans, the fact being the first to indicate the near approach of the enemy.

"Versailles has honourably capitulated." Such was the next intelligence to reach us. Confusion thereupon became general. A grand review of forces of the Defence of Paris forthwith ordered; information circulated by authority that the several forts beyond the line of ramparts were fully armed and manned by sailors under command of their own proper officers. As extemporised battalions marched towards the general rendezvous they presented in their ranks two types of manhood—the Parisian and the provincial: the former poor in physique, and undisciplined; the latter, strong and active, but unacquainted with anything beyond elementary stages of military drill. A captive balloon established on Montmartre from which to observe the movements of the enemy. A furore of destruction suddenly set in, resulting in that of bridges, houses, and everything destructible on the immediate outskirts of the city, including a considerable strip of the Bois de Boulogne.

Stores and provisions were collected to enable Paris to withstand a siege of two months' duration, that being thought the limit to which such an emergency could extend, should it happen at all. Cattle and stock of all kinds were brought within the walls; fodder and grain for them collected, and food of all kinds, available for human consumption, stored; a census of "mouths" taken at the same time.

Already had evils shown themselves as a result of billeting armed men on the people; huts were therefore prepared in the boulevards and other open spaces for the former. Disinclination was soon apparent in a suggestively large number of the men to occupy their proper places on parade. From the city there was reported exodus of men whose names were enrolled for military service. On the walls were posted codes of instructions as to the correct manner of loading rifles. Authority was given to the system now introduced whereby improvised battalions of National Guards elected their own officers—a system from which deplorable results were soon to arise.

Gates along the line of fortifications were now closed against traffic, except to persons bearing special permits. Musters taken of so-called "effective" combatants, prepared, according to declarations by themselves, to defend the capital to the death, gave their number, including all classes [1] of troops, approximately at 400,000. Among us foreigners

[1] According to Regulations at that time in force, conscripts and volunteers for the line, having served therein seven years, or on attaining the age of twenty-nine years, passed thence to the Garde Mobile; over that age they pass into the Garde Nationale.

hints circulated that neither by Trochu nor other superior officer were hopes of ultimate success entertained, taking into account the kind of material so extemporised. M. Thiers had proceeded on his mission to the Governments of Europe; hopes accordingly entertained that intervention by England, Russia, and Austria, singly or united, might be brought about. It was an open secret that sympathy of the principal leaders, civil and military, within the capital were more in favour of the past regime than of that now entered upon, their hopes that by some means or other restoration might be effected, a siege and probable bombardment averted. Those hopes were soon destroyed; information circulated that the terms on which further proceedings on the part of the Germans could be arrested, included such items as a heavy money indemnity,[1] the retrocession of Alsace and Lorraine, as also of half the French fleet.

In the streets and everywhere else within the city filth and otherwise objectionable matters had accumulated to a very unpleasant degree; means of conservancy and cleansing were deficient; the atmosphere polluted by odours of decomposition. A separate police force to take the place of the Gens d'Armes extinguished on the day of Revolution had not yet been established; crimes of violence were the more remarkable in their infrequency when that circumstance is taken into account, together with the heterogeneous elements of which the defensive forces were now composed.

The plot thickens; information reaches us which leaves no doubt but that Paris is encircled by the enemy. Within the city there is general commotion; in battalions and smaller bodies newly raised levies march towards Vincennes; trains of ambulance carriages wend their way in the same direction. Official notices affixed to walls direct that all men liable to military service should report themselves within twenty-four hours at the rendezvous of their respective corps, under penalty of being proceeded against as deserters. In striking contrast to all this turmoil was the sight of several elderly men and others calmly and peacefully fishing in the Seine; their prize an occasional gudgeon two inches long or thereabout!

At this point some representatives of Great Powers quitted the beleaguered city with the intention of proceeding to Tours, where it was stated another Government than that of the capital was in process of

A soldier of the line engages in the first instance for the term of seven years; he may at its expiration re-engage for other seven or fourteen years. At the end of twenty-five years in the service he becomes entitled to a pension equal in amount to *ninepence* per day.

[1] Five milliards of Francs; equal to two hundred millions of pounds sterling.

formation. Among those who did so was the British Ambassador. The Consul of Paris had already proceeded on leave of absence, the outcome of the state of affairs so created being that upwards of two thousand persons claiming the rights and privileges of British subjects were left without official representative. Colonel Claremont, Military Secretary, to his great credit, speedily returned within the ramparts, and remained with the besieged until the defeat at Champigny left the question of capitulation a matter of only a few weeks to be decided. By no means did all the Foreign Representatives quit the capital. Among those who remained were the Minister and Consul-General of the United States; the Ministers of Belgium, Spain, Portugal, Switzerland, Denmark, Sweden, and Norway. Neither did the Persian Ambassador withdraw from his official position in Paris.

The corps of Sergeants de Ville is re-introduced; itinerant musicians parade the streets, their favourite instruments the barrel-organ, harp, and violin; beggars become numerous and demonstrative. Parties of Mobiles march excitedly, and in an irregular manner, in various directions, no one knowing the why or wherefore of their movements; some to the sound of drum and bugle, others without such instruments. A report circulates that outside the ramparts the members of that force fired upon each other instead of *at* the enemy; they were said to have arrested their commander on the plea that he held communication with the Prussians. A tax was put upon meat and bread sold in shops; supplies from without had all but ceased; Rentes were down to 54.15. The general demeanour of the masses in ill accord with the conditions in which their capital now was.

From the day on which intelligence of the great defeat at Sedan reached Paris, a degree of enthusiasm became manifest among official classes and private individuals, in regard to arrangements for possible sick and wounded, which contrasted very favourably with the confusion and indecision in military affairs already recorded. The ordinary military hospitals under administration of the Intendance were equipped to their utmost extent; various large buildings fitted up as *annexes* thereto; societies of various kinds, and pertaining to different nationalities, established hospitals, or *ambulances sedentaires* as such places came to be called, at different points throughout the city; several clubs were similarly transformed, and numerous private families made what arrangements they could for the reception of sick or wounded men in case of emergency. The medical faculty of the capital volunteered their services in a body; ladies devoted themselves to "ambulance" work in a manner and on a scale never before witnessed, while volunteers as *brancardiers* gave their names in numbers beyond requirements even according to the most liberal estimates of probable casualties, Thus it came about that provision was complete for 37,000 patients.

At a later period so numerous became the "nurses" that "to carry a *brassard*[1] turned into a fashion; young women *played* the nurse with wounded soldiers as little girls play the mother with their dolls." Many earnest women devoted themselves to the work, but that the remark just made was not without grounds was no less true. In some instances the declared object with which they undertook such work was to release men therefrom, so that they might join the active ranks in combat, or become *ambulanciers*. In other instances it was said of the ladies so employed that they restricted their *performances* to mere show, leaving all real work in the wards to men, but ready to accept credit really due to the latter. Instances occurred of wounded Frenchmen submitting a formal request to be moved to wards in which their attendants should be men only. Up to a certain time a halo of romance attached itself to the movement as a whole; latterly the brightness of that "glory" became less dazzling.

Unfortunately some of the larger ambulance establishments drew upon themselves suspicion; a report circulated that while above them, as also some huts or barraques erected for similar purpose, waved the Red Cross flag, side by side with or in close proximity to them were stores for combatant purposes,—in at least one instance artillery ready equipped for battle. There were cynics who said that the profusion of Geneva flags on private houses was indicative of a desire on the part of the inmates to claim protection under that emblem, as much as the wish to share their rapidly diminishing quantity of food and "comforts" with sick and wounded men. The fact that brancardiers were "neutral" by virtue of the brassard worn by them was considered by pessimists to account for the great popularity attached to the Corps of Ambulanciers as compared to the fighting battalions. Nor were there wanting persons who expressed views that the entire system of "Sociétés des Secours" had in it the objection that by their means responsibility in respect to the care of sick and wounded soldiers was withdrawn from Governments concerned, and so war protracted beyond what would otherwise be possible.

[1] Red Cross badge worn on the arm.

CHAPTER XXVII

1870. SEPTEMBER. SIEGE OF PARIS

An Alsacienne—Action at Chatillon—The dangerous classes—"*Mourir pour la patrie*"—Contrasted conditions—Batteries open—Theatres and Louvre—Food and prices—More contrasts—Action at Villejuif—Again the Alsacienne—Historical sieges.

AMONG the "ambulances" visited by me while being prepared for their intended purpose was one in the near vicinity of the Luxembourg Palace. A particular club was in process of transition accordingly; its members, socially distinguished in Parisian society, had arranged among themselves to undertake the entire management and work, professional and otherwise, in connection therewith, the female members of their respective families devoting themselves to the performance of such functions as pertained more properly to them. In a spacious apartment of that club-ambulance, a number of ladies were variously occupied in arranging articles of bedding, night-dresses, bandages, etc. Among them was one, an Alsacienne, young, fair, and so gentle in manner, that as she accompanied me through the several apartments about to become wards, I took leave to ask whether she had formed any idea as to the nature of the duties that might fall upon her in relation to wounded men, and, if so, whether she felt that she was physically capable of them. "Of course," so she said in reply, "she could not tell what those duties might be, or if she would be able to fulfil them; but in such circumstances as now threatened, it was the duty of every one, man and woman alike, to do their best, and she hoped to do hers."

In the early hours of the 19th, the French forces, some 60,000 strong, occupying the heights of Meudon and Chatillon, were attacked, and driven away by the Germans. It subsequently transpired that although considerable numbers of the regular soldiers of the line stood their ground as became them, others, including some Zouaves, fled panic-stricken; their example was quickly followed by the Mobiles, and so, as day advanced, great numbers of those classes were seen in flight along the great thoroughfares of the city, a few of them carrying their arms, but the great majority without weapons of any kind, shouting as they fled, "*Nous sommes trahi!*" themselves saluted by the populace with cries of "*Lâches.*"[1] The sight was a melancholy one, its tendency to impair whatever belief existed in regard to the successful issue of the defence now entered upon. Still later, ambulance carriages passed along the streets, bearing their loads of men wounded in this the first serious engagement in the near vicinity of the capital, the siege of which begins as a result of that action. As subsequently expressed by newspaper correspondents, there is little doubt that had the Prussians followed up the fugitives on this occasion they might with them have entered Paris.

In the evening of that day the sound of shots fired in the streets was heard; report spread that two thousand of "the dangerous classes" were abroad, a report so far confirmed that they were being marched under escort to the gates, and so expelled, to take their chances between the lines of besieged and besiegers. It was deemed unsafe for foreigners to appear, lest, being taken for Prussians, they might vicariously suffer for the success of the morning. Cafés and such places were ordered to close early; a declaration published that persons convicted of pillage should be held liable to death penalty. The discovery was made that telegraphic communication with the outer world was cut off. Under all these circumstances there existed an impression that the risks to life had been lessened to those within the city by the repulse sustained by our "defenders" in the morning.

On September 21 was celebrated in Paris the outbreak in 1792 of the Republic, and massacre of French nobles. Placards declared that the successors of men of that day will prove themselves worthy of their ancestors; other *affiches* expressed determination to resist to the death, to accept no armistice, to yield neither a stone of a fortress nor an inch of territory. In the Place de la Concorde a battalion of the Garde Nationale presented arms to the statue of Strasbourg, sang in chorus the Marseillaise, decorated the emblem itself with floral wreaths; having done so, they marched away! Soon there came a body of "patriots"; their task to drape the figures of Marseilles and Lyons in red, in token of the Republic declared at both those places. Along the Rue Rivoli came a battalion of newly-enrolled citizen soldiers, their destination said to be the front. At the head of the column marched

[1] Of the Mobiles billeted in the hotel where I resided, some re-entered quietly smoking their pipes or cheroots. One of them remarked that he had fired three shots against the enemy; but as his companions bolted, he did not see the fun, as he expressed it, of remaining to be killed.

in gorgeous and picturesque costume a cantinière. The men's rifles were decorated with evergreens; accompanying them were their wives and children, all in tears; the brave men loudly singing, "*Mourir pour la patrie.*" As they reached the Rue Royale an affecting and sad parting was witnessed; the column resumed its march, but now in silence; but, as subsequently transpired, not to come in conflict with the enemy.

A strange contrast between conditions was now observable. Considerable numbers of the fugitives from Chatillon were marched along some thoroughfares, their coats turned outside in, their hands tied behind them, the word "*Lâche*" placarded on their backs. Masses of men, including old and young, the strong, decrepid and malformed, gathered in front of the Hôtel de Ville, and along the boulevards extending thence to the Place de la Bastille. After a time the crowds dispersed, but the reason alike of their gathering and of their dispersion did not then transpire.[1] Meanwhile, the aspect of the boulevards was bright and gay with women fashionably dressed, and men in uniform; the cafés crowded, their inmates laughing and joyous. At the kiosks people eagerly purchased papers of the day, and laughed at the caricatures of Germans, executed in even worse style, if that were possible, than anything previously seen. In the Champs Elysées goat carriages and merry-go-rounds, Mobiles playing games of sorts, nursery maids neglecting their charges, men squabbling, songs, patriotic and ribald, half-drunken men everywhere.

Events developed rapidly. The sound of heavy guns at different points around the outskirts told its own tale. The heaviest firing came from the direction of Meudon. Crowds of people gathered at the Trocadero, and there watched for explosions of Prussian shells as they burst in mid air or crashed through the leafy woods adjoining the Seine, though at some distance from the city. A balloon dispatched from within glided westward at an elevation beyond the reach of Prussian fire; the balloon, as we subsequently learned, being guided by M. Nadar, who, while passing over their camp, dropped showers of his own advertisements among them.

Now the theatres were in some instances turned to another purpose than that of mere amusement; they were transformed into ambulances, the male portion of the usual performers taking their places in the fighting ranks, the ladies adopting the brassard as nurses. Another significant incident was the barricading of doors and windows of the Louvre Museum, a number of water reservoirs being prepared near it, in case of fire, and with evident regard to possible bombardment.

[1] The object of the demonstration was to demand that municipal elections should be immediately proceeded with.

The inhabitants of villages within the line of investment were admitted inside the ramparts; there they became established as so many communities, each under its own administration. Conditions, present and prospective, pointed to the necessity of systematising the issue of food stores; meat was unobtainable at butchers' establishments and restaurants. A register was established on which was inscribed the names and residence of persons authorized to remain within the walls, these numbering two millions, exclusive of *bouches inutiles* already expelled.

From academies and medical schools students enrolled themselves as artillerymen and ambulanciers. So popular was the last-named corps that many fictitious "members" were soon arrested for bearing its brassard. In some instances it was said of citizen "soldiers" that they showed small desire to take post in advanced positions; in a few, that Gardes Nationaux and Mobiles objected to proceed beyond the barriers. While on the one hand certain enthusiasts endeavoured to set on foot a League of Peace, others proposed schemes of mutual assurance against casualties incidental to a state of siege. Still went on the work of destroying emblems and changing the names of streets associated with that of Napoleon. A proposal was made to strip from the column in the Place Vendome the historical scenes on its metal casing, and utilise the bronze for purposes of defence. Wives of workmen on barricades and other defences might be seen carrying the implements of their husbands, while the latter lounged about unencumbered, and in all respects unlike earnest *ouvriers*. In the long hours of inactivity that intervened between short periods of indifferent work, tongues and idle hands became in their respective ways so demonstrative that, as a counterpoise, a series of cheap performances "for the benefit of the masses" was organized. In the pages of *Le Combat* was a proposal that a subscription list should be opened, with a view to present a *fusil d'honneur* to the man who should shoot the King of Prussia, the subscriptions to be limited to five sous per person. Prussian helmets were offered for sale in such numbers that people asked each other how far off was their place of manufacture.

Ten days elapsed since the Prussians gained their position on the heights of Chatillon. Meanwhile it would seem that beyond slight combats nothing of importance occurred between besieged and besiegers. Rumour ran that "the people"—within Paris—demanded to be led against the enemy by whom their city was surrounded, while the daily journals advocated such a demonstration, if for no other object than to quiet such of the disaffected as declaimed against the past inaction. On September 30 a combined force of the line, artillery, cavalry,

National Guards and Mobiles, said to number in all 10,000 men, attacked the Prussians at Villejuif, where at first they were successful. At another point, however,—namely, Choisy-le-Roi,—the result of the incautious rush made by them was unfortunate to themselves; they sustained heavy loss in killed and wounded,—General Guilhém being among the former,—and were constrained to withdraw behind the adjoining forts.

During the interval between those actions I visited several ambulances, containing considerable numbers of wounded, and now much added to by those from the sortie just mentioned. Among those visited was the one near the Luxembourg Palace already noticed. But the Alsacienne was no longer there. On the fatal day of Chatillon, among the wounded carried thither from the field was an officer whose injury was of the gravest nature. To him was assigned an apartment; he was placed under sole charge of the young nurse, whose first patient he thus became. Night closed in; the surgeons attended to his injuries; then patient and "nurse" were left together. With return of daylight came the morning visit. On the bed lay stiff and cold what had been the wounded man; kneeling beside the bed, her face buried in the sheets, herself in a state of catalepsy, was the nurse, her condition so sad and extreme that she was straightway taken to her friends, with whom, as subsequently transpired, she long remained an invalid.

All of us recognised the fact that the attendant conditions of a siege were upon us, that with regard to their future course everything was uncertain. Under such circumstances we read with interest a resumé of the history of past sieges of Paris, published apparently for our encouragement in one of the morning journals.[1] It appears that Paris has undergone seven different sieges; namely, in A.D. 856–7, by the Normans, for thirteen months, at which date its population numbered 60,000 persons; on that occasion, though the besiegers committed great destruction in its immediate environs, they were ultimately obliged to withdraw. In 970, the Emperor Otho II., with 60,000 troops, appeared before its walls; but he was routed by King Lothaire, and pursued as far as Soissons. In 1359 Charles of Navarre blockaded the city, and tried to reduce it by famine; the population suffered intensely, but in the end, Charles, learning of the approach of relieving armies, raised the siege, and with his forces withdrew. In November of the same year, Edward III. of England invaded France with 100,000 men, and marched on Paris the following spring. At that

[1] *La Cloche.*

time Paris contained 200,000 inhabitants. During the siege, which lasted three months, they suffered the horrors of famine, but the troops of Edward, having devastated all the surrounding country, became themselves short of provisions, and were consequently compelled to withdraw. A century later, the English, under Edward IV., who became possessed of the city, were attacked by Charles VII., whom they had before driven to Bourges, and Joan of Arc was wounded at the head of a storming party. Finally the French were repulsed. For seven years Paris was "between the hammer and the anvil," till at last the citizens revolted against the exactions of the English, and let the French into the place. In 1589, at which time Henry IV. laid claim to the throne of France, the king's army attacked the Faubourg St. Germain; after which the siege was raised for a few months, to be renewed in 1590. On that occasion the siege lasted eighty-five days; namely, from May 30 to August 23. The populace were reduced to such straits that animals of all kinds, clean and unclean, were slaughtered; soldiers chased children, and put them to death as food; bones were dug up and prepared as *patés;* an instance related of a woman who devoured some of the flesh of her own offspring, and shortly afterwards died mad—and no wonder. At the end of that time the approach of the Duke of Parma forced Henry to raise the siege. In 1814 and in 1815 the city capitulated without a battle. The seventh siege is now in progress. It is for us to fulfil our destiny to the best of our ability.

CHAPTER XXVIII

1870. *OCTOBER. SIEGE OF PARIS*

Ceinture Railway—Advanced post—First Prussian—St. Cloud Palace—Historical associations—Signs of the times—Balloon and pigeon post—*Le don Anglais*—British Charitable Fund—Two emergencies—Defences and workmen—Superior officers—Other officers—Rank and file—Federals—Extemporized "troops"—*Francs Tireurs*—*Amazones de la Seine*—Council of Hygiene—Sortie on Malmaison—The days following—Excursion to Boulogne—Stirring events—Minor measures—Numerous sick and wounded.

EARLY in October two [1] of us proceeded some way by Ceinture Railway, the more conveniently to see conditions beyond the walls. The Bois de Boulogne was sadly transformed in aspect; trees recklessly cut down, flower beds destroyed, troops already established in camps, others preparing for themselves bowers of branches, while from Mont Valérien the frequent recurring boom of heavy guns told of missiles directed therefrom upon strong positions of the enemy on the heights of Meudon.

Descending at Porte Montrouge, it was with some difficulty we obtained permission from the Etat Major to go outside that part of the fortifications. Proceeding along what once had been the road to Bicètre, we came upon and passed a succession of barricades. On either side of our route were gardens and fields now laid waste, hamlets and villages deserted, houses dilapidated, and in many instances destroyed, the better to clear the way for artillery fire upon our besiegers; at short intervals a thin layer of earth concealed a torpedo. Still further towards the front, outlying sentries of the contending forces exchanged stray shots with each other.

At Arcueil the Dominican College, transformed to an ambulance, was filled with wounded men. Among them was a German soldier, he belonging to the 23rd Infantry, the first of the enemy with whom, so far, we had become acquainted. He was not only well cared for, but petted by those around him, and, to judge by expression, was well

[1] Mr. Whitehurst, of the *Daily Telegraph*, and myself.

contented with his surroundings. In course of our trip we came upon various parties of troops of the line marching to their front; for already we were within range of the Prussian needle gun. In one of those parties was a man upon whose knapsack was perched a cat, which clung to its position as best it could. It was probably the creature the man loved best.

On another occasion of an excursion by the Ceinture we witnessed the conflagration by which the palace of St. Cloud utterly perished. From various positions artillery fire was continuous. As we watched, first a mass of dense smoke, then of lurid flame, burst from the edifice, and speedily the whole was in a state of ruin. Subsequently it was said that to the French themselves was due this great mishap; whether by intention or accident did not transpire.

Among the historical associations connected with that palace the following may be noticed: In it on July 29, 1589, Henry III. was murdered by the monk Jacques Clément; Henrietta of Orleans died; Peter the Great was received by the Regency in the time of Louis XIV. There was signed the capitulation of Paris in 1815; Queen Victoria was received by Napoleon III. in 1855; and in 1870 the Declaration of War against Prussia was signed. Strangely enough, the table used on the last-named occasion was among the few articles saved from the conflagration just witnessed.

Signs of the times multiplied apace. Sounds of firing by heavy guns became more and more distinct and continuous, conversation turning upon the circumstance as if it were an ordinary though interesting subject. Precautions against *incendie* were pressed on. Demonstrations of various kinds took place in the different parts of the city, the people composing them comprising numbers of those from Belleville and Mobiles bearing arms. At most of them the Marseillaise with other *patriotic* music mingled with denunciations against the besiegers, against whom, however, those who most loudly denounced seemed to consider further personal action unnecessary. Nor did the Provisional Government escape their declamations, the expressions against it being in some instances no less strong than those against the Prussians.

A post by balloon and the employment of carrier pigeons had been already introduced, the first for the dispatch of communications, the second for their conveyance to the authorities within the city. The first so brought in was a Proclamation by Gambetta, who had by means of aerial transit proceeded to Tours. By photography it was reduced to a minimum size, and so attached to a pigeon; by a reverse method it was enlarged, and so made legible. Throughout the remaining period of the siege letters were regularly dispatched by balloon to those dear to me; but weeks had to elapse before intimation from the outside world was received.[1]

The arrival of Colonel Lloyd Lindsay in the middle of October as bearer of £20,000, a donation from England to the sick and wounded in Paris, was an important event. He entered the city in the uniform of his rank. The spy mania was still strong; he was captured as such, and underwent various unpleasant experiences notwithstanding the philanthropic character of his mission. By order of General Le Flo, Minister of War, I became a member of the Committee appointed to distribute "le don Anglais," and fulfilled the duty as best I could. Looking back through the vista of many years doubts occur as to the actual amount of good effected by that *don*. While it was in process of distribution, jealousies were expressed among institutions[2] to which portions of it were given, while among various classes of persons the remark was heard, "It is all very well to send us money, but France expected aid of another and more active kind." Nor were the French singular in the views expressed, if information subsequently gained is correct.

Those who, as already alluded to, claimed rights and privileges as British subjects had to be seen to by countrymen able to afford partial help in the circumstances of the time. Previous to the departure ot their Representative, intimation was sent to them that they also were at liberty to quit the threatened city; but if they preferred to remain, they

[1] The following form is that of letters permitted to be so dispatched:—

Paris, le 187

PAR BALLON MONTÉ

Placer ici le timbre-poste.
*Affranchissem*t. *France et Algerie: 20 centimes. Etranger: taxe ordinaire.*

M ....

....

à ....

*dép*t ....

[2] The fact transpired that certain ambulances were established rather for the advantage of their *fondateurs* than the good of sick and wounded. Others acted altogether independently, but had neither *personnel* nor *matériel* to fit them for their professed purpose. With such at were allied to military hospitals it was sufficiently easy to deal and adjust; not so with the others alluded to.

did so on their individual responsibility. So stringent were orders left with regard to the "British Charitable Fund" that help therefrom could only be given under authority of that Representative, and it impossible to obtain after his departure. As expressed by some of the persons alluded to, "What could they do by quitting Paris? All their possessions were in the city; so were their homes; if they were to die of starvation, better do so there than away, shelterless and wanderers among strangers and possibly enemies. Their means of obtaining or earning income had for the time being ceased; unless aided by compatriots, they must perish." An extemporized Board of Assistance[1] obtained for and distributed among them help, and to those suffering from illness professional aid. But in all this the official element had no part.

The current of events had made two points clear: the first that in the annihilation of her army at Sedan, France was subjected to an emergency not calculated upon or provided against; the second, equally unforeseen, that a powerful army was rapidly strengthening an investing circle around her capital. Such measures as were adopted under the combined circumstances must needs be taken on the spur of the moment, and from materials ready at hand, these facts to be borne in mind by those of us who were mere lookers-on.[2]

Works of defence included the strengthening of forts and ramparts already existing; the erection of barricades, and other operations incidental to conditions at the time existing. Workmen unused to such requirements had to be employed, the results being disproportion between labourers numerically and in their performances, alike in quantity and in quality. Much of their time was spent in trifling, in "demonstrations," in drinking, singing, and fighting with comrades who had joined the ranks as "soldiers"; others of them were loud in demands for arms, though, as subsequently shown, those given to them were misused. The general result of these conditions was that when October had came to an end defensive works were still incomplete.

The line of action, and of what was looked upon as inaction by some of the higher military officers, was subject of talk and com-

[1] Composed of Sir Richard Wallace, Honourable Allan Herbert, Dr. Shrimpton, Sir John Rose Cormack, and the Rev. S. Smyth.

[2] How strangely similar the circumstances alluded to to those of Prussia in the early years of the 19th century! Then "Prussia had made no provision for defeat. Her fortresses, though garrisoned, were ill commanded and unprepared for serious resistance. Passion and sentiment had dictated her war, in which prudence and foresight had no part. Her territory was reduced to a fragment, her army to a mere residue."—*Quarterly Review*, October, 1893, page 425.

ment. Of the Governor[1] it was said that in these respects his policy was enigmatical; his sympathies were more with the deposed Emperor than towards the Republic, holding communication with the Empress and her enemies, but abandoning her in her time of greatest difficulty. Little fitted to conduct the duties of a leader; more able to detect administrative faults than to remedy them; vacillating in opinion; liable to adopt the views of the latest speaker in an interview; making promises which he left unfulfilled; substituting phrases for action; circulars and proclamations for force of arms; his demeanour between opposing factions so equivocal that he was doubted and mistrusted by all. Having little confidence in the "armed men" under his command, and in ultimate success of the defence, his object in continuing it was that he might so "maintain the honour of France." Disbelieving in the continuance of the Republic, his hopes were in restoration of the deposed Emperor: an event towards which the policy of Bazaine at Metz was deemed likely to conduce. Towards his officers, personal feelings rather than public considerations dictated his demeanour; thus his supersession of Vinoy by Ducrot at Chatillon was considered to have led to misfortune on that occasion, as ill-feeling towards Bellemere did subsequently at Le Bourget. It was said of another general officer that on September 4 he was in command of the line at the Corps Legislatif, who fraternized with the National Guards, and on the 19th abandoned his position at Chatillon, re-entering Paris with other fugitives.

That among staff and other officers were men whose reputation stood high was acknowledged. But an impression was abroad that the former class were so numerous that individual efficiency was thereby impaired, while battalions suffered in consequence of their withdrawal. That there were some who scarcely gave the impression of efficiency was no less apparent. These were to be seen lounging about cafés and boulevards, usually in exaggerated uniform and trappings, their hands encased in *manchons*.[2] On the line of march towards advanced positions, the frequency with which a few of the latter resorted to the artistes who *acted* as *vivandières* was subject of not admiring wonder to foreigners who looked on. While in actual movement the process of electing their officers was gone through by some battalions of "Federals." On such occasions, political considerations seemed to outweigh those of military efficiency. Men have been seen soliciting votes with bottle in hand; in some instances men "elected" refused to accept the distinction; in others, altercations were to be seen between individuals.

[1] See *Guerre de* 1870–1871, Paris. *Par* Alfred Duquet. [2] Muffs.

The rank and file of the "defenders" were more formidable in numbers than efficiency. It was felt that in creating such a force arms of precision were placed in the hands of men belonging to recognised "dangerous classes," nor was the difficulty that might possibly arise in getting from them again those arms unperceived by responsible authorities. Subsequent events sufficiently proved it would have been better for Paris and for France had such a force not been organized, had terms of peace been arranged prior to the calling together of "Federal" elements. With the exception of relatively small numbers of the old army and marines, the defence was to be carried out by levies, of whom it was said that "they comprised the old and the young; the hale and the lame, gamblers, and the disturbers of the peace." These elements thrown together promiscuously were formed into battalions, but otherwise they were without cohesion or affinity.

Of the regular cavalry, the numbers available for service were small, not exceeding some 5,000 men, and not all these were employed in the face of the enemy. The artillery was made up in part of regular soldiers of that branch, partly of marines, and partly of Mobiles; thus it presented the two extremes of excellence and non-efficiency—the old soldiers presenting the former of these characteristics, those newly drafted into the ranks the latter. The Zouaves, of whose achievements we were already accustomed to hear so much, and from whom so much was expected, failed altogether to fulfil those anticipations; in some instances showing defection and panic in the face of the enemy, in others such feeble resistance that they came to be looked upon as useless against trained soldiers inured to battle.

The National Guard [1] was distinct from the army proper; it had its own laws and code of regulations. The Mobile Guard was assimilated to the active army for purposes of pay and discipline—like the line, organized in distinct battalions. While the German forces were at a considerable distance from the capital, several corps of Mobiles were brought thither from the provinces. No sooner had the Republic been declared than several of their members were among the first of the insurgents to force their way into the Tuileries, from which the escape of the Empress had not yet been effected. When, immediately thereafter, orders were issued within Paris for the enrolment of such troops, those orders were obeyed to a partial extent only; evasions were frequent, desertions numerous. If in their ranks there were some trustworthy men, report stated that there was also a dangerously

[1] The militia force so-called comprised the Garde Nationale Sedentaire, and Mobiles, the first named having its own "organization," if such a term is applicable, the last being affiliated to the regular army.

large proportion of fugitives from justice, and of the criminal classes. Subsequent experience proved that such elements were more ready to declare for the Commune than to face the besiegers; that when led to the front they speedily withdrew therefrom, although on such occasions their casualties were *nil*.

To many of the extemporized troops the declaration of the Republic was looked upon as giving them the right to trangress law and order, to claim whatever they chose at the moment to desire, but to give nothing in return. Fraternizing with the worst elements of Belleville and Vilette, they early joined them in demonstrations against existing government; and being billeted upon the civil population, evil influences were spread from class to class, to the serious danger of public administration.

Various corps of Francs Tireurs were extemporised. With regard to them as a body, it has been said that for the most part the men were bad soldiers, acting according to their individual pleasure; marauders not only with regard to the enemy, but to the French, whom they were supposed to assist. By the Germans they were looked upon as assassins, and dealt with accordingly, whenever they fell into the hands of our besiegers. It is true that among them there were good men, but so relatively small their numbers that their influence upon the general *morale* was imperceptible. There was at least one corps among them whose bearing and efficiency was unquestionable, namely, Franchetti's *Eclaireurs à Cheval de la Seine*; but, unfortunately for them, their gallant commander fell in battle before the operations were nearly over. As a body, the reputation accorded to the Francs Tireurs was that they fled before small bodies of the Germans, by whom in consequence they were looked upon with contempt.

A movement of very unusual kind was suggested, and although never carried out deserves to be noticed in these reminiscences. The intended movement was none other than a demand on the part of a number of women that in the first place they should be granted "social solidarity," whatever that may mean; and in the second, should be drafted into a series of battalions, armed and clothed suitably to their sex; that those battalions should have the designation from one to ten of the "Amazones de la Seine"; that they should "man" the ramparts, and so take the places of battalions proceeding more to the front.[1]

A Council of Hygiene was early organized to take upon itself the

[1] It will be remembered that on the outbreak of mutiny among the sepoys at Dinapore, it was contemplated to arm the "Amazones" of the 10th Regiment of Foot, and that men had every confidence in their fighting qualities.

various duties relating to public health, that is so far as it could be protected under the circumstances in which the city was placed. The gradually diminishing food supplies, including milk, produced evil effects in the aged, the very young, and the sick; ordinary diseases incidental to the season of the year increased in prevalence, while smallpox did so to an extent which ultimately merited the name of a pestilence. Vaccination became compulsory, and it was a somewhat amusing sight, even under the conditions of the time, to see whole battalions of citizen soldiers being marched to the École de Médecine, there to undergo that operation.

An important sortie [1] against Prussian positions on the west of Paris took place on October 21, the first on a large scale that had as yet been made. The several ambulances established within the city dispatched to the field no fewer than two hundred carriages of sorts in anticipation of a severely contested battle. Among them were eight from the American, situated in the Avenue de l'Impératrice, the carriages well and elegantly built, each horsed by four high-bred animals from the stables of wealthy Americans, the *personnel* in smart uniform, the *matériel* provided on a most liberal scale, the whole in a state of completeness for its expected work. As the cavalcade stood, drawn up in regular order, all eyes were turned towards Mont Valérien, from which three guns fired in quick succession were to be the signal for the general advance. About noon the appointed signal was given. Away started, in their assigned order, the line of carriages; down by the Avenue de la Grande Armée towards Port Maillot, they went at rapid pace, attracting the admiration of pedestrians, many of whom waved their hats in token thereof. Arrived at Courbevoie, the appointed rendezvous of the ambulance services, we [2] were directed by an Intendant to take up position on a vine-clad ridge behind Mont Valérien, midway between Reuil and Bougeval, towards both of which places the active forces were advancing. Two French batteries in our immediate front opened fire upon the enemy; one of the two, consisting of mitrailleuses being so directed as to sweep the valley that intervened between the ridges on which were respectively posted the guns of besiegers and besieged. Across that valley, but partly hidden by vine bushes, a strong infantry force of Germans was in progress towards us, while stretching away on our right battalions were making progress towards the enemy. The fight quickly became developed, artillery and infantry fire from contending sides becoming increasingly rapid and destructive. That

[1] Under the command of General Ducrot.

[2] I was with the Americans on this occasion.

from the batteries close to our position, though less regular than what in actions in the Mutiny campaign we had opportunities of observing as directed against the rebels, was so to a degree beyond what we had been led to expect, considering the materials of which the defending and extemporized forces were composed. The mitrailleuses were new to us, hence their performances were observed with all the greater interest; the general impression left upon us that their destructiveness in the open fell short of anticipations. In our immediate vicinity and along the line of combat, casualties became so numerous that the best energies of our ambulanciers were fully taxed. The approach of evening told that hostilities must soon cease. Our carriages now filled with wounded, sixty-four in all were collected, and so began their journey back towards Paris. It was dark when we re-entered the gate by which a few hours earlier we had emerged; the great thoroughfare towards the Arc de Triomphe was dimly lighted by oil lamps, for the manufacture of gas had ceased with the expenditure of reserve coal. From the crowds at Port Maillot came loudly expressed inquiries for friends who perchance might be among our wounded. As we continued our progress, people formed dense lines on either side of the broad avenue; hats were respectfully raised; our further progress was between rows of uncovered heads—a touching and spontaneous mark of appreciation and deference to the Red Cross establishments of which we were members. The results to the French of this great sortie were unfortunate, the casualties on their side very heavy. Among the subjects of those casualties were an ex-consul at Stettin, two popular landscape painters, and a sculptor, all of whom fought in the ranks as private soldiers.

The events during the next few days were in their several ways characteristic of the time and circumstances. The press boasted that seventy German soldiers had been captured at, and brought into the city from, the late battle, while rumour ran that the captives were cast into the ordinary prisons, there to associate with the criminal population of such places. Seasonal cold was rapidly increasing in severity; the supply of fuel giving way, the issues of food, already under strict supervision, were still more rigidly superintended; the quantities allowed per ration curtailed, not only in respect to persons in health, but for the sick and wounded. The explosion of an establishment devoted to the manufacture of Orsini bombs caused a good deal of injury to life and property, at the same time that the attention of the authorities was thereby drawn to the circumstance that those implements were being prepared on an extensive scale, but for use within the walls, rather than against the enemy still beyond the lines of fortification. The diminishing supply of materials for the manufacture of gunpowder directed attention to the catacombs as a possible source whence in greater emergency saltpetre might be obtained. Between National and Mobile Guards quarrels occurred from the circumstance that the former were employed only on the fortifications, while the latter were sent to the front, there to engage against the enemy. As the readiest way of solving the difficulty it was ordered that "the citizen soldiers should in their turn be taken beyond those lines, in order that they might be gradually accustomed to the sight of the enemy."

An excursion to the village of Boulogne brought me face to face with an incident new to me in "civilized" warfare. That small town, once the favourite resort of visitors, was now reduced to utter dilapidation; its ordinary occupants fled; its ruins giving shelter more or less complete to defending troops; its streets barricaded; garden and other walls loopholed. Through some of those loopholes sentries took aim at isolated Germans, as the latter came into view among the woods in which they were posted; at others, a sentry for a small "tip" handed his rifle to a stray visitor to have a shot at *le Prusse*. It was not long, however, before a rattle of rifle bullets on the wall put a stop to this kind of "sport." From Valérien and other forts heavy continuous firing went on, their missiles directed upon particular points of the German position, where siege batteries were in course of erection for possible bombardment of our city; from those positions an equally active shell-fire upon French outposts went steadily on.

Among the minor events of the time, one was the addition of several battalions of Federals to those already existing. Another, an attempt made to suppress the extent to which cantinières had come to march at the head of battalions. The grounds of that attempt included the fact that in all instances such followers were young girls, many of them little more than children, who were thus exposed to temptation while beyond the observation and care of their parents or other guardians.

For once in a way our besiegers appear to have been taken unawares. At Le Bourget, towards the end of October,[1] a small body was successfully attacked by Francs Tireurs and Mobiles. But their success was of brief duration. Report circulated that reinforcements applied for by Bellemere were refused by Trochu, that refusal the outcome of personal feeling. Be that as it may, an attack in force was speedily delivered by the Germans; the position carried,[2] with great slaughter of the occupants. There was consternation in Paris. All through the 31st the streets were in a state of turmoil. Masses of people, the great majority armed, marched towards the Hôtel de Ville; that building

[1] On 28th. [2] On 30th.

surrounded by them; the members of the Defence made prisoners; cries of "Vive la Commune!" interspersed with yells, and clarion blasts everywhere; the Commune was in fact declared. But not for long. The 106th Battalion of National Guards forced their way through the insurgents, rescued the Government, and so saved the capital from scenes which were to disgrace it four months later on, in which scenes the same battalion was to play so iniquitous a part.

The extent to which sickness prevailed within the city had become alarming. Accommodation and other necessities for the suffering were severely taxed; for although regular combats between the opposing forces were not frequent, the results from collisions of daily occurrence, and of almost continuous fire from the batteries of the enemy, were a large influx of wounded men. Funeral processions along the cold sloppy streets were of constant occurrence. Certain maladies, among them small-pox, prevailed to a great and fatal extent. As if to emphasize these conditions, news circulated that Metz had capitulated;[1] a large portion of the investing force thus set free on its way to increase that of the besiegers around Paris. So ended the month.

[1] Namely, on the 27th.

CHAPTER XXIX

1870. *NOVEMBER. SIEGE OF PARIS*

Le Jour des Morts—Requiem—Political excitement—Conditions within the city—Progress of affairs—Porte St. Denis—Intended sortie—Battle of Champigny—Night on the field.

LE Jour des Morts was devoted to visiting the cemetery of Père la Chaise. That vast city of the silent was more than usually crowded with mourners and other visitors. Recently covered graves were numerous; around many such stood sorrowing relatives and friends, some of whom placed thereon wreaths or other tokens of affection; around others stood similar groups, some of whom re-decorated tombs of those longer numbered among the dead. The assembled crowds were grave and demure, as befitted the occasion. At intervals the sound of heavy guns came as if floating on the air. On reaching the higher ground within the cemetery, the sharp *ping* of German rifle shots came sharply and often, as the missiles passed over-head or fell among us; for it seemed as if they were directed upon the mourners by the more advanced posts of the besiegers out of a spirit of wantonness—not unlike, it must be confessed, that already shown by French sentries *and others* at Boulogne. But "it was not war" in either instance.

A requiem mass in the Madeleine for victims of the war up to that date was a most impressive service. That beautiful church, draped in black for the occasion, was filled to crowding by men and women, be-longing to all social grades, those of the higher classes wearing deep mourning, all having lost members of their families on the field of battle, or by disease which had already assumed the character of pestilence; in near proximity to the altar sat some few mutilated men, who had so far escaped with their lives. While the service was in progress, the rich music of the recently erected organ, then used for the first time, was broken in upon from time to time by the sound of heavy artillery from the outer forts. During the address delivered by the Abbé Deguerry the same accompaniment continued. In less than four months thereafter the venerable and respected Abbé was numbered among the victims of the Commune.[1]

Political excitement was rampant within the city; serious outbreak by the inhabitants of Belleville and Vilette was dreaded; but on the result being declared of elections rendered necessary by recent events at the Hôtel de Ville, the disturbing elements accepted for a time the defeat thereby given to their cause, and gradually became less demonstrative in behaviour. But not for long. The publication of orders for reorganization of the National Guard was immediately followed by renewed disturbances in those localities, from neither of which did men volunteer for the ranks in obedience to the call do so; some battalions, already including members from those quarters, refused to take their turn of duty on the ramparts, declaring their intention to plunder the city if such orders were persisted in. The difficulties of the existing Government had become very great. Public loans for purposes of the defence were called for and subscribed. Negotiations were carried on for an armistice, whether with or without *ravitaillement*. These proved unsuccessful;[2] but, as events were subsequently to show, acceptance of the terms of Bismarck, hard as they were, would have saved much suffering and loss of human life.

Winter weather rapidly advanced; strong winds, rain, and sleet gave way to snow and bitter frost. Clothing had to be supplemented in various ways; skins of animals slaughtered were utilised, and articles of various kinds "converted" in a manner heretofore unknown. Fuel had become scarce. The public markets were bare of all things eatable; horses and other draught animals belonging to private individuals were requisitioned; licences issued by the municipality to official classes and others permitted to retain and draw rations for particular specified numbers; an embargo was placed upon the small fish already mentioned as furnishing sport for anglers on the Seine. All persons were placed on the universal ration scale,[3] but "the poor" had the additional advantage of gratuitous meals provided at certain places by mairies. The more respectable classes refused to so declare themselves; the consequence was that little, if any, advantage in the way of free meals reached them, whereas the disturbing elements of Belleville and Vilette reaped the full advantages of the scheme, while the classes alluded to became gradually reduced to direst poverty and privation. The wounded in-

[1] According to a tablet erected in the Madeleine: "Mort pour la Foi et la Justice, en la Prison de la Roquette le XXIV Mai MDCCCLXXI."

[2] *Le Journal Officiel*, November 5, 1870.

[3] The following is a transcript of the "ticket of authority" to receive their daily

creased rapidly in numbers; disease in ordinary forms and as epidemics acquired alarming prevalence, various hotels and other large buildings being taken up as additional hospitals. Some schools and colleges still remained open; the Théâtre Française and a few similar establishments presented the ordinary scenes of performances in one portion of the buildings, while in others lay wounded men, sick, dying, and dead.

From outside came evidences that our besiegers were actively at work. Intervals between rounds of fire from Prussian guns became shorter as time wore on. From French outposts came reports that siege batteries were being erected, and armed with Krupp guns of large calibre, with the evident object of bombarding the city. Additional measures were taken to interfere with communication, such as it was, between Paris and the provinces, even to the extent of keeping a more than usual sharp look-out upon messenger pigeons, many of these birds having failed to arrive. Two, if not more, of our balloons, while floating across positions occupied by our enemies, were brought to earth by their bullets, or otherwise fallen into their hands, their occupants threatened with trial by Court-Martial on charges of unauthorizedly attempting to traverse the circle of investment.

In the year 1814, and again in 1815, the allied army entered Paris by the Porte St. Denis. The impression arose that an entrance by our besiegers was possibly intended on the present occasion to take place from the same direction; the defences on that side were accordingly strengthened to so great an extent that those of us able to do so took an opportunity of visiting them. One entire cold foggy day was so spent by me, the Red Cross card procuring for me ready admittance, and "circulation" everywhere. Rumour said that on some of the advanced posts in this direction, men of the opposing forces were wont, during the long weary hours of night, to meet in friendly intercourse and partake of such small hospitality as they could, leaving for the morrow their

allowance of meat granted by mairies to persons authorized to remain within the walls, namely:—

ARRONDISSEMENT

NO. D'ORDRE

M................

Nombre de personnes..................

Demenre..................

Nom de boucher..................

Demeure..................

Quantité de viande { Bœuf / Mouton

Jours de distribution..................

Heure de la distribution..................

TIMBRE DE LA MAIRIE.

respective transition from "friends" to "enemies." Records of the Peninsular War relate similar stories in reference thereto.

As the end of November drew near, rumour spread that the outer gates of the city had been closed; that a sortie on a greater scale than any of those preceding was about to take place; that the investing circle was to be broken, and the victorious army from Paris to march triumphantly into the provinces. Along the thoroughfares of the city leading eastward marched battery after battery of artillery and battalion after battalion of infantry; the crowds cheered, general excitement prevailed; high-sounding promises were expressed that our isolation from the outside world was about to cease. Towards evening orders reached those concerned that early on the morrow the attack was to be delivered; at the same time the publication of a subsequently much jeered at "Proclamation" by a general officer became the subject of comment. At the early hour of one o'clock the following morning a heavy cannonade was opened upon the positions held by the enemy from the whole line of forts on the west and south of the city, and continued during the succeeding hours, so heavy indeed that according to calculation some two hundred missiles per minute were discharged upon them, while a no less furious bombardment was opened upon our outposts, the continuous bursting of shells in mid air of a grey foggy morning having a most weird effect. Throughout those weary hours equipages of all kinds to be used in the removal of wounded were being collected and arranged by the Intendance; while on the river, rows of *bateaux mouches*, ready prepared for similar work, were moored to the embankment. At length morning broke, and such a morning! bitterly cold, a dense fog hanging over us; we, several hours without shelter or refreshment, our innate powers of maintaining animal warmth materially reduced by privation of food. Hour after hour passed, and we were still in our assigned positions; some few conveyances and boats took their departure for the front, but that was all. Noon passed; afternoon advanced. Rumour spread that the intended attack on the position at Champigny had miscarried; that during the previous night the Marne had come down in flood, available pontoons proved insufficient in the emergency, the passage of the forces across the stream had to be postponed. We knew that on the morrow the attempt would be renewed, but all perceived that meantime preparations against that attack would be made by those upon whom it was to be directed.

As daylight broke on November 30 heavy cannonading as on the previous day began. Now the long line of conveyances was set in motion eastward, along the road between Charenton and the Seine. As we neared Joinville we met an escort party conveying to the city a considerable number of German soldiers who had fallen into their hands. At the same time we learned, what subsequent information confirmed, that the first onslaught by our besieged troops was so far successful, the village of Champigny being attacked by them; the mitrailleuse sweeping its streets, the Wurtembergers and Saxons by whom it was occupied were driven from it with extremely heavy loss to their numbers. During the past night the bridge across the Marne that had suffered from the mania of destruction already mentioned was temporarily repaired, a bridge of boats completed, so that the troops, together with thirty-three batteries of artillery, had crossed in the darkness and begun their attack at an unexpectedly early hour. There was no great difficulty connected with the transit of Red Cross conveyances. As we advanced towards Champigny, appearances betokened continued success on the part of the French; and although wounded men were being carried to the rear in great numbers, the general impression was that the endeavours of our citizen forces against their enemies were on this occasion attended by success. Thus matters continued during the next two hours; our establishments moving little by little onwards, following as we then considered the victorious progress of those with whom our sympathies naturally were. The fight now raged with great fury, its scene covering a vast extent of ground, the ridges that stretch from Brie to Champigny, and beyond the latter place still further to our right, presenting an almost uninterrupted line of batteries from which the deadly missiles fell thickly upon the troops engaged, and upon the ground occupied by us, while from the forts in rear of us similar showers of projectiles directed against those positions whizzed over our heads. Now there came a pause; brancardiers carrying wounded, and conveyances of sorts similarly laden, came from the front, and continued their journey rearward. There is confusion. The range of some of the enemy's guns has changed; so has the line of fire. Shells fall more and more near to us; Spahis gallop in an irregular way among us. There is confusion among the ambulance conveyances; brancardiers are unable to discover those to which they respectively belong. For the time being means are unavailable for the removal from the field of men who had fallen wounded. After a short time there was a rally. Again it was evident that the French were attacking the German positions; but ere night closed in they were everywhere repulsed. It was during the state of confusion just described that the commander of the 4th Zouaves, having received what proved to be his death-wound, was dropped and so left by the men who had brought him so far from the front. A shell had burst in their close vicinity. They abandoned the unfortunate officer, helpless as he was, and themselves disappeared in the general confusion. Some few of us expressed indignation in no doubtful terms. We rallied to the aid of the dying man, to whom we gave such aid as we were able to render.[1] A gentleman connected with one of the Embassies who was present succeeded in finding his brougham; in it was placed our patient, and so we started back to Paris for further help. Having re-crossed the Marne, we were driven by the road traversing the Parc de Vincennes, and so entered the city by the Place du Trone. Denser and more dense became the crowd as we neared the city; people in uniform and in bourgeois dress, waggons, and troops in disorder, all served to impede our progress. When near enough to the bulwarks to observe what was taking place upon the slopes connected with them, a scene of the most astounding character presented itself. Crowds of people, male and female, were there, indulging in games as if the occasion were a holiday; and yet within a very short distance from them their brothers and other relations were engaged in deadly combat, torn and mangled, in many instances, into shapeless masses of humanity. Having entered the city, we were driven quickly to the American ambulance, and there within a few short hours the sufferings of the poor *Chéf de Battalion* had ceased. He entered his rest.

Before we could regain the field of battle, darkness had set in. Firing had much diminished, though still proceeding heavily, the flames from guns and burning buildings around us lighting up from time to time portions of the plain on which the events of the day had taken place. A considerable number of Red Cross men had returned in the hope of succouring such of the wounded as were left on the ground. Bitterly cold was the night, as hour after hour, till well past midnight, all of us, with lamp in hand, and in small separate bodies pursued our search, our own frames benumbed, unsupported by sufficient food, and without the possibility of obtaining such comfort as hot coffee or tea could afford. While so engaged, to our surprise, there flashed over us from the Faisanderie a beam of bright white light. For a moment it illumined the Prussian position upon the heights of Villiers, then suddenly ceased. A shell flew through the air. There was a loud explosion, preceded by a blaze of flame. We were made aware that for the first time the electric light was made use of in this way. At last, wearied, tired, exhausted by cold, we were able in the early hours of morning to reach our respective hotels.

[1] This episode was subsequently illustrated in one of the pictorial scenes relating to the siege exhibited in London.

CHAPTER XXX

1870. *DECEMBER. SIEGE CONTINUED*

The day after battle—Disaster—Next day—Paris "dead"—Benevolence and clamour—Citizen soldiers—A possible significance—Spy mania—A duel—Sortie on Le Bourget—A lady on the field—After the battle—An Irishman in French Navy—Christmas—Public opinion—First shell in Paris.

FROM early morning, and all next day,[1] ambulance equipages and men patrolled the field of battle in the performance of their merciful work, their search for wounded made difficult by the dense fog prevailing. Hostilities had ceased for the time, to permit of interment of the dead and succour to the wounded. But unhappily the truce was taken advantage of by stragglers of many kinds, some of whom were bent on plunder. Everywhere on and near the scene of recent combat there was devastation; houses burnt and otherwise dilapidated; boundary walls reduced to fragments; trees broken and torn by shot; the ground furrowed by shells. Bivouacking in the open, or in small groups taking advantage of such shelter as remained against the bitterly cold wind, were soldiers, who, after the fight of yesterday, so spent the night where they had fought; more than half benumbed by cold, they kept up camp fires by means of fragments of furniture, some of great value, taken from neighbouring ruins. Their cooking utensils were supplied for the occasion by *viande* freshly cut from horses killed by Prussian shells. The carriages were soon filled with wounded. They were driven back to Paris, their loads appropriately disposed of; after which a second trip was made to the field, the carriages again filled, the wounded in them similarly distributed, the horses getting over more than thirty-six miles in the double journey. Rumours spread that in some few instances the rôle of the Red Cross had been departed from; intrenching tools conveyed in carriages bearing that emblem; information interchanged between contending forces, communication of which was beyond its proper sphere. The rumours applied to the one side as to the other.

[1] December 1.

Throughout the dreary night that followed, the French troops had to remain in bivouac among the scenes and wreck of battle, their physical strength, already lowered by privation, still further reduced by fatigue and cold, for the weather was now bitterly cold; their *morale* impaired by the scenes around them, added to the experiences of the previous day. As subsequently learned, conditions of the German troops were very different. All who had survived on the 30th were withdrawn from the field of battle and positions near it, their places taken by others who had not seen the carnage of that day, well fed, comfortably sheltered, and thus, in physical condition as in *morale*, better fitted than their opponents to renew the combat. At break of day on December 2 a furious onslaught was made by them upon the French, hundreds of whom were so benumbed by cold as to be unable to stand to their arms. No wonder, therefore, that to them the day became one of disaster. During all that day wounded in great numbers arrived from the field in Paris, all available accommodation for them became crowded. Eminent surgeons were busy in the performance of needful operations among the five thousand six hundred so brought to them. As to the dead, their probable numbers did not transpire; but at one point of the extensive range over which the fight extended, eight hundred were interred in one long trench. During the succeeding night the troops recrossed the Marne and bivouacked in the Bois de Vincennes.

The most determined effort yet made to break the besieging circle having failed, the fact was now apparent that unless aid came from the provinces, all within the beleaguered city were about to enter upon a condition of things more desperate than we had as yet experienced. On the day immediately following what undoubtedly was a withdrawal from the field of combat, the aspect of Paris and of its people was that of sadness, mourning, and uncertainty. The day was cold, a thick fog overhung the city, with occasional falls of snow. Along the great thoroughfares the usual traffic was replaced to a great extent by conveyances engaged in the transport of wounded; funeral processions, more or less imposing in their surroundings, met with in different parts of the city. The absence of sound of heavy guns in the early part of the day seemed to add to the sombreness of our conditions. It was in a manner a "relief," as afternoon advanced, to hear the familiar boom from outlying forts, as their guns opened fire upon the German positions in front of them.

A week of sadness passed; Paris "dead"; its shroud a thick covering of snow; not a wheeled carriage in the streets; scarcely a foot-passenger to be seen. Winter more than usually severe was upon us; even the more unsettled classes of the populace seemed to give a thought to the seriousness of conditions present, and more particularly to those of the near future. As time advanced, so did the prevailing miseries among the besieged increase and assume different forms; in some disease and death, in others starvation in respect to food and fuel, insufficient clothing, want of necessary care and attendants among the poorer classes, and so on. As a result of exhausted fuel supplies, the streets were dimly lighted by oil or petroleum lamps; shops closed at nightfall; in streets and boulevards pedestrians had to grope their way along the distance that intervened between the flickering lamps. Meanwhile, by day and night, with hardly an interruption, the sound of heavy cannonading was heard with suggestive distinctness. An occasional hope expressed that help from the provinces would soon arrive, only to be destroyed by the receipt by pigeon post of news of defeat near Orleans.[1] Riot and a spirit of upheaval became manifest; the places where "demonstrations" by the dangerous classes were most pronounced, the Halles Centrales, and others where food was issued. Within the churches scenes of a different kind were enacted: some were nearly filled with men, women, and youths engaged in private devotion; in others were groups in the midst of which the Service for the Dead was being performed over a more or less richly draped coffin, according to the social position of him or her whose body it enclosed.

Now it was that noble efforts were made by individuals, municipalities, and by the Assistance Publique to lessen, as far as that was possible, some of the greatest straits prevailing among particular classes. Large sums of money were presented to the Paris Administration for that purpose by some wealthy residents, of whom Sir Richard Wallace gave 80,000 francs. Places of distribution of such fuel as could be procured, and of food to the poor, were arranged; nor was it long before the discovery was made that the persons who obtained the lion's share in these respects were the most clamorous and dangerous, rather than the most necessitous for whom those measures of philanthropy were intended. But among all classes, notwithstanding everything possible in the way of help, the difficulties and privations incidental to our position increased apace.

In the ranks of the citizen "soldiers," more especially those of Belleville, disaffection and insubordination took various new developments. They established among themselves a so-called Committee of Admin-

[1] On November 28 General d'Aurelle de Paladine, at the head of the army of the Loire, while endeavouring to force his way from Orleans to Fontainebleau, whence he hoped to advance to the rescue of Paris, was attacked near Beaune la Rolande by the army under Prince Frederick Charles, and defeated, with a reported loss to the French of 1,000 killed, 4,000 wounded, and 1,600 prisoners.

istration, by which all orders were thenceforward to be issued, and promotions made. They once more clamoured to be sent to the front against the enemy; their demand was acceeded to; their conduct when face to face with their opponents so objectionable in more respects than one that they were hastily recalled. The particular corps most implicated were disbanded; a general reorganization, as far as practicable, applied to the whole body of the Garde Nationale.

A possible significance in respect to other forces than those of Paris under similar complications of circumstances attached to the occurrences just mentioned; it was emphasized by conditions pertaining to other classes of citizen soldiers whose reputation stood higher than that alluded to. It was said of those enrolled under such titles as *Amis de France*, *Francs Tireurs*, and so on, that so far from being recognised by the Germans as soldiers, properly so called, when they fell into the hands of the latter they were looked upon as brigands and assassins; dealt with accordingly, that is, taken to the rear and shot. It was said of them that "if the franc tireurs will indulge in Red Indian warfare, they must take the consequences."

The spy mania acquired renewed activity, experiences among us foreigners becoming again unpleasant, though never to the extent already mentioned. Such was the degree to which the new development prevailed that certain aristocratic ladies who had taken upon themselves the part of *vivandières*, in place of those to whom allusion has already been made, were subjected to unpleasantness as a result of suspicion that fell upon them. Houses in the windows of which lights were detected in the course of the long nights of midwinter were disagreeably overhauled by order of "the authorities"; those occupied by Germans, or by French suspected of German proclivities, were in some instances invaded by roughs, and that without interference by the police, who were passive spectators of violence done to person or property, or both. It was necessary for all who desired some measure of individual safety to obtain at the office of the Governor a "*Laissez passer*," and to have the card so named viséd from time to time at the same bureau.

Arising out of what seemed to us outsiders a very silly quarrel in connection with the tittle-tattle and can-cans of a club a duel took place, while the circumstances around us were as have just been described. The principals and their "friends," all French, every endeavour made by the latter to prevent the encounter having failed, the meeting took place in a garden within the city. The adversaries, each with foil in hand, took their places as arranged by their "friends," the foils of the latter held so as to be under those of their respective opponents, and so, ready to strike up the weapon in case of "accident," undue advantage, or other sufficient cause. Stripped to the shirt, the combatants lunge, parry, and thrust at each other in the grey mist of morning, while the sound of heavy firing from outlying forts was borne through the air. From their persons perspiration issues, to be converted by the cold of a December morning into visible vapour; the shirt of one is pierced, his side grazed; the fight lasts forty-five minutes; the bared arm of the other principal is suddenly raised quivering in the air, blood trickles. "*Je suis touché!*" he exclaims; the weapon falls; "honour" has been satisfied.

From forts and other positions around the city firing increases in degree; it is continuous by day and throughout the night. Within, there are large bodies of troops in motion to the sounds of drum and bugle; orders issued that all gates of the fortifications shall be closed alike to egress and ingress, these incidents being precursors of another attempt against the enemy. Long before daybreak on December 21 the Rue Lafayette was crowded by troops and ambulance establishments making their way to the Porte de Pantin. Soon thereafter a combined force,[1] comprising this and other portions, took up position on the open field, triangular in form, at the angles of which stand respectively Aubervilliers, Le Bourget, and Drancy. On the left of the French position the combat immediately became terrific in its violence, the interchange of fire from guns and rifles on each side amounting to a continuous roar and shower of missiles. Heaviest of all was the bombardment of Bourget, then in possession of the Germans, from the fort of Aubervilliers. After a time the marine battalion, led by Admiral de la Roncière, made a rush, hatchets in hand, cheering as they went, upon the village, with the result that out of six hundred men, of whom their force consisted when their charge began, two hundred and seventy-nine lay dead or wounded within a few minutes, the position still retained by the enemy. At other places also the French attack failed; a third defeat had been sustained. The intensity of cold was the greatest hitherto experienced.

While the fight was at its hottest a lady bearing the Red Cross brassard came upon the scene, her precise object and purpose not apparent. Wounded men were being brought to and attended by members of ambulance societies under circumstances to which most of us had become accustomed. Not so the lady, to whom the scene around and its general accompaniments proved altogether "too much"; her demeanour and style of action showed how unsuited she was to

[1] The chief officers in command were Vinoy, Ducrot and De la Roncière.

the position into which, no one knew how or why, she had come. She was taken in charge by a courteous surgeon, and guided with gentle firmness to the rear, after which ambulance work proceeded with regularity and system, as usual.

On the day following the scene presented by the battlefield was one that fancy could have hardly pictured. The village of Drancy a mass of ruin; fire and smoke everywhere rising therefrom; the church destroyed, but in the midst of ruin the figure of the Madonna and Child erect upon its pedestal, and untouched. Parties of troops who had bivouacked during the night sheltered themselves as best they could, some by pieces of *tentès abri*, others by pieces of doors and furniture; camp fires kept up by means of fragments of cabinets, costly furniture, and pianos. Among the men some had possessed themselves with sheep-skins, blankets, rugs, or carpets, with pieces of which their heads and bodies were protected, giving to them a strange and wild appearance. Everywhere the deeply frozen ground was torn by shells, or had in it pits formed by the explosion of those missiles.

Accompanied by a Staff officer I visited two of the largest barracks within the city, meeting in both of them from the soldiers through whose rooms I passed such a display of civility and hospitality as I had heretofore been unaccustomed to. In the Caserne de Papinière, in accepting the cup of wine proffered by a soldier, I drank "Success to the French army," feeling as I did so how little likely was that sentiment to be realized. From the further end of the room came the inquiry, expressed in the English tongue, "How do you like our wine, sir?" A brief talk with the speaker followed. In the course of it he said he was by birth an Irishman; had left his wife in Dublin; had served twenty years in the French navy; was well satisfied with that service, in which there were a good many of his countrymen; that his period for pension was very nearly complete; but in all that time he had never been so near "losing his number" as "there at Bourget."

Christmas is upon us. Weather bitterly cold; many of the troops in bivouac suffer from frost-bite; the Seine thickly covered with ice; fuel expended; pumping machinery, like other kinds, at a standstill, hence water supply materially interfered with, personal ablution and laundry work all but impossible. Marauding parties break down and rob wood wherever they can; trees newly cut down are placed on the hearth; they refuse to burn, but yield smoke in abundance, which irritates and inflames the eyes. Food difficulties have increased in urgency; the daily ration insufficient in quantity to maintain strength and animal warmth. In the hospitals upwards of 20,000 sick and wounded; mortality in those establishments greater than on the field of battle; *pourriture* among the wounded prevailing to an alarming extent.[1] The health of besieged had become impaired by semi-starvation; hands, feet, and ears were chapped and painful. These were among the conditions in which our great festival was celebrated; affectionate thoughts wafted towards those from whom no communication had reached us since the unhappy day of Chatillon.

Public opinion manifested itself in ways opposed to religion, law, and order. Classes of people belonging to, or of similar type to those of Belleville and Vilette, broke into ribaldry of expression that seemed to approach in profanity that of 1792; in that also they were joined by some of the daily papers, the position assumed by the Communists so violent as to menace the existence of the Provisional Government. Meantime there was increased activity in the batteries of the besiegers, indicating that the circle of "fire and steel" beyond the city had narrowed; yet, with all this, the dangers, present and prospective, were looked upon as at least equal in gravity from enemies within as from those beyond the walls.

On the 27th of December newly unmasked batteries opened heavy fire on Avron and other places in its vicinity; shells began to fall within the *enceinte* of the city, and so the long-expected bombardment began. So heavy was the volume of fire on that position that during three days of its continuance it was estimated that 7,000 missiles—all of large size—fell upon it. Manfully for a time did the defenders stand their ground; very great their losses in killed and wounded when at last they were forced to abandon their forts on the north-eastern side, their wounded serving to still further crowd the overcrowded ambulances. The ultimate issue of the siege, never very doubtful to us foreigners, had now become less so than before. Men asked each other, "How is it that 600,000 Frenchmen permitted themselves to be blockaded by 200,000 Germans?" The mystery seemed to be solved by a writer[2] of that day, somewhat according to this manner: "It is confessed that the Governor (Trochu) has shown unfortunate hesitations; but to do good work the tools must be good, and in these respects he is deficient. To fight the Prussians we should have old soldiers, well disciplined and inured to war, reliable and instructed officers; not young soldiers of three months, poorly fed and sickly, and officers who have been too recently promoted to properly understand their duties." In gloom and sadness to us the year 1870 ended.

[1] Notwithstanding the free use of antiseptics and disinfectants of many kinds.

[2] *Journal du Siége par un Bourgeois de Paris*, p. 573.

CHAPTER XXXI

1871. *JANUARY. SIEGE. BOMBARDMENT. CAPITULATION OF PARIS*

Bombardment begun—Its progress and effects—"The terrible battery of Meudon"—Sundry particulars—Conditions of the besieged—A telegram—Increasing privations—Disaffection and corruption—Routine of every-day life—Our food supplies—Photographic messages—Personal circumstances—Night march—A Proclamation—Sortie on Montretout and Bugeval—Defeat—The killed and wounded—Armistice declared—*Vive la Commune!*—General events—At our worst—Ambulances—Ward scenes and statistics—Unexpected recognition.

INCESSANT firing between the enemy's positions and outlying forts during the last night of 1870 and first day of 1871, increasing in violence as the day advanced; additional batteries unmasked on the German side, thus giving visible signs of what was to come. At 3 a.m. on the 5th, the first shell of actual bombardment fell within the city; then followed similar missiles in quick succession, chiefly falling and exploding near the Panthéon, Luxembourg, and market of Montrouge. In the course of that day a Government Proclamation was issued, the terms of which as they are transcribed seem almost childish in their simplicity: "The bombardment of Paris has commenced. The enemy, not content with firing upon our forts, hurls his projectiles upon our houses; threatens our hearths and our families. His violence will redouble the resolution of the city, which will fight and conquer. The defenders of the forts, exposed to incessant firing, lose nought of their calmness, and know well how to inflict terrible reprisals upon the assailants. The population of Paris valiantly accept this new token. The enemy hopes to intimidate it; he will only render its bound the more vigorous. It will show itself worthy of the Army of the Loire, which has caused the enemy to retire; of the Army of the North, which is marching to our relief.[1] *Vive la France! Vive la République!*"

[1] Referring to confusedly expressed news received by pigeon, which was interpreted to the effect that Faidherbe had repulsed the enemy in the Pas de Calais; Chansy and Bourbaki were at Nevers "watching" on either flank of the army of Prince Frederick Charles; at Nuits, "a French general" had with 10,000 French beaten 25,000 Prussians.

Bombardment increased in violence and rapidity during the nights and days immediately following, the shells falling nearer and nearer to the centre of the city. With reports of casualties among men, women, and children, came accounts of buildings struck and penetrated by shells, including private dwellings, hospitals, ambulances, churches, and convents, all situated on the left side of the Seine. An exodus of people from the places struck was a natural result. They flocked to parts of the city situated on the right side of the river, and there, in the face of great difficulties, were provided with accommodation; food being obtained for them with even greater difficulty than accommodation. Sick and wounded had similarly to be provided for; so had the inmates of maternity establishments. Hotels, business establishments, churches, and public buildings of all sorts were rapidly transformed for the reception of the several classes alluded to; private houses belonging to persons who had quitted the beleaguered city were "requisitioned" for the same purpose, while in many instances private families gave shelter and aid to refugees from the bombarded quarters.

Then opened upon the city what speedily became known among us as "the terrible battery of Meudon," on account of the great violence of bombardment by it; the missiles therefrom committed greater havoc than anything previously experienced, and fell nearer and nearer to the centre of Paris as "practice" went on. Day and night continuously, with varying intensity, but always greatest during the night, did the bombardment continue. Answering fire from the forts around was scarcely less actively directed upon the German positions, the incessant rolling sound of heavy guns varied by that of exploding shells, the tremor of houses so caused rendered the hours of darkness somewhat "hideous."

So passed twelve days and nights. On the 17th of January there was a slackening of fire from the forts. Rumour in different shapes spread in regard to the cause: that to which most ready belief was given being that ammunition had begun to fail; the meaning of such a report significant. At this time certain published records appeared in which statistics of casualties purported to be given; those during the first eight days of bombardment 51 killed and 138 wounded, the damage to buildings unexpectedly small. Some of us set to work to calculate arithmetically our individual chances of being struck, and so made them out to be relatively little. Those chances would no doubt have been materially increased had the intentions assigned to the German artillery been carried out of discharging incendiary bombs upon Paris—an intention frustrated by order of the Emperor—for that dignity had recently been assumed by him.[1] Fortunately

[1] On January 18, 1871, at Versailles.

for us not more than three out of every five *obuses* discharged upon us exploded; whether as a result of defects in themselves or other cause did not matter to us upon whom they were directed.

It was now that the terms of a telegram said to have been sent by "King William to Queen Augusta" was everywhere exhibited in the great thoroughfares. That message intimated that "the bombardment of Paris proceeds satisfactorily, thank God." The comments passed with reference to it were at the time distinctly expressive, and no wonder. But now, long years after the event, the question arises—Was such a telegram ever sent?

Meanwhile the conditions of the besieged, as already noticed, had increased in severity. The season of mid-winter was of unusual inclemency; sickness and mortality by disease had acquired alarming rates, irrespective of casualties in battle; fuel was unobtainable, the want of it a cause of increased suffering and illness. The best energies of arrondissements, public institutions, and private individuals were directed to the mitigation of these and other evils incidental to a people besieged and under bombardment; but, alas! while the cause remained, the ordinary effects could only be averted in a very small degree, if in any.

It was under these circumstances that a renewed spirit of disaffection towards the existing Government broke out violently among the classes who were the chief recipients of help in various ways specially granted to them by that Government, even to the relative neglect of those who, equally needy, were less clamorous. There arose dissensions among the sectional Representatives; distrust of, and ill-feeling towards, the foreign residents on imaginary grounds that the latter carried on a system of communication with the besiegers. Signs of disaffection and corruption were manifest among the citizen soldiers, those signs giving peculiar signficance to the extravagant terms in which official orders made mention of the services performed by them; for the facts were popularly known that an attempted sortie on the 10th miscarried because information regarding it had reached the enemy; that a second, planned for the 14th, had to be abandoned on account of some of those citizen "soldiers" having failed to be in their assigned positions at the appointed time. So far as indications pointed, revolution and civil war were imminent, while heavy bombardment by the enemy was still in progress.

Meanwhile the ordinary routine of everyday life went on much as if besiegers outside and various dangerous elements within our gates were non-existent, with the difference that to more common subjects of talk was added *obuses*, including probable size, distance at which from the speaker, and places of their explosion, damage to property and life caused thereby, and so on. As time went on the bombardment became, to some degree, a substitute for the weather as subject of first remark between acquaintances when meeting each other for the day; for example: "The bombardment is rather lively to-day," or "it is rather slow." People met at dinner, if that term can be applied to the fare procurable. Walking became a necessity, for the reason that the horses of omnibuses and other public conveyances had been requisitioned for purposes of food; hence, those of us who had duties to perform, experienced increasing difficulties in carrying them out. But these conditions were not altogether unrelieved by an incident having in it much of the ludicrous. An order was published declaring that widows of "soldiers" of the Mobile and National Guards should thenceforward be deemed entitled to pension, the immediate result being a great outcrop of marriage ceremonies among the classes concerned.

All ordinary supplies of *viande* had now become expended, the small reserve store being retained for the sick and wounded. Animals of all kinds, excluding the carnivora,[1] were requisitioned, their carcases exposed for sale in boucheries, but only issued to persons provided with the required *billet de rationnement* from the mairie of his arrondissement. Supplies of grain were in like manner "requisitioned" and issued under authority; armed sentries guarded retail establishments, their services on various occasions required against rioters, as already alluded to, from Belleville and Vilette. In the southern parts of the city long queues of women were to be seen, each individual waiting her turn to receive her "ration"; not a few of the elderly and weak among them falling where they had stood, exhausted as their physical powers were from cold and insufficient food. In some localities, more especially near the Luxembourg, casualties among them occurred by the explosion of Prussian shells. The daily "ration" for which they scrambled consisted latterly of about ten ounces of bread, one ounce of horseflesh, and a quarter litre of *vin ordinare.* The bread contained $\frac{1}{8}$ flour, $\frac{4}{8}$ *fecula* of potatoes, rice, peas and lentils, $\frac{1}{8}$ of ground straw, the remaining fraction made up of water and "sundry" materials. Women of all social classes aided the *real* poor in every possible way, and in other respects maintained the reputation of their sex in times of danger and difficulty.

An improved and ingenious method by which news from the outer

[1] The remark refers to those in the Jardin des Plantes and Jardin d'Acclimation. The flesh of these animals was sold at exorbitant prices.

world could be brought within access to the ordinary people within the city was now introduced, through the instrumentality, it was said, of the *Times*. A series of advertisements addressed to individuals appeared in that journal; these having been reduced at Tours to minimum dimensions by photography, the sheet containing them was thence transmitted by pigeon-post. On arrival within Paris the whole was enlarged by means of the camera, after which the messages were copied and dispatched to their several addresses. In this way a message reached me from my beloved wife—the first I had received for upwards of four months—it was, "Your family are well; most anxious about you." I fully appreciated the significance of these few words.

In respect to privations and risks, my individual experiences were neither more nor less than those to which many others within the bombarded city had perforce to submit. My stock of cash had become exhausted; to all intents and purposes I was a pauper, only able to obtain the requirements of life by giving to the *maitre d'hôtel* in which I resided written authority to my London agents, that in the event of my death they should pay all his claims upon me. I subsequently learned that, in response to my urgent requests sent *par ballon monté*, my wife had vainly endeavoured to have money transmitted to me, until, having applied to the American Embassy in London, a remittance was at once sent through that channel; in due time received by me from Mr. Washbourne, and so my pecuniary obligations discharged. As pressure in respect to food increased, I fear that on some few occasions I partook of *bifteck de cheval*, and once,—only once,—of *paté de chien*; but against both of these appetite rebelled, and latterly I had to put up with the one salt herring with which I was supplied as "meat rations" for three days. Prior to the complete investment of the city, I had procured and hidden away such small supplies as I could lay hands on, of anchovies, mushrooms, sailors' biscuits, and oatmeal; the quantities of each were small, but such as they were, they served their purpose.

All through the night of the 18th, large bodies of troops marched silently towards positions previously assigned to them with reference to coming events. The night was unusually dark; the streets presented only glimering lamp-lights at distant intervals; the city enshrouded in dense mist; beyond the gates the ground saturated with rain, the roads by which the forces had to proceed encumbered with guns, waggons, and other obstructive objects.

Daylight revealed to "all concerned" the Proclamation as follows, not only published in the journals, but affixed to walls in various places, namely: "Citizens, the enemy kills our wives and children, bombards us night and day, covers with shells our hospitals. One cry, 'To Arms!' has burst from every breast. Those who can shed their life's blood on the field of battle will march against the enemy; those who remain, jealous of the honour of their brothers, will, if required, suffer with calm endurance every sacrifice, as their proof of their devotion to their country. Suffer and die if necessary, but conquer! *Vive la République!*"

Three *Corps d'Armée*, comprising more than one hundred thousand men, under the commands of Ducrot, Vinoy, and Bellemere, had taken, or were in progress of taking up positions under cover of Mont Valérien against the Prussian lines between Montretout and Bugeval, the prevailing fog so dense that assigned routes could not be maintained; several hours were thus lost. The French troops were consequently worn out with fatigue; portions of them had not arrived in position, among others considerable bodies of artillery, so that when about 9 a.m. the fight began, they had not been consolidated. On the other hand, the larger forces against whom they were led were unfatigued by night march and other difficulties; they had passed the night in relative quiet, had good and ample rations, and were in full physical strength. With all these disadvantages the first onslaught against the enemy's positions at Montretout and Fouilleuse was successful. Thence, toward the French right, the combat quickly developed in fury; no fewer than five hundred cannon, including both sides, were estimated as engaged in their deadly work, excluding those of Mont Valérien, missiles from which whizzed above our heads in their flight towards the German lines. On our side, shells from the latter fell as it were from the zenith among the masses of advancing infantry, making great gaps, as each successive cloud of débris from their explosions cleared away. From Fouilleuse we were able to see the terrible violence with which the fight now raged. There the Société Internationale des Secours aux Blessés established a field ambulance; many wounded received first aid, and thence were dispatched to "fixed" establishments within the city. To reinforce the troops engaged, whose losses were already very great, large bodies of men from those in reserve marched laboriously towards the front. The ground was soaked by rain, their progress slow and difficult, themselves weary, fatigued, and physically weak. In their advance they came upon many carcases of horses killed by German shells, some of the men falling out of their ranks to cut from them slices of bleeding flesh; having secured them on their backs, they resumed their places, and so onward towards the enemy. Meanwhile, a horrible scene was taking place in close proximity to the place where, mounted, I stood with a group of Staff officers.

A private of the 119th regiment of the line shot the captain of his company while their battalion was advancing, and torn by vertical fire as already mentioned. Ducrot ordered the man to be put to death on the spot. A party of his own regiment was at once detailed for the purpose; by it he was taken aside—not more than a few feet from the left of the advancing column; he was seen to fall. A party of brancardiers approached; they were warned off; one of the execution party levelled his rifle and fired at him as he lay struggling on the ground; then another; then a third, and now the unhappy man lies still in death. We speculated among ourselves as to the circumstances that may have led him to commit the crime so expiated.

As day advanced the thick mist of morning cleared away, revealing the progress of battle and extent of field on which it raged. That the French were more exposed than were the enemy was at once apparent; yet, though suffering greatly by shot and shell from unseen batteries, they stood their ground with obstinacy, inured as they had now become to combat by their four months of experience. Later on, however, hesitation is shown in their ranks; stragglers drop away; needlessly large numbers[1] accompany to the rear their wounded comrades; unsteadiness affects battalions; and now the sad spectacle is seen of one such body in flight down the declivity adjoining Montretout. Officers make frantic efforts to rally their men; daylight fades in gloom; soon night closes in, mist again covers the scene; firing from both sides have ceased; all around is dark and silent.

In the darkness for hours did the ambulance men of various societies traverse the field in pursuance of their work. As conveyances were in progress towards the general rendezvous, confusion and crush increased, as a combined result of darkness and an absence of regular roadways; progress consequently so retarded that night was far advanced when we reached the rampart gates, our conveyances *complet* with wounded men. As on the first occasion, roadsides and avenues within Port Maillot were crowded with people. Loud and anxious inquiries for relatives and friends who had taken part in the recent battle were frequent; frivolity in abeyance, as if experience had impressed upon them the significance of combat against our besiegers. That the result of the day had been disastrous to the French was speedily realized. Next day the casualties among the forces engaged were estimated at 1000 killed, the greater number by artillery fire; the wounded as "very many."

Meanwhile the work of bombarding Paris, scarcely if at all interfered

[1] On one occasion thirteen were so counted, bringing to the rear a wounded comrade.

with by the incident of severe conflict just narrated, was increased rather than diminished in its intensity; new batteries opened upon the city, with *acharnement*, shells falling upon places hitherto untouched. St. Denis was assailed, and underwent greater destruction in respect to property and life than had been sustained by the capital itself. A rush of people from that suburb took place, causing serious inconvenience to those whose duty it was to provide them with accommodation and food. All hopes of deliverance had become extinguished; negotiations were accordingly opened with the German Chancellor in view to an armistice being arranged. While they were in progress, bombardment continued with its usual violence. Early in the night of the 26th there was a sudden lull; a few minutes before midnight there was discharged upon us a volley from all points of the circle, such as we had never previously experienced; then followed stillness. Bombardment had ceased; we knew that the Convention had been signed. For 130 days Paris had been besieged; during thirty, the advanced forts had been bombarded; during twenty-one, the city.[1]

Demonstrations by "the dangerous classes" of Belleville and Vilette took place; their plea, the terms on which the armistice had been concluded. The Hôtel de Ville was menaced by crowds of excited men, gesticulating wildly as they shouted, "*Vive la Commune!*" They are dispersed by force of arms; several of their numbers killed, many more wounded. There is a flight towards the Mazas prison; an entrance thereto is effected, some of the more noted of its inmates released. A rush is made upon the small remaining food stores of their arrondissements; they are broken into, their contents distributed among the assailants. After a time these disturbances are suppressed. Trochu has resigned his command; Vinoy is his successor.

When on January 27, 1871, the morning papers published the terms of amnesty, the fact was one of common knowledge that the stock of food remaining was not equal to more than six or seven days' "rations," even according to the reduced scale to which the besieged were at the time brought down; in fact, all were now at starvation point as a result of gradually diminishing allowances of food. Next day the Germans occupied Mont Valérien as the French troops marched out of it. Some hours later appeared a proclamation by the Govern-

[1] The following places were those that chiefly suffered within Paris, viz., The Luxembourg quarter, Boulevard St. Michel, Rues St. Jacques, d'Enfer, Vaugirard, Hôpital Val de Grace, Théâtre Odéon, Church of St. Sulpice, the Jardin des Plantes, Panthéon, Ministère de Commerce, Invalides, Church of St. Germain, Rue Boissy d'Anglais.

ment of the Defence announcing that "the Convention which terminates the resistance of Paris will be signed in a few hours"; that "we could not have prolonged the resistance without condemning to certain death two millions of men, women, and children. Mortality has increased threefold." "We come out with all our honour," the same document said, "and with all our hopes, in spite of our present grief." In accordance with the terms agreed upon, the process began of disarming the citizen soldiers, of whom groups along the thoroughfares showed by their gloomy style and demeanour those pent-up feelings of disaffection which were soon to break out in the horrors of the Commune.

The conditions to which Paris and its people had been reduced were urgent. Severe cold, absolute want of fuel, the insufficient scale of food to which all were officially limited, prevailing sickness and mortality by disease, added to the recurring influx of wounded as a result of desultory conflicts beyond the line of fortifications, combined to render further resistance impossible.

All establishments set apart for the reception of wounded were overcrowded. Not alone food, but appliances were insufficient in quantity and kind. In many instances private families had received wounded into their houses, and so crippled their own resources. The result of the recent sortie and action at Montretout was an accession to the numbers requiring care and accommodation of three to five thousand, for actual statistics were unobtainable; professional and other attendants were insufficient to meet the demands on their services; while, as if still further to complicate matters, the Germans sent several hundred wounded French into the city, and so lightened the work of their own establishments.

In some ambulances such scenes were to be seen as French and German wounded occupying adjoining beds; no longer "enemies," but helpless; unable to communicate with each other; many destined to quit the place in death, for hospital diseases setting at defiance disinfection and all other supposed preventive measures proved fatal to a large proportion of patients within those establishments. A heavy offensive odour, that of *pourriture*, pervades wards and corridors of the buildings, extending to the streets or boulevards immediately adjoining. In the mortuary of a large hospital the scene presented was too horrible for detailed description.

The defence now ended had been carried on at a cost in human life in respect to which reliable statistics were unobtainable. According to one account, deaths on the field of battle and in ambulances amounted among troops of the line and Mobiles to 50,000; to another to 63,000; to a third to 73,000; neither estimate taking into account mortality by disease and privation among the non-military inhabitants. On the capitulation of Paris the troops who became prisoners of war numbered about 180,000; the fortress guns "captured" by the enemy 1,500 field pieces and 400 mitrailleuses; in addition the gun-boats on the Seine, locomotives, and rolling stock.

While making my round among the ambulances, I was somewhat surprised to hear myself accosted by name by a wounded man who occupied one of the beds past which I was moving. At once I entered into conversation with him, naturally enough expressing sympathy for him. He briefly informed me that he was in the 101st (British) Regiment, and landed with that corps at Gosport on the occasion of its first arrival in England from India; that he remembered me on duty there; that having left the regiment he joined the Francs Tireurs of Paris at the beginning of the siege; that fifty per cent. of his comrades had perished by shot, disease, or at the hands of the Germans, into which they may have fallen as prisoners; that he himself had not slept in a bed for three months until brought to the ambulance wounded. He was but one example of the material of which such volunteers were composed, and a similar story to his could doubtless be told by many others.

Under the circumstances to which we were now reduced, welcome was the news that supplies of food sent to the besieged from England and elsewhere had arrived in proximity of the outskirts; credit must be accorded to the supreme officers of the investing force for the rapidity with which those supplies were forwarded to the now starving people within, so that on the last day of January many waggon loads were received, and forthwith distributed. On that day also postal communication with the outer world was re-established, though with the proviso that letters dispatched should be unsealed.

CHAPTER XXXII

1871. *FEBRUARY. PARIS AFTER CAPITULATION*

Food in abundance—Theatrical parody—Contrasted conditions—Preparations for German entry—Causes assigned for defeat—Citizen and regular soldiers—Distributing food.

RENEWED disturbances inaugurated the month of February. The central market, in which were the food stores arriving from without, was again attacked and pillaged; nor were the rioters dispersed until a strong military force arrived on the spot. Further supplies came pouring into the city, until within a few days there was abundance everywhere; all restrictions on sale removed; restaurants recovered much of their ordinary aspect. From London came large quantities of food, and of appliances for wounded; a donation from the city to the Municipality of Paris. The whole of those supplies, in accordance with such terms, were divided among the twenty arrondissements of Paris, with the result that a large share fell to the dangerous classes so often alluded to; comparatively little to the professional and other respectable classes who all through the times of greatest trial had borne their privations in silence. Within a few days thereafter, so profuse had been the supplies issued that large quantities, exposed for sale in shops, could be purchased at less than their ordinary retail price. But money wherewith to make purchases had not yet come into the hands of those most in want.

The urgency of conditions among the "better" classes alluded to was known to those of us who had passed through the difficulties of the siege now at an end; proffered suggestions in regard to issuing food and other requirement to them were ignored by those in charge. Thus came about the undesirable state of things that the disaffected and dangerous among the population had more than they could make use of; the orderly and reputable obtained little, if anything, to relieve their necessities. An Englishman applied at the mairie of the 9th

Arrondissement for help in food from the *don anglais* received. He was asked, "Are you really much in want to-day?" "Very much," was his reply, "or else I should not have wasted the day by coming here." So they gave him a halfpenny biscuit, a square inch of cheese, and three lumps of sugar, but not until he had been kept waiting several hours! That is but one illustration.

While on the one side the scenes just mentioned were in progress as an outcome of well-meant liberality on the part of our own country, others were to be seen, the style of which presented to us foreigners a phase of Parisian characteristics altogether new. In a theatre close to the Porte St. Martin, the privations and various other painful incidents of the siege were parodied much to the apparent amusement of the crowded house. Comment on the "performances" in question is best omitted.

Fugitives who had abandoned their houses while investment of the city was incomplete returned in daily increasing numbers, to find for the most part that stores of food and wine they had left behind were non-existent, they having been taken possession of meanwhile. Railway passenger traffic was resumed; on the Seine the *bateaux mouches* conveyed crowds of sightseers to the various river stations, near which the most interesting relics of the siege might be seen, including dismantled forts, dilapidated houses, devastated grounds, and burial places of victims of the war. For the payment of the indemnity to the Germans in accordance with terms of Convention it became necessary to raise a special loan. No sooner were the terms[1] of that Convention published than the people took it up with enthusiasm; from morning till night queues of intending subscribers,[2] from sums of a few francs to thousands, occupied the pavements in the vicinity of the offices where their contributions were to be received. Nothing could better indicate the frugality of the Parisian masses in respect to available money than the fact that a sufficient sum was thus quickly and readily obtained to enable the municipality to pay to the German authorities at Versailles the first moiety—namely, one hundred millions of francs—of that indemnity. Return to the ordinary conditions of the capital went on; shops were re-opened; the windows made gay with mer-

[1] "The city of Paris is to pay a contribution of 200,000,000 francs (equal to £8,000,000 sterling) within a fortnight. Public property is not to be removed during the armistice. All German prisoners of war shall immediately be exchanged against a proportionate number of French prisoners; also captains of vessels and others, as well as civilian prisoners on both sides."

[2] At this very time the ordinary 3 per cent. Rentes stood at 51·20; while the new loan for the indemnity stood at 52·40.

chandise; gas re-lighted in the thoroughfares at night. Supplies of provisions and of money in large sums, sent from various sources, continued to arrive, one noteworthy contribution of the latter kind being 112,000 francs from Mexico. The process of disarming the troops was still in progress, until the numbers should be reached in accordance with the preliminaries already determined. The Government of the Defence gave place to the National Assembly. The armistice was extended, first from the 19th to 24th of February, then from the latter date to March 12, the Treaty of Peace being signed on 26th of that first named. Part of that Convention was that German troops should enter Paris, and occupy part of the capital until the ratification of the Treaty by the Assembly. Great excitement and threatened outbreak among the lower orders was the immediate result, while the papers of the day fanned rather than moderated popular ill-feeling by rhodomontade and calumnies in their columns.

Preparatory to the entrance of the German forces, it was determined that those of Paris should occupy quarters for the time being on the left side of the Seine; that the duty of maintaining order should be confided to the Garde Nationale. The citizen soldiers "magnanimously" offered to take charge of the artillery guns, for the removal of which horses were non-existent; the whole were collected and "parked" in the Parc de Monceau, though at the time questions arose as to the means by which they were again to be got from the hands of those to whom they had so fallen. Signs of probable disturbance multiplied apace; barricades were erected in some of the principal thoroughfares; fights occurred between the most violent elements of the populace and the Garde Nationale, with the result that some of the guns were taken possession of by the former.

Brought in contact with representatives of various classes of society, political and religious opinion, opportunity was afforded me to note the views expressed by them respectively as to the causes to which the present humiliation of Paris and of France was considered to be due. It was my custom to record the several opinions expressed in conversation as soon as I had an opportunity of doing so. I reproduce them as follows, rather than in a classified order, namely :—

1. The empire was looked upon as "expended."

2. The manhood of Paris and of France had become degenerated in physique; the sick and the relatively weak having been alone left after the wars of the 1st Napoleon to propagate their kind.

3. The study of the military sciences had been neglected; officers underwent examination rather for the purpose of obtaining appointments than to attain proficiency in knowledge of their profession.

4. Defects in administration by the Intendance, and general obstructiveness in that branch of the service.

5. Over-centralization, so that when emergency of war occurred, no corps was complete in itself; *materiel* had to be obtained from Paris, means of transport and roads being at once blocked in consequence.

6. The soldiers being allowed to give their votes at elections, their sympathies were diverted to their political parties rather than with their military commanders.

7. Want of mutual confidence between officers from the highest to the lowest rank; between officers and their men, and between the men themselves.[1] In fact, general mistrust prevails where confidence should exist.

8. The officers to a great extent being members of the same class of society to which the rank and file belong, there is an absence of that deference towards them by the latter, such as is considered essential to the maintenance of the highest order of discipline. From this and other circumstances there was said to exist a deplorable state of indiscipline, of which indeed some striking illustrations occurred during the siege.

9. Laxity of discipline among the higher officers, due to the (assigned) circumstance that the deposed Emperor manifested hesitancy and uncertainty with regard to punishments for shortcomings and offences on their part.

10. A spirit of impatience of control and of opposition against authority, fostered by the conditions of social life in France, including the absence of domesticity, and, as a consequence, of lively affection between parents and children, and among children themselves, many of whom spend their early years among strangers.

11. The expenses connected with the unfortunate expedition to Mexico had so far exceeded the estimate, that the Emperor "feared" to make public the whole of the circumstances connected therewith; hence it was considered necessary to divert to their liquidation money obtained nominally for current military purposes. Thus it was asserted

[1] Among other circumstances to which this want of confidence was assigned, on various occasions I heard enumerated "The Confessional" of the Romish Church, to which the great majority of the people belong. The direct effect of that observance is said to be the breaking of confidence between members of the same family, and so on upwards throughout public, as in private life. In connection with this allegations made by so many with whom I had communication, the circumstance is significant that whenever and for whatever political end a "Revolution" takes place in Paris, the class of persons who are first and invariably attacked are the clergy of that particular denomination.

the actual condition of military establishments differed from that represented on paper.

12. A general lowering of the moral sense, of which the religious sentiment is the first great principle.

To this somewhat imposing list I append the subjoined, which was subsequently collated while perusing various works relative to the Franco-Prussian war, namely:—

(*a*) Absolute unpreparedness of a war, which was begun "with frivolity without parallel."

(*b*) General maladministration.

(*c*) Antagonism between the Paris and Provincial Governments.

(*d*) Misrepresentations of actual conditions contained in official Proclamations and in organs of the Press.

(*e*) Political divisions and sub-divisions among the people, whether official or non-official.

(*f*) Antagonism of interests and personal considerations among the higher administrators and commanders.

(*g*) Disturbances fomented and brought about by agitators.

(*h*) The inferior military qualities of a large portion of the citizen-soldiers.

(*i*) Social immorality. For a long time past piety and moral earnestness have been much shaken in French society; the cancer of frivolity and immorality has eaten into the heart of the people.

That several of the defects above enumerated are real is beyond all question, even when allowance is made for those which are perhaps more theoretical than actual. Some had special reference to the episode of the war from which France was about to emerge heavily crippled; others have a prospective significance; nor is it easy to conceive of success, so long as they are permitted to continue.

Adverting to the non-military qualities already mentioned, and to the conduct in face of the enemy displayed by the extemporised citizen-soldiers, to whom per force of circumstances the defence of Paris had to a considerable extent to be confided, the fact is noteworthy and suggestive that, having become to some extent acquainted with the use of arms and with war, they became transformed into very dangerous elements when the Commune was declared. It was then that they fought resolutely against the Versailles forces, and committed many of the atrocities by which that occasion was to be disgraced.[1] Of the

[1] One of the first measures of the Government of M. Thiers, after crushing the insurrection by the Communists, including the National Guard, was to suppress the militia "force," so called.

troops belonging to the regular army, however, it is their due to observe that in actual combat the gallantry displayed by them could not be exceeded; no more could their patient endurance under the difficulties, privations, and general hardships incidental to the siege. But individual qualities were overbalanced by the disadvantages and evils just enumerated.

No sooner had the gates of Paris been opened, under provision of the armistice, than my coadjutor [1] with the Germans performed to me the good and brotherly act of bringing for myself, and for distribution among my friends and other persons whom I knew to be in necessitous circumstances, not only liberal supplies of food, but also considerable sums of money, contributed by charitable persons to me unknown. It was a source of lively satisfaction to be able thus to aid individuals and some institutions; and in the performance of that most pleasant task several incidents occurred the recollection of which is still fresh. A few examples must suffice. One lady, to whom I carried a fowl, among other articles, was prostrate in bed, her physical powers reduced by starvation to an extremely low ebb. When I told her that she was simply dying from want of food, her reply was that she really had no appetite; she did not think she could eat anything if she had it; yet when I supplied her with some savoury morsels to be used at once, and then the fowl to be cooked later on, her face brightened, she half raised herself in bed, and clutched the little articles I had brought to her. Another lady, to whom I presented some balls of butter, rolled up separately in bits of newspaper, did not delay to unfold the packet, but took a mouthful of the whole, including butter and paper. Being informed that I had a few red herrings for distribution, she next day drove to my hotel in her well-equipped carriage to receive *one* [2] of those savoury fish. The "Little Sisters of the Poor" were astounded and delighted to be presented with a small cartload of mutton, bread, eggs, butter, and various other articles; for the aged paupers, to whose care till death they devoted themselves, had been reduced to extreme want, not a few having succumbed under their privations. In accordance with invitation from the Lady Superior, I visited their establishment to receive expressions of gratitude from its inmates, and in the course of my visit was shown through a ward in the uppermost storey into which a Prussian shell had penetrated, and where some of the old, decrepid inmates had there and then died of fright. A Roman Catholic Seminary sent a representative to express the thanks of its inmates for supplies given to them. As I subsequently was informed,

[1] Surgeon-General Sir J. H. Innes, C.B.

[2] The only one that remained.

the nurses in an ambulance that I similarly aided danced round the table on which the supplies were displayed, while they invoked blessings on my head. Some British subjects to whom I was able to give assistance in food and money were most grateful. As regards myself, what I most craved for, and indulged in when opportunity offered, was fried fat bacon and fruit, more especially apples.

CHAPTER XXXIII

1871. *MARCH. ENEMIES WITHIN PARIS*

German troops enter—"Occupation" ended—Troubles within—Officier de la Légion d'Honneur—Destruction by war—Visit to Versailles—Review by German Emperor—Railway ambulance—Communists on Montmartre—Mission ended.

THE representative statues in the Place de la Concorde were enshrouded; guards placed on either side of positions to be occupied by the Germans. On the morning of March 1, the head of a dense column of troops was seen approaching the Arc de Triomphe; that monument passed, the "Army of Occupation" steadily made its way downwards along the Champs Elysées. In front of all rode a young officer, fair in complexion, his face pale, lips compressed, expression grave and resolute; his name, as we subsequently learned, Bershardy, lieutenant in the 14th Prussian Hussars. Some signs of disturbance were shown among French onlookers; they were quickly suppressed; all knew that the guns of Mont Valérien pointed towards the city; that by them stood German gunners. All through the morning troops *poured* in, until 30,000 men—the number agreed upon—were within their assigned places; among them the Leib Regiment of Bavaria, the losses of which in the war exceeded numerically its strength when leaving Germany. It was now that the striking contrast in physique, *tenue*, and discipline presented by the newly-arrived forces, as compared with those to whom we had been so long accustomed, was strikingly apparent to all spectators; doubtless to Parisians themselves.

Forty-eight hours, including one entire day, was the period mutually agreed upon as that during which the German forces were to remain within Paris. Precautions against collision between them and the populace were so successfully taken that crowds looked on and quietly listened to the foreign bands within their precincts. In other parts of the city, however, signs of restiveness were visible. Among the German troops, on the contrary, all was orderly and soldierlike. Early on the morning of the 3rd, "evacuation" of the city began, and within a few hours was completed. Not until the rear column had passed the Arc de Triomphe did the mob, that meantime hung upon their flanks, begin to "demonstrate"; a section of the withdrawing troops faced round; the demonstrators fled helter-skelter. The work of sweeping and burning refuse in the great thoroughfares was soon begun; it continued during the day; by evening Paris looked as if it had not been entered by a victorious army.

During the following night, internal troubles assumed the first definite shape of that in which they were soon to culminate. The National Guards withdrew from the Parc de Monceau some of the guns entrusted to them, together with their equipment and ammunition, to arrange them in order on Montmartre; others were taken to the disaffected quarters, as Belleville and Vilette; while a definite plan of further action was come to by the Communists. In the emergency so presented, no apparent action was taken by the responsible authorities; citizen "soldiers" were permitted to retain arms, the use of which they had recently learned; with what result was speedily to be seen. During the next few days scenes of pillage were enacted, wherever stores, of whatever kind, existed; barricades were thrown up; other preparations, in various ways, made alike for defence and offence. As events developed, the commandant appointed to the National Guards was repudiated by the men; they demanded that they should have the right to elect their own commander and other officers. Battalions displayed the red flag; marched to the Place de la Concorde; placed the emblem of Revolution upon the statues there, and upon public monuments elsewhere. On the 10th, as the Germans marched from Versailles, the Communists placed on Montmartre the remaining guns, making a total of 417. Seven days thereafter the horrors of the Commune began.

While the German army was entering Paris, I had the honour of being entertained at a *déjeûner* by the members of the Ambulance de la Presse, on the occasion of the distinction of Officier de la Légion d'Honneur[1] being conferred upon me by the Provisional Government. The venerable Professor Ricord was pleased to make me the subject of a toast, alluding in kind terms to my association with the French army and ambulances; then, taking from his own button-hole the rosette of the Order so highly prized, he placed it in mine.

An excursion to a little distance beyond Montrouge revealed a sad example of destruction: houses reduced to heaps of rubbish, with here and there a fragment of cracked wall left standing among them; masses of charred timbers; furniture and what had been ornamental pieces

[1] Date of gazette, February 21, 1871.

strewn about in fragments among débris of various kinds, including dead animals. From among ruined walls of gardens and conservatories green young shoots of plants, revived by sunshine of early spring, served, by contrast with the scene of destruction around, to impress us the more. Were it possible for crowned heads of Europe to make a similar round, it might ensure peace for one generation. So thought we as we continued our walk through miles of devastation.

Making a journey to Versailles, the party of which I was one passed by the heights beyond Meudon, on which were ranged the guns until recently employed in bombarding Paris, but now parked preparatory to being sent back to Germany. Several of them were seriously damaged; others presented traces of work done by them in "the terrible battery," also visited by us; its condition, abandoned to ruin. Thence we looked towards Vaugirard and vicinity, where greatest destruction by its shells took place. At Versailles, while dining in the *grande salle* of the Hôtel des Reservoirs, then filled with Prussian officers, we saw among them Prince Leopold of Hohenzollern, the nomination of whom to the Spanish throne was the ostensible cause of the needless war now ended. Visiting in the Chateau the Galerie of Louis XIV., it was seen converted into an ambulance ward, its paintings damaged and torn as a result of wind and weather admitted through windows kept open for purposes of ventilation. The less severely wounded had been dispatched to Fatherland; those remaining were too seriously injured to admit of being removed; in cots, above the heads of which stood canvas representations of the "glories of France," shattered frames of recent conquerors lay in agony.

Under the wing of a *Times* correspondent, I witnessed on the heights of Villiers a review by the German Emperor of three *corps d'armée*, consisting respectively of Bavarians, Saxons, and Wurtembergers, all under command of the Crown Prince of Prussia. As the troops took positions assigned to them, it was observed by our friend, who had accompanied them from Rhine to Seine, that their numbers scarcely equalled half of those who entered France. An impression was said to exist among the Bavarians that more frequently than other corps they were so placed as to bear the first brunt of battle, and thus exposed to more than was fair of risks in action. It was further said that considerations of creed and politics had much to do with such an arrangement; hence some fears were expressed lest unpleasantness might now occur. All present, therefore, felt a sense of relief when, as the Emperor, surrounded by his brilliant staff, rode on to the ground, a cheer burst from all ranks assembled. The inspection over, the troops marched off, the Crown Prince at their head. Next day the return to

Berlin began, the pride of victory no doubt saddened by memories of thousands from among them, to be left buried in alien soil.

Being given an opportunity of testing railway arrangements for transport homewards of German wounded, I embarked at Pantin station in a train of that description. It was fully occupied by wounded men, for whose requirements and comfort every arrangement was complete, including staff and attendants. While in the train I was most courteously and hospitably received by the staff. The journey taken was somewhat long, nor did I get back to disturbed Paris till late at night.

A visit to Montmartre enabled me to see the manner of disposal and position of guns from the Parc de Monceau, now in hands of the Garde Nationale, who have openly declared for the Commune. My companion [1] and myself, recognised as foreigners, were courteously escorted, first to one battery, then to another, comments meanwhile freely made by those accompanying us in regard to their plan of action. Still, as far as we were able to understand, no counter-measures were taken by the authorities; and so the rising flood of revolution increased in volume and power, to burst disastrously three days thereafter.

In obedience to orders I quitted Paris for England by evening train on March 14. Early next morning I was with my beloved wife, whose anxieties and fears during my absence had told upon her health. So ended the important episode in which I had taken part.

[1] The late Mr. Laurence Oliphant.

CHAPTER XXXIV

1871-1874. *DOVER. ALDERSHOT*

Ordered to Dover—Garrisons—Short service—"Golden Rules"—Administrative duties—Lady de Ros—Alas! Alas!—M. Henry Dunant—Aldershot.

THE official Report of the mission performed had to be sent in, that done, orders directed me to take over duty in the South-eastern District, of which Dover is Headquarters. A few weeks elapsed, when I received an order of readiness for India. For the first and only time in my career I had to plead inability to proceed; long-continued semi-starvation in Paris had so lowered physical strength that reluctantly I was forced to plead the circumstance. The authorities were pleased thereon to consider that episode equivalent to a tour of foreign service; my name was placed at the bottom of the roster, and so the next three years were spent at the favourite station of England.

All that time the quiet routine of duty was more of an agreeable occupation than arduous or unpleasant work. Among some of the resident families acts of civility towards myself and family were numerous; intercourse with staff and regiments most pleasant, so that recollections of place and people remain agreeable.

Military positions and Departmental establishments connected with the ancient town itself had to be visited from time to time; so also had several throughout the "district," including Shorncliffe camp, whence had proceeded in the early years of the century the force destined for Spain, under command of Sir John Moore; Canterbury, with its associations connected with St. Augustine; Maidstone, provincial capital of England's garden; Brighton, etc.

Gradually was the system of short service in the ranks of the Army taking the place of that to which most officers of considerable standing had been accustomed. Complications and friction occurred in such a stage of transition among departments concerned in giving the change effect. In the ranks themselves all was not propitious; the old class of non-commissioned officers gave place to young and inexperienced, whose authority, even when rightly exerted, was not always tacitly accepted by the youthful and unbroken elements concerned. Moral influence such as emanated in many instances from old and experienced sergeants had all but died out; trivial shortcomings on the part of young lads were magnified into "crimes"; more than ordinary difficulty experienced by officers in keeping things smooth, yet "going."

In matters of administrative routine difference of views between officers concerned seemed inevitable; a satisfactory phase of official life, however, was that in the few instances in which such divergence occurred it was limited to official relations. Previous experience induced me to formulate certain principles in accordance with which correspondence submitted for decision should be dealt with; to them I endeavoured to adhere.[1] Another point taught by experience was that, in directing particular administrative ends to be attained, to leave to officers concerned the details of means by which instructions were to be carried into effect; in that way responsibility attached to the executive, while at the same time it left to them freedom of action.

As a matter of history relating to an important episode, and some personages connected therewith, it is worth while to refer to the account of the famous ball in Brussels on June 15, 1815, related to me by Lady de Ros, daughter of the Duke of Richmond, and who was present on the occasion in question. How, while dancing and conviviality proceeded, sounds of waggons and other heavy conveyances, guns and tumbrils among them, broke upon the ears of the gay throng; how small groups of the higher officers entered into grave and subdued talk; how, without exciting notice, singly they slipped away; how in the early hours of morning of the 16th, "the Duke" himself took his departure; how, as the remaining guests left the room, the turmoil in the streets of the Belgian capital resounded with the bray of bugles, trumpets, and military movements;[2] and how, before the day was over, several of those who had so left were brought back wounded, some dead, from Quatre Bras.

[Subsequently, taking advantage of the sixty-one days' leave to which officers are entitled, I visited the house, now a convent, which

[1] The following rules were those alluded to: 1. Never write in a hurry. 2. Be unswayed by personal feeling. 3. Judge charitably. 4. Never act upon a one-sided statement; *audi alteram partem*. 5. Avoid irritating expressions. 6. Obtain, if possible, "the last word." 7. In giving decision, take nothing for granted; have clear grounds for that decision. 8. Confine remarks and recommendations to their proper sphere.

[2] The 5th Division, or that of Picton, as also the Duke of Brunswick's contingent, both left Brussels at 5 a.m. of the 16th. Doubtless, therefore, the noises referred to were caused by the various arms belonging to it. (Horsford's *Waterloo*.)

stands on the site of the ball-room just mentioned—40–42, Rue de la Blanchisserie.]

It was while at Dover that one of those sad bereavements befel my dear wife and myself which leave their after-impress upon memory and affection. The taste for sea life had been early developed in my second son. As far as possible it was discouraged, but that having failed, he was permitted to carry his wishes into effect. Alas! alas! the result was very grievous. The ship in which he was proceeding was ultimately "declared missing" at Lloyd's; the dear, affectionate boy was never heard of. It is too painful to write even this brief notice.

A short visit by M. Henry Dunant gave me the opportunity of hearing from his own lips the story of the Red Cross convention, of which he has the distinction of being Founder. To his experiences gained among the thousands of wounded left on the field in and near Solferino without necessary help from the Austrians or Allies between whom that most sanguinary battle was fought,[1] and afterwards in extemporized ambulances for reception of those for whom provision could be made, M. Dunant assigned his resolve to institute, if possible, an Association whereby to mitigate in some measure at least the horrors of war such as he then witnessed. Of medical officers and their work as seen by him on that occasion he expressed himself in this way: "Certes, si tuer les hommes est un titre de gloire, les guerir, et cela, souvent au peril de sa vie, mérite bien l'estime et la reconnaissance." But in numbers they were altogether insufficient for the task required of them, supplemented as they soon were by volunteers, not only from the countries immediately concerned, but from others, including Belgium, Switzerland, and even Canada. Bearing these matters in mind, he asked himself the question, "Is it not possible to found through all the nations of Europe societies the object of which shall be aid to the wounded in times of war; that care the most prompt possible, not by mere mercenaries, but by persons devoted by high principles to so high a vocation." His appeal, formulated in a most touching narrative [2] of what he had seen in Lombardy, produced the effect desired by him; the subject he had at heart was earnestly taken up by all classes of persons, from crowned heads to peasants, and soon he had the reward of seeing organizations according to his own model in active operation. It was while he was occupied in observing the working of volunteer ambulances in Paris that I had the pleasure of being introduced to M. Dunant.

[1] June 24, 1859.

[2] *Convention de Genève: Un Souvenir de Solferino.* Paris: Hachette & Cie.

At long last came the "gazette" of my promotion, and almost simultaneously an order to take up at Aldershot the duties pertaining to my new rank.[1] The chief event during my short stay at that important military camp was the annual review and exercise of the troops composing it. For some time previous the old system of regimental hospitals and medical officers was in gradual process of abolition, and now that destructive policy had been so far matured as to be experimentally acted upon in the present manœuvres. My own duty was limited to carrying into execution orders received. But sympathies were altogether on the side of soldiers and their officers, who raised their voices against it. By what was now called the system of unification the fact became unpleasantly apparent that thenceforward the sick soldier, together with his wife and child, must depend in times of illness upon the aid of strangers, instead of, as heretofore, obtaining the help of those who personally knew them, and whose self-interest, even in the absence of higher motive, enhanced the care and attention shown towards them.

[1] Surgeon-General, April 1, 1874.

CHAPTER XXXV

1874-1875. *BURMAH*

Ordered to India—Bombay—Malabar coast—Madras—Intended expeditions—Rangoon—Shoay Dagon—Delhi Royal family—A coming race—Up the Irawaddy—Donabew—Hansadah—Akouk-tong—Prome—Thyet Myo—History—Petroleum wells — Great forest—Our progress—Mengee Sekan—Night shelters — Wandering Karens—Tonghoo—"Complication" with the King—The Sitang River—Boats and crews—Shoay Gheen—Sitang town—Its associations—Kadouk—Kyatsoo creek—Back to Rangoon—Comments.

SUDDENLY, and without note of warning, the contents of one of those long blue War Office envelopes informed me that in consequence of a death vacancy in India, I was to proceed without delay to Madras. The immediate result was a good deal of inconvenience and expense, arrangements having been made for a somewhat longer stay in camp than under the circumstances was now possible.

Leaving Portsmonth by the Indian troopship *Euphrates* early in September, in due time, and without adventure, we [1] landed at Bombay. Arrived at the capital city of the Western Presidency, the hospitality of one of India's merchant princes [2] was extended to us, a letter of introduction [3] having preceded us. It so happened that an unusually heavy rainstorm had passed over that part of India a few days previous, causing complete destruction of railways, besides much damage in other respects. Our departure was accordingly delayed several days, it being necessary that we should proceed by steamer towards our destination. Meanwhile, however, the kind civility of our host was unrelaxed; short trips were organized by him for our pleasure—one to the famous Caves of Elephanta on the island of Gharipuri, the sculptures in which represent nearly, if not all, the mythology of Hindooism.

The first month of the "cold" season was well advanced, the cold being rather in name than reality. Otherwise our sea trip along the coast of Malabar was pleasant enough; the bold scenery of the western

[1] My wife, daughter, and self. [2] Mr. Oliphant. [3] From Mr. John Ogilvie.

ghats in some places striking, in others grand; the cities, towns, and natural harbours, at several of which our ship made a brief stay to land and take on board goods and passengers, became so many objects of interest to us and a few others, who, like ourselves, had been also forced to adopt this mode of travelling.

Arrived off Beypore, we disembarked; thence took train, and so in due time reached Madras. The formality of reporting arrival to the authorities concerned once got over, duty was entered upon, our residence temporarily taken up in one of the large but otherwise comfortless hotels with which the place was provided, all such establishments being the property of, and managed by, natives.

Rumours circulated that a military expedition was likely to proceed *via* Burmah towards Yunnan, to co-operate with a corresponding force to be dispatched thither by the Yangtse kiang, with a view to inflict punishment on those by whom Mr. Margery had recently been murdered in that province. As a preliminary measure, the Commander-in-Chief, Sir Frederick Haines, determined to make a tour through what was then British Burmah, to satisfy himself in regard to the capabilities of the country to meet requirements of an army, including food, transport, supplies, and accommodation.

Together with other members of the staff with whom special details relating to the expected expedition would rest, His Excellency and party embarked; the pier on the occasion being crowded with his numerous friends, a guard of honour, in accordance with his rank and position, also drawn up. The *Oriental* quickly steamed away; in due time touched at Coconada and Vizagapatam respectively, then away across the Bay of Bengal, landing us safely at Rangoon on the seventh day from that on which we had gone on board. Hospitable friends awaited our landing, and by the kindness of Surgeon-General and Mrs. Kendall I was made comfortable as their guest.

Various objects and places of interest in and around this modern but prosperous city were visited and examined, so soon as relaxation from official duties permitted us to do so; but it is not intended in these notes to give more than a very brief record of experiences in these respects.[1] The first to claim attention was the famous Golden Temple, the Shoay Dagon, the most important Buddhistic memorial in Burmah, originally erected, according to legend, as a monument over eight hairs from the head of the Sage. In the course of our wanderings among the many smaller temples by which the dagon proper is surrounded, we met at intervals female devotees,—nuns, in fact, who had given themselves up to the service of the temple, their object in doing so, accord-

[1] These are given in detail in *Our Trip to Burmah.*

ing to our informant, that in the next transmigration they might be born men!

In the course of the day's excursion we came upon a very unroyal-looking "palace," now the residence of the Delhi Begum, and then upon an equally unroyal-looking personage, described as the remaining prince, his brothers having been shot by Hodson in 1857. The residence of other political prisoners were pointed out to us, including the house in which the deposed "Grand Mogul" of Delhi died.[1]

The extent to which the Chinese element monopolized various kinds of business and industry was remarkable; it was no less evident that the best portion of the town was theirs. In course of our rounds we met with several examples of what may in a sense be looked upon as a new race; namely, fruits of unions between Chinese men and Burmese women. Those with whom we met were young women, comely in appearance; their costumes a happy mixture of styles of the nationalities personified in themselves. It is probable that the males adopted the costume pertaining to one or other nationality, and so were undistinguishable from these.

Our journey upwards by steamer on the Irawaddy was pleasant, and in some respects interesting. The early portion was through a succession of narrow creeks before getting into the main stream, somewhat after the manner of the Soonderbunds, but on a small scale as compared to them. As we advanced, a rich, well-cultivated country opened up on either side of us. The fresh cool air on deck made thick clothing desirable. On either side well-to-do villages rose at short intervals as if out of the river, while on it were thickly dotted boats of various sizes transporting goods of many kinds. Rafts of timber, consisting of several portions ingeniously united, and well steered, were met with winding, as it were in folds, along the current. Fields of rice and gardens of banana gave place to patches of forest, separated by tracts covered by tall reed grass; then dense bamboo jungle, while from some of the riverside villages odours wafted off which told that in them various delicacies from fish, such as Burmans love, but other people abominate, were in course of preparation. Such a place was Pantanau, at which we spent a night.

Resuming our journey, the somewhat large towns of Yandoon and Donabew were passed in quick succession, the latter associated with the history of the first Burmese War, 1824–26. There, one of the most severely contested battles of that war took place; the Burmese

[1] There was a rumour that his head had been disinterred and carried away, perhaps to be made use of after the manner of the Scythians.

leader, Bundoola, was killed. At the same place in the war of 1852 severe fighting took place, heavy losses being inflicted upon our forces by the native troops under command of Myot Zoon.

In due time we are off Hansadah, also associated with the wars of 1825 and 1852; the name of the place itself—namely, *Hansa—anser*, goose—being derived from Turanian mythology. At a little distance from that place a halt was made to replenish the stock of firewood; the time so spent enabling us to take a short excursion in the near vicinity. Animal life in great profusion existed everywhere; cattle in excellent keeping, for the Burmese are extremely kind to them; poultry of all sorts in abundance; sparrows in myriads, and if possible more bold than are their kind in our own country; water birds in great numbers; land birds equally so are everywhere, nor are they as yet slaughtered in the name of "sport," as doubtless they will be when British guns become more numerous here than, luckily for the wild creatures, they are at present.

On either side the country changes gradually in appearance; at first an uninterrupted level, then undulating, the inequalities greater and greater as we proceed. Now the dim outline of the Arracan Yoma range looms in the distance; we reach the high bold promontory of Akouk-tong, round the base of which the Irawaddy rushes violently. On its river-face several rude carvings represent Buddha; on its summit and landward declivity stand pagodas of various sizes, the whole connected with each other by winding pathways. During the war of 1852 the Burmese erected a powerful battery upon the summit of that promontory, for the capture of which a party, under command of Captain Gardener, was landed from the *Enterprise*. Unhappily it fell into an ambuscade, its commander beheaded, his head carried away as a trophy of victory. More and more distinctly the hills of Prome came into view; forests of teak, interspersed with patches of custard-apple trees, were seen clothing their sides, tracts of underwood everywhere. Now we obtain glimpses of a well-made military road, to be used if need be by troops from Akayab to this place.

Prome is a city or town of considerable importance; its chief products, lac, petroleum, silk, and lacquer. Occupying an elevated site is "The Holy Hair Pagoda," smaller in dimensions than its counterpart the Shoay Dagon at Rangoon; like it, approached by an extensive flight of steps, on either side of which is a long series of mythological figures. A variety of bells, large and small, swung from stands, at short intervals among the buildings connected with the temple proper. These bells, when struck by a mallet of deer's horn, suspended from their stands for the purpose, emit a sound of surprising sweetness. In the second Burmese War, namely that of 1852, Prome was taken possession of by our troops on October 11.

Thyet Myo is reached after a few such mishaps as are incidental to travel on the Irawaddy; among them breaks-down of machinery, leaking of steam boilers, running "fast" upon sand-banks, getting doubled up in the coils of rafts, and so on. As on the occasion of our departure from Madras, so on disembarking here, a guard of honour, with regimental band and colour, salutes the chief; hospitable friends[1] invite us to their houses; our party is comfortably and well provided for.

Thyet Myo, otherwise "Mango city," has a history which dates back to A.D. 250. In 1854 cantonments for British troops were erected near to it, on a site so situated as to command the passage of the Irawaddy. In 1857 the river deserted its old bed, making for itself a new one at least a mile and a half distant, thus destroying the purpose originally in view.

A tedious ride through thorny jungle, then along what was intended to become a main line of road to Mendoon, took us to a series of petroleum wells at Pendouk-ben. Regarding them great expectations were entertained, and energetic endeavours were in progress accordingly; but so far, their produce was limited to the oozing in small quantities of "oil" from the sides of wells in course of formation in the schistoze rock. Subsequently, that industry, there and elsewhere in the country, has attained great importance.

Official duties over at Thyet Myo, our journey was resumed, all arrangements made beforehand for an expected interesting if somewhat arduous progress through the extensive forest that occupies the tract of territory between the rivers Irawaddy and Sitang, including what is called "the great Yoma range" of mountains, or more properly speaking, hills. Our first move was to cross the first-named river and encamp on its further bank. Next morning, we four[2] began our real trip, all mounted, the large body of "followers" of all sorts composing our escort making their way on foot.

Our progress during the next four days was along "roads" the roughness and other difficulties of which rapidly increased as we went on; villages and patches of cultivation became smaller and less frequent; the people showed themselves curious to see the *kalas*, or white foreigners, their own state of raggedness and dirt offensive to look upon.

We had reached the densest part of the forest, at a point whence our

[1] I by Dr. Lamprey of the 67th.

[2] General Sir F. Haines, Brigadier-Generals Howlett and Stewart, and myself.

further progress was to be by elephants, a track being made in the jungle by a number of men sent before us for that purpose. We reached a stockaded village, such a defence in this secluded spot being very necessary against marauders. The forest resounds with the voices of birds, from the resplendent plumage of some of which the sunlight is reflected in flashes. Later on all becomes silence, save from the voices of our own party, and so we reach, as afternoon advances, the halting place of Mengee Sekan.

Hitherto we have taken advantage for accommodation overnight of such buildings as we found, in the shape chiefly of deserted Buddhist monasteries, in various stages of decay. It became necessary to extemporize a hut or bower in which to pass the night. Such a place was quickly prepared for us by natives attached to our party, who, by means of their *dahs* — half-knife, half-sword — cut down branches of bamboos and trees; these they arranged and secured by ropes made of bark and creepers: thus they made quarters in which we were by no means uncomfortable.

Our elephant steeds carry us onwards, along the half-dried bed of what in the rainy season is a mountain torrent, confined on either side by precipitous cliffs, our progress at times interrupted by deep pools, at others by boulders singly or in masses in the river bed; these obstacles having to be circumvented as best was practicable, but always causing much delay and inconvenience. Coming upon a pathway, evidently used by wandering Karens, and made passable for us by our dah-men already mentioned, our elephants have to scramble as best they can upwards along the steep face of a mountain spur of the Yoma range. We gain the summit, and from it obtain a wide and extensive view of rich dense forest stretching far away, around, below the level of the point from which we took our survey. We pass the watershed that divides the tributaries to the Irawaddy and Sitang. Our descent is rough and precipitous; we arrive at the Kyat-Moung creek, and for some miles travel eastward along its bed; the forest on either side dense as before, the brushwood and lower vegetation consisting chiefly of ferns and stemless palms. After a day of somewhat arduous toil we reach an open space, and there a bower being quickly prepared for us we rest for the night.

Our journey resumed, the roadway we take is once again the bed of a mountain stream, the banks high and steep; vegetation still dense, huge creepers stretching from branch to branch, masses of parasitical plants hanging from the highest arms. Soon the forest becomes less dense; isolated houses, then villages, surrounded by patches of cultivated ground, are reached. Such a village is Pyagone. It is under the jurisdiction of Tonghoo, from which place letters have been sent for us, and so we hear of those we care for. Here we part with our elephants and other establishments belonging to Thyet Myo, exchanging the former for small Burmese ponies, on which the remaining part of our journey is performed. Several more marches were performed, differing in no particular characteristic from those already alluded to. Then, glittering in the sun, but still a long way in front of us, the pinnacle of a gilded pagoda indicates the position of Tonghoo. As we plod along the dusty way, we overtake a caravan of Shans, their bullocks laden with merchandise to market. We reach the remains of what was once the fortified wall by which the city was surrounded, but is now a series of dilapidated fragments. Friends [1] come out to receive and offer us hospitality; baths and good cheer soon set us up; we look back amused at such small discomforts as we had recently undergone.

Tonghoo marks the eastern limit of what was, three centuries B.C., the empire of Asoka. The modern town, however, dates *only* from the tenth century of our era; its position, upon a peninsula round which winds the river Sitang. At a distance eastward, the Karenee range of mountains some four thousand feet in height, their sides thickly covered by forest; the general aspect of the locality and its surroundings forlorn and unattractive.

At the time of our visit a political "complication" with the king of Burmah was considered likely to be the outcome of a different interpretation as to the boundary line between Native and British Burmah entertained by the Indian and Burmese officials; while the Karens lay claim, in opposition to both, to a tract of territory said to have been occupied by them from time immemorial. Some months subsequently this matter was amicably arranged.

Our duties performed, our homeward journey began; we start away to Tantabin, where long, narrow boats lie moored to the bank, awaiting to take us on board, and so down the Sitang River. But the hospitality of friends at Tonghoo has yet another demonstration to the Chief and his party ere we finally take leave. A sumptuous and costly *déjeûner* awaits us in the *zyat*, or travellers' rest-house at the ghat. When the meal is over and we get on board each his particular boat, many expressions of mutual good-will exchanged, much waving of hands and handkerchiefs, and then—our river trip begins.

The kind of craft in which the next few days and nights must be spent is peculiar. Mine consists of the scooped-out trunk of a tree,

[1] Major Kingsley, 67th Regiment, kindly extended his hospitality to me.

[2] By the hospitality of Major and Mrs. Lloyd.

its inner arrangements fitted up according to Burmese ideas of comfort, or it may be, luxury. The measurement of the boat, or rather canoe, is three tons, itself so narrow and crank that practice is needed to move without tilting it over to a dangerous degree; yet on further experience this became sufficiently easy. The crew comprised six Burmese, active in body, cheery in disposition, well acquainted with their particular work; ready to joke and chaff with brother boatmen, as we glided pleasantly down the stream.

A short halt is made at Shoay Gheen, an important town, at which in due time we arrive. Here we find the remains of a stockade, held in considerable strength against our troops by the Burmese in 1825, though surrendered by them without a struggle in December of that year. There are two respects in which Shoay Gheen is famous: the one, that from here direct to Yunnan a trade route extends; the other, that in the district to which the town gives its name is the chief habitat of that most dreaded of poisonous snakes, the hamadryad (*Ophiophagus elaps*).

Another day and night and we are at the town of Sitang; its streets and houses are arranged in regular order, the streets wide, sheltered, boulevard like, by a row of spreading trees on either side; everywhere flocks of poultry, large and small, especially of the particular breeds for which Burmah is famous. On the more prominent points are pagodas, several undergoing repair and being regilded. Near each is a group of hideous stucco figures of *nats*;[1] among these, people in attitudes of devotion, presenting to the images offerings, sprigs of sacred flowers, jasmine and jonesia (the asoka tree), and other plants.

In the first Burmese War a strong position was taken up by them at this place. On January 7, 1826, it was unsuccessfully attacked by our forces, who sustained severe loss, including their commander; on the 11th, however, the attack was renewed, the position captured, with a loss to the enemy of six hundred in a strength of four thousand defenders. In 1852, after peace had been declared, a British detachment was stationed here, and so remained for some time.

Time presses; tide waits for no man. Our boatmen, aware of the latter fact, press on by means of sail and paddle throughout the night; we arrive at Kadouk soon after daylight. Considerably to our surprise, our boats are quickly turned from the main stream into a narrow creek, and there made fast. But the detention is only for a little; our boatmen resume their work; our boats re-enter the stream, and for a time keep close to the right bank. A rushing sound comes upon us from the

[1] Demons.

distance; it increases; the tidal wave of the Sitang is upon us; not in its full volume, however, for from a point just ahead of us it breaks with a roar, and then, curling with foam as it advances, it rushes irresistibly to the opposite bank. It was to avoid this "bore," for so the wave is named, and being probably swamped by its force, that our boatmen had pushed on.

Communication between the Sitang and Pegu rivers was by means of the Kyatsoo creek, and that only during the three days of spring tides at the present season of the year. A canal was in progress of construction, and railways were being extended in various directions; yet neither was usable for our purpose. One suggestive circumstance, however, we learn: that, anticipating enhanced value of land as a result of such works, a precocious native agriculturist is making extensive purchases along the line of the new waterway. Our passage along the Kyatsoo creek was marked by nothing more stirring than a succession of groundings, bumps against other craft, and such trifles. On either side of us cultivated fields extend away to the distance; on some of them the blue flower of the flax plant is bright and fresh. Isolated huts and small villages occur at small distances from each other, and high up in the azure firmament a lark pours forth its volume of song, as in our own island.

As we proceed, the tapering summits of pagodas are seen reflecting the sunlight ahead; they indicate the site of the once important city of Pegu, capital of the Talain kingdom. A little further and we experience the tide as it comes from the river so named, to meet that from the Sitang, by which so far we have been conveyed. A little more and we are back in Rangoon, the members of our small party hospitably received by newly-made friends, Mr. and Mrs. Wilkinson kindly taking me to their house.

The next few days were passed mostly in the performance of official duties, spare intervals being taken up in visiting places of interest previously passed over from want of time. Our journey and observations made during it supplied subject alike for official and for ordinary talk, giving zest to forecasts variously expressed in regard to the probable issue of events which may follow upon the death or deposition of the king. The prevailing view was that Government will place upon the throne the legitimate heir, and having done so will carry on administration by means of a Commission. In such an event, it is anticipated that Burmah will be one of the best fields for British energy and capital, that communication will be opened up, and resources of the country developed.

CHAPTER XXXVI

1875-1880. *MADRAS PRESIDENCY*

Return to Madras—Death of Lord Hobart—Lord Pigot's tomb and story—Interregnum—Duke of Buckingham—H.R.H. the Prince of Wales—Commanders-in-Chief—Famine—A relief camp—Ootacamund—Fever among British troops—Thebaw—Affghanistan—Sir N. Chamberlain as Envoy—Young soldiers *versus* old—Suggested scheme—Medical system—Inspection tours—New barracks—Calicut — Cannanore — Maliaporam — Bangalore — Bellary — Secunderabad — "Confidential" reports—Indication of illness—"New brooms"—Official demeanour—In the hills—Pleasant recollections—Back at Portsmouth—Finale.

WE embark on the *Mecca*. A week passes; we land at Madras, bearing with us pleasant recollections of friendly hospitality received during our now bygone "Trip to Burmah." [1]

The death of Lord Hobart,[2] Governor of the Presidency, was an event regretted by those of us who had come to know his amiable though retiring character, and much sympathy was expressed towards the widowed Lady Hobart on her bereavement. The remains of the deceased were carried to the tomb with all the pomp and ceremony due to the high office he had occupied, and estimation in which he was generally held, the coffin committed to the tomb in St. Mary's Church, Fort St. George.

While clearing out a place for the purpose, the workmen came upon the coffin of Lord Pigot, whose death took place in 1776, and whose place of burial, if not intentionally concealed, had long since ceased to be remembered. The story of his death was thus resuscitated, and reference made to history relating how the Council deposed him, how he was arrested by the Commander-in-Chief, placed in confinement, and there forcibly kept during eight months, at the end of which he died. No wonder that this audacious proceeding on the part of the chief actors in the drama produced astonishment and indignation at home.

An interregnum followed, during which the senior member of

[1] Under that title an account of it was published by Baillière, Tindall & Cox, London.

[2] On April 27, 1875.

Council[1] became head of the Government, the headquarters of which, together with those of the Commander-in-Chief, were shortly thereafter transferred to Ootacamund, where they remained until the following "cold" season, as it is called in Madras.

In the latter part of the year arrived His Grace the Duke of Buckingham and Chandos, appointed Governor. On the occasion of his landing, together with his daughters, the three Ladies Grenville, there was an immense gathering at the pier to receive the distinguished party. The assemblage comprised His Excellency the Commander-in-Chief, staff, high military officers, and heads of departments, a guard of honour, Government and municipal officers, representatives of the native princes and nobility, and, in addition, a large concourse of the community.[2]

The arrival of the Prince of Wales was an important event in the history of Madras. During the stay of His Royal Highness at the provincial capital, the best endeavours of all classes, official and non-official, natives and British, were directed to manifest duty and loyalty to the Heir Apparent. In addition to official entertainments and receptions given by Governor and Commander-in-Chief, the civil society, native princes and community, did all they could to do honour to him and to themselves on the occasion.

The next events of importance in reference to official affairs in Madras comprised a change in the head of the Army, Sir Frederick Haines being moved to Simla, and succeeded by Sir Neville Chamberlain. The departure of the former was much regretted by all classes, military, civil, and non-official; all honour and welcome were given to the latter, whose great military reputation and high character were known to and acknowledged by all.

In 1877 the Madras Presidency, as well as other parts of India, was visited by famine, large numbers of natives falling victims, notwithstanding the exertions by the Governor and officers acting under the orders of His Grace to combat the misfortune. Private associations and individuals added their endeavours to those by Government; missionary bodies provided for large numbers of orphans and other victims, with the result that many "converts" were added to their lists. The necessity for extended and improved systems of irrigation being shown, steps were taken in both directions. While not a few of the ancient methods had been abandoned, the modern substitutes were, in some instances, far from effectual for their purpose. Now also an important

[1] Mr., afterwards Sir William Robinson, K.C.S.I.

[2] By the *London Gazette* was announced my appointment as Honorary Physician to the Queen, March 22, 1876.

financial measure was adopted: a special fund against famine was established, the equivalent of eight million pounds sterling set aside for that purpose, and if some time thereafter that fund was otherwise absorbed, its original devisers and founders had passed from office before the change in question took place.

In obedience to orders, I visited a camp situated a few miles from the city of Madras for the reception and care of sufferers from the famine, the object being the somewhat technical one of making a report on the phenomena of starvation. In tents provided for their accommodation lay prostrated men, women, and children in all stages of absolute starvation. Carts were bringing in from the surrounding districts persons who, while proceeding along the highways in search of food and other aid, had fallen exhausted, and so lay on the roadsides. Altogether, the sights presented were very sad.

There being a prospect that Ootacamund would shortly become the permanent seat of the Presidency Government, His Grace the Governor appointed a Committee,[1] of which I was senior member, to inquire into and report upon the general condition of that place. The subject was carefully gone into, the respects pointed out in which improvements were suggested, the nature of those improvements given in detail. In due time our report (written by me) was officially submitted; it passed through the usual official channels, and, having done so, was *not* acted upon. Years have passed away since then; the public prints record that evils have occurred at this beautiful locality which, it is safe to believe, would have been averted had our recommendations been carried out; those evils, moreover, definitely predicted in that report.

Another subject on which it fell to my lot to submit a report, related to the prevalence of fevers among our troops:, a duty which caused myself much unpleasantness, inasmuch that practical experience was brought into somewhat violent collision with pure theory. All that need be noticed in this place is that, according to what is called the "scientific" school, the actual cause of those affections is *dirt*, and apparently *dirt* alone. According to the practical school, the *causes* are various, including the youth of the men, translation to an alien climate and alien conditions, exposure, indiscretions, etc. In accordance with the views first-named, numerous works to which the term "sanitary" was applied were undertaken at a cost to the Indian Government of many thousands, nay millions, of rupees. According to the second, many of those expensive improvements have been without

[1] The other members were Mr. Macallum Webster, I.C.S., and Surgeon-General Cornish, C.I.E.

their intended result, nor have they in any degree touched the root and origin of the evil, comprised in the general conditions just named.

The king of Burmah having died, the legal heir Thebaw was duly acknowledged his successor. No sooner had he attained to power than acts of maladministration and of atrocity drew upon him extreme displeasure of the Indian Government. Milder measures having proved ineffectual, a military force was sent to his capital, with the result that in due time it was captured, he himself deposed, and brought to India as prisoner of State. For a considerable time before that expedition was dispatched, preparatory arrangements for such a contingency had been as far as practicable matured—those of the department under my own supervision included.

Relations between the Government of India and the Ameer of Affghanistan had been in a more or less strained condition since 1873, when "after the return of Noor Mahomed Shah from Simla, the Ameer's language was very unsatisfactory" to Lord Northbrook. "A sum of £100,000 placed to the Ameer's credit at Peshawur by the British Government was allowed to remain there, and never drawn."[1] During the early months of 1878 the general state of those relations was much discussed in military society and in civil, two different views being expressed regarding it: the one by officers and others of long Indian experience and practical acquaintance with frontier matters; the other, chiefly by those of shorter Indian experience, and less practical acquaintance on the border.

Later in that year, our much-esteemed Commander-in-Chief, Sir Neville Chamberlain, was ordered by Lord Lytton to proceed as Envoy to Sheer Ali, the Ameer. He did so, and now the Madras command fell during his absence to General Elmhirst, formerly of the 9th Foot, a good officer and amiable man. After much ineffectual negotiation by Sir Neville Chamberlain, in the hope of averting armed intervention, Lord Lytton declared war against the Ameer. Forces were meanwhile being gathered for the purpose of the campaign, the 67th Regiment with some other troops being sent from the Madras Presidency. Their equipment and the general arrangements for active service had to be provided under orders of the responsible officers concerned, of whom I was one. In due time, Sir Neville was received with welcome back from the important, but unhappily futile, mission upon which he had been sent.

While the general subject of young soldiers *versus* old was occupying the War Office authorities, the opinions held regarding it from personal experience of certain senior officers were called for, mine among them.

[1] *Affghanistan*, by P. F. Walker, p. 62.

To a number of definite questions, definite answers were submitted by us individually; but the tone of all was identical,—namely, that for the purpose of field service in India men of mature growth, and who had already been some years in the country, were most capable of withstanding the wear and tear incidental to war. Sufficient grounds for that opinion are casually stated in reference to incidents relating to the Mutiny campaign, and to the Siege of Paris.

In connection with the same subject, the question arose whether or not advantage might accrue from the introduction of a double system of recruiting; namely, short service for home, long service for India. Some of us elaborated a series of calculations, the outcome of which was that on the score of expense, including pensions, the latter scheme would be more economical than the system, then as still in operation, involving as it does the constant influx and efflux of men to and from India, the maintenance of expensive systems of transport, hill stations and sanatoria. This, however, is but one among several points relating to the important question now touched upon.

The process of "divorcing" medical officers from regiments had become general, notwithstanding representations and protests from men of long experience. In the early part of the nineteenth century, the defects incidental to "general" hospitals and methods relating thereto having declared themselves in the Peninsular campaign, what was called the regimental system was introduced in addition to, and partial supersession of that method, the better to meet the requirement professionally of the several classes pertaining to regiments. With the abolition of that system a retrograde step is taken, to the serious disadvantage of the soldier and all other persons concerned. No sufficient reason exists why the double system, staff and regimental, should not continue as before, and so fulfil alike the purposes of war and of peace.

Inspection duty to military stations within the command occupied the greater part of each "cold" season. In the performance of this somewhat invidious function, the agreeable far outbalanced the unpleasant, hospitality and every consideration by the officers with whom I came in contact going far to make each such tour a pleasure trip.

Barracks, hospitals, and other buildings for accommodation or other use by soldiers had recently been erected in accordance with plans and instructions formulated by the Sanitary Commission in Calcutta, of which I was a member, as already mentioned. In the majority of instances they had been in use by the troops during six to eight years; but so far, liability to endemic illness of their occupants showed no decrease statistically from what had occurred among occupants of "the old style" of barracks. With regard to several other matters connected with them, evidence was apparent that anticipations by that Commission had yet to be realized.

Beyond the objects of routine duty there was much of interest connected with the majority of places visited. On the west coast the history of what are now civil or military stations carries us back to a period when Tadmor in the wilderness, the ancient Palmyra, was a depôt for merchandise and goods imported in the days of Solomon from this part of India. It was off Calicut, at which there is now stationed a small force of British troops, that in May, 1498, Vasco da Gama came to anchor after a voyage of eleven months from Lisbon. In 1509, Albuquerque having failed in one attack upon that place proceeded to Goa, which he captured, and has ever since that time remained in Portuguese possession.

Cannanore, situated further up along the Malabar coast, is also a place of great antiquity, though now of small importance. From the days of Pliny, and long before then, the inhabitants of the whole district so named were known to be sea robbers and wreckers. At the present day, however, the descendants of those early pirates may be seen quietly at study, and learning useful handicrafts in the establishments belonging to the Basel Mission, which are in a very flourishing condition, if we can form an opinion on the subject from a cursory visit to them.

An isolated military post is Maliapuram, situated in a district mostly covered with dense jungle, at the distance of a night's journey from Calicut. The result to me of the trip there and back through malarious forests was an attack of illness, recovery from which was due to the hospitable attentions received from Mr. and Mrs. Wigram. The object of the little garrison alluded to is to preserve peace among the Moplas, a manly, lawless race, whose descent is believed to be from Arab sailors who, in ancient times, formed connections with native (Tier) women. They are noted for their zeal as Mahomedans, for the rapidity with which "risings" take place among them, and the bloodshed incidental to those occasions.

Bangalore has been already mentioned in these notes. The large cantonment for British troops, in respect to completeness of arrangements, is unsurpassed in India. In near proximity to it is the residence of the representative of Government at the Court of Mysore.

From this place the routine usually is to proceed to Bellary, situated in the centre of the Indian Peninsula. Smaller than Bangalore, yet of considerable importance, it is the military centre of the Berar district, assigned in 1853 to the Government of India represented by Lord Dalhousie on account of certain subsidies then in arrear on the part of the Nizam.

Secunderabad, perhaps the largest military station in India, is situated at a distance of nine to twelve miles from Hyderabad. That important native city was visited after duty had been gone through, the visit performed on elephants, a guard of sowars furnished for our safe conduct; nor was the precaution unnecessary, if an opinion could be gathered from the expression of men's countenances as we proceeded along the narrow winding streets. Our excursion was varied by a short trip by steam launch on the Meer Alum tank, and afterwards by a short visit to the mosques at Golconda.

An unpleasant duty connected with my position, but one which fortunately had only at rare intervals to be performed, was that of reporting otherwise than favourably on officers within my sphere of superintendence. Such occasions only arose at the periodical inspections, and then the method I adopted was to read to the officer concerned the portion of the usual official report relating to the particular point commented upon, requesting him at the same time to furnish his explanation regarding it, so that the explanatory document should be transmitted together with the adverse comment. Otherwise, as it seemed to me, an injury would be inflicted without the officer concerned being aware of the grounds or extent of it, and without an opportunity being afforded him to defend himself. In fact, the whole system of "confidential" reports is open to very grave objection, as by their very nature they more or less "strike a man in the dark."

In some instances, fortunately of rare occurrence, it was found that an officer, previously known to be zealous, painstaking, and otherwise efficient, suddenly displayed impatience of administrative control, and in other respects brought himself unpleasantly before the authorities. In the course of experience I came to know various instances in which the sudden change alluded to was in reality the premonitor of illness; others in which it was the first indication of actual disease; consequently I was at the outset prepared to look upon such a change in one or other of these lights. This remark may apply to all classes of officers, more especially in the tropics, and I believe that much unnecessary disciplinary severity towards individuals under such circumstances could be with advantage exchanged for more considerate methods.

In my own branch of the general service, and in others, I had various opportunities of seeing the results of so-called "sweeping" reforms by "new brooms" and particular officers whose moving principle seemed to be that whatever is, is wrong, and therefore must be abolished. Happily for the personal comfort of all concerned, and for the benefit of the service as a whole, the great majority of administrative officers have learnt that reasons are forthcoming, if sought for, to account for whatever may not be at first sight evident in reference to particular modes of routine; therefore the officer of experience, as opposed to the mere "reformer," endeavours, in the first place, to ascertain the nature of those conditions, and having done so, to introduce slowly and gradually such changes as altered conditions may suggest.

There are certain other points relating to administration which I may note. I had long ago become aware that in conducting duties, the making of promises other than such as could there and then be performed is a bad one; circumstances are apt to arise which render it quite impossible to carry out those made in anticipation. In such cases great disappointment and often chagrin to the officer concerned was the result. Very bitterly as a young man had I felt rough and cavalier action towards me by senior and official superiors. It was accordingly my endeavour to avoid similar demeanour towards my juniors. In communicating expressions of official dissatisfaction, it was an object of my endeavour to avoid giving such an expression the tone of personality.

During the greater part of the five years comprising my tour of service in the Madras Presidency, my family occupied a house in Ooty, for by that almost loving abbreviation was Ootacamund known. There my wife and daughter remained continuously, their occupation and enjoyment comprising horses, dogs, a farmyard, and garden. Thither in the hot season I repaired, as one of the officials entitled to that great privilege; and there, while carrying on departmental duties, I was able to participate in the various occupations and enjoyments special to the place. Among those were rides, drives, excursions, and picnics, visits to various Government and other gardens and plantations, including tea gardens; while to a lover of nature there was a never-failing source of interest in the phases of plant and animal life as we rode or walked along the various mountain faces by which the station was encircled.

Society was pervaded by a spirit of sociability and friendliness; that tone given to it by its leaders, the Ladies Grenville and Lady Chamberlain. Official duty was conducted in a spirit of kind consideration between officials, at the same time that it was well and honestly performed. It was, then, with great regret that my period drew to a close; that having ended, my "relief" arrived. My five years in the Madras Presidency were indeed "the green spot" in my somewhat long period of service. In December, 1879, I embarked for England.

In the early days of January, 1880, we landed at Southampton, whence we proceeded to Portsmouth, to which district I found myself again appointed. It was now the dead of winter. The rapid change from the heat of Madras to the bitter cold of this part of England caused severe illness in the person of my dear wife—a circumstance which gave rise to a fellow-feeling for the many soldiers' wives and children who undergo the same transition between extremes, but without sufficient provision in clothing and other requisites to enable them to withstand its effects. The routine of duty was much the same as it had been some ten years previous; the one respect in which a change was visible referred to my own special department, into which alterations introduced seemed to tend neither to the well-being of the soldier nor comfort of the officer.

My period of service drew to a close under the terms of a recently issued Royal warrant. Arrangements were made accordingly for handing over to a successor duties the performance of which had become in a manner second nature to me, so much so that their cessation was looked forward to as a blank in prospect. In the early days of April the Army Estimates for the current year were published. In accordance with them I was one of six to whom was authorized the reward for "Distinguished Military Services." On May 25, as the clock struck the hour of noon, I resigned my seat to the officer ordered to relieve me. In the succeeding *Gazette* the notification appeared that I was placed on retired pay. My active career was ended.

[P.S.—In the Jubilee *Gazette*, 1897, the distinction of K.C.B. was conferred upon me. On August 11 following, at Osborne, Her Most Gracious Majesty was pleased to invest me with the Insignia of the Order. On December 2 I had the additional honour of receiving the Jubilee medal, transmitted by command of the Queen, to be worn in commemoration of the sixtieth anniversary of Her Majesty's Reign.]

THE END.

INDEX

A

B

C